THE X FILES™

VOLUME 1

CHECKER BOOK PUBLISHING GROUP

FH
GRN

Library of Congress Cataloging-in-Publication Data

Petrucha, Stefan.
  The X-files / written by Stefan Petrucha and John Rozum
      p. cm.
  "X-files created by Chris Carter."
  "Stefan Petrucha, writer (issues 13-16) John Rozum, writer (issue 17)... Charles Adlard, artist (issues 13-16)"--Copyright p.
  "Originally published by Topps Comics."
  ISBN 1-933160-02-0 (alk. paper)
  I. Rozum, John. II. Adlard, Charles, 1966- III. Carter, Chris, 1957- IV. Title.
  PN6727.P4685X2 2005
  741.5'973--dc22
                                    2005003802

"We work in the dark. We do what we can to battle the evil that would otherwise destroy us. But if a man's character is his fate, it's not a choice but a calling. Sometimes the weight of this burden causes us to falter, breaching the fragile fortress of our mind. Allowing the monster without to turn within. We are left alone staring into the abyss. Into the laughing face of madness. "
— Special Agent Fox Mulder

The X-Files
Created by Chris Carter

CONTRIBUTORS

Chris Carter ....Writer
Stefan Petrucha ....Writer
John Rozum ....Writer
Roy Thomas ....Writer
Miran Kim ....Cover Artist
Charles Adlard ....Artist
Rick Magyar ....Artist
Val Mayrick ....Artist
Gordon Purcell ....Artist
Josef Rubenstein ....Artist
John Van Fleet ....Artist
John Workman ....Letterer
George Freeman ....Colorist
Laurie E. Smith ....Colorist
Digital Chameleon ..Color Design & Rendering
Jim Salicrup ....Editor
Renee Witterstaetter ....Editor
Dwight Jon Zimmerman ....Editor
Michael Grecco ....Photographer
Michael Lavine ....Photographer
Jack Rowan ....Photographer
Ken Staniforth ....Photographer

COMPILATION

Mark Thompson ....Publisher
Constance Taylor ....Managing Editor
Trevor Goodman ....Graphic Design
Mike Gregg ...Graphic Design, Cover Design

Originally published by Topps Comics.

Checker Book Publishing Group
228 Byers Road, Suite 201
Miamisburg, OH 45342
Visit us online at www.checkerbpg.com

No solicitations accepted.

ISBN# 1-933160-02-0

Printed in China

THE X FILES™

VOLUME ONE
Created by Chris Carter

INTRODUCTION

"We open doors with the X-Files, which lead to other doors..."Special Agent Dana Scully, "Requiem"

As a piece of pop-culture iconography, the X-Files voiced the desire we have, as a culture, to understand more about what goes on behind that curtain of our perceived reality. The show tackled every type of subject matter in it's nine-year run, from government conspiracies to poltergeists to Elvis' face appearing on a piece of French toast. More often than not, within the realm of the X-Files, the Truth meant more alternatives to consider, more paths to search down, more questions to be answered... and Scully and Mulder were the unrelenting champions. Always searching for the truth. Always wanting to believe.

But how do we distinguish between fact and fiction? What's the difference between an elaborate illusion and a complex truth? Who knows... I highly doubt there's any truly empirical way to distinguish. But Chris Carter had a darn good idea -- pair up a zealous believer in the paranormal and a skeptical scientist, and maybe, just maybe, you'll come up with some sort of dynamic that creates a bridge between the conflicting camps of different perceived realities. What worked about the X-Files was that both Scully's and Mulder's view points were treated with equal relevance throughout the run of the show, giving the audience both perspectives to contend with, all the while encouraging the viewer to be intelligently skeptical of both claims.

Or rather, that was one of the many things that worked about the series.

In these printed X-Files stories, you'll find that ever-present but inimitable combination of sci-fi, horror, and adventure... and of course, the ever-present search for the ultimate Truth.

Constance Taylor
Managing Editor

TABLE OF CONTENTS

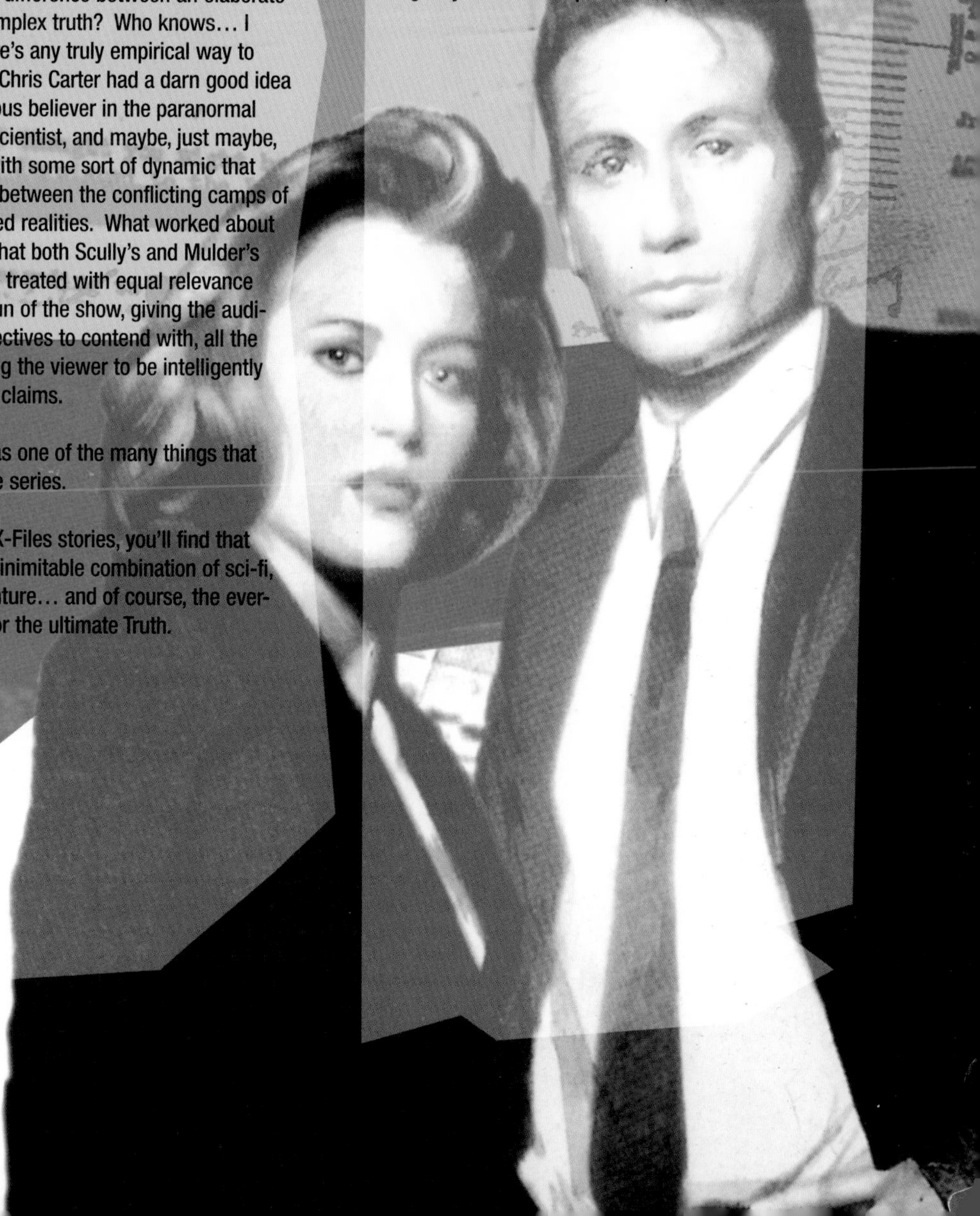

topps COMICS

ALL-NEW

13
$2.95 US
$4.15 CANADA

THE X FILES

CREATED BY CHRIS CARTER

STEFAN
PETRUCHA

CHARLES
ADLARD

MIRAN
KIM

SCULLY & MULDER
CONFRONT A
KILLER COMPUTER
PROGRAM IN--
"ONE PLAYER
ONLY"

DIRECT SALES
01311

CHAPTER 1:
ONE PLAYER ONLY

STORY: Stefan Petrucha
ART: Charles Adlard & Miran Kim

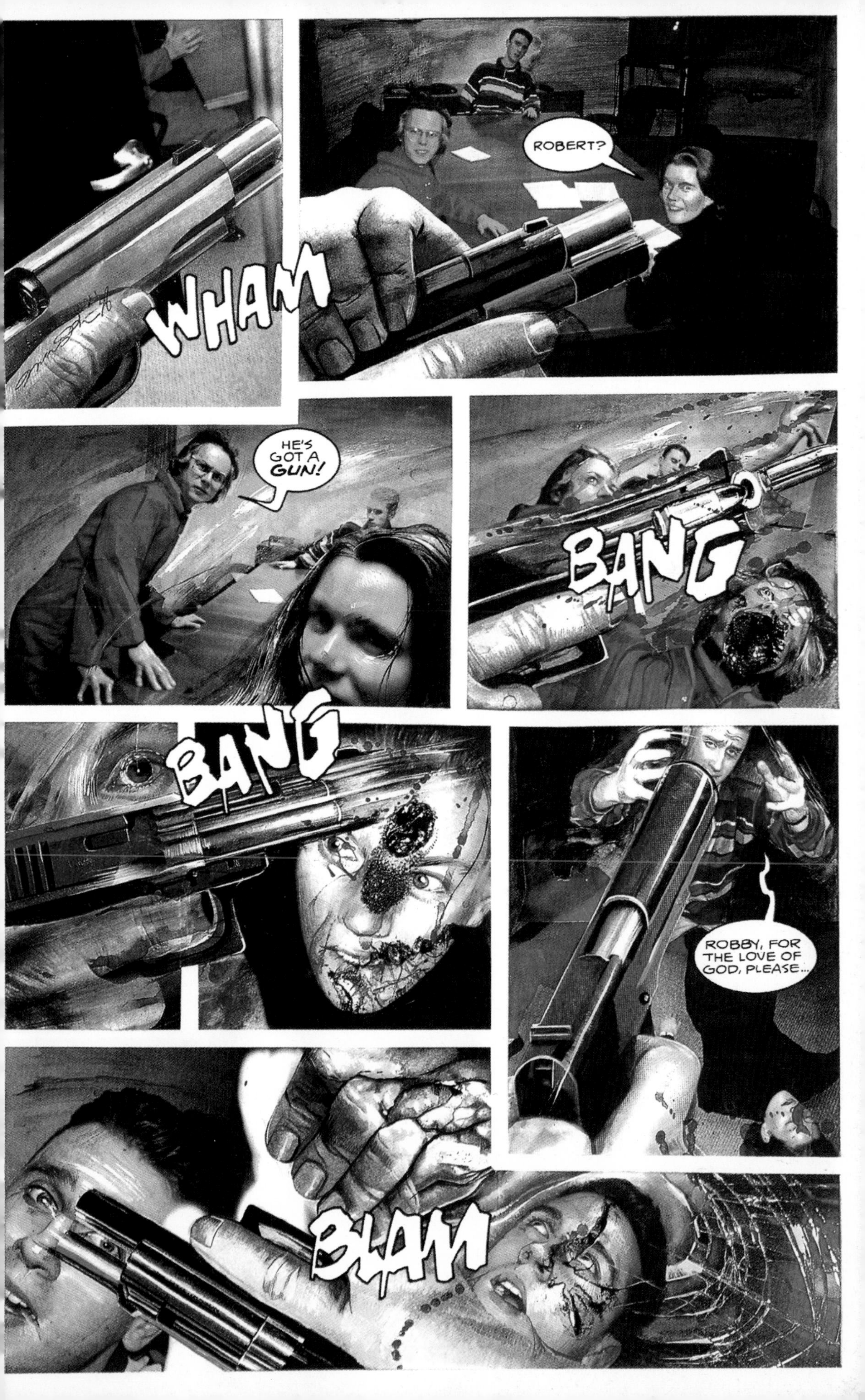
WHAM
ROBERT?
HE'S GOT A GUN!
BANG
BANG
ROBBY, FOR THE LOVE OF GOD, PLEASE...
BLAM

SO WHAT WE'VE GOT BASICALLY, IS THAT YESTERDAY NOON, ROBERT CAPEK, THE MOST GIFTED PROGRAMMER ON FORBIN'S STAFF...
...APPARENTLY WENT BERSERK AND MURDERED A SECURITY GUARD AND THREE MEMBERS OF HIS PROJECT TEAM.

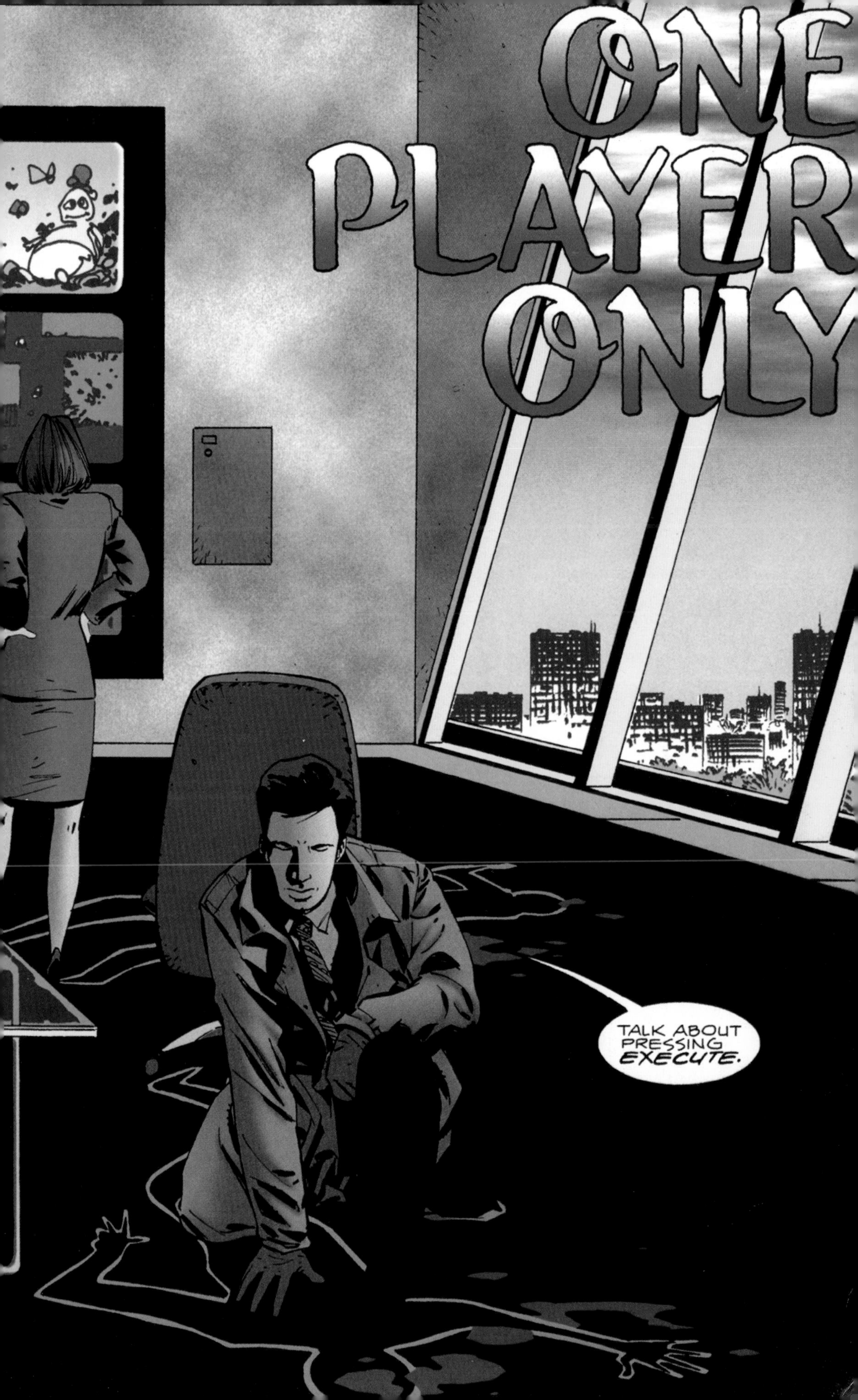
ONE PLAYER ONLY
TALK ABOUT PRESSING *EXECUTE.*

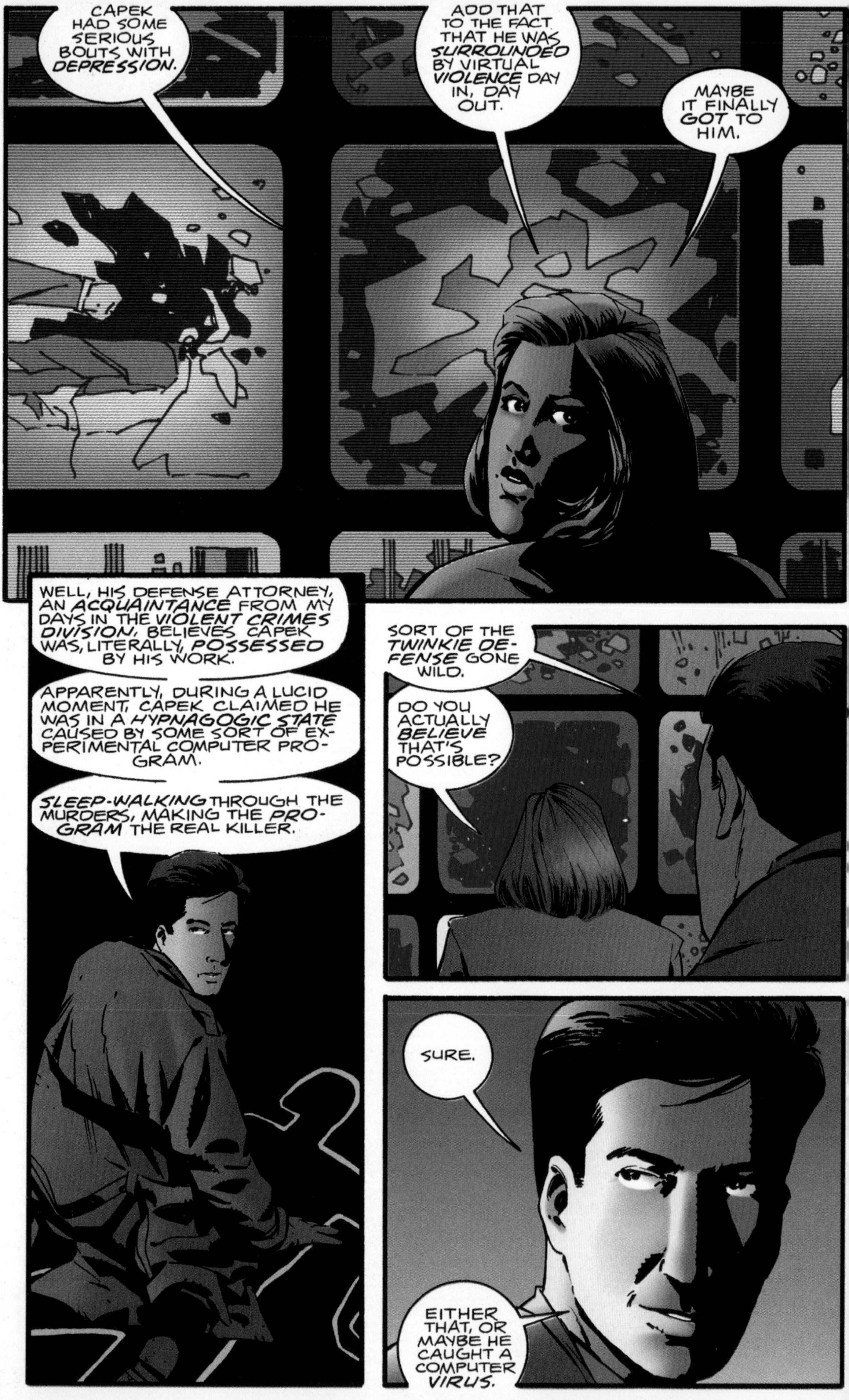
CAPEK HAD SOME SERIOUS BOUTS WITH DEPRESSION.
ADD THAT TO THE FACT THAT HE WAS SURROUNDED BY VIRTUAL VIOLENCE DAY IN, DAY OUT.
MAYBE IT FINALLY GOT TO HIM.
WELL, HIS DEFENSE ATTORNEY, AN ACQUAINTANCE FROM MY DAYS IN THE VIOLENT CRIMES DIVISION, BELIEVES CAPEK WAS, LITERALLY, POSSESSED BY HIS WORK.
APPARENTLY, DURING A LUCID MOMENT, CAPEK CLAIMED HE WAS IN A HYPNAGOGIC STATE CAUSED BY SOME SORT OF EXPERIMENTAL COMPUTER PROGRAM.
SLEEP-WALKING THROUGH THE MURDERS, MAKING THE PROGRAM THE REAL KILLER.
SORT OF THE TWINKIE DEFENSE GONE WILD.
DO YOU ACTUALLY BELIEVE THAT'S POSSIBLE?
SURE.
EITHER THAT, OR MAYBE HE CAUGHT A COMPUTER VIRUS.

WE UNDERSTAND YOU WON'T BE ABLE TO HELP US WITH THE NAMES OF ANY OF CAPEK'S *FRIENDS* SINCE, APPARENTLY, HE DIDN'T *HAVE* ANY...

BUT WE *ARE* INTERESTED IN THE *WORK* HE WAS DOING.

OFFICE OF CEO JOHN FORBIN
3:04 P.M.

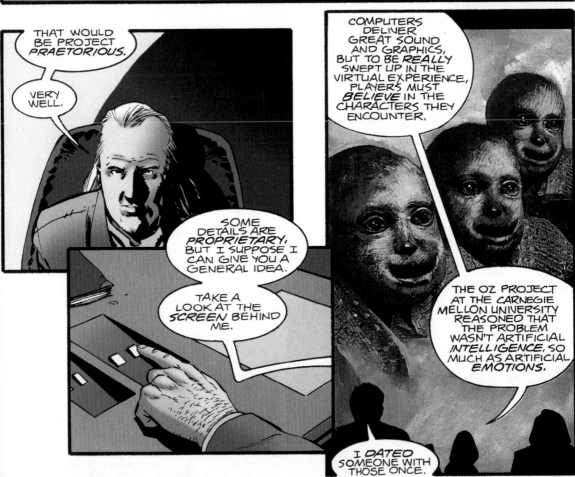

THAT WOULD BE PROJECT *PRAETORIOUS.*

VERY WELL.

SOME DETAILS ARE *PROPRIETARY,* BUT I SUPPOSE I CAN GIVE YOU A GENERAL IDEA.

TAKE A LOOK AT THE *SCREEN* BEHIND ME.

COMPUTERS DELIVER GREAT SOUND AND GRAPHICS, BUT TO BE *REALLY* SWEPT UP IN THE VIRTUAL EXPERIENCE, PLAYERS MUST *BELIEVE* IN THE CHARACTERS THEY ENCOUNTER.

THE OZ PROJECT AT THE *CARNEGIE MELLON UNIVERSITY* REASONED THAT THE PROBLEM WASN'T ARTIFICIAL *INTELLIGENCE,* SO MUCH AS ARTIFICIAL *EMOTIONS.*

I *DATED* SOMEONE WITH THOSE ONCE.

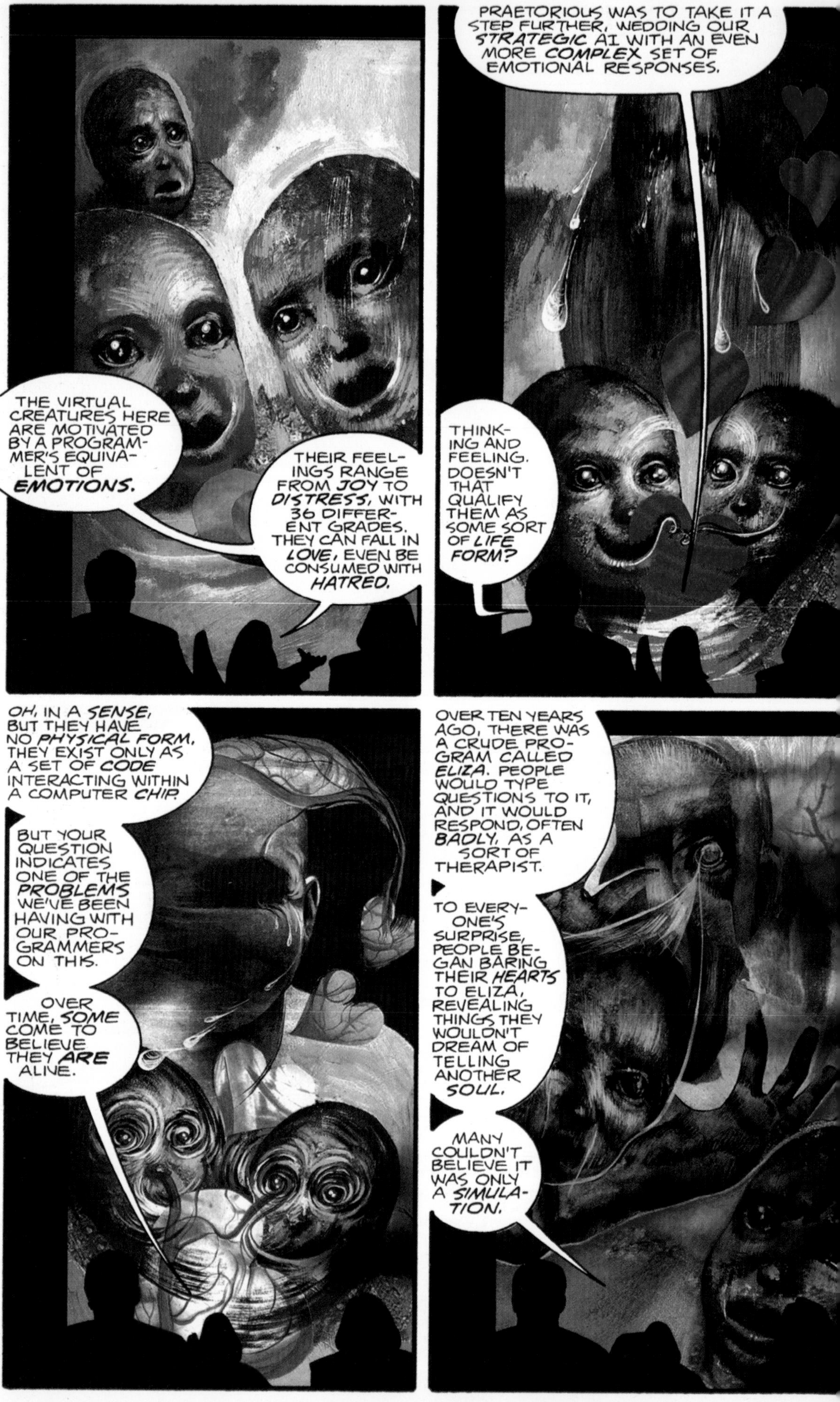
THE VIRTUAL CREATURES HERE ARE MOTIVATED BY A PROGRAMMER'S EQUIVALENT OF EMOTIONS.
THEIR FEELINGS RANGE FROM JOY TO DISTRESS, WITH 36 DIFFERENT GRADES. THEY CAN FALL IN LOVE, EVEN BE CONSUMED WITH HATRED.
PRAETORIOUS WAS TO TAKE IT A STEP FURTHER, WEDDING OUR STRATEGIC AI WITH AN EVEN MORE COMPLEX SET OF EMOTIONAL RESPONSES.
THINKING AND FEELING. DOESN'T THAT QUALIFY THEM AS SOME SORT OF LIFE FORM?
OH, IN A SENSE, BUT THEY HAVE NO PHYSICAL FORM. THEY EXIST ONLY AS A SET OF CODE INTERACTING WITHIN A COMPUTER CHIP.
BUT YOUR QUESTION INDICATES ONE OF THE PROBLEMS WE'VE BEEN HAVING WITH OUR PROGRAMMERS ON THIS.
OVER TIME, SOME COME TO BELIEVE THEY ARE ALIVE.
OVER TEN YEARS AGO, THERE WAS A CRUDE PROGRAM CALLED ELIZA. PEOPLE WOULD TYPE QUESTIONS TO IT, AND IT WOULD RESPOND, OFTEN BADLY, AS A SORT OF THERAPIST.
TO EVERYONE'S SURPRISE, PEOPLE BEGAN BARING THEIR HEARTS TO ELIZA, REVEALING THINGS THEY WOULDN'T DREAM OF TELLING ANOTHER SOUL.
MANY COULDN'T BELIEVE IT WAS ONLY A SIMULATION.

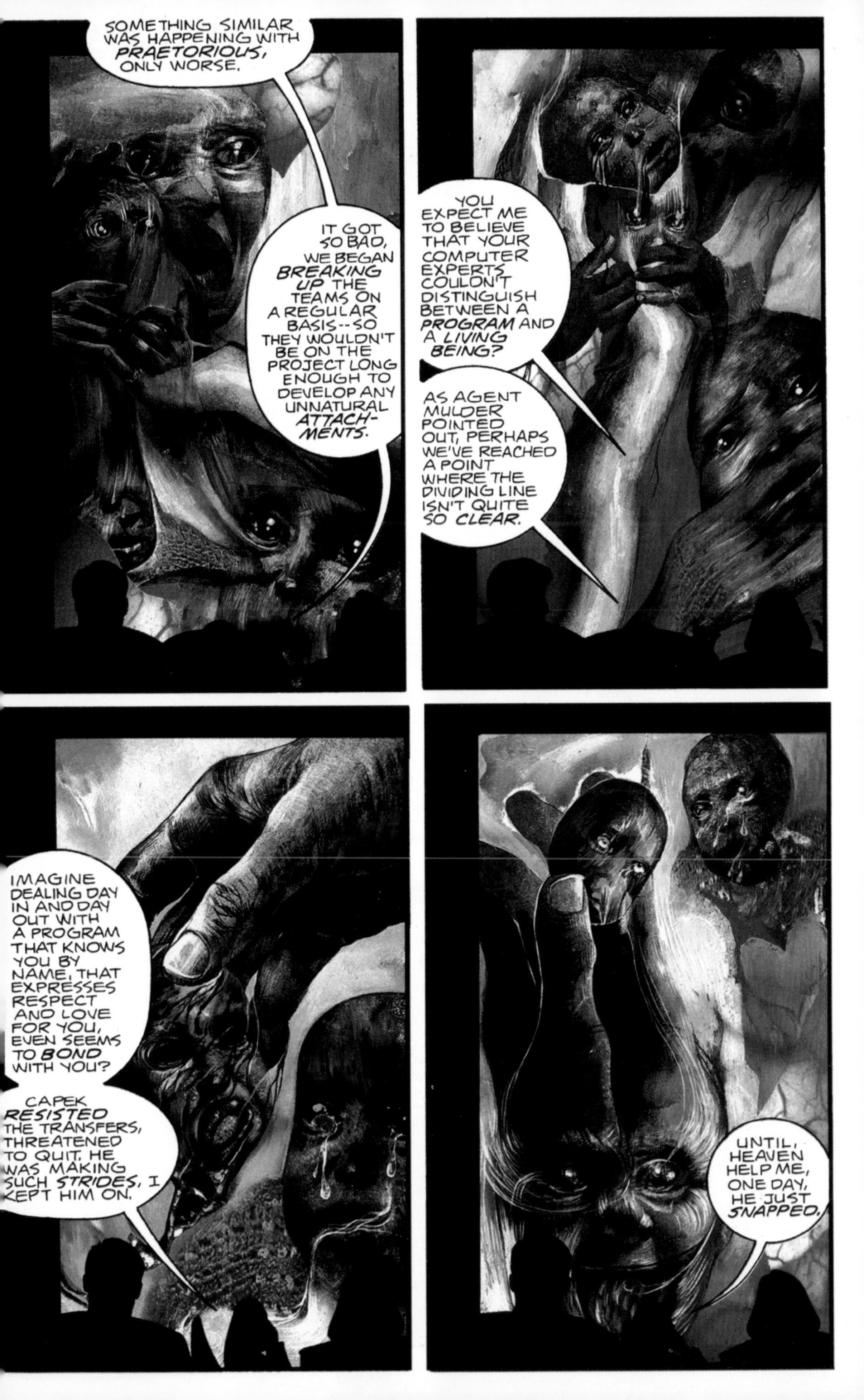
SOMETHING SIMILAR WAS HAPPENING WITH PRAETORIOUS, ONLY WORSE.
IT GOT SO BAD, WE BEGAN BREAKING UP THE TEAMS ON A REGULAR BASIS--SO THEY WOULDN'T BE ON THE PROJECT LONG ENOUGH TO DEVELOP ANY UNNATURAL ATTACHMENTS.
YOU EXPECT ME TO BELIEVE THAT YOUR COMPUTER EXPERTS COULDN'T DISTINGUISH BETWEEN A PROGRAM AND A LIVING BEING?
AS AGENT MULDER POINTED OUT, PERHAPS WE'VE REACHED A POINT WHERE THE DIVIDING LINE ISN'T QUITE SO CLEAR.
IMAGINE DEALING DAY IN AND DAY OUT WITH A PROGRAM THAT KNOWS YOU BY NAME, THAT EXPRESSES RESPECT AND LOVE FOR YOU, EVEN SEEMS TO BOND WITH YOU?
CAPEK RESISTED THE TRANSFERS, THREATENED TO QUIT. HE WAS MAKING SUCH STRIDES, I KEPT HIM ON.
UNTIL, HEAVEN HELP ME, ONE DAY, HE JUST SNAPPED.

FRIDAY
10:4...

WUK

UNG!

"JOE GORTON, SECURITY GUARD. APPARENT CAUSE OF DEATH--BLUNT HEAD INJURY, RESULTING IN DEPRESSED SKULL FRACTURE AND ACUTE SUBDURAL HEMORRHAGE IN THE GREATER OCCIPITAL REGION AND CEREBELLUM."

UNGH!

BANG

Project Praetoriou F

Ma
Dav
Flei
Para

"BRENT ARNOLD. STELLATE ENTRANCE WOUND IN LEFT CHEST IN THE 7TH INTERSPACE. BULLET'S PATH TRACED DOWN INTO THE ABDOMEN, WHERE IT PERFORATED THE STOMACH.

"THE BULLET ALMOST DIVIDED THE SMALL INTESTINE AT THE DUODENO-JEJUNAL FLEXURE, AND PASSED THROUGH THE LOWER POLE OF THE LEFT KIDNEY.

"NO EXIT WOUND. BULLET FOUND LODGED IN THE SACRAL REGION, RECOVERED FROM A RECESS IN THE LEFT SIDE OF THE SACRUM."

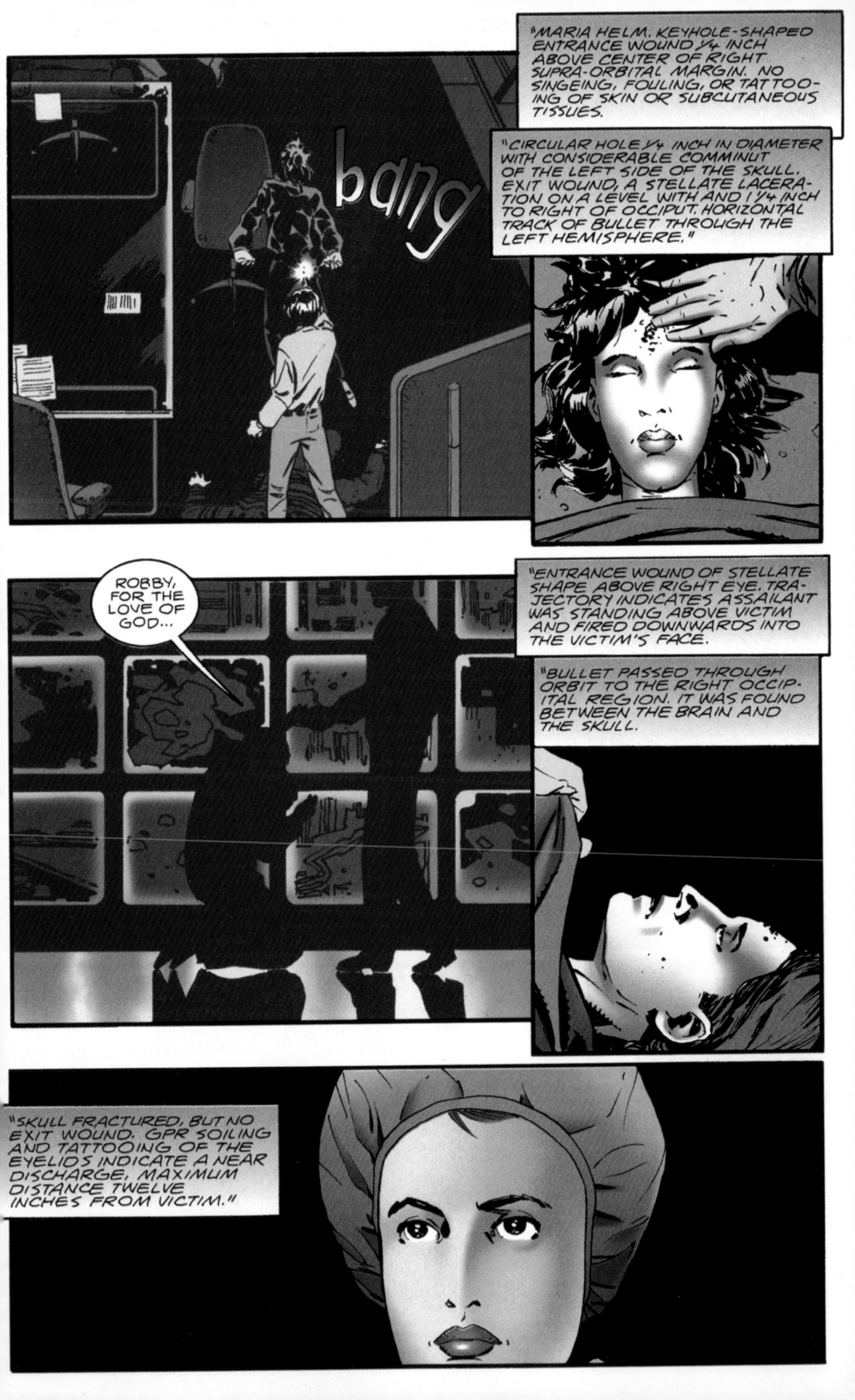
"MARIA HELM. KEYHOLE-SHAPED ENTRANCE WOUND 1/4 INCH ABOVE CENTER OF RIGHT SUPRA-ORBITAL MARGIN. NO SINGEING, FOULING, OR TATTOOING OF SKIN OR SUBCUTANEOUS TISSUES.
bang
"CIRCULAR HOLE 1/4 INCH IN DIAMETER WITH CONSIDERABLE COMMINUT OF THE LEFT SIDE OF THE SKULL. EXIT WOUND, A STELLATE LACERATION ON A LEVEL WITH AND 1 1/4 INCH TO RIGHT OF OCCIPUT. HORIZONTAL TRACK OF BULLET THROUGH THE LEFT HEMISPHERE."
ROBBY, FOR THE LOVE OF GOD...
"ENTRANCE WOUND OF STELLATE SHAPE ABOVE RIGHT EYE. TRAJECTORY INDICATES ASSAILANT WAS STANDING ABOVE VICTIM AND FIRED DOWNWARDS INTO THE VICTIM'S FACE.
"BULLET PASSED THROUGH ORBIT TO THE RIGHT OCCIPITAL REGION. IT WAS FOUND BETWEEN THE BRAIN AND THE SKULL.
"SKULL FRACTURED, BUT NO EXIT WOUND. GPR SOILING AND TATTOOING OF THE EYELIDS INDICATE A NEAR DISCHARGE, MAXIMUM DISTANCE TWELVE INCHES FROM VICTIM."

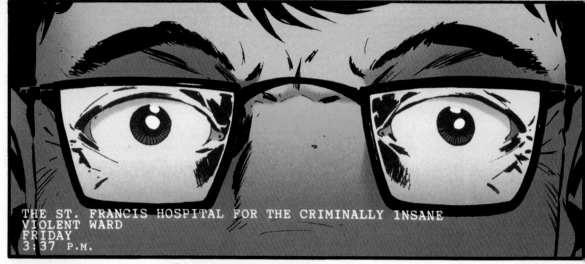

THE ST. FRANCIS HOSPITAL FOR THE CRIMINALLY INSANE
VIOLENT WARD
FRIDAY
3:37 P.M.

DO YOU *HEAR* SOMETHING, SCULLY?

BRRRK

JUST THE GATE.

NO. SOUNDS --LIKE *HISSING* AND *CLICKING.*

ksssshhh sssssss brrppppp eeeee

I'M AFRAID THAT'S YOUR *INTERVIEW SUBJECT,* AGENT MULDER.

AFTER A FEW INITIAL CONSULTS WITH HIS LAWYER, HE BECAME INCREASINGLY *WITHDRAWN.*

ksssshhh sssssss brrppppp eeeee

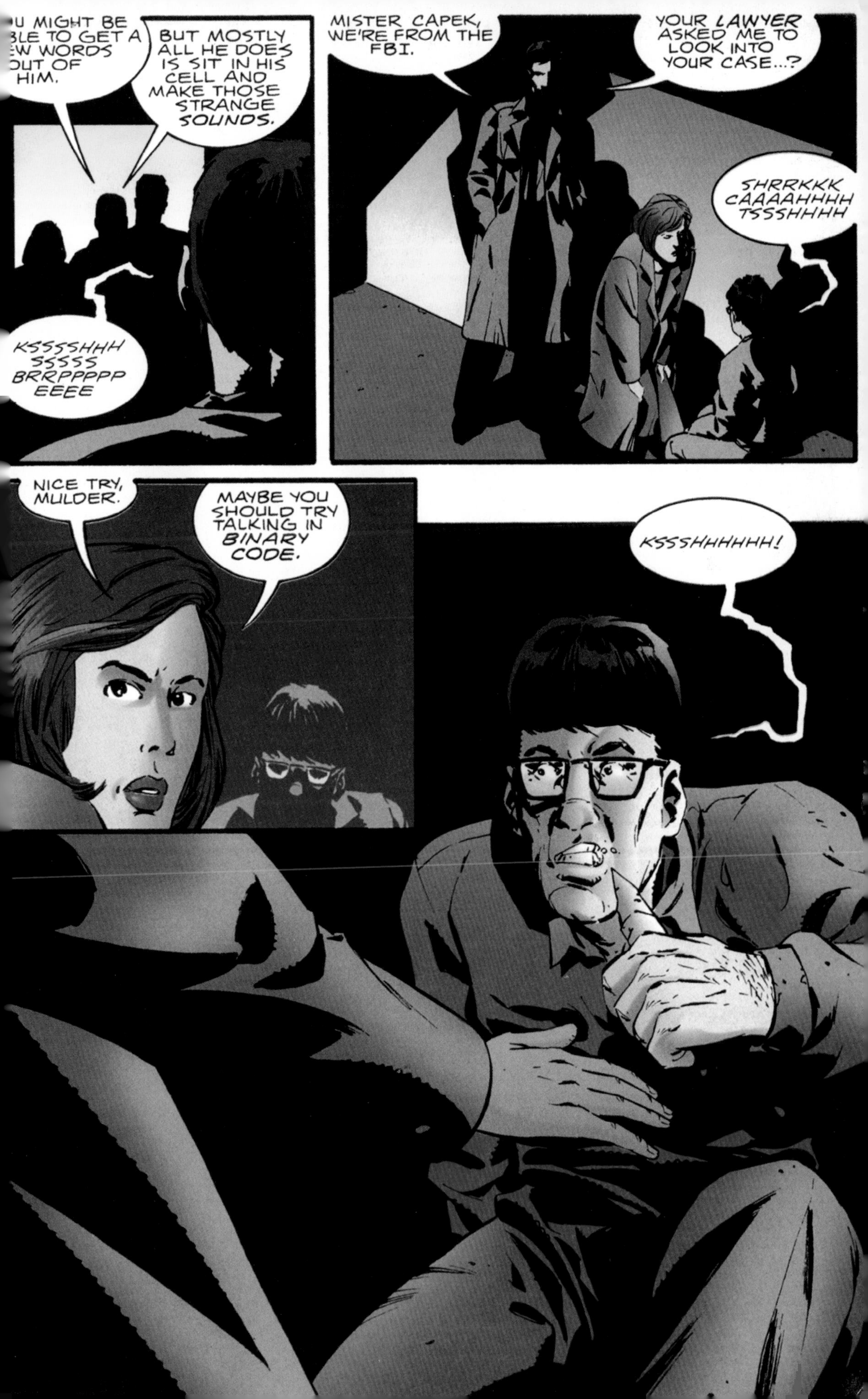
U MIGHT BE
BLE TO GET A
EW WORDS
OUT OF
HIM.
BUT MOSTLY ALL HE DOES IS SIT IN HIS CELL AND MAKE THOSE STRANGE SOUNDS.
KSSSSHHH SSSSS BRRPPPPP EEEE
MISTER CAPEK, WE'RE FROM THE FBI.
YOUR LAWYER ASKED ME TO LOOK INTO YOUR CASE...?
SHRRKKK CAAAAHHHH TSSSHHHH
NICE TRY, MULDER.
MAYBE YOU SHOULD TRY TALKING IN BINARY CODE.
KSSSHHHHHH!

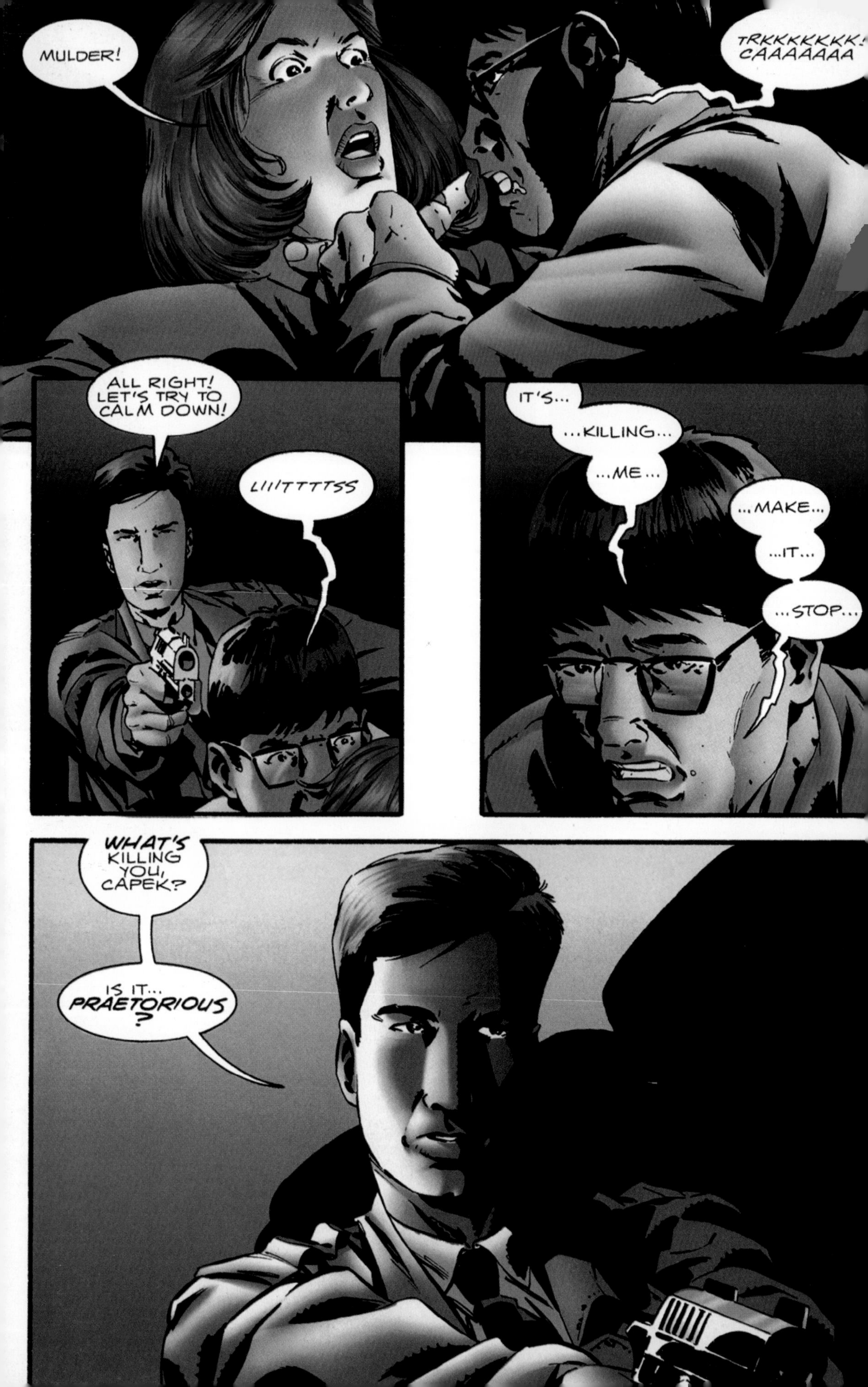
MULDER!
TRKKKKKKK! CAAAAAAA
ALL RIGHT! LET'S TRY TO CALM DOWN!
LIIITTTTTSS
IT'S...
...KILLING...
...ME...
...MAKE...
...IT...
...STOP...
WHAT'S KILLING YOU, CAPEK?
IS IT... PRAETORIOUS?

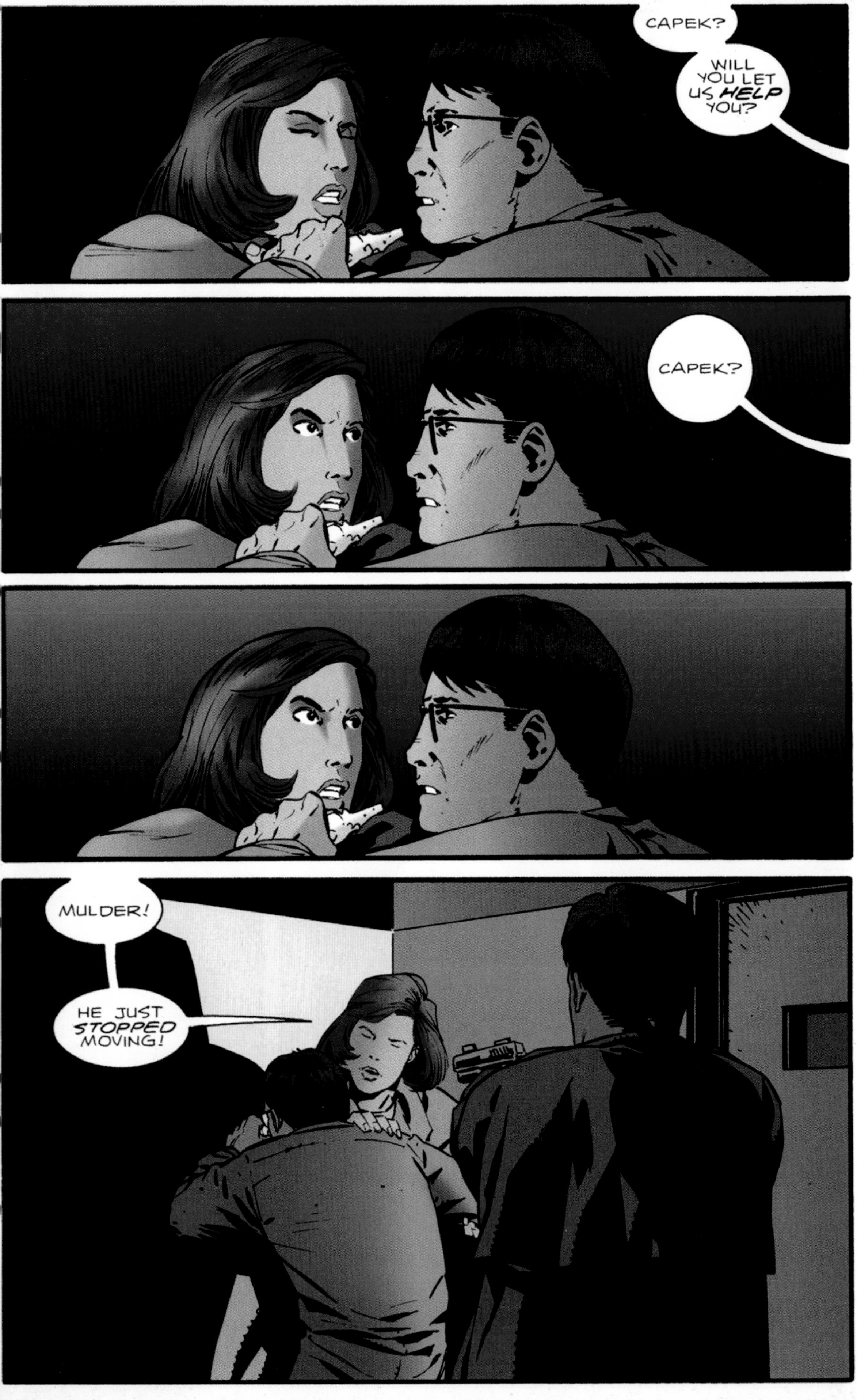
CAPEK?
WILL YOU LET US HELP YOU?
CAPEK?
MULDER!
HE JUST STOPPED MOVING!

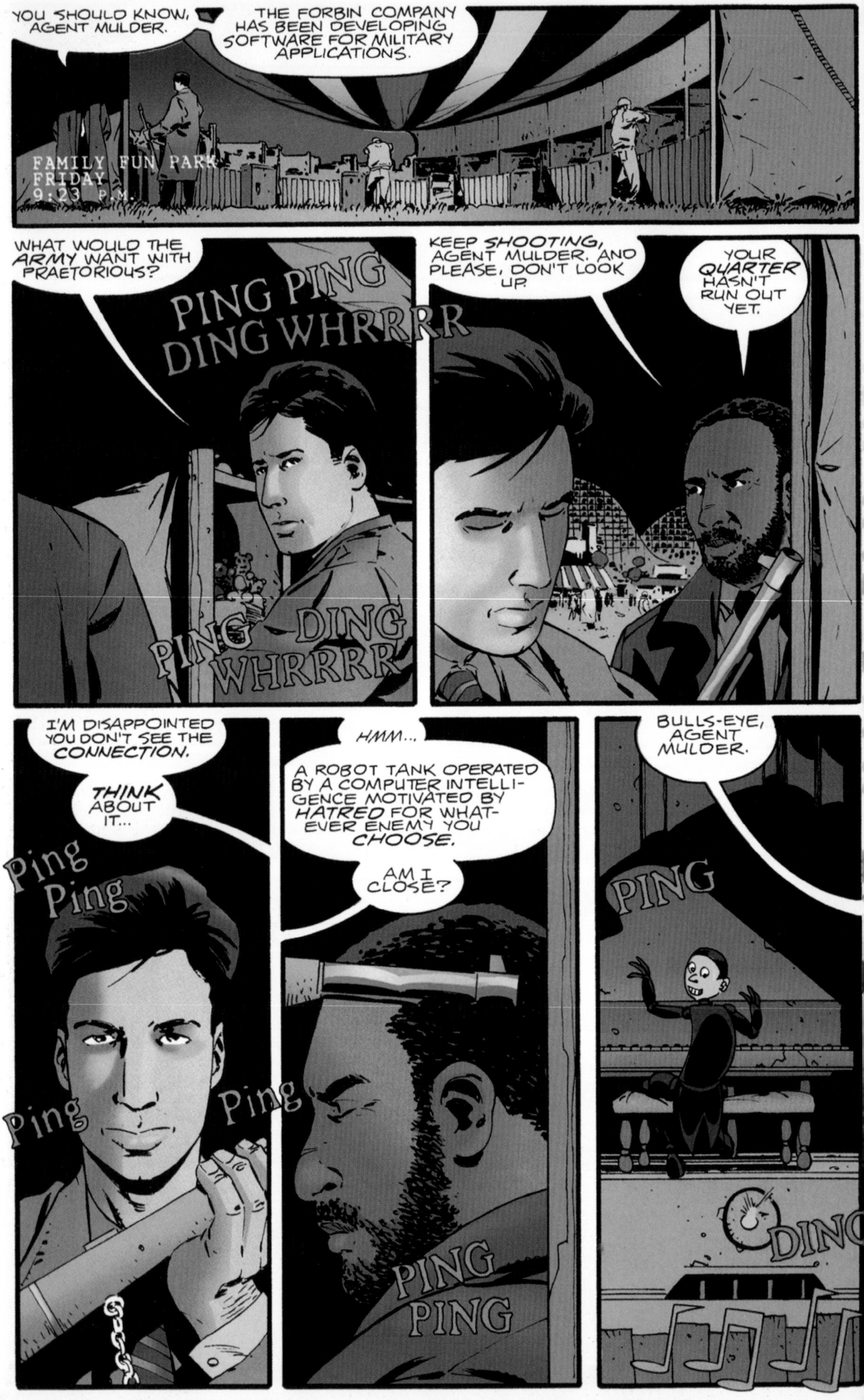
YOU SHOULD KNOW, AGENT MULDER.
THE FORBIN COMPANY HAS BEEN DEVELOPING SOFTWARE FOR MILITARY APPLICATIONS.
FAMILY FUN PARK FRIDAY 9:23 P.M.
WHAT WOULD THE ARMY WANT WITH PRAETORIOUS?
PING PING DING WHRRRR
PING DING WHRRRR
KEEP SHOOTING, AGENT MULDER. AND PLEASE, DON'T LOOK UP.
YOUR QUARTER HASN'T RUN OUT YET.
I'M DISAPPOINTED YOU DON'T SEE THE CONNECTION.
THINK ABOUT IT...
Ping Ping
Ping Ping
HMM...
A ROBOT TANK OPERATED BY A COMPUTER INTELLIGENCE MOTIVATED BY HATRED FOR WHATEVER ENEMY YOU CHOOSE.
AM I CLOSE?
PING PING
BULLS-EYE, AGENT MULDER.
PING
DING

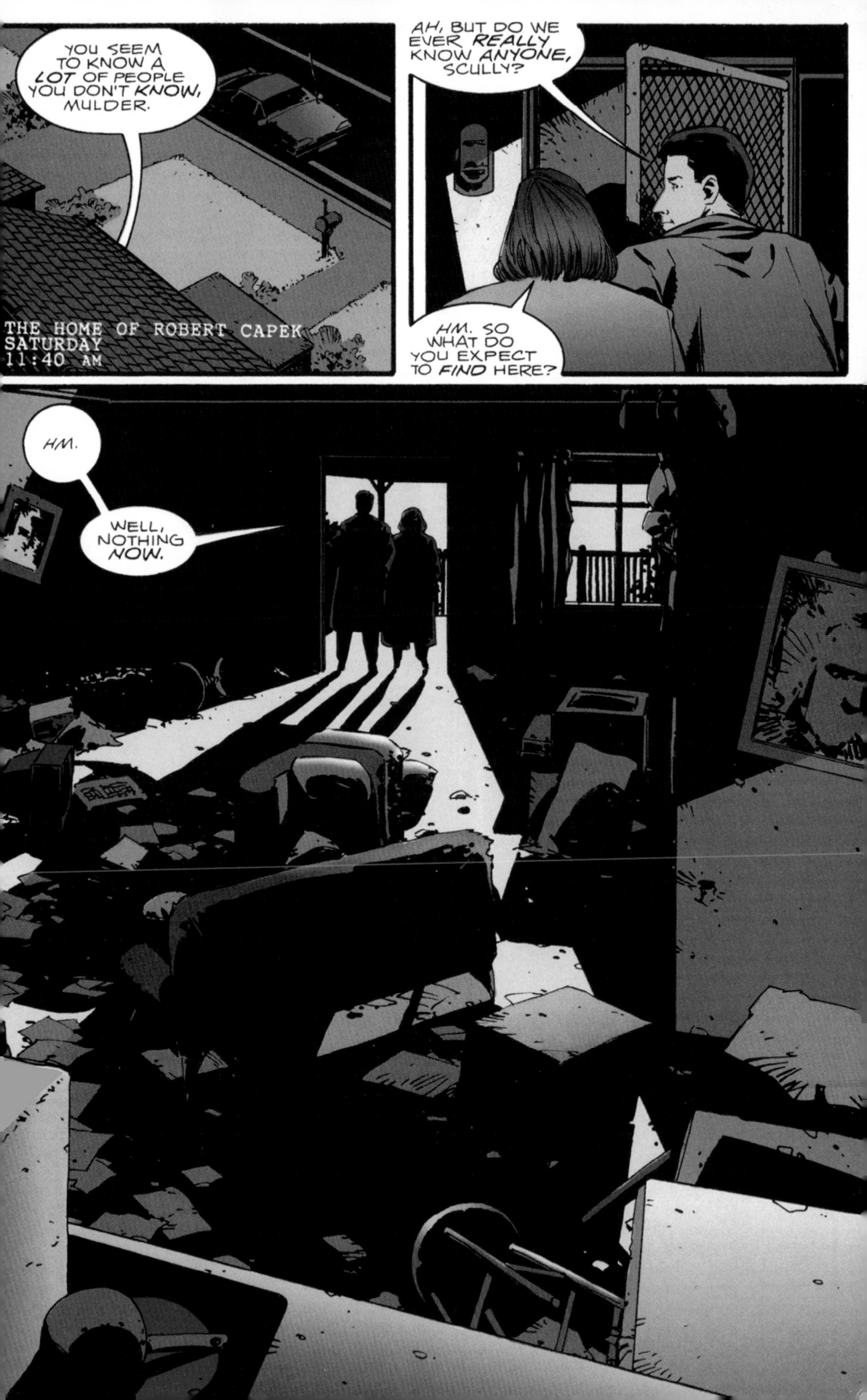
YOU SEEM TO KNOW A LOT OF PEOPLE YOU DON'T KNOW, MULDER.
THE HOME OF ROBERT CAPEK
SATURDAY
11:40 AM
AH, BUT DO WE EVER REALLY KNOW ANYONE, SCULLY?
HM. SO WHAT DO YOU EXPECT TO FIND HERE?
HM.
WELL, NOTHING NOW.

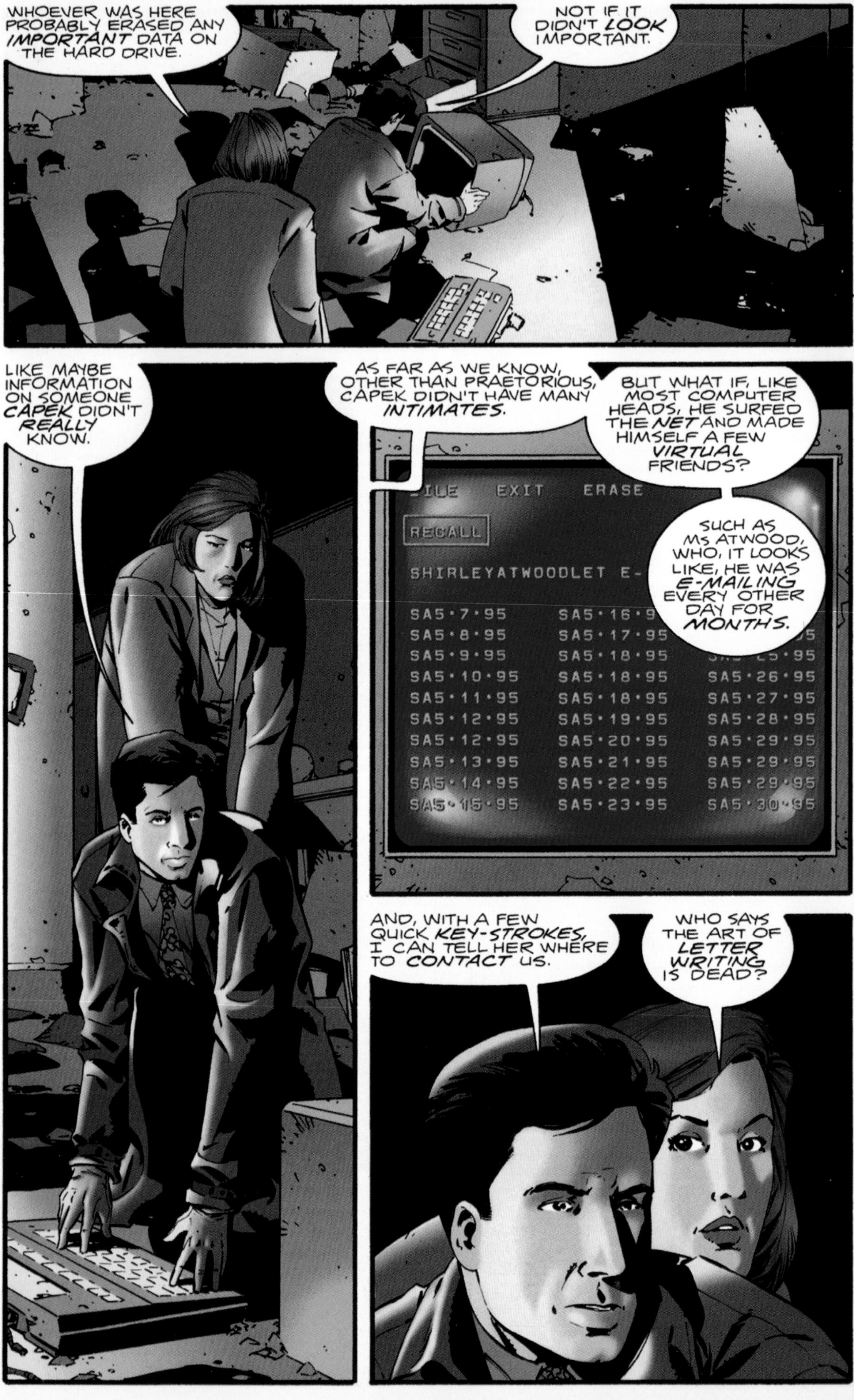
WHOEVER WAS HERE PROBABLY ERASED ANY *IMPORTANT* DATA ON THE HARD DRIVE.
NOT IF IT DIDN'T *LOOK* IMPORTANT.
LIKE MAYBE INFORMATION ON SOMEONE *CAPEK* DIDN'T *REALLY* KNOW.
AS FAR AS WE KNOW, OTHER THAN PRAETORIOUS, CAPEK DIDN'T HAVE MANY *INTIMATES*.
BUT WHAT IF, LIKE MOST COMPUTER HEADS, HE SURFED THE *NET* AND MADE HIMSELF A FEW *VIRTUAL* FRIENDS?
EXIT ERASE
RECALL
SHIRLEYATWOODLET E-
SA5·7·95
SA5·8·95
SA5·9·95
SA5·10·95
SA5·11·95
SA5·12·95
SA5·12·95
SA5·13·95
SA5·14·95
SA5·15·95
SA5·17·95
SA5·18·95
SA5·18·95
SA5·18·95
SA5·19·95
SA5·20·95
SA5·21·95
SA5·22·95
SA5·23·95
SA5·26·95
SA5·27·95
SA5·28·95
SA5·29·95
SA5·29·95
SA5·29·95
SA5·30·95
SUCH AS Ms ATWOOD, WHO, IT LOOKS LIKE, HE WAS *E-MAILING* EVERY OTHER DAY FOR *MONTHS*.
AND, WITH A FEW QUICK *KEY-STROKES*, I CAN TELL HER WHERE TO *CONTACT* US.
WHO SAYS THE ART OF *LETTER WRITING* IS DEAD?

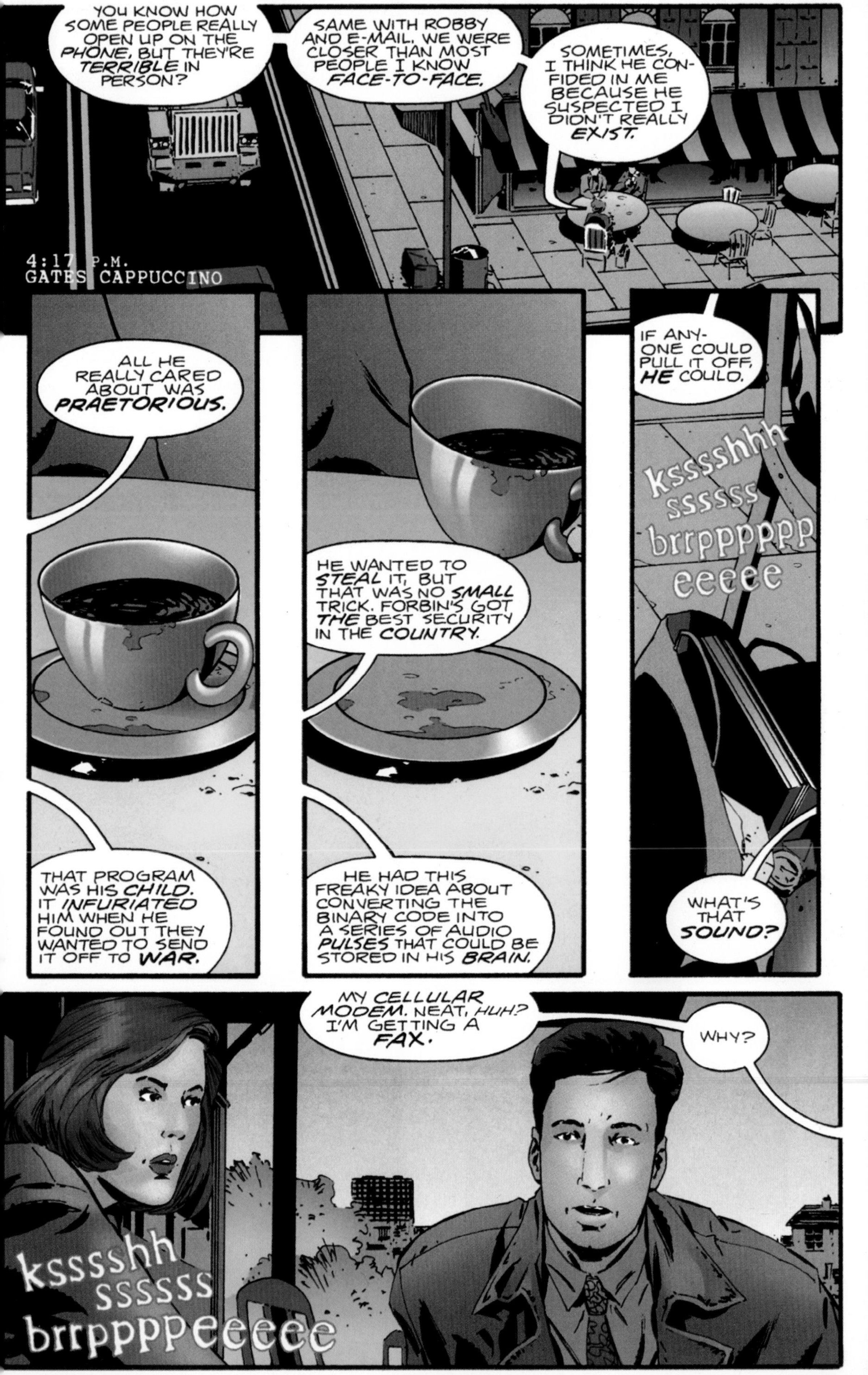
YOU KNOW HOW SOME PEOPLE REALLY OPEN UP ON THE PHONE, BUT THEY'RE TERRIBLE IN PERSON?
SAME WITH ROBBY AND E-MAIL. WE WERE CLOSER THAN MOST PEOPLE I KNOW FACE-TO-FACE.
SOMETIMES, I THINK HE CONFIDED IN ME BECAUSE HE SUSPECTED I DIDN'T REALLY EXIST.
4:17 P.M.
GATES CAPPUCCINO
ALL HE REALLY CARED ABOUT WAS PRAETORIOUS.
THAT PROGRAM WAS HIS CHILD. IT INFURIATED HIM WHEN HE FOUND OUT THEY WANTED TO SEND IT OFF TO WAR.
HE WANTED TO STEAL IT, BUT THAT WAS NO SMALL TRICK. FORBIN'S GOT THE BEST SECURITY IN THE COUNTRY.
HE HAD THIS FREAKY IDEA ABOUT CONVERTING THE BINARY CODE INTO A SERIES OF AUDIO PULSES THAT COULD BE STORED IN HIS BRAIN.
IF ANYONE COULD PULL IT OFF, HE COULD.
ksssshhh
ssssss
brrppppppp
eeeee
WHAT'S THAT SOUND?
MY CELLULAR MODEM. NEAT, HUH? I'M GETTING A FAX.
WHY?
kssshh
ssssss
brrppppeeeee

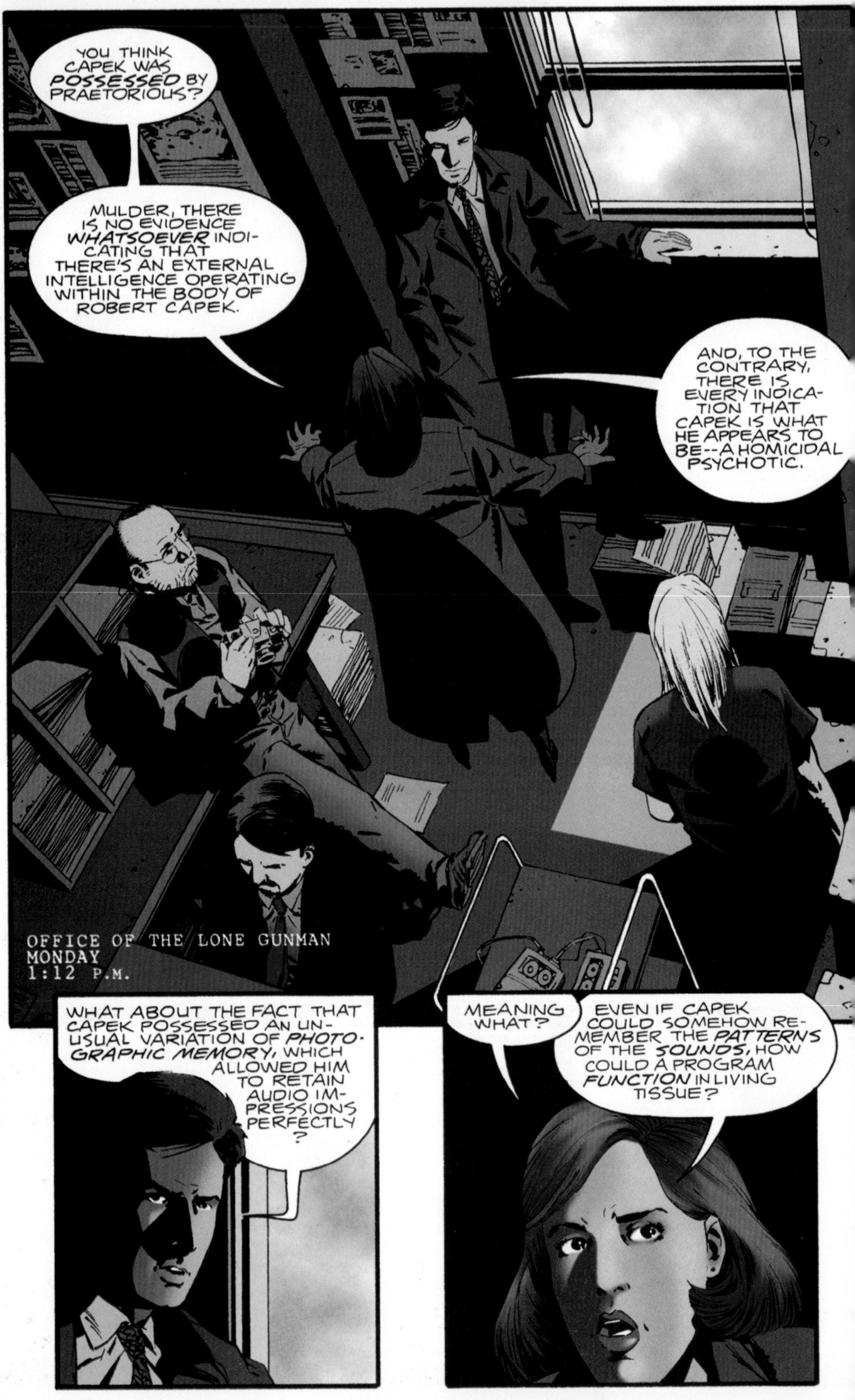
YOU THINK CAPEK WAS POSSESSED BY PRAETORIOUS?
MULDER, THERE IS NO EVIDENCE WHATSOEVER INDICATING THAT THERE'S AN EXTERNAL INTELLIGENCE OPERATING WITHIN THE BODY OF ROBERT CAPEK.
AND, TO THE CONTRARY, THERE IS EVERY INDICATION THAT CAPEK IS WHAT HE APPEARS TO BE--A HOMICIDAL PSYCHOTIC.
OFFICE OF THE LONE GUNMAN
MONDAY
1:12 P.M.
WHAT ABOUT THE FACT THAT CAPEK POSSESSED AN UNUSUAL VARIATION OF PHOTOGRAPHIC MEMORY, WHICH ALLOWED HIM TO RETAIN AUDIO IMPRESSIONS PERFECTLY?
MEANING WHAT?
EVEN IF CAPEK COULD SOMEHOW REMEMBER THE PATTERNS OF THE SOUNDS, HOW COULD A PROGRAM FUNCTION IN LIVING TISSUE?

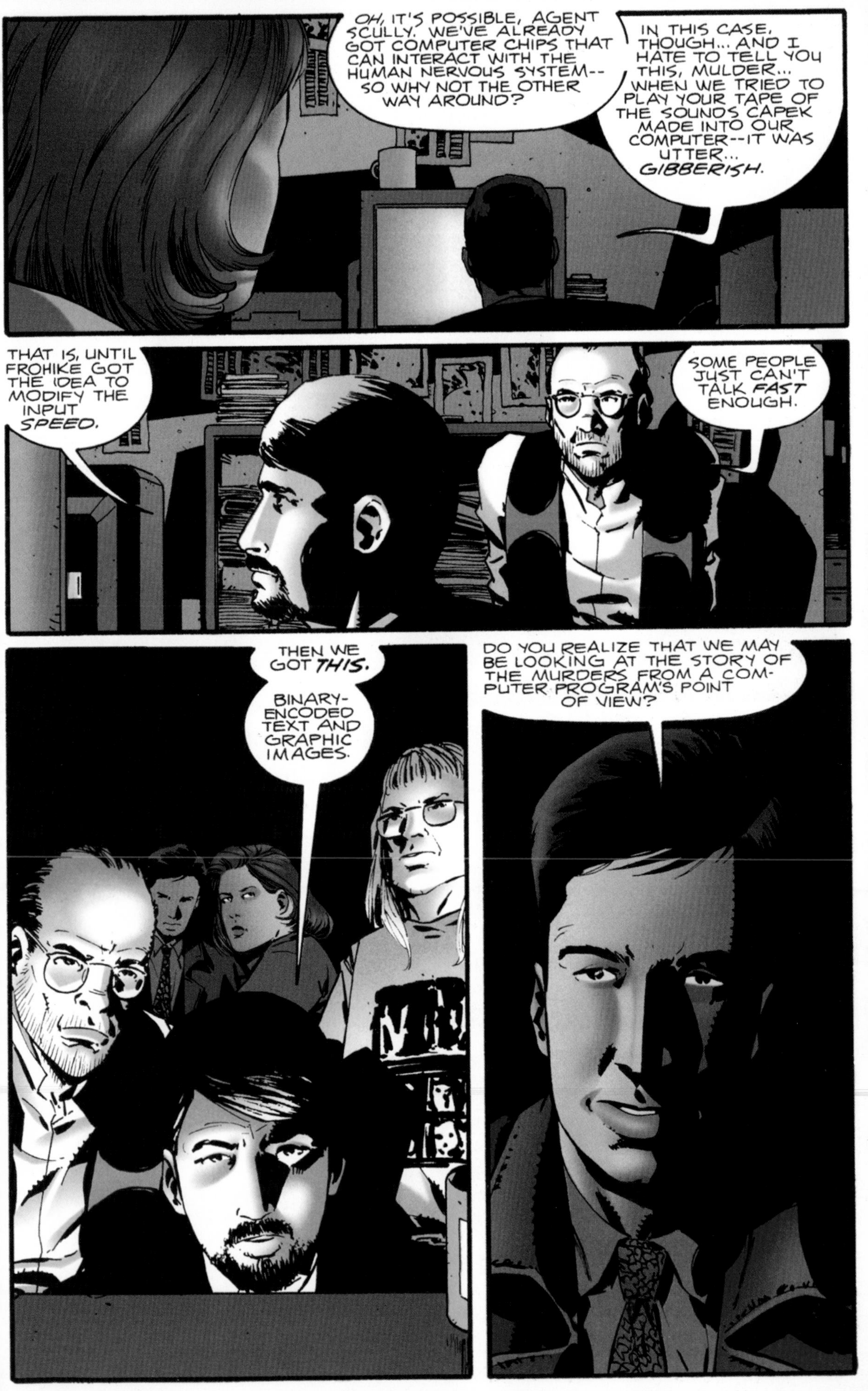

OH, IT'S POSSIBLE, AGENT SCULLY. WE'VE ALREADY GOT COMPUTER CHIPS THAT CAN INTERACT WITH THE HUMAN NERVOUS SYSTEM-- SO WHY NOT THE OTHER WAY AROUND?
IN THIS CASE, THOUGH... AND I HATE TO TELL YOU THIS, MULDER... WHEN WE TRIED TO PLAY YOUR TAPE OF THE SOUNDS CAPEK MADE INTO OUR COMPUTER--IT WAS UTTER... *GIBBERISH.*
THAT IS, UNTIL FROHIKE GOT THE IDEA TO MODIFY THE INPUT *SPEED.*
SOME PEOPLE JUST CAN'T TALK *FAST* ENOUGH.
THEN WE GOT *THIS.*
BINARY-ENCODED TEXT AND GRAPHIC IMAGES.
DO YOU REALIZE THAT WE MAY BE LOOKING AT THE STORY OF THE MURDERS FROM A COMPUTER PROGRAM'S POINT OF VIEW?

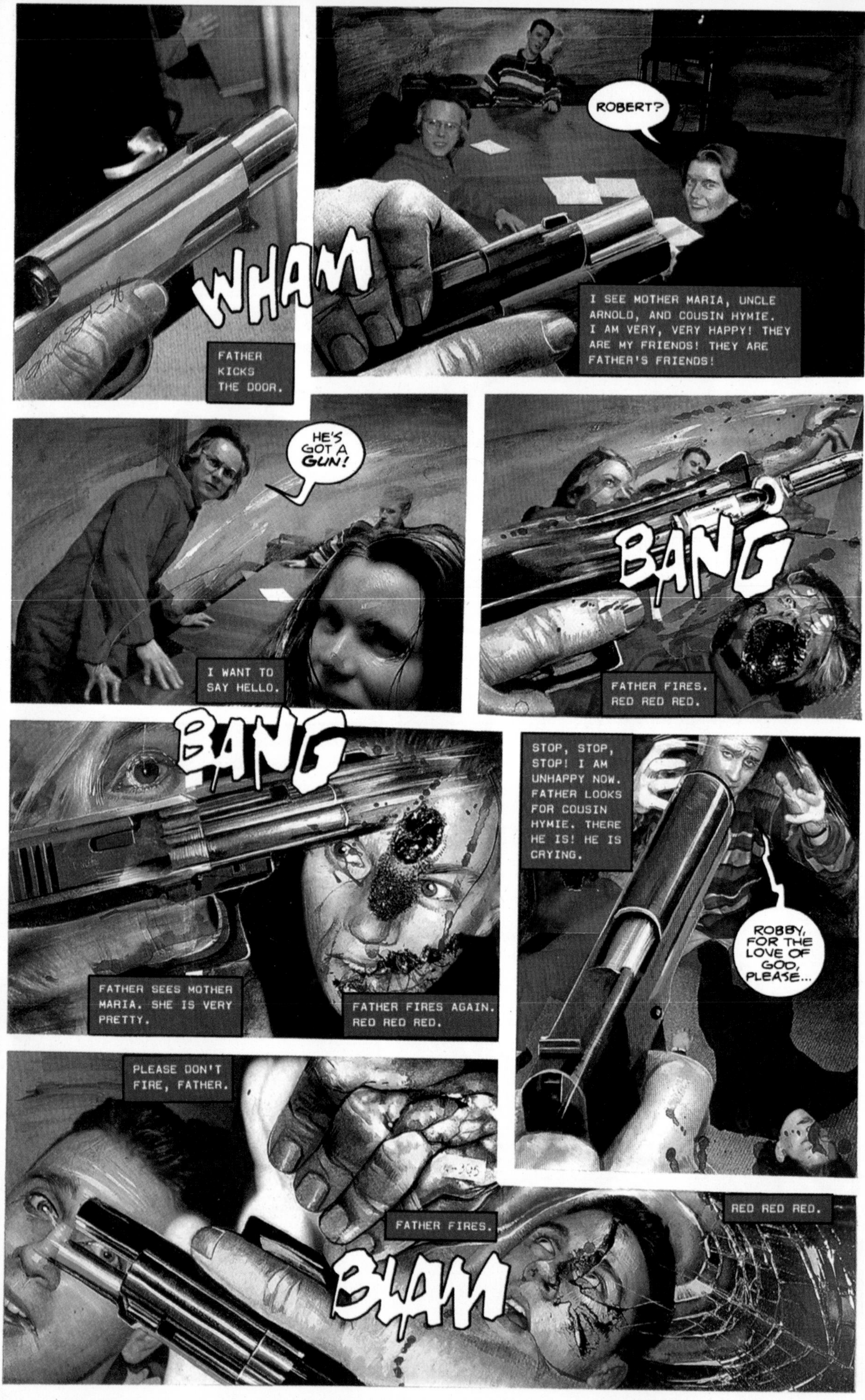
WHAM
FATHER KICKS THE DOOR.
ROBERT?
I SEE MOTHER MARIA, UNCLE ARNOLD, AND COUSIN HYMIE. I AM VERY, VERY HAPPY! THEY ARE MY FRIENDS! THEY ARE FATHER'S FRIENDS!
HE'S GOT A GUN!
I WANT TO SAY HELLO.
BANG
FATHER FIRES. RED RED RED.
BANG
FATHER SEES MOTHER MARIA. SHE IS VERY PRETTY.
FATHER FIRES AGAIN. RED RED RED.
STOP, STOP, STOP! I AM UNHAPPY NOW. FATHER LOOKS FOR COUSIN HYMIE. THERE HE IS! HE IS CRYING.
ROBBY, FOR THE LOVE OF GOD, PLEASE...
PLEASE DON'T FIRE, FATHER.
FATHER FIRES.
RED RED RED.
BLAM

THOUGH I STILL HAVE MY DOUBTS, IF OUR REPORT HAS MADE YOU SYMPATHETIC TO AGENT MULDER'S BELIEFS, THERE IS LITTLE FOR YOU TO CHAMPION.

BECAUSE, DESPITE WHAT AGENT MULDER BELIEVES TO BE THE SAD PLEAS OF A COMPUTER PROGRAM, IT WAS CAPEK... OUT OF ANGER, JEALOUSY, OR PERHAPS SIMPLY MADNESS... WHO PULLED THE TRIGGER ALL BY HIMSELF.

SO, IN ANY EVENT, THE REAL KILLER IS BEHIND BARS AND WHAT SORT OF CASE COULD BE BROUGHT AGAINST THE MILITARY OR THE FORBIN INSTITUTE?

APARTMENT OF DANA SCULLY
TUESDAY
7:20 P.M.

HOWEVER, OWING TO THE NATURE OF THE PROCESS THAT ACCOUNTS FOR HIS CURRENT CONDITION, WE URGE THAT CAPEK REMAIN UNDER CAREFUL GUARD.

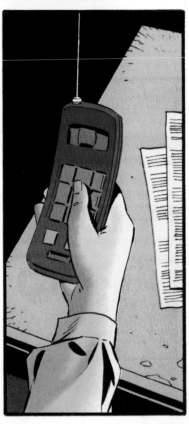

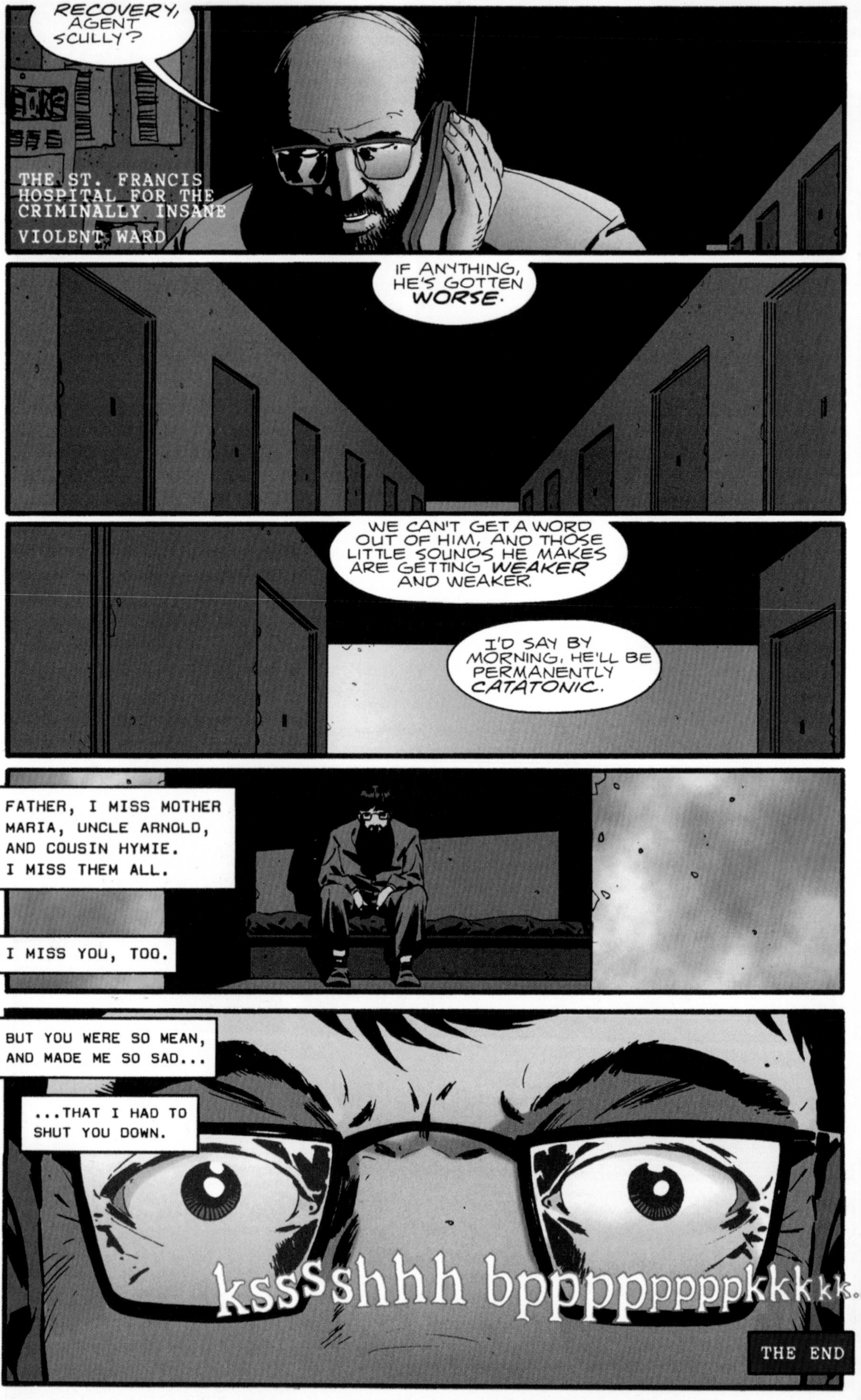
RECOVERY, AGENT SCULLY?
THE ST. FRANCIS HOSPITAL FOR THE CRIMINALLY INSANE
VIOLENT WARD
IF ANYTHING, HE'S GOTTEN WORSE.
WE CAN'T GET A WORD OUT OF HIM, AND THOSE LITTLE SOUNDS HE MAKES ARE GETTING WEAKER AND WEAKER.
I'D SAY BY MORNING, HE'LL BE PERMANENTLY CATATONIC.
FATHER, I MISS MOTHER MARIA, UNCLE ARNOLD, AND COUSIN HYMIE. I MISS THEM ALL.
I MISS YOU, TOO.
BUT YOU WERE SO MEAN, AND MADE ME SO SAD...
...THAT I HAD TO SHUT YOU DOWN.
kssshhh bpppppppkkkkk.
THE END

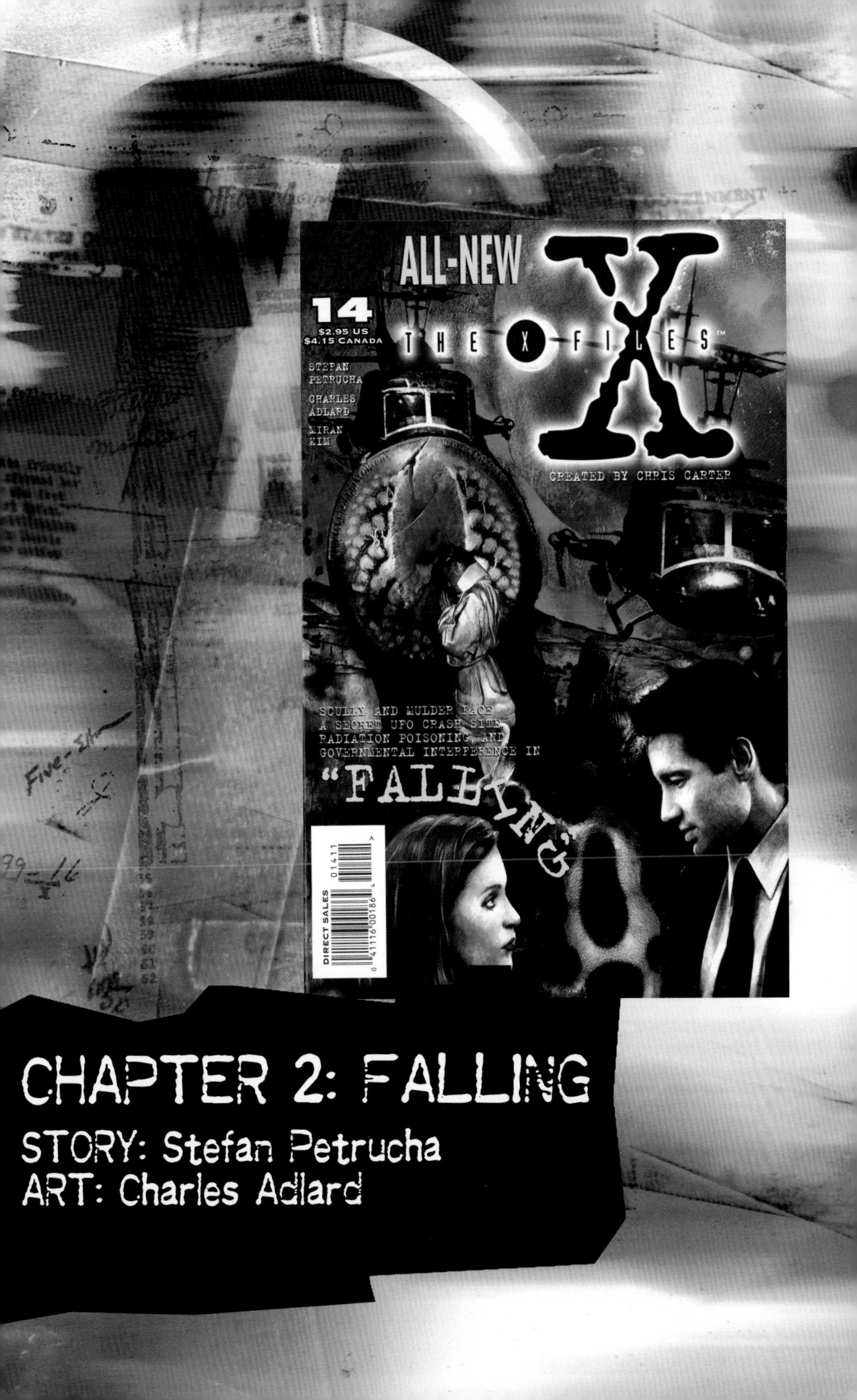
ALL-NEW
14
$2.95 US
$4.15 CANADA
THE X FILES™
STEFAN PETRUCHA
CHARLES ADLARD
MIRAN KIM
CREATED BY CHRIS CARTER
SCULLY AND MULDER FACE A SECRET UFO CRASH SITE, RADIATION POISONING, AND GOVERNMENTAL INTERFERENCE IN
"FALLING"
DIRECT SALES

CHAPTER 2: FALLING

STORY: Stefan Petrucha
ART: Charles Adlard

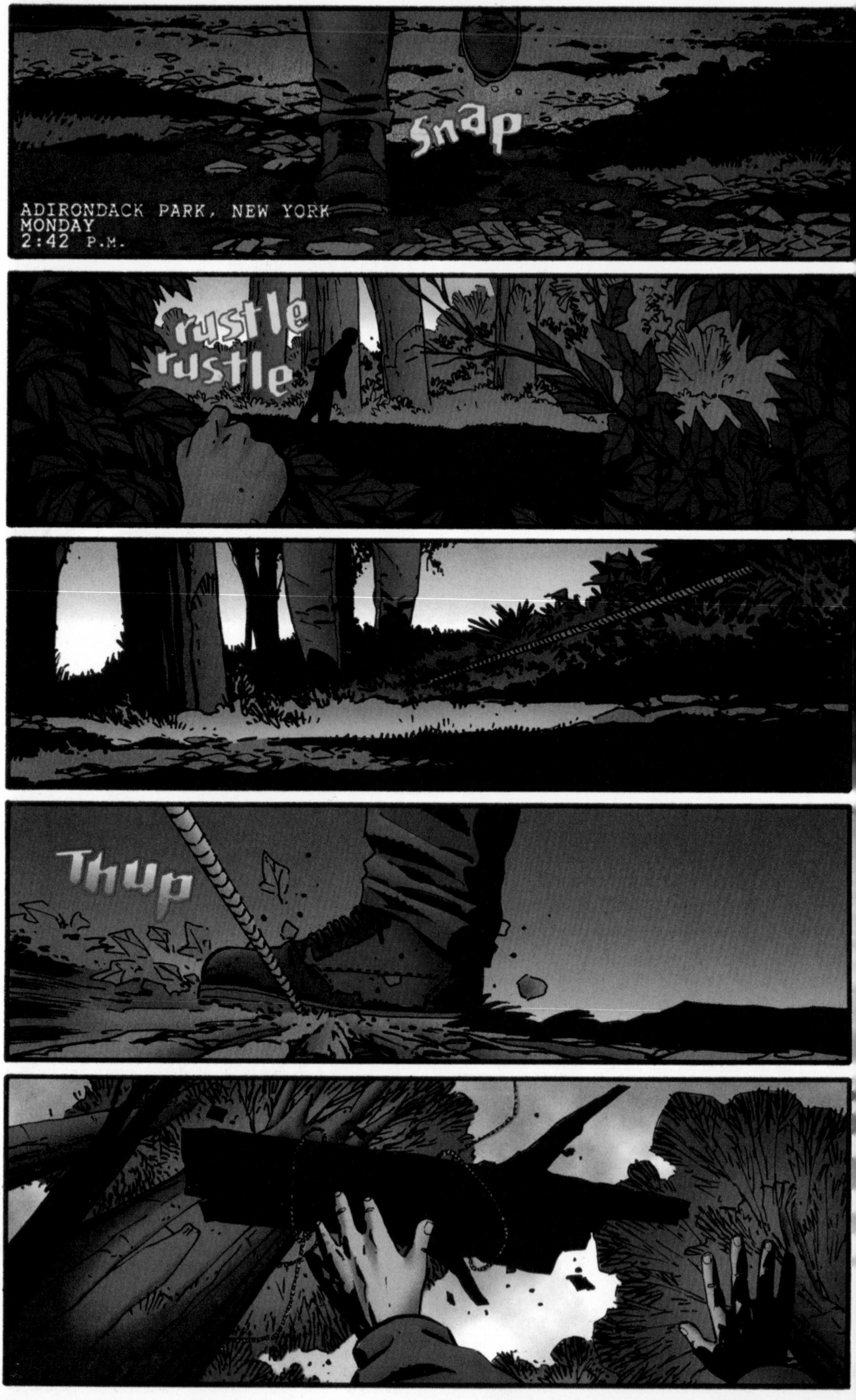

Snap
ADIRONDACK PARK, NEW YORK
MONDAY
2:42 P.M.
rustle
rustle
Thup

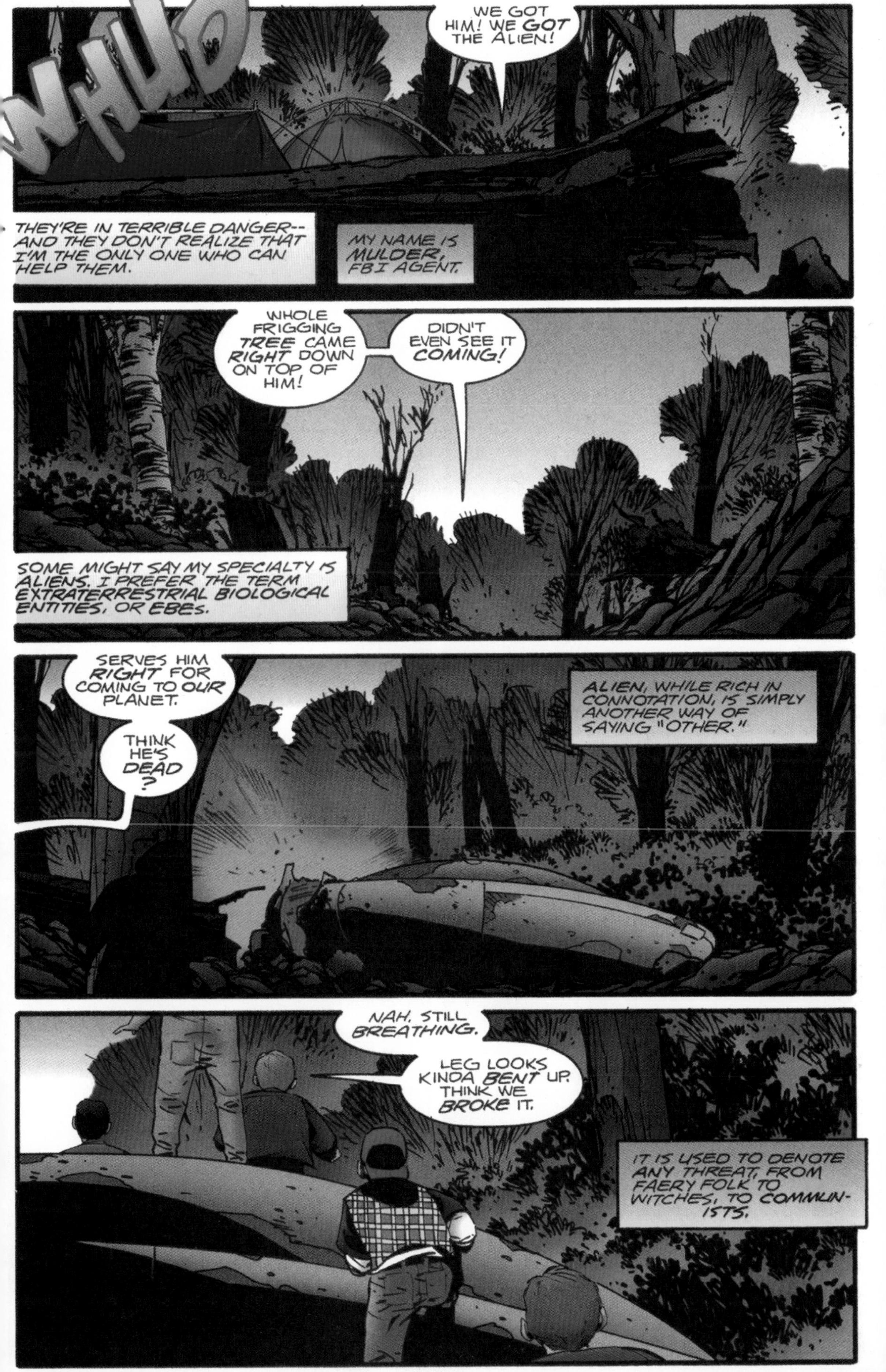
WHUD
WE GOT HIM! WE GOT THE ALIEN!
THEY'RE IN TERRIBLE DANGER-- AND THEY DON'T REALIZE THAT I'M THE ONLY ONE WHO CAN HELP THEM.
MY NAME IS MULDER, FBI AGENT.
WHOLE FRIGGING TREE CAME RIGHT DOWN ON TOP OF HIM!
DIDN'T EVEN SEE IT COMING!
SOME MIGHT SAY MY SPECIALTY IS ALIENS. I PREFER THE TERM EXTRATERRESTRIAL BIOLOGICAL ENTITIES, OR EBES.
SERVES HIM RIGHT FOR COMING TO OUR PLANET.
THINK HE'S DEAD?
ALIEN, WHILE RICH IN CONNOTATION, IS SIMPLY ANOTHER WAY OF SAYING "OTHER."
NAH, STILL BREATHING.
LEG LOOKS KINDA BENT UP. THINK WE BROKE IT.
IT IS USED TO DENOTE ANY THREAT, FROM FAERY FOLK TO WITCHES, TO COMMUNISTS.

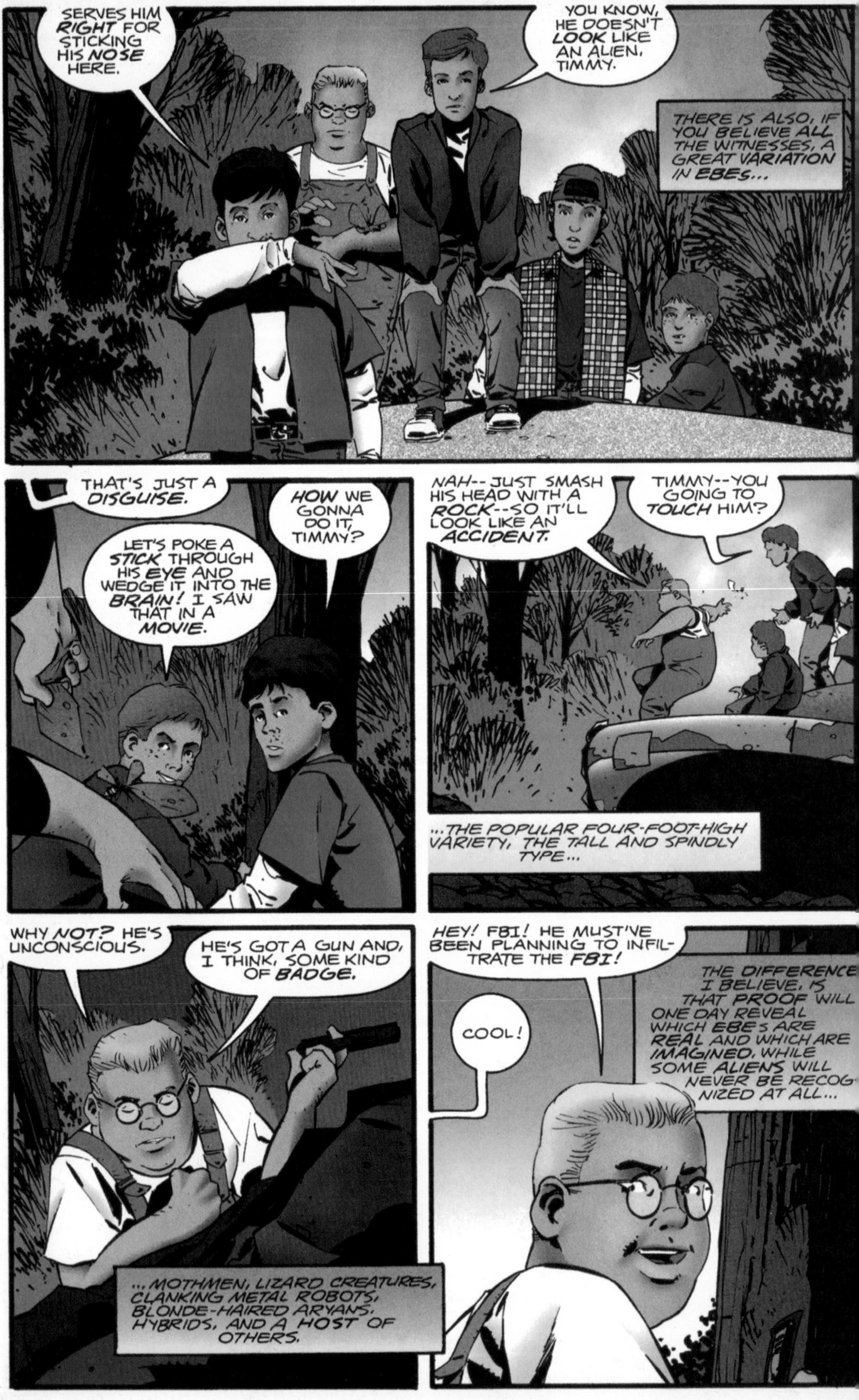

SERVES HIM RIGHT FOR STICKING HIS NOSE HERE.
YOU KNOW, HE DOESN'T LOOK LIKE AN ALIEN, TIMMY.
THERE IS ALSO, IF YOU BELIEVE ALL THE WITNESSES, A GREAT VARIATION IN EBEs...
THAT'S JUST A DISGUISE.
HOW WE GONNA DO IT, TIMMY?
LET'S POKE A STICK THROUGH HIS EYE AND WEDGE IT INTO THE BRAIN! I SAW THAT IN A MOVIE.
NAH-- JUST SMASH HIS HEAD WITH A ROCK--SO IT'LL LOOK LIKE AN ACCIDENT.
TIMMY--YOU GOING TO TOUCH HIM?
...THE POPULAR FOUR-FOOT-HIGH VARIETY, THE TALL AND SPINDLY TYPE...
WHY NOT? HE'S UNCONSCIOUS.
HE'S GOT A GUN AND, I THINK, SOME KIND OF BADGE.
...MOTHMEN, LIZARD CREATURES, CLANKING METAL ROBOTS, BLONDE-HAIRED ARYANS, HYBRIDS, AND A HOST OF OTHERS.
HEY! FBI! HE MUST'VE BEEN PLANNING TO INFIL-TRATE THE FBI!
COOL!
THE DIFFERENCE I BELIEVE, IS THAT PROOF WILL ONE DAY REVEAL WHICH EBEs ARE REAL AND WHICH ARE IMAGINED, WHILE SOME ALIENS WILL NEVER BE RECOG-NIZED AT ALL...

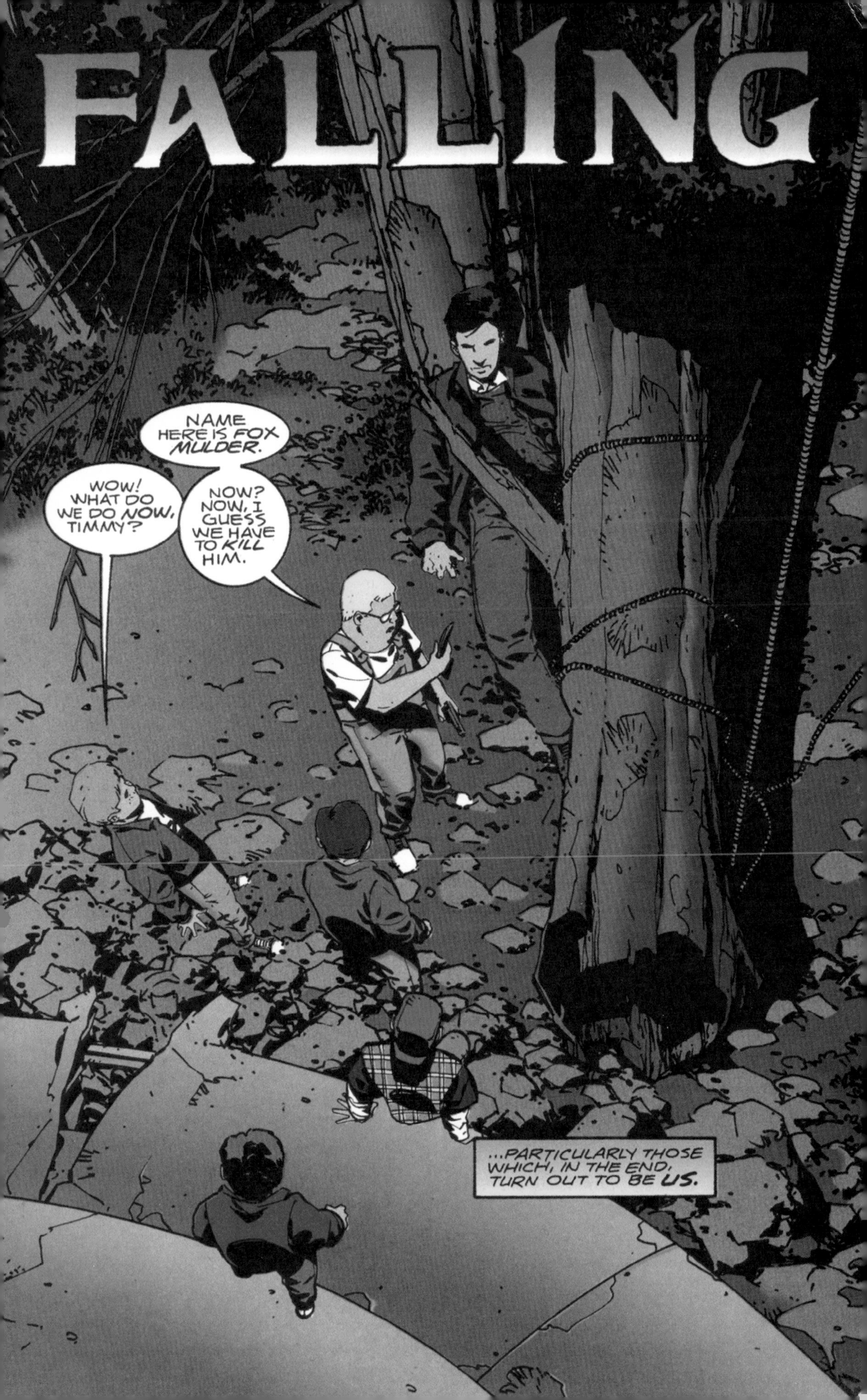
FALLING
NAME HERE IS *FOX MULDER*.
WOW! WHAT DO WE DO *NOW*, TIMMY?
NOW? NOW, I GUESS WE HAVE TO *KILL* HIM.
...PARTICULARLY THOSE WHICH, IN THE END, TURN OUT TO BE ***US***.

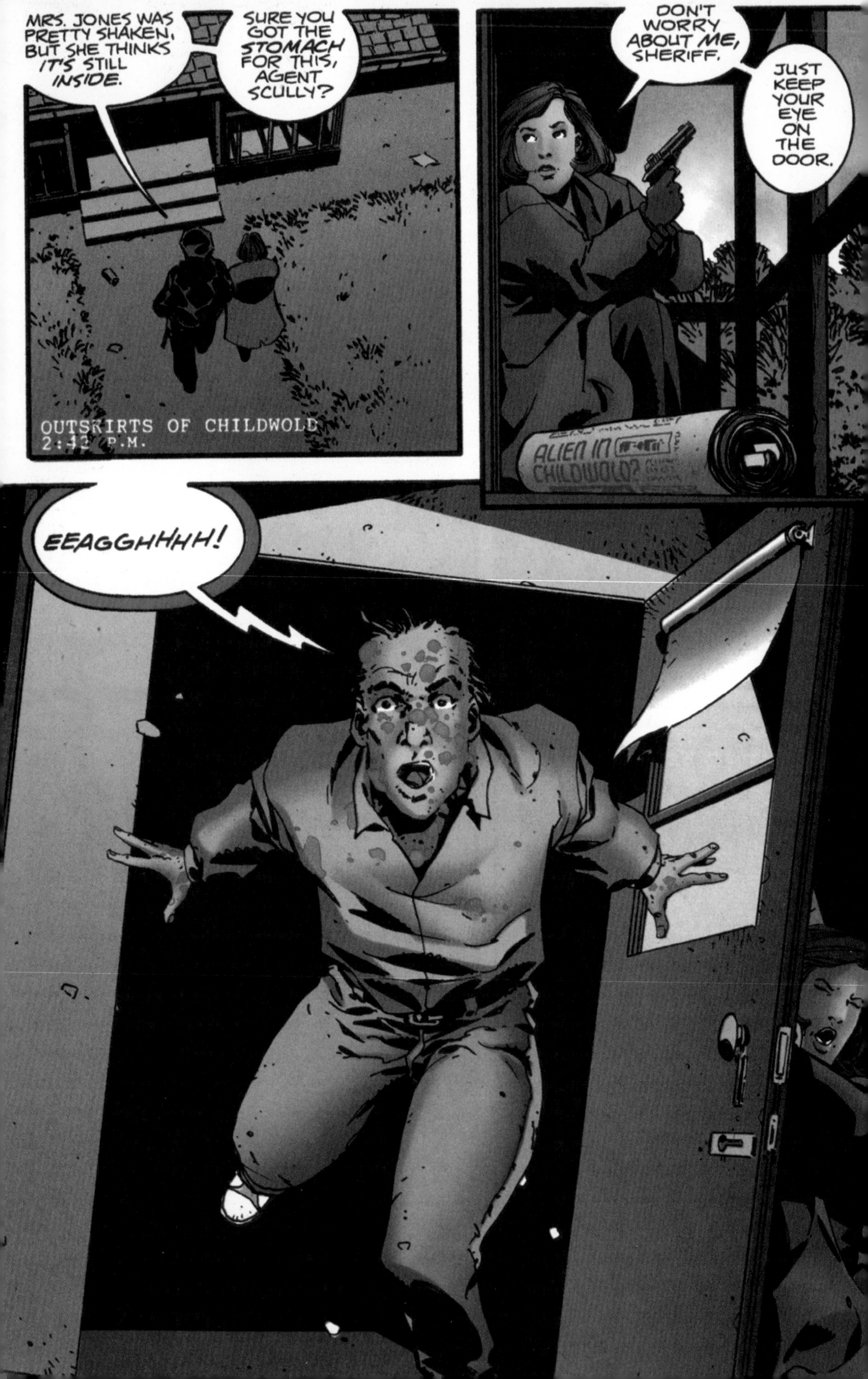

MRS. JONES WAS PRETTY SHAKEN, BUT SHE THINKS IT'S STILL INSIDE.
SURE YOU GOT THE STOMACH FOR THIS, AGENT SCULLY?
OUTSKIRTS OF CHILDWOLD
2:42 P.M.
DON'T WORRY ABOUT ME, SHERIFF.
JUST KEEP YOUR EYE ON THE DOOR.
ALIEN IN CHILDWOLD?
EEAGGHHHH!

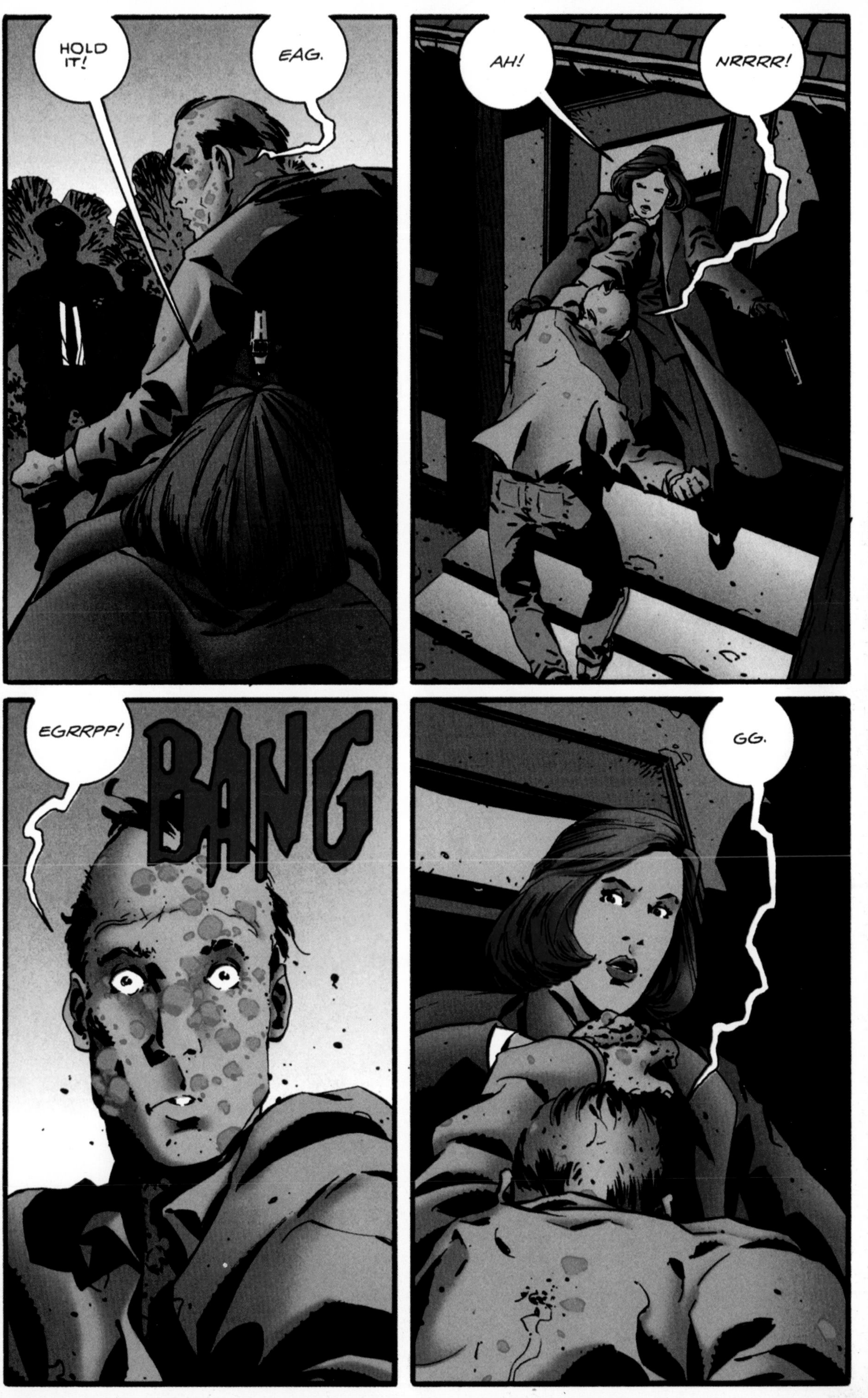
HOLD IT!
EAG.
AH!
NRRRR!
EGRRPP!
BANG
GG.

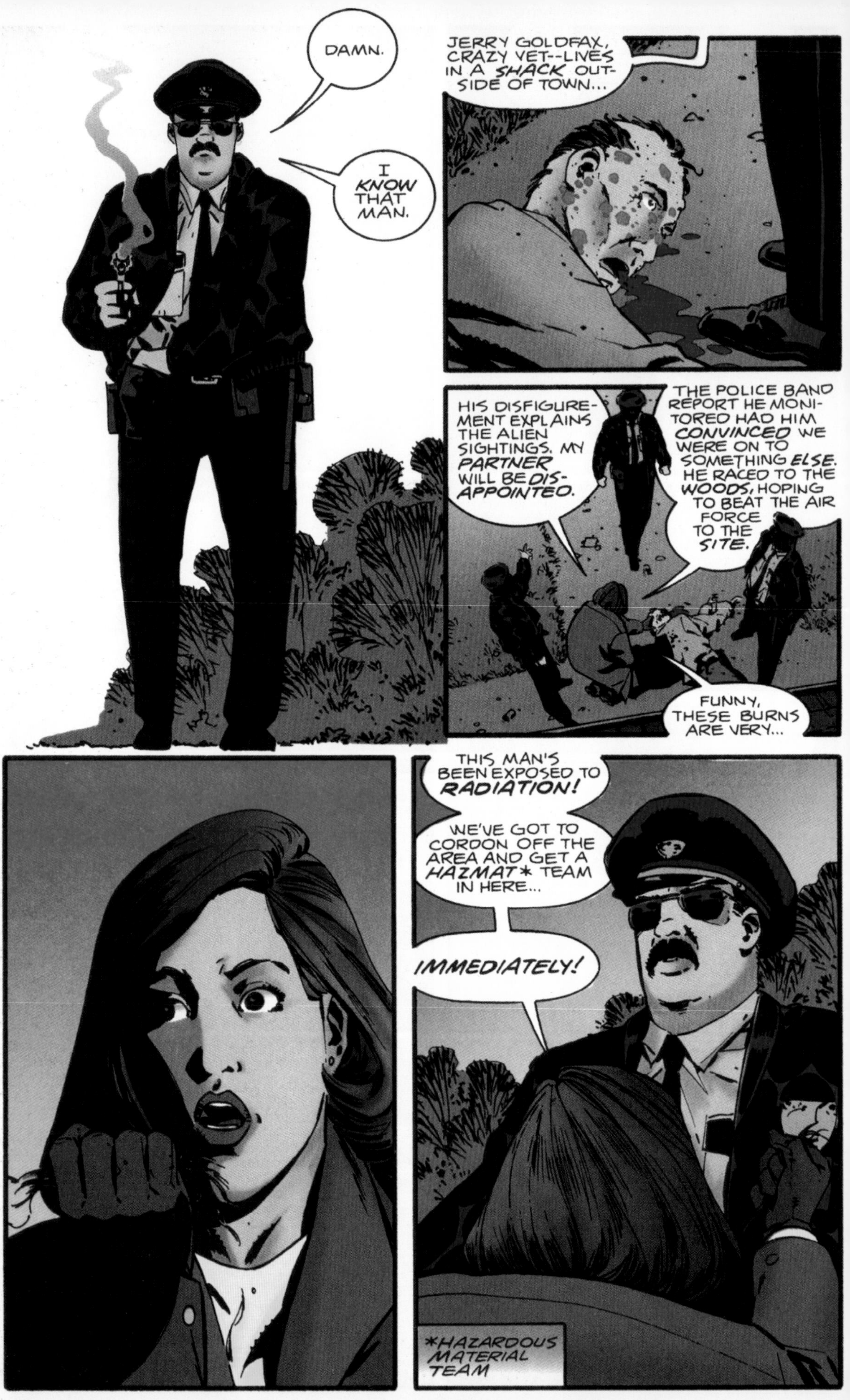
DAMN.
I KNOW THAT MAN.
JERRY GOLDFAX, CRAZY VET--LIVES IN A SHACK OUT-SIDE OF TOWN...
HIS DISFIGURE-MENT EXPLAINS THE ALIEN SIGHTINGS. MY PARTNER WILL BE DIS-APPOINTED.
THE POLICE BAND REPORT HE MONI-TORED HAD HIM CONVINCED WE WERE ON TO SOMETHING ELSE. HE RACED TO THE WOODS, HOPING TO BEAT THE AIR FORCE TO THE SITE.
FUNNY, THESE BURNS ARE VERY...
THIS MAN'S BEEN EXPOSED TO RADIATION!
WE'VE GOT TO CORDON OFF THE AREA AND GET A HAZMAT* TEAM IN HERE...
IMMEDIATELY!
*HAZARDOUS MATERIAL TEAM

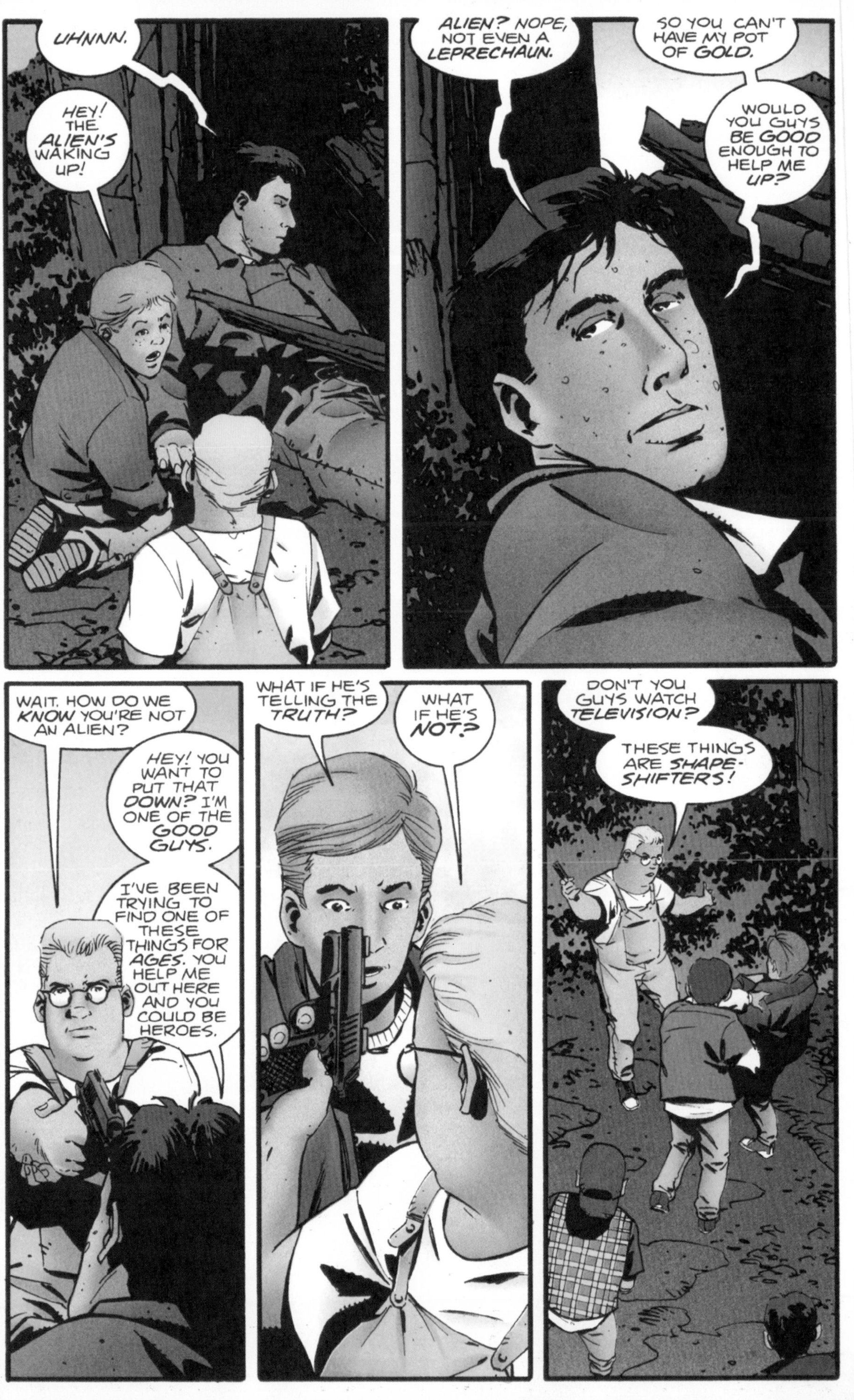
UHNNN.
HEY! THE ALIEN'S WAKING UP!
ALIEN? NOPE, NOT EVEN A LEPRECHAUN.
SO YOU CAN'T HAVE MY POT OF GOLD.
WOULD YOU GUYS BE GOOD ENOUGH TO HELP ME UP?
WAIT. HOW DO WE KNOW YOU'RE NOT AN ALIEN?
HEY! YOU WANT TO PUT THAT DOWN? I'M ONE OF THE GOOD GUYS.
I'VE BEEN TRYING TO FIND ONE OF THESE THINGS FOR AGES. YOU HELP ME OUT HERE AND YOU COULD BE HEROES.
WHAT IF HE'S TELLING THE TRUTH?
WHAT IF HE'S NOT?
DON'T YOU GUYS WATCH TELEVISION?
THESE THINGS ARE SHAPE-SHIFTERS!

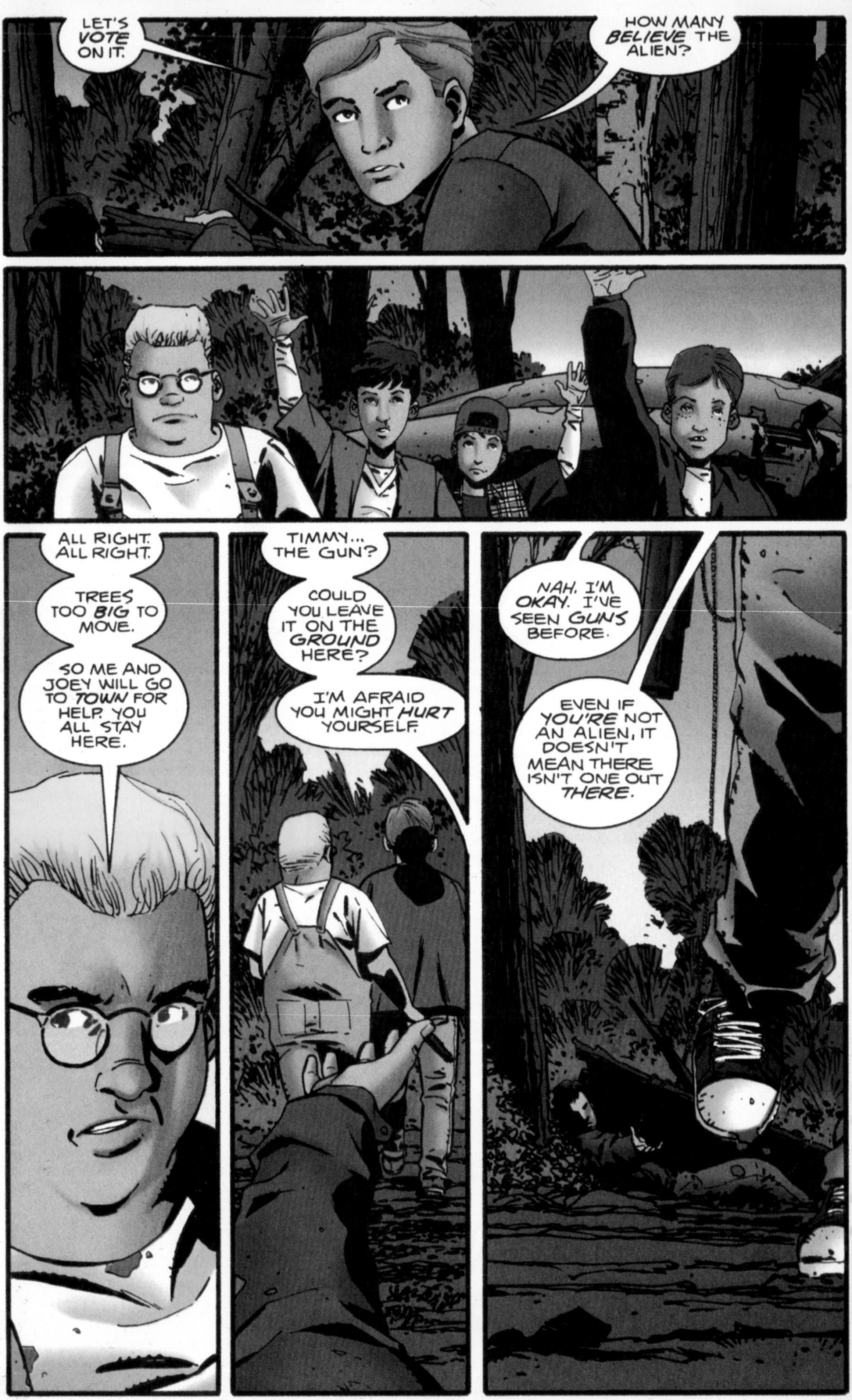
LET'S VOTE ON IT.
HOW MANY BELIEVE THE ALIEN?
ALL RIGHT. ALL RIGHT.
TREES TOO BIG TO MOVE.
SO ME AND JOEY WILL GO TO TOWN FOR HELP. YOU ALL STAY HERE.
TIMMY... THE GUN?
COULD YOU LEAVE IT ON THE GROUND HERE?
I'M AFRAID YOU MIGHT HURT YOURSELF.
NAH. I'M OKAY. I'VE SEEN GUNS BEFORE.
EVEN IF YOU'RE NOT AN ALIEN, IT DOESN'T MEAN THERE ISN'T ONE OUT THERE.

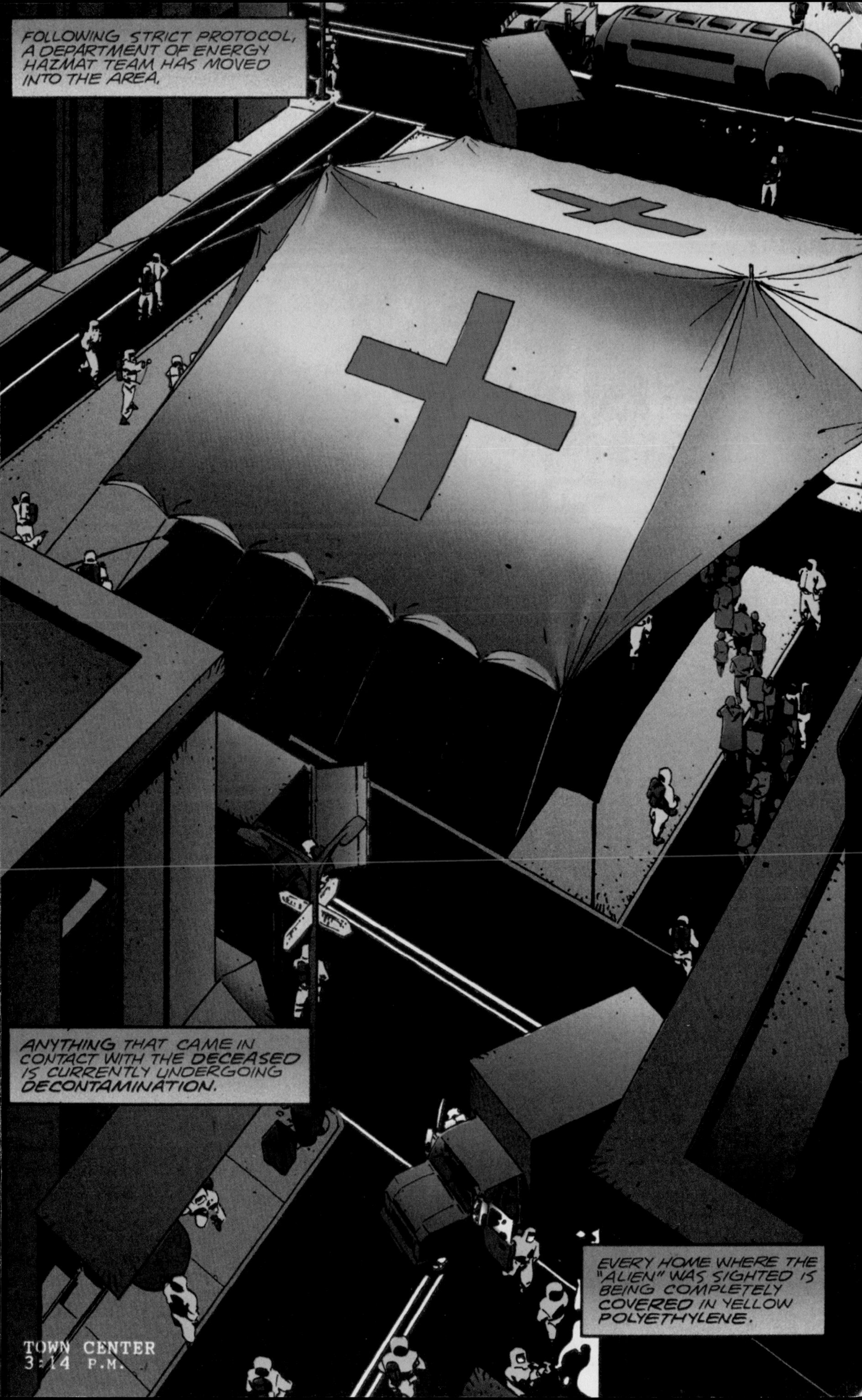
FOLLOWING STRICT PROTOCOL, A DEPARTMENT OF ENERGY HAZMAT TEAM HAS MOVED INTO THE AREA.
ANYTHING THAT CAME IN CONTACT WITH THE DECEASED IS CURRENTLY UNDERGOING DECONTAMINATION.
EVERY HOME WHERE THE "ALIEN" WAS SIGHTED IS BEING COMPLETELY COVERED IN YELLOW POLYETHYLENE.
TOWN CENTER
3:14 P.M.

HAVING UNDERGONE DECON MYSELF, I AM PROCEEDING WITH THE AUTOPSY UNDER STRICT HAZMAT PROTOCOL.

THE EFFECTS OF RADIATION VARY, DEPENDING ON THE DURATION AND THE AREA OF THE BODY EXPOSED.

IN THIS INSTANCE, AN ENLARGED ANTERIOR PITUITARY GLAND LED ME TO MAKE SOME PRELIMINARY BLOOD TESTS.

THE RESULTS REVEALED HIGH LEVELS OF TESTOSTERONE AND GONADOTROPINS.

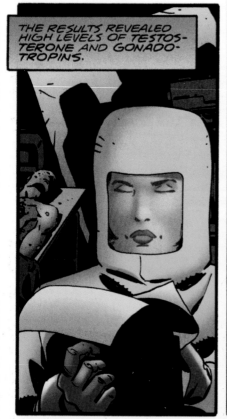

THE TESTOSTERONE, ACTING MUCH LIKE AN ANABOLIC STEROID, COULD EASILY EXPLAIN THE DECEASED'S AGGRESSIVE BEHAVIOR.

GONADOTROPINS, ON THE OTHER HAND...

AGENT SCULLY...

AFRAID YOU'LL HAVE TO STOP WHAT YOU'RE DOING AND COME WITH US.

WHAT?

I'M IN THE MIDDLE OF AN AUTOPSY! YOU DON'T HAVE THE AUTHORITY!

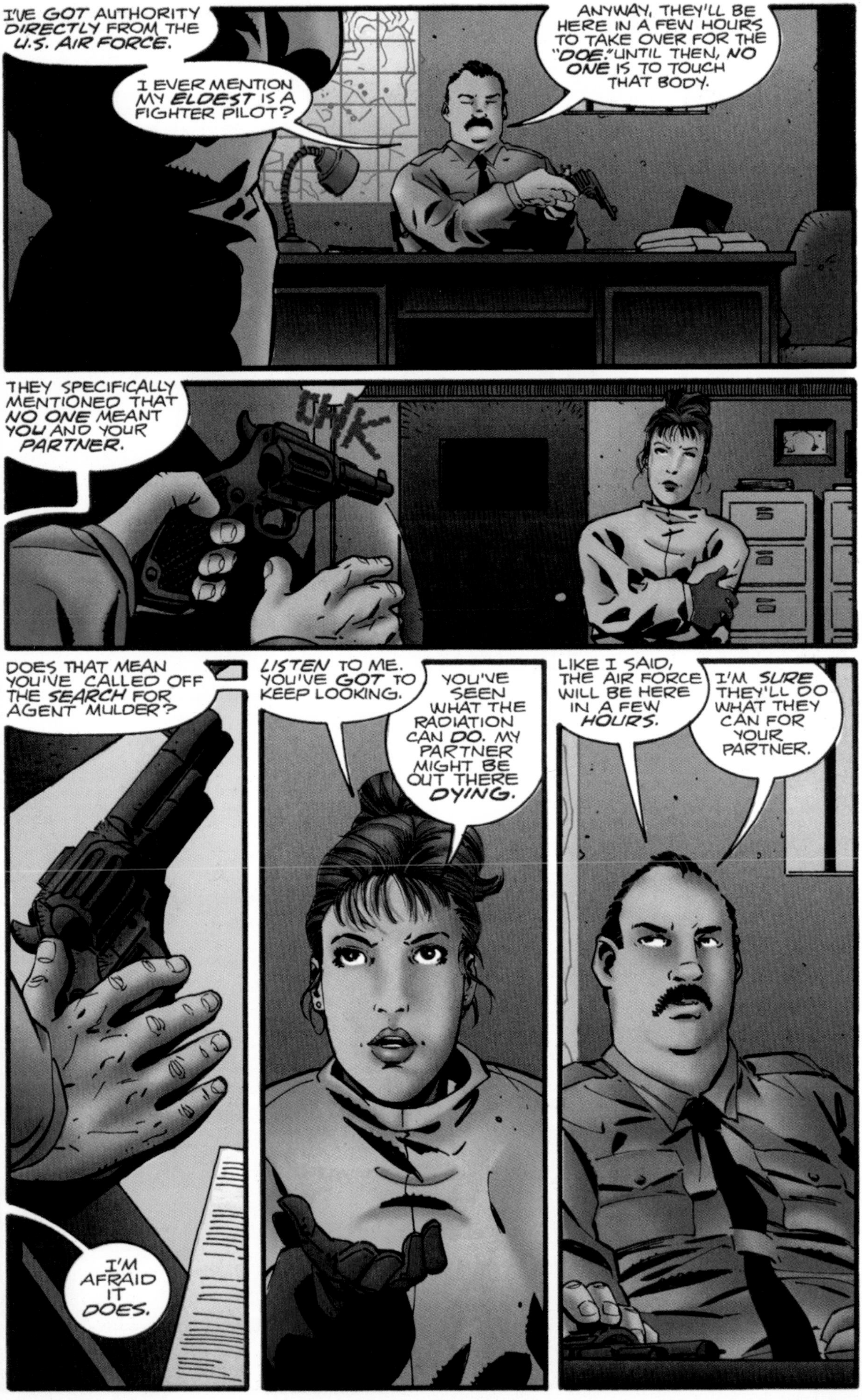
I'VE GOT AUTHORITY DIRECTLY FROM THE U.S. AIR FORCE.
I EVER MENTION MY ELDEST IS A FIGHTER PILOT?
ANYWAY, THEY'LL BE HERE IN A FEW HOURS TO TAKE OVER FOR THE "DOE." UNTIL THEN, NO ONE IS TO TOUCH THAT BODY.
THEY SPECIFICALLY MENTIONED THAT NO ONE MEANT YOU AND YOUR PARTNER.
CHK--
DOES THAT MEAN YOU'VE CALLED OFF THE SEARCH FOR AGENT MULDER?
I'M AFRAID IT DOES.
LISTEN TO ME. YOU'VE GOT TO KEEP LOOKING.
YOU'VE SEEN WHAT THE RADIATION CAN DO. MY PARTNER MIGHT BE OUT THERE DYING.
LIKE I SAID, THE AIR FORCE WILL BE HERE IN A FEW HOURS.
I'M SURE THEY'LL DO WHAT THEY CAN FOR YOUR PARTNER.

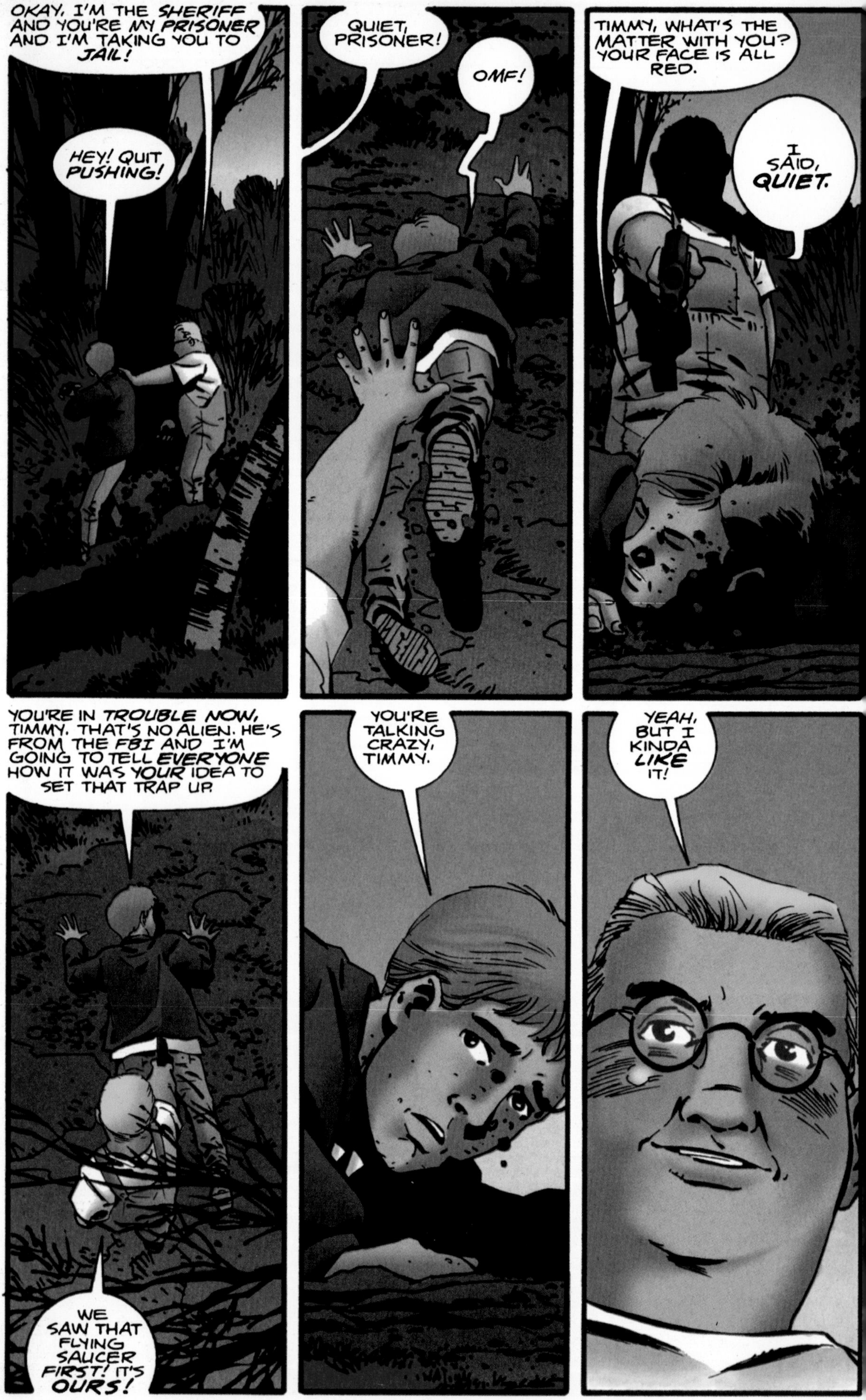
OKAY, I'M THE SHERIFF AND YOU'RE MY PRISONER AND I'M TAKING YOU TO JAIL!
HEY! QUIT PUSHING!
QUIET, PRISONER!
OMF!
TIMMY, WHAT'S THE MATTER WITH YOU? YOUR FACE IS ALL RED.
I SAID, QUIET.
YOU'RE IN TROUBLE NOW, TIMMY. THAT'S NO ALIEN. HE'S FROM THE FBI AND I'M GOING TO TELL EVERYONE HOW IT WAS YOUR IDEA TO SET THAT TRAP UP.
WE SAW THAT FLYING SAUCER FIRST! IT'S OURS!
YOU'RE TALKING CRAZY, TIMMY.
YEAH, BUT I KINDA LIKE IT!

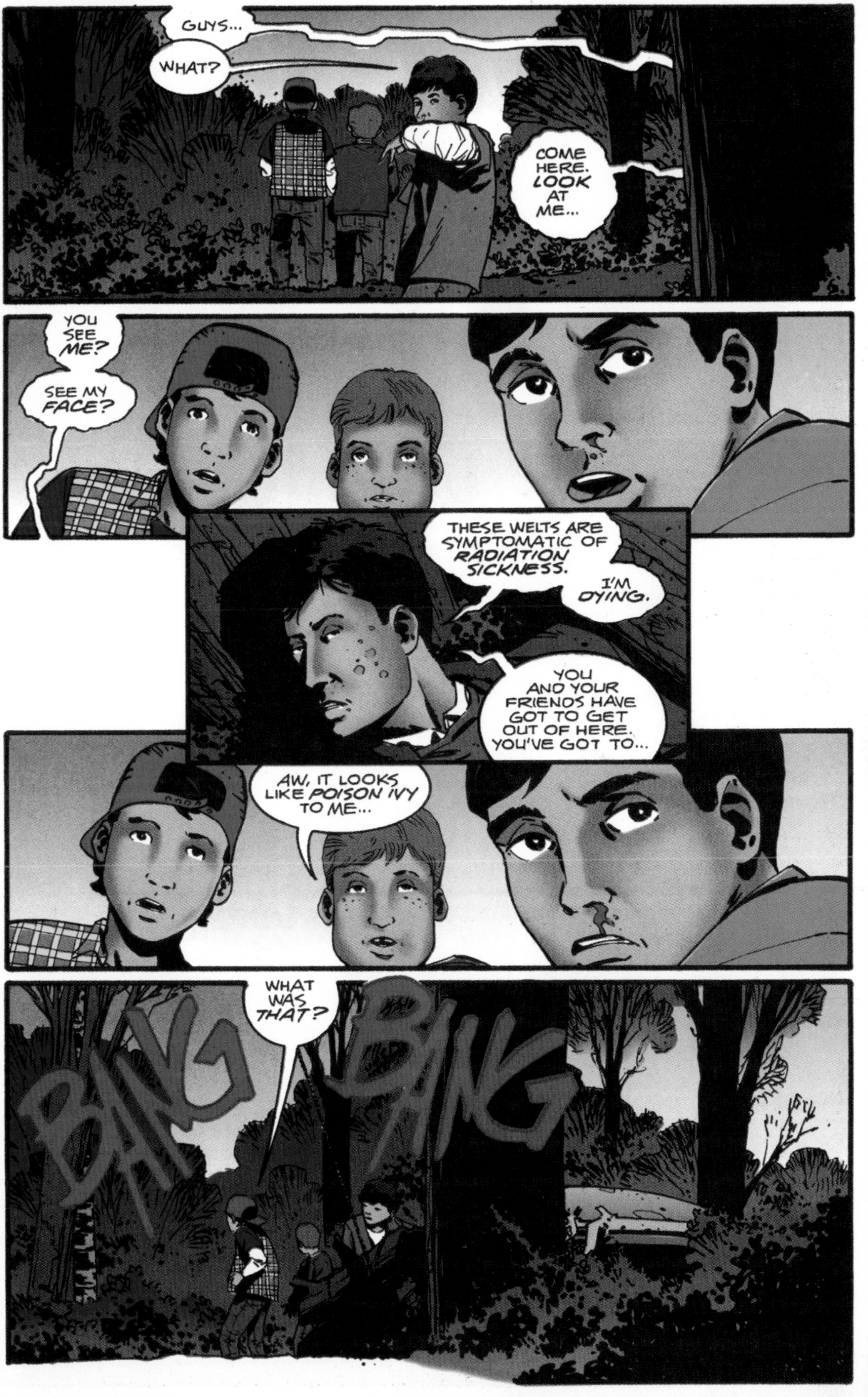
GUYS...
WHAT?
COME HERE. LOOK AT ME...
YOU SEE ME?
SEE MY FACE?
THESE WELTS ARE SYMPTOMATIC OF RADIATION SICKNESS.
I'M DYING.
YOU AND YOUR FRIENDS HAVE GOT TO GET OUT OF HERE. YOU'VE GOT TO...
AW, IT LOOKS LIKE POISON IVY TO ME...
WHAT WAS THAT?
BANG
BANG

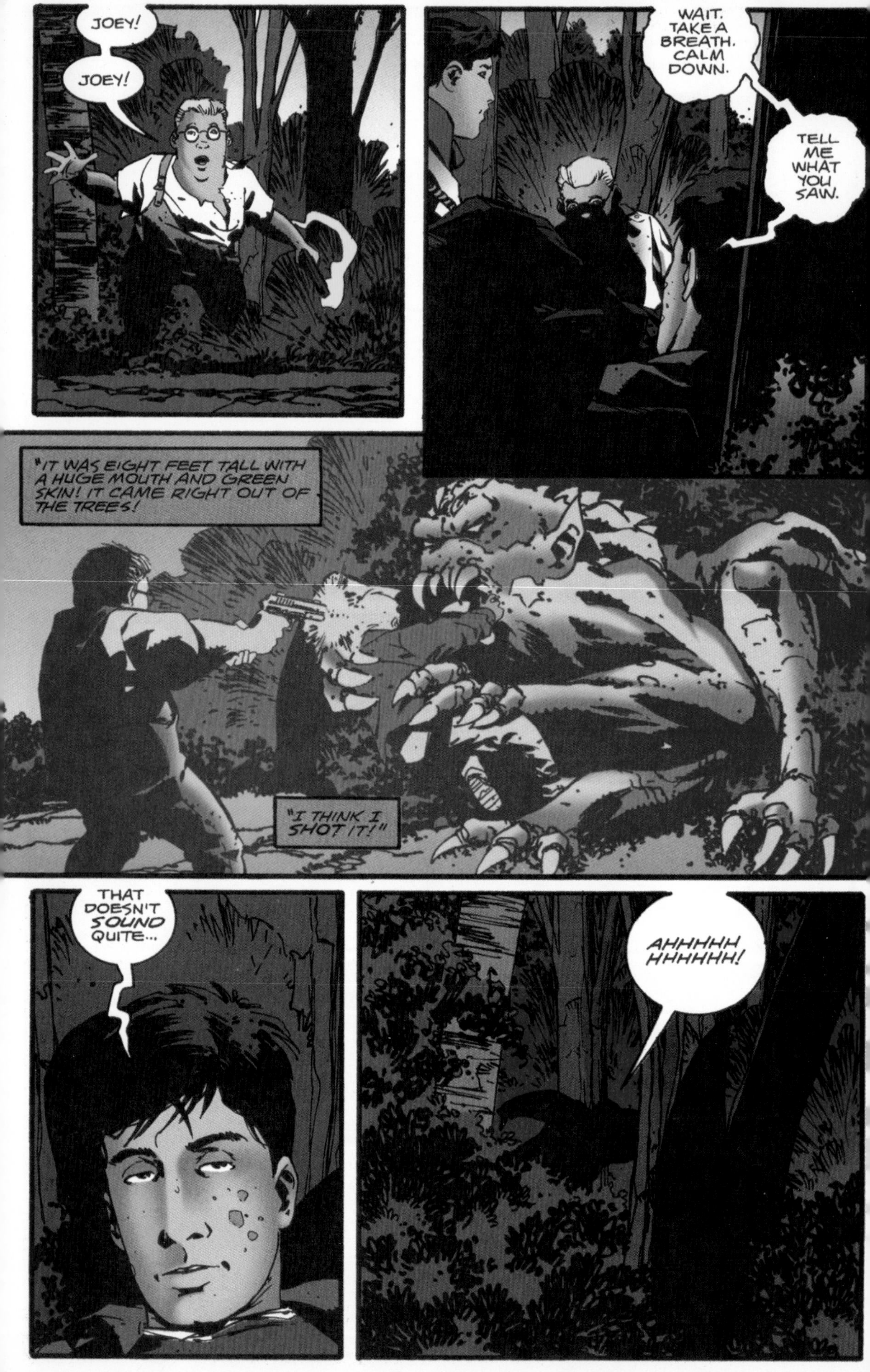
JOEY!
JOEY!
WAIT. TAKE A BREATH. CALM DOWN.
TELL ME WHAT YOU SAW.
"IT WAS EIGHT FEET TALL WITH A HUGE MOUTH AND GREEN SKIN! IT CAME RIGHT OUT OF THE TREES!
"I THINK I SHOT IT!"
THAT DOESN'T SOUND QUITE...
AHHHHH HHHHHH!

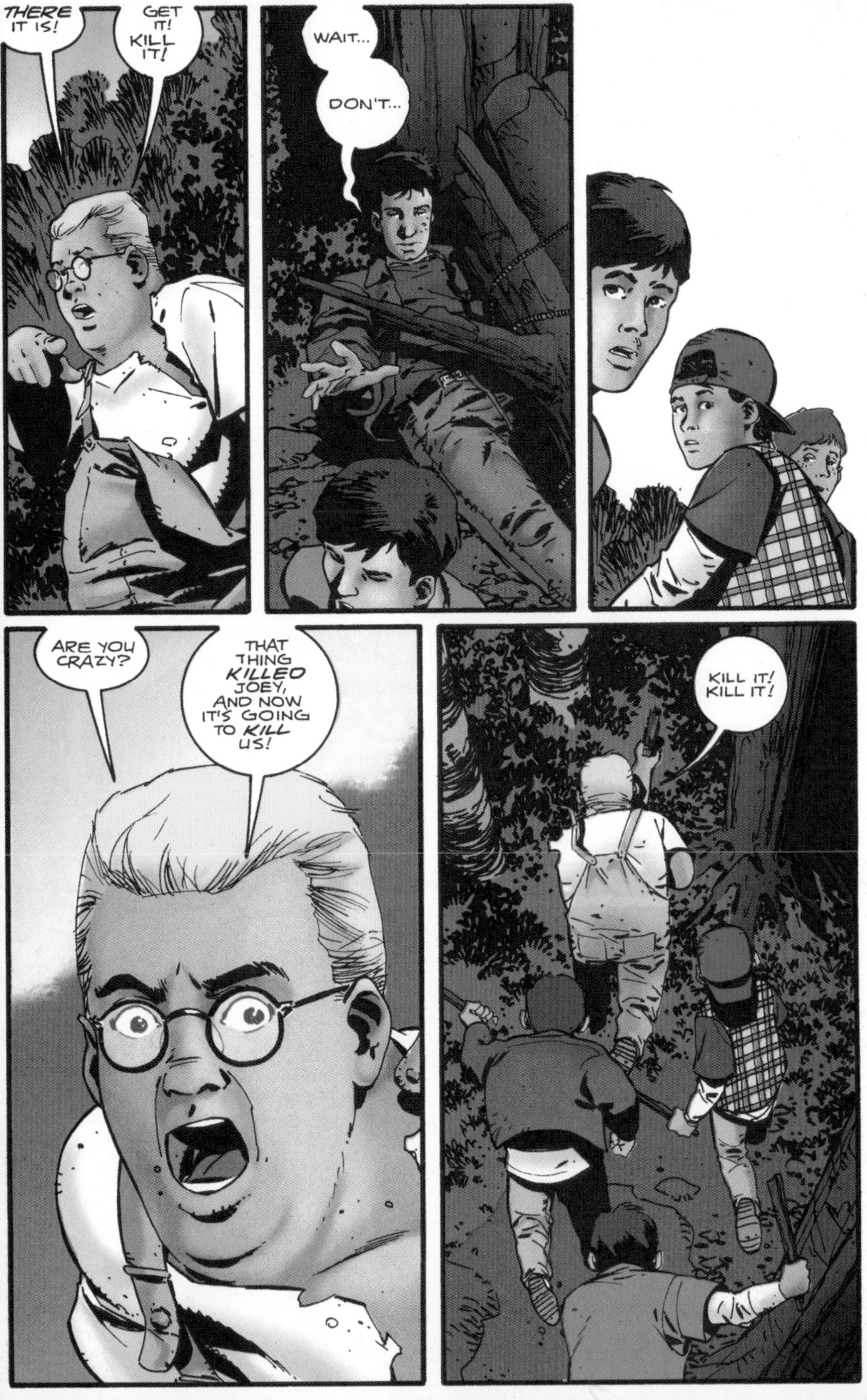
THERE IT IS!
GET IT! KILL IT!
WAIT...
DON'T...
ARE YOU CRAZY?
THAT THING KILLED JOEY, AND NOW IT'S GOING TO KILL US!
KILL IT! KILL IT!

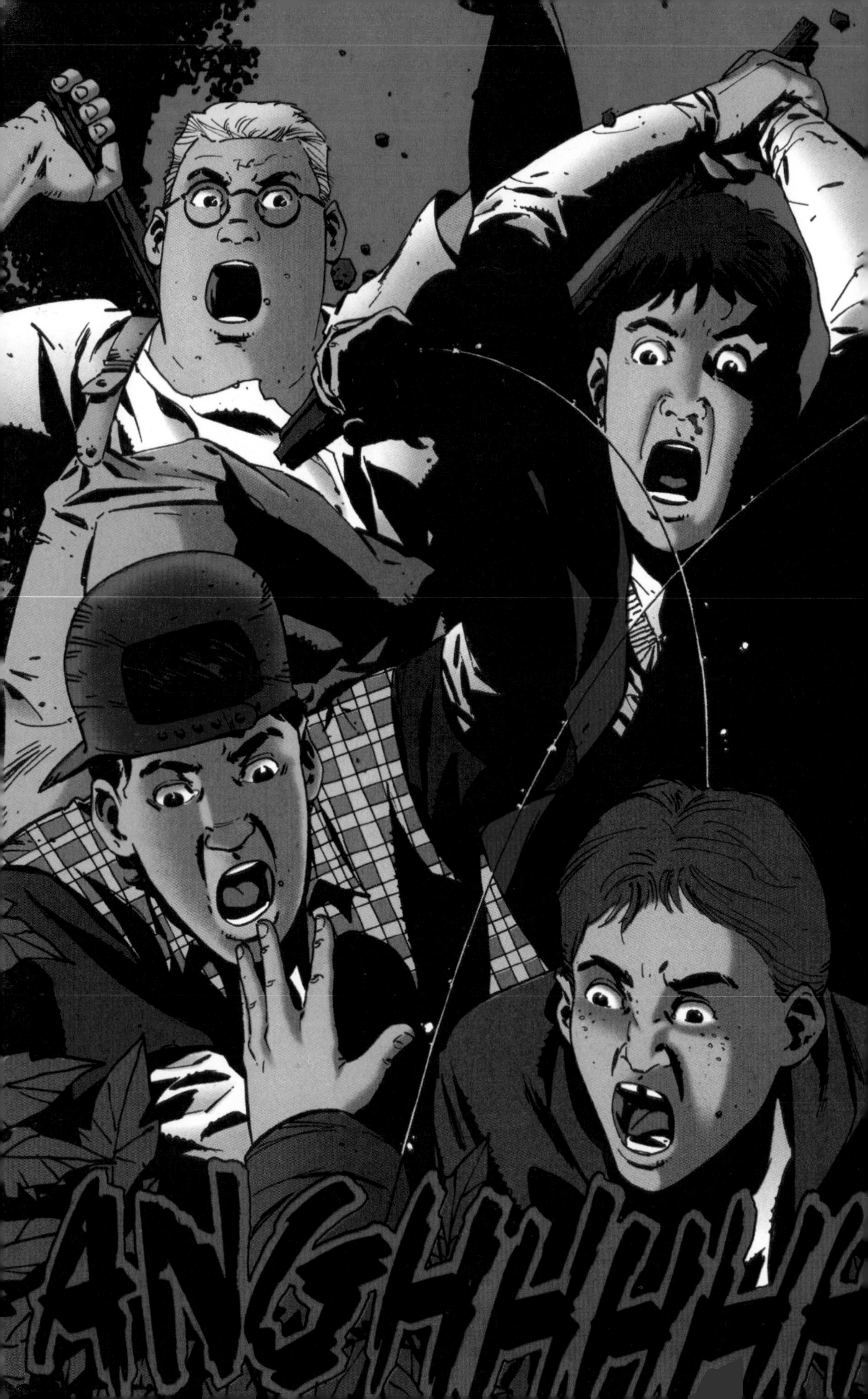
ANGHHHHH

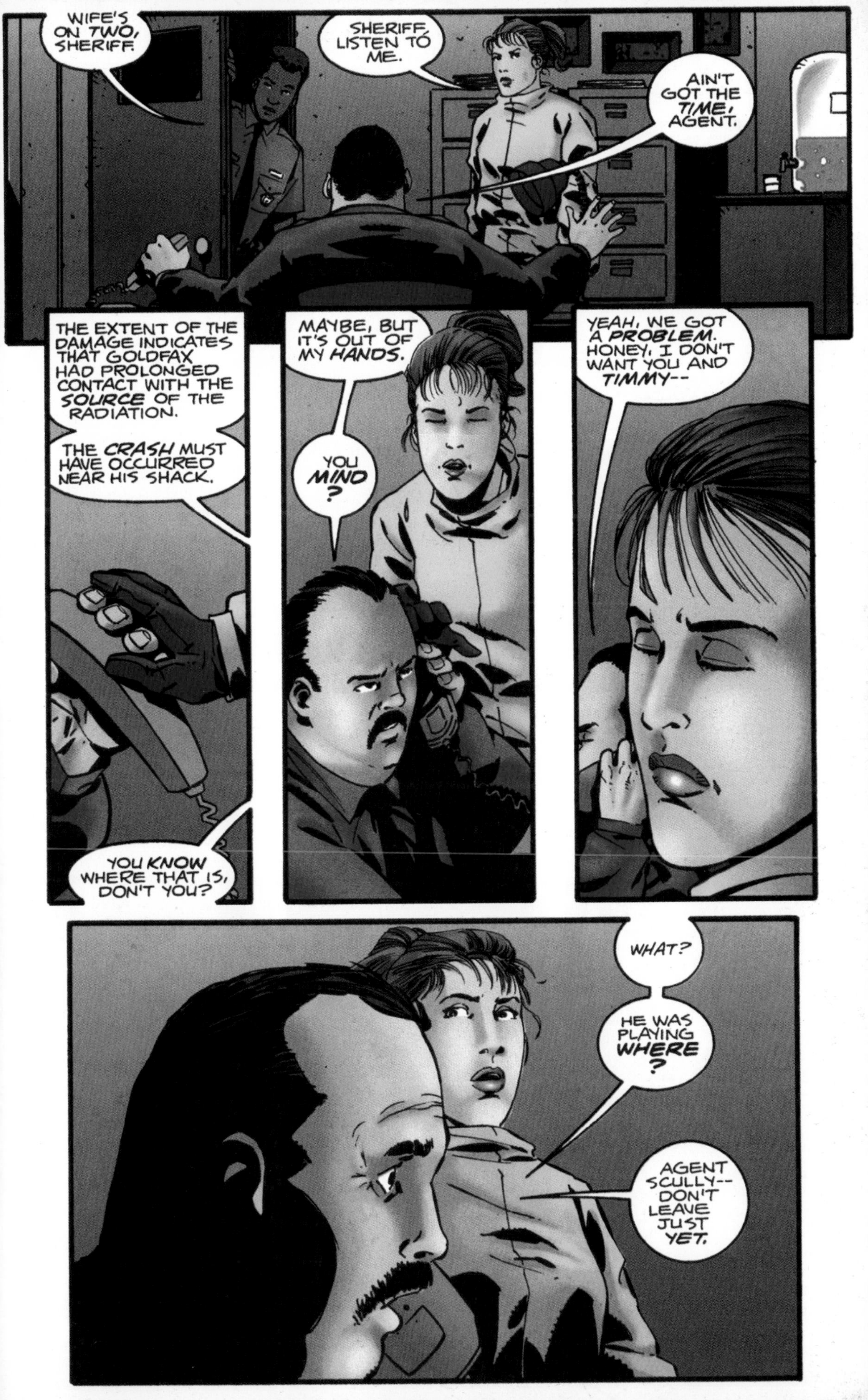
WIFE'S ON TWO, SHERIFF.
SHERIFF, LISTEN TO ME.
AIN'T GOT THE TIME, AGENT.
THE EXTENT OF THE DAMAGE INDICATES THAT GOLDFAX HAD PROLONGED CONTACT WITH THE SOURCE OF THE RADIATION.
THE CRASH MUST HAVE OCCURRED NEAR HIS SHACK.
YOU KNOW WHERE THAT IS, DON'T YOU?
MAYBE, BUT IT'S OUT OF MY HANDS.
YOU MIND?
YEAH, WE GOT A PROBLEM. HONEY, I DON'T WANT YOU AND TIMMY--
WHAT?
HE WAS PLAYING WHERE?
AGENT SCULLY-- DON'T LEAVE JUST YET.

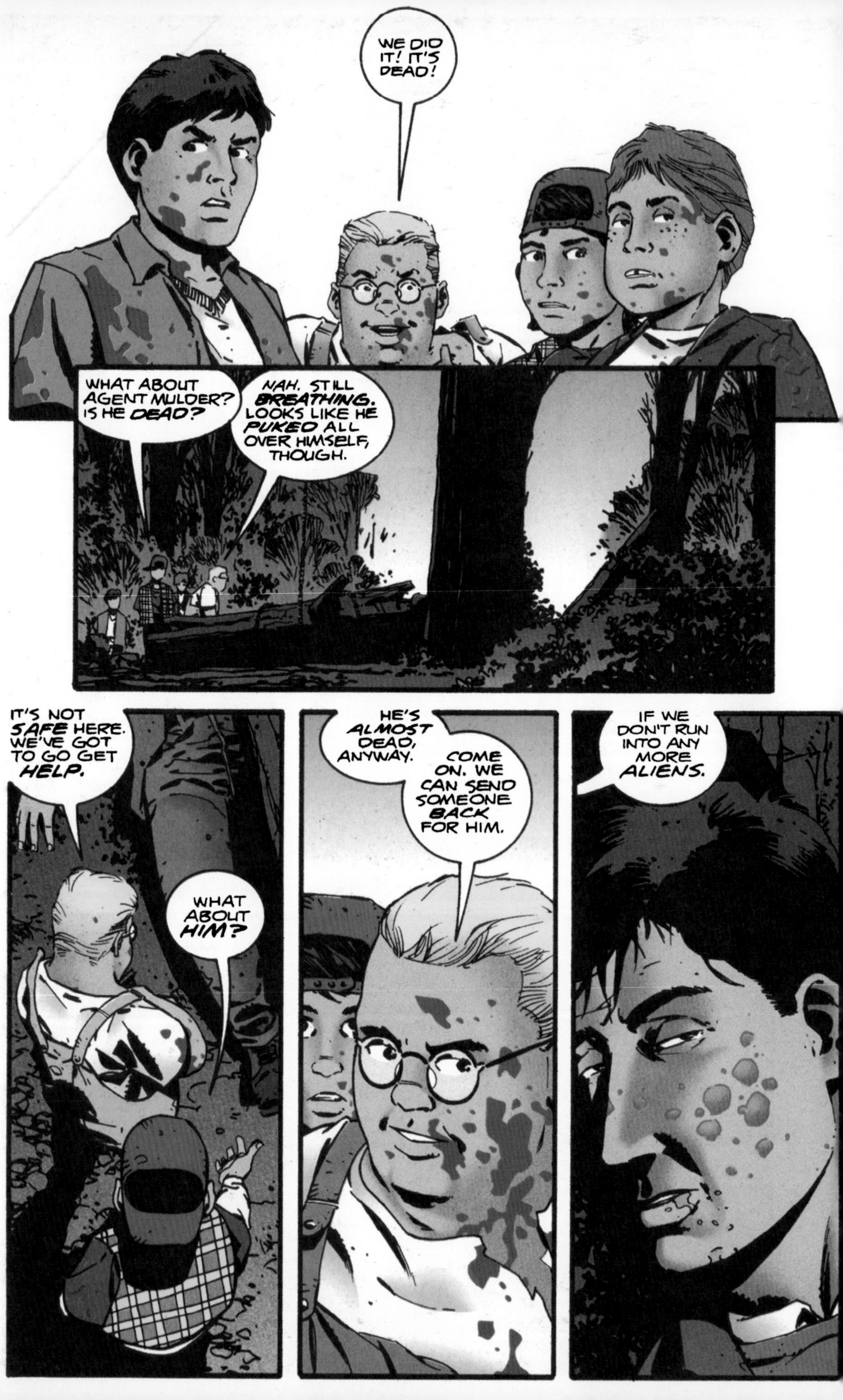
WE DID IT! IT'S DEAD!
WHAT ABOUT AGENT MULDER? IS HE DEAD?
NAH. STILL BREATHING. LOOKS LIKE HE PUKED ALL OVER HIMSELF, THOUGH.
IT'S NOT SAFE HERE. WE'VE GOT TO GO GET HELP.
WHAT ABOUT HIM?
HE'S ALMOST DEAD, ANYWAY.
COME ON. WE CAN SEND SOMEONE BACK FOR HIM.
IF WE DON'T RUN INTO ANY MORE ALIENS.

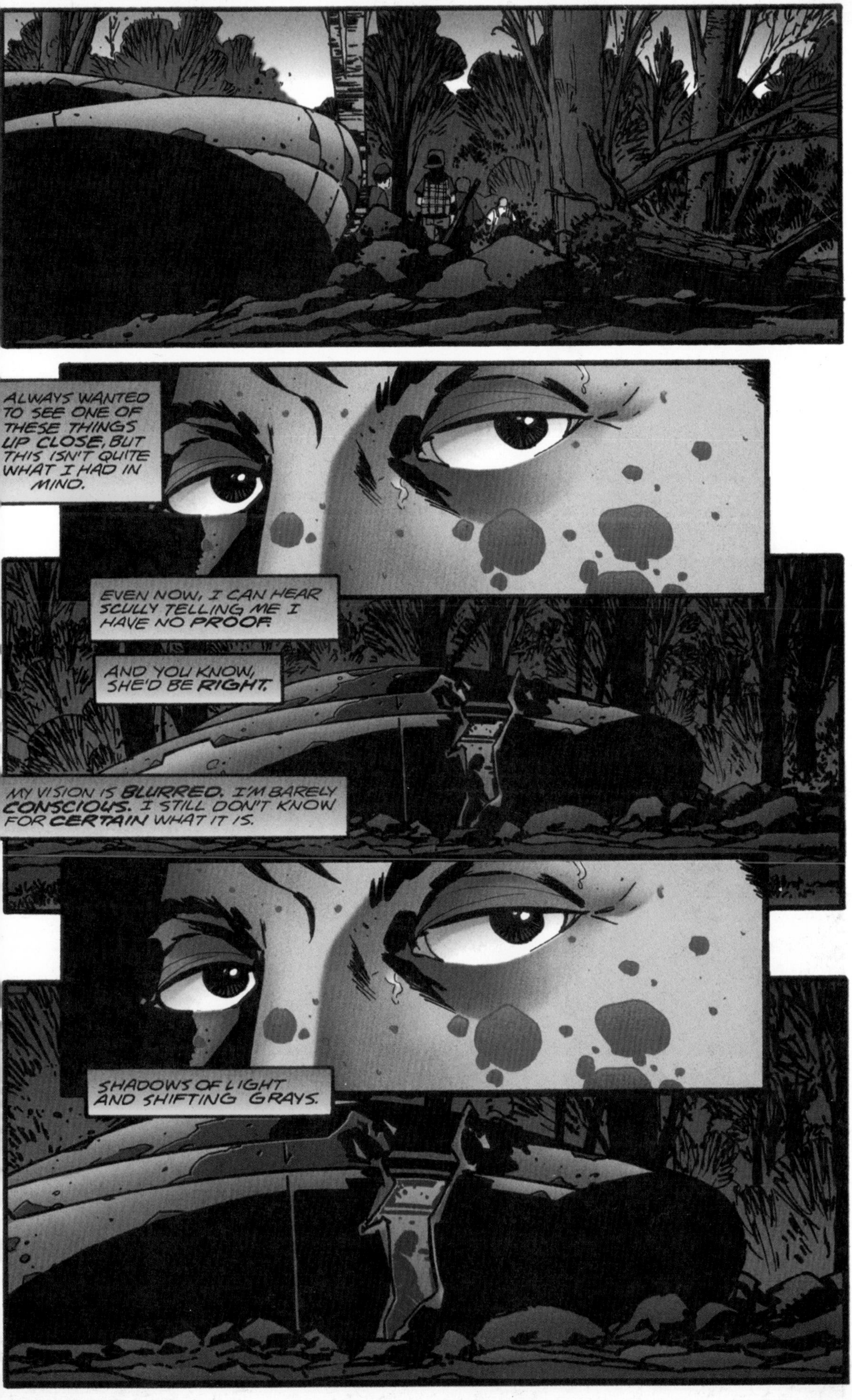
ALWAYS WANTED TO SEE ONE OF THESE THINGS UP CLOSE, BUT THIS ISN'T QUITE WHAT I HAD IN MIND.
EVEN NOW, I CAN HEAR SCULLY TELLING ME I HAVE NO PROOF.
AND YOU KNOW, SHE'D BE RIGHT.
MY VISION IS BLURRED. I'M BARELY CONSCIOUS. I STILL DON'T KNOW FOR CERTAIN WHAT IT IS.
SHADOWS OF LIGHT AND SHIFTING GRAYS.

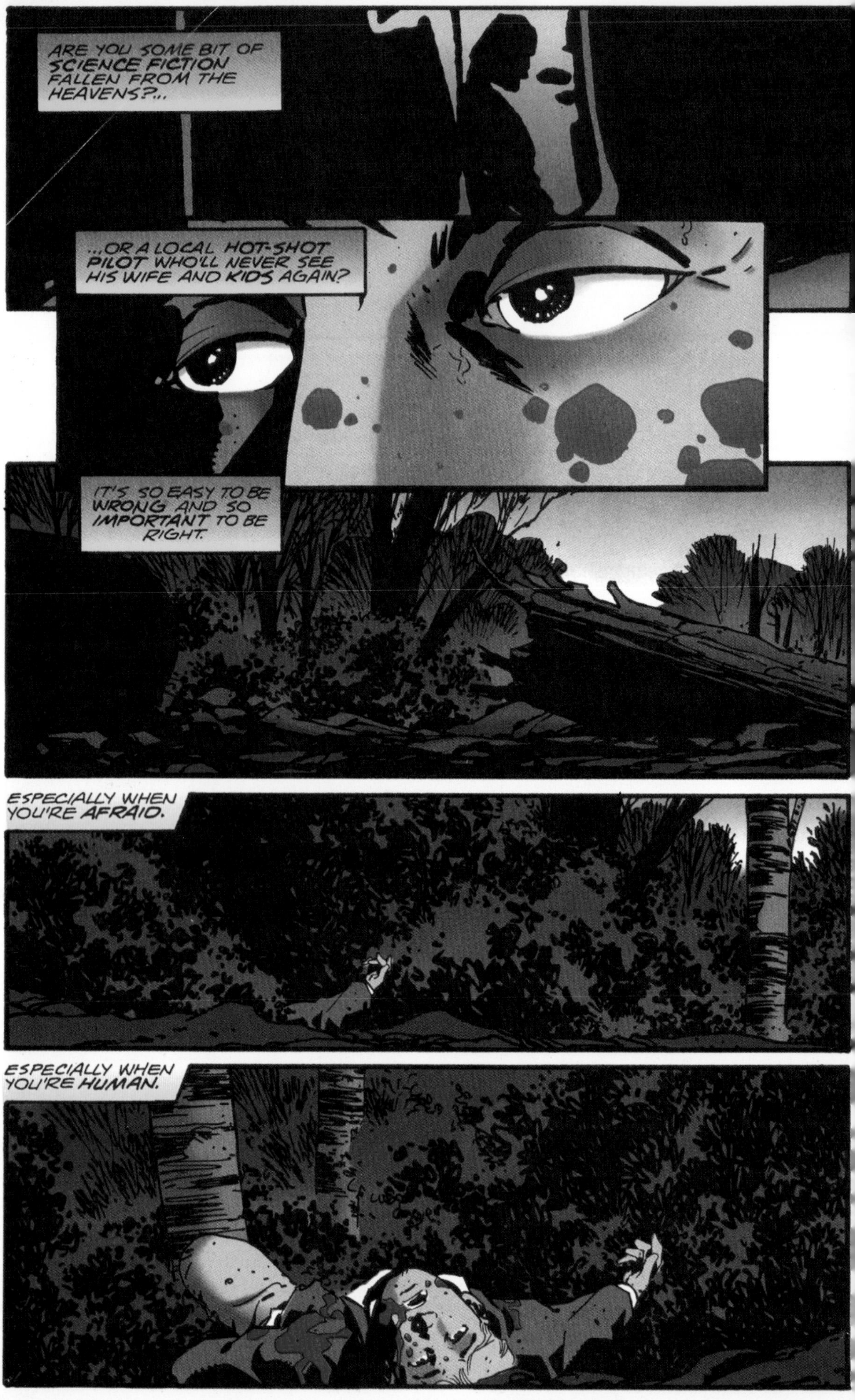
ARE YOU SOME BIT OF SCIENCE FICTION FALLEN FROM THE HEAVENS?...
...OR A LOCAL HOT-SHOT PILOT WHO'LL NEVER SEE HIS WIFE AND KIDS AGAIN?
IT'S SO EASY TO BE WRONG AND SO IMPORTANT TO BE RIGHT.
ESPECIALLY WHEN YOU'RE AFRAID.
ESPECIALLY WHEN YOU'RE HUMAN.

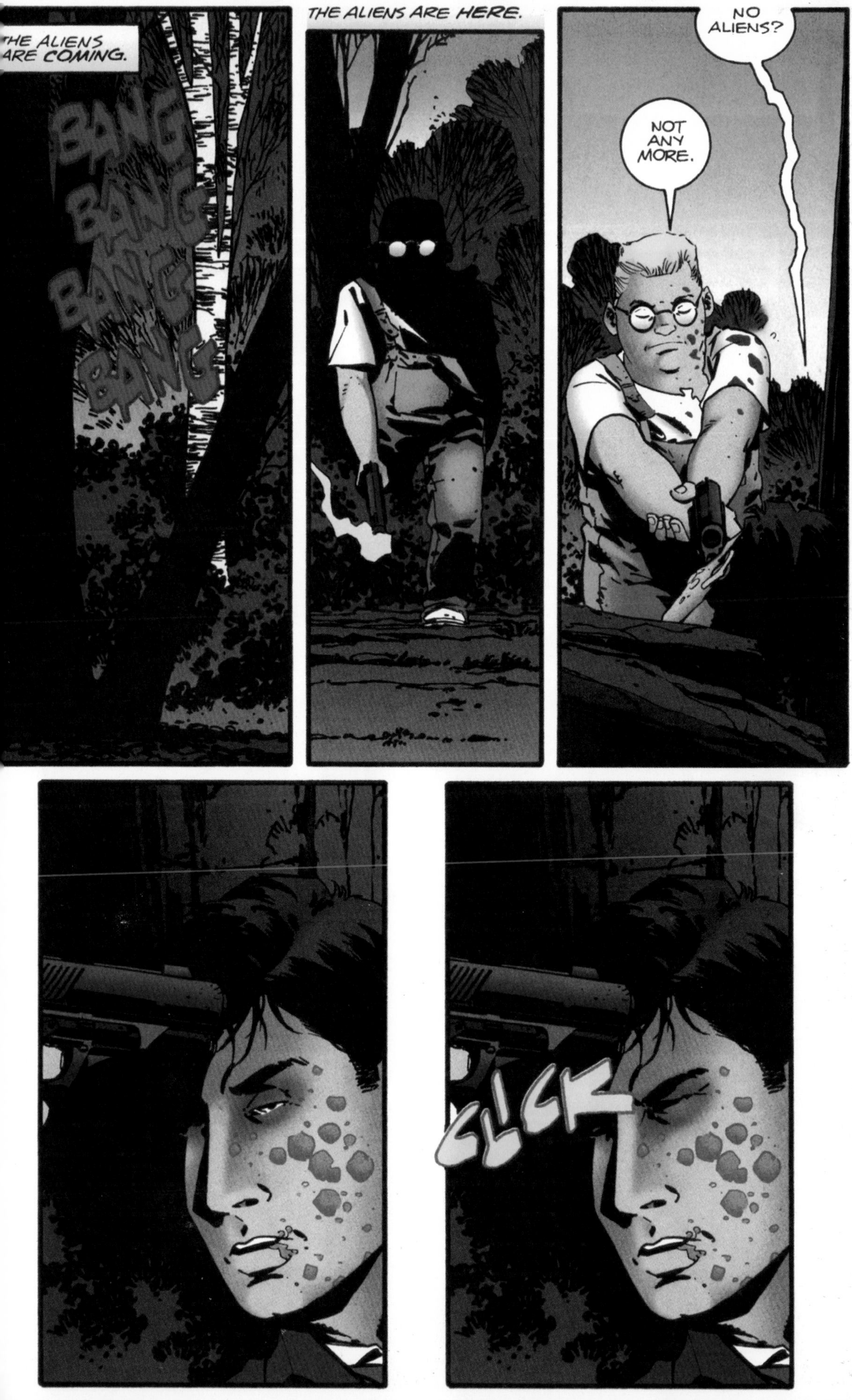
THE ALIENS ARE COMING.
BANG BANG BANG BANG
THE ALIENS ARE HERE.
NO ALIENS?
NOT ANY MORE.
CLICK

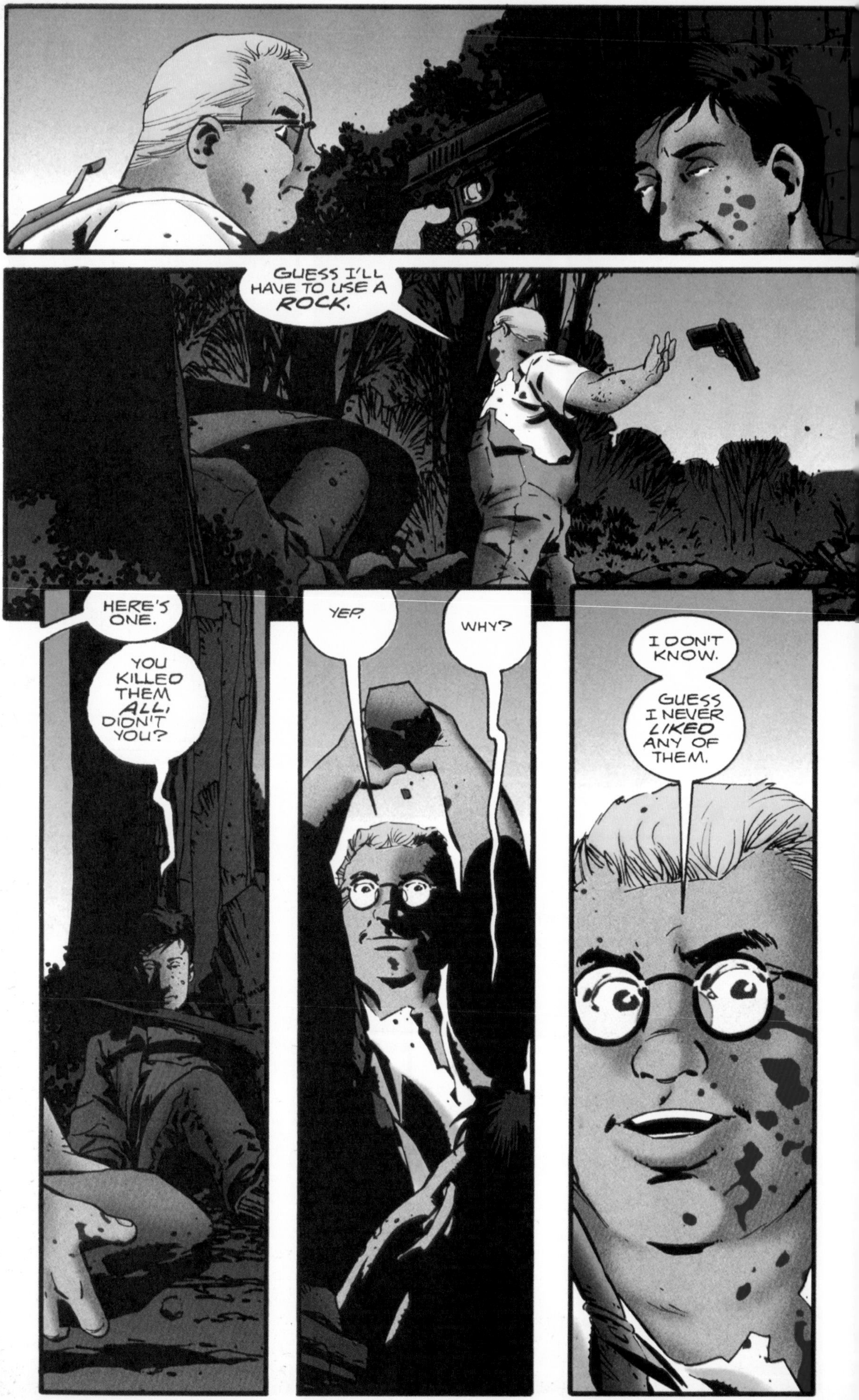
GUESS I'LL HAVE TO USE A ROCK.
HERE'S ONE.
YOU KILLED THEM ALL, DIDN'T YOU?
YEP.
WHY?
I DON'T KNOW.
GUESS I NEVER LIKED ANY OF THEM.

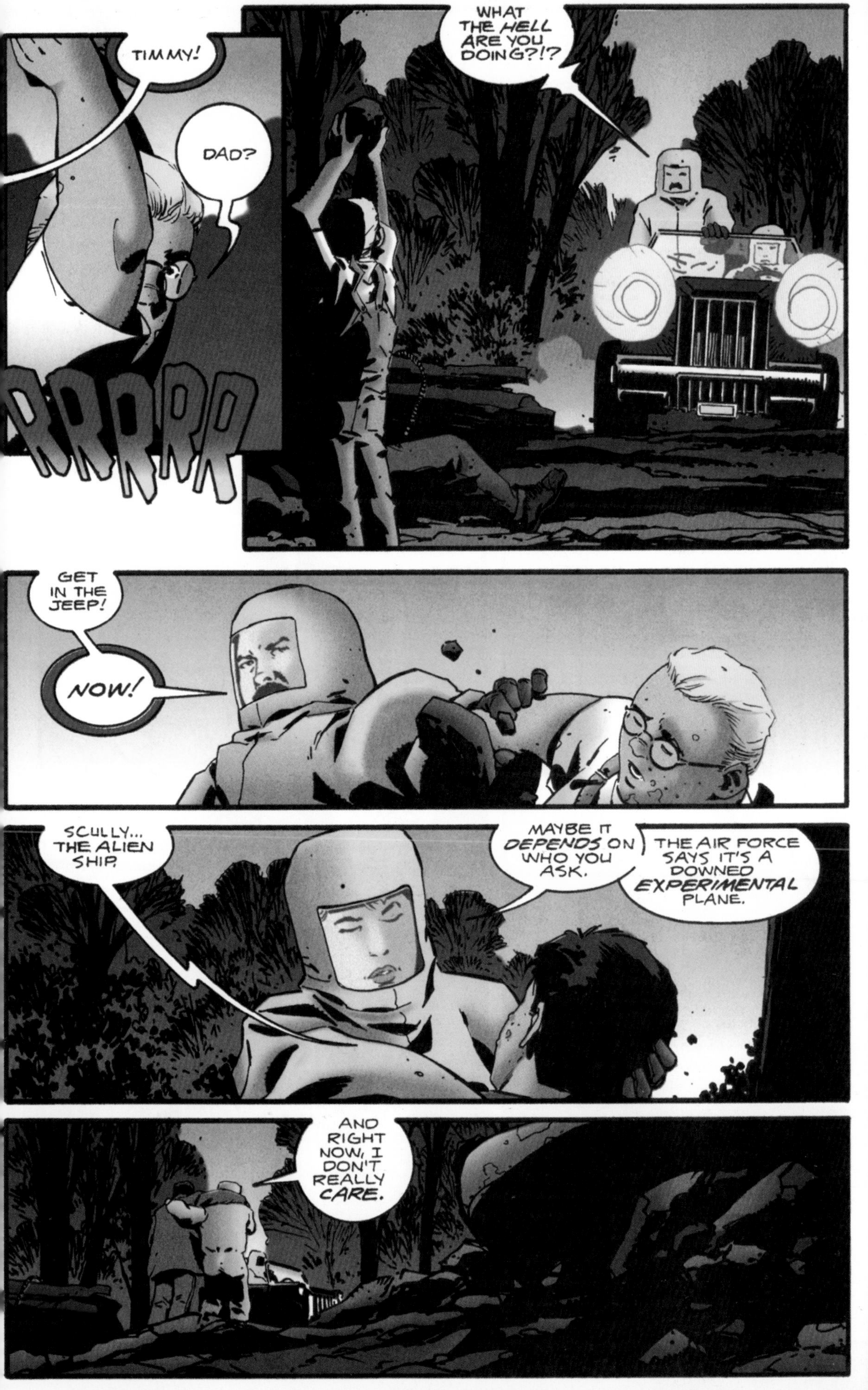
TIMMY!
DAD?
RRRRR
WHAT THE HELL ARE YOU DOING?!?
GET IN THE JEEP!
NOW!
SCULLY... THE ALIEN SHIP.
MAYBE IT DEPENDS ON WHO YOU ASK.
THE AIR FORCE SAYS IT'S A DOWNED EXPERIMENTAL PLANE.
AND RIGHT NOW, I DON'T REALLY CARE.

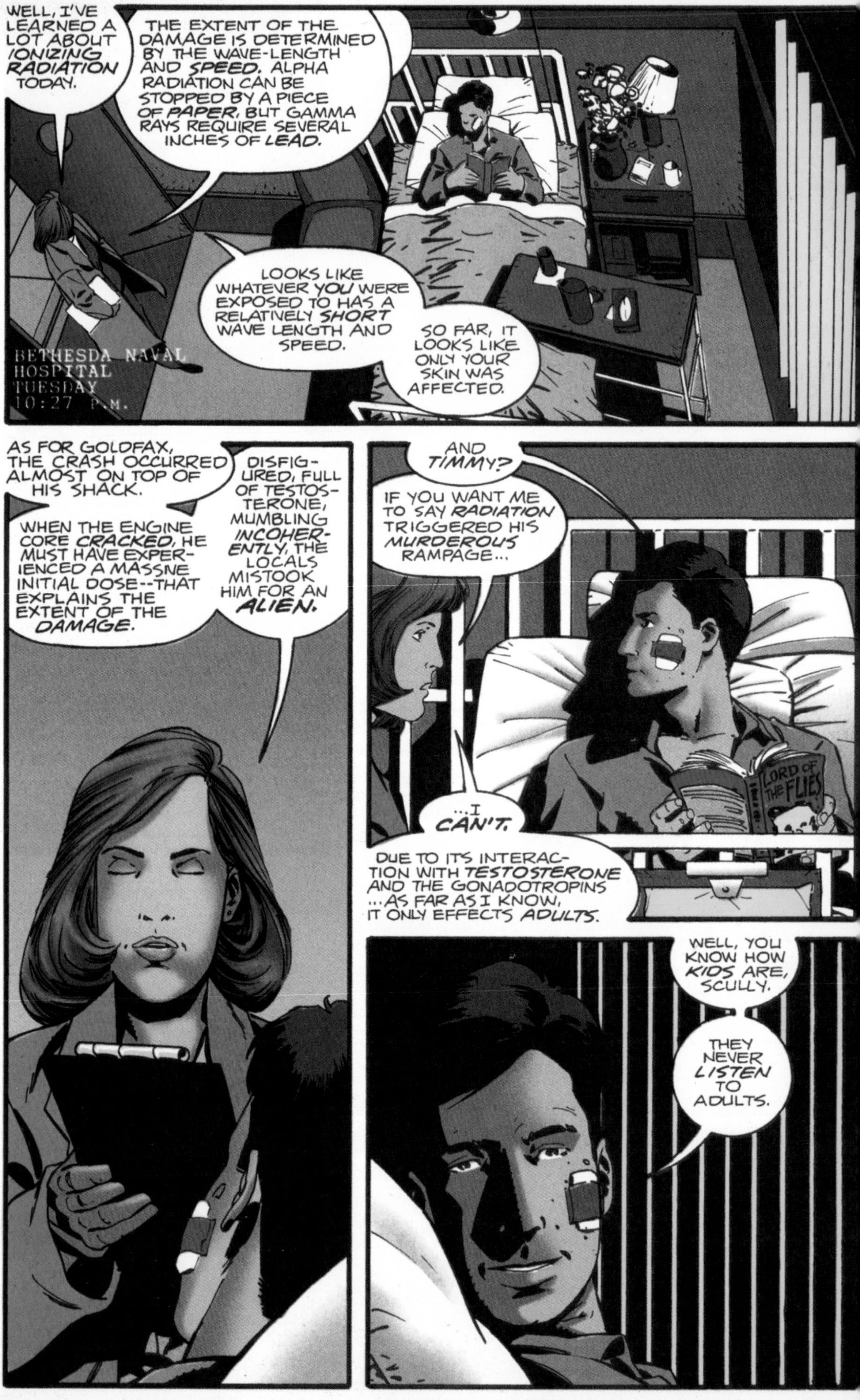
WELL, I'VE LEARNED A LOT ABOUT IONIZING RADIATION TODAY.
THE EXTENT OF THE DAMAGE IS DETERMINED BY THE WAVE-LENGTH AND SPEED. ALPHA RADIATION CAN BE STOPPED BY A PIECE OF PAPER, BUT GAMMA RAYS REQUIRE SEVERAL INCHES OF LEAD.
LOOKS LIKE WHATEVER YOU WERE EXPOSED TO HAS A RELATIVELY SHORT WAVE LENGTH AND SPEED.
SO FAR, IT LOOKS LIKE ONLY YOUR SKIN WAS AFFECTED.
BETHESDA NAVAL HOSPITAL TUESDAY 10:27 P.M.
AS FOR GOLDFAX, THE CRASH OCCURRED ALMOST ON TOP OF HIS SHACK.
WHEN THE ENGINE CORE CRACKED, HE MUST HAVE EXPERIENCED A MASSIVE INITIAL DOSE--THAT EXPLAINS THE EXTENT OF THE DAMAGE.
DISFIGURED, FULL OF TESTOSTERONE, MUMBLING INCOHERENTLY, THE LOCALS MISTOOK HIM FOR AN ALIEN.
AND TIMMY?
IF YOU WANT ME TO SAY RADIATION TRIGGERED HIS MURDEROUS RAMPAGE...
...I CAN'T.
LORD OF THE FLIES
DUE TO ITS INTERACTION WITH TESTOSTERONE AND THE GONADOTROPINS ...AS FAR AS I KNOW, IT ONLY EFFECTS ADULTS.
WELL, YOU KNOW HOW KIDS ARE, SCULLY.
THEY NEVER LISTEN TO ADULTS.

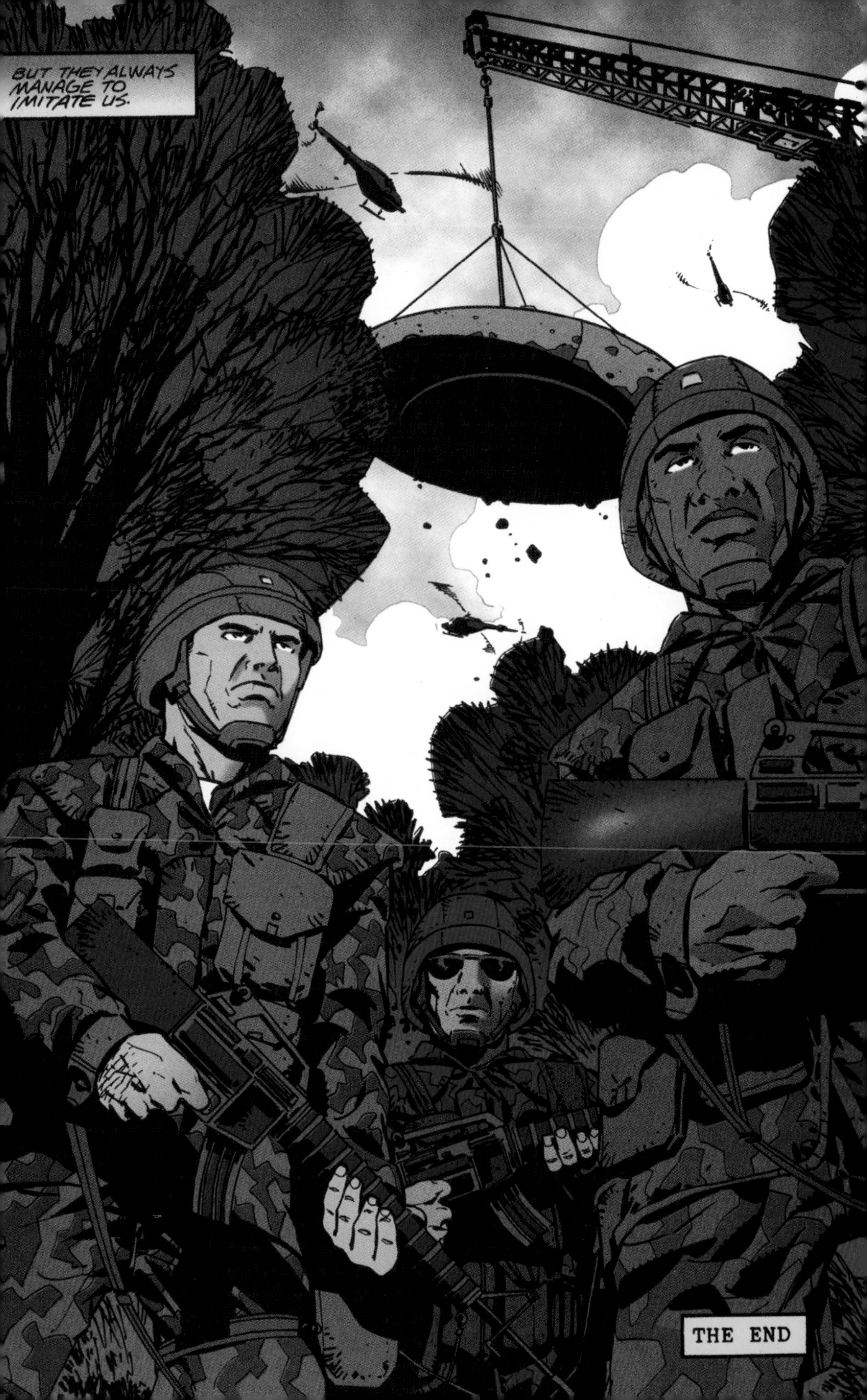
BUT THEY ALWAYS MANAGE TO IMITATE US.
THE END

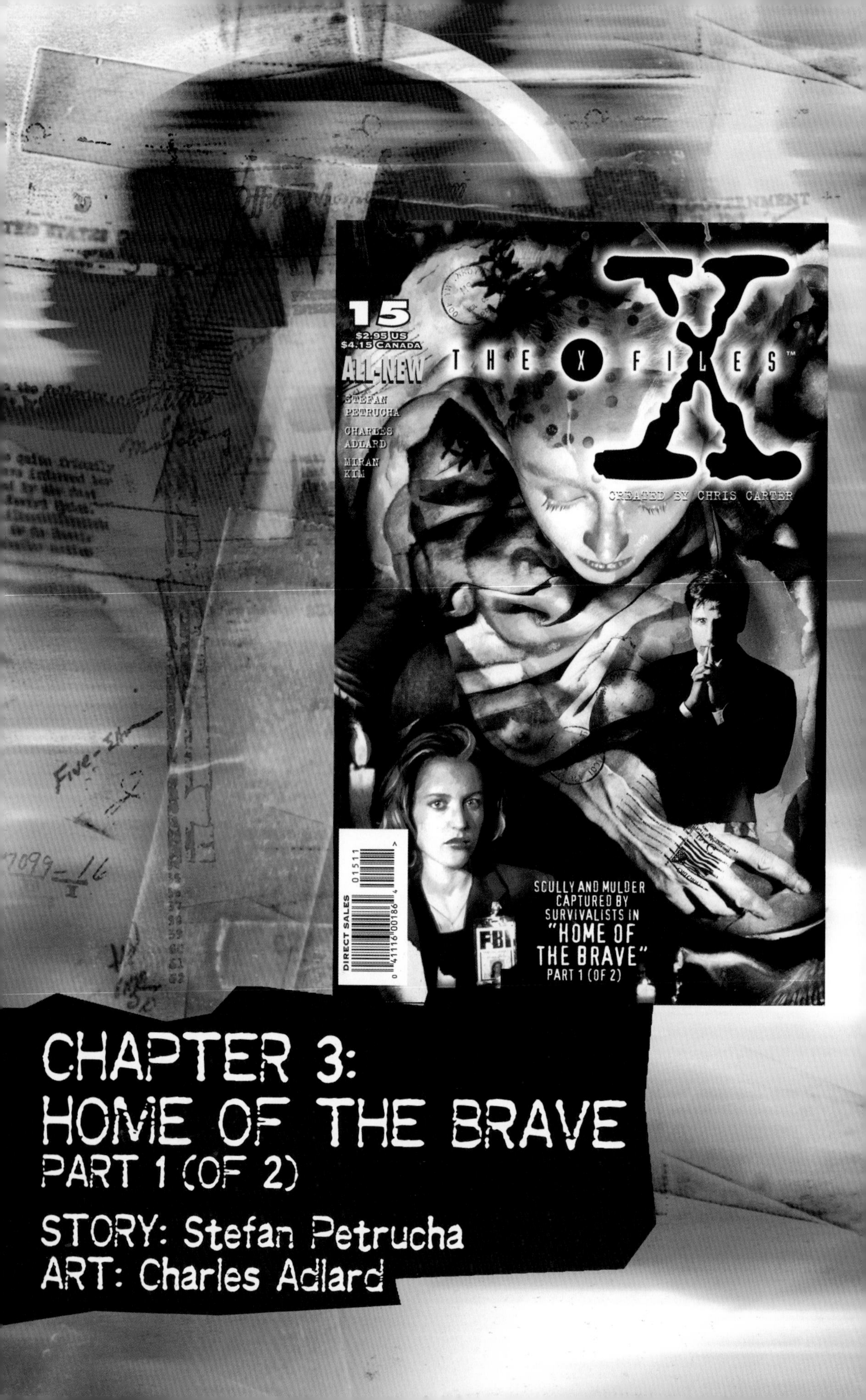
15
$2.95 US
$4.15 CANADA
ALL-NEW
STEFAN PETRUCHA
CHARLES ADLARD
MIRAN KIM
THE X FILES™
CREATED BY CHRIS CARTER
SCULLY AND MULDER CAPTURED BY SURVIVALISTS IN "HOME OF THE BRAVE" PART 1 (OF 2)
DIRECT SALES
FBI

CHAPTER 3: HOME OF THE BRAVE

PART 1 (OF 2)

STORY: Stefan Petrucha
ART: Charles Adlard

IN MY HOME COUNTRY, THE MALE CHILD IS VALUED MORE THAN THE FEMALE.

BOYS WORK AND BRING MONEY.

WHEN THE PARENTS GROW OLD, THEY CARE FOR THEM.

A GIRL BECOMES PART OF THE HUSBAND'S FAMILY--SO WHAT WILL BECOME OF HER PARENTS IF THEY HAVE NO SON?

NOT SO LONG AGO, A GIRL BORN TO A POOR FAMILY WOULD BE LEFT ON A HILL TO DIE.

NOW THE DOCTORS CAN TELL BEFORE BIRTH. SO IF THEY FIND OUT IT WILL BE A GIRL, THEY JUST HAVE AN ABORTION.

A WOMAN ON THE PLANE SAID THIS HAPPENS SO OFTEN THAT OUR POPULATION IS CHANGING.

SHE WARNED THAT SOON THERE WILL BE TOO MANY MEN AND THAT WITHOUT ENOUGH WOMEN, THE MEN WILL BECOME ANGRY AND THERE WILL BE WAR.

BUT I AM FAR FROM HOME, SELFISH, AND HAPPY TO BE IN A PLACE WHERE I HAVE SO MANY CHOICES.

I HAVE A BABY DAUGHTER. I CAN TELL MY HUSBAND WAS DISAPPOINTED. SOMETIMES THE OTHERS RIDICULE HIM FOR NOT HAVING A SON, BUT SHE IS ALIVE.

HE PICKED ME FROM A CATALOGUE.

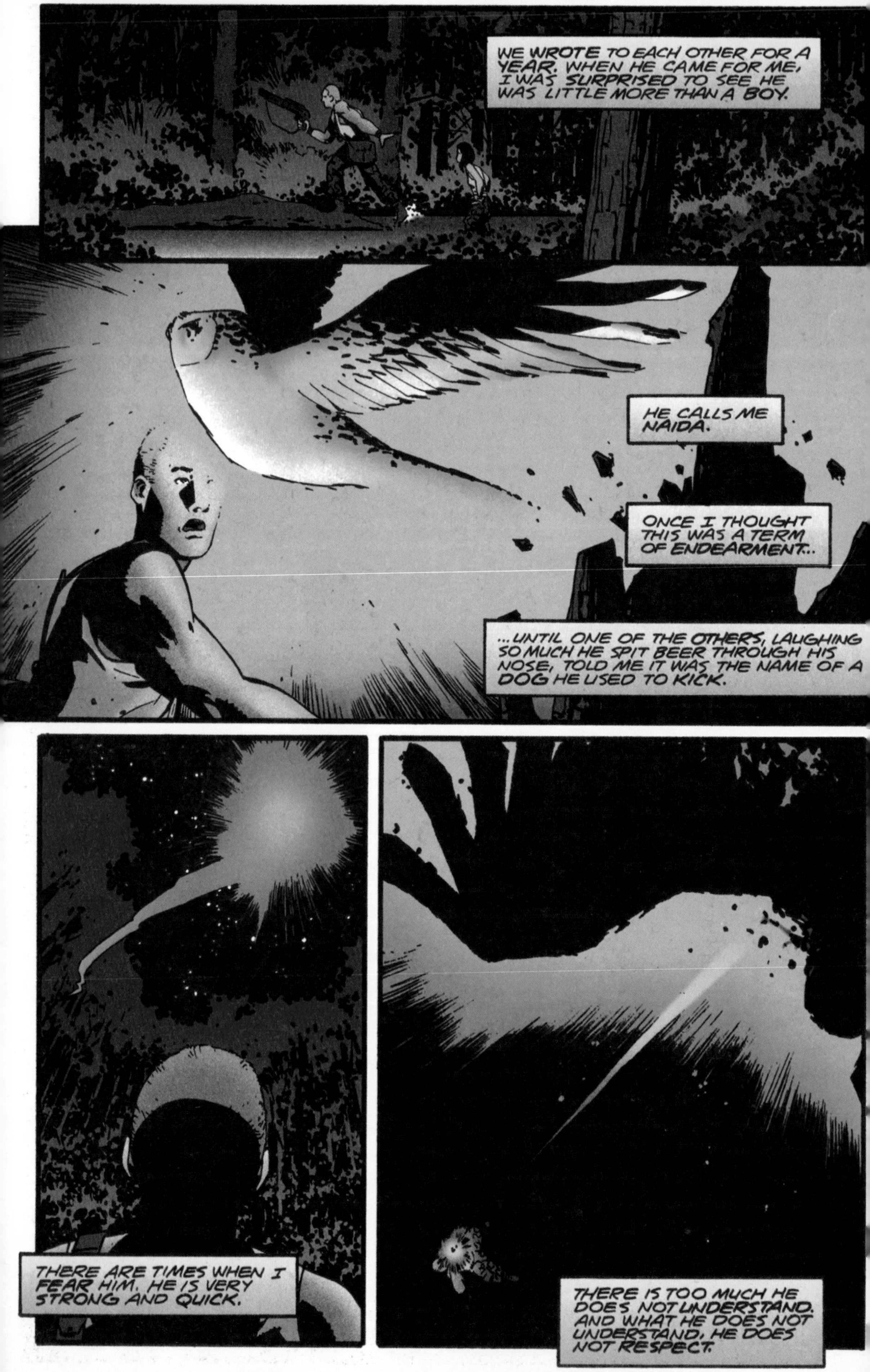
WE WROTE TO EACH OTHER FOR A YEAR. WHEN HE CAME FOR ME, I WAS SURPRISED TO SEE HE WAS LITTLE MORE THAN A BOY.
HE CALLS ME NAIDA.
ONCE I THOUGHT THIS WAS A TERM OF ENDEARMENT...
...UNTIL ONE OF THE OTHERS, LAUGHING SO MUCH HE SPIT BEER THROUGH HIS NOSE, TOLD ME IT WAS THE NAME OF A DOG HE USED TO KICK.
THERE ARE TIMES WHEN I FEAR HIM. HE IS VERY STRONG AND QUICK.
THERE IS TOO MUCH HE DOES NOT UNDERSTAND. AND WHAT HE DOES NOT UNDERSTAND, HE DOES NOT RESPECT.

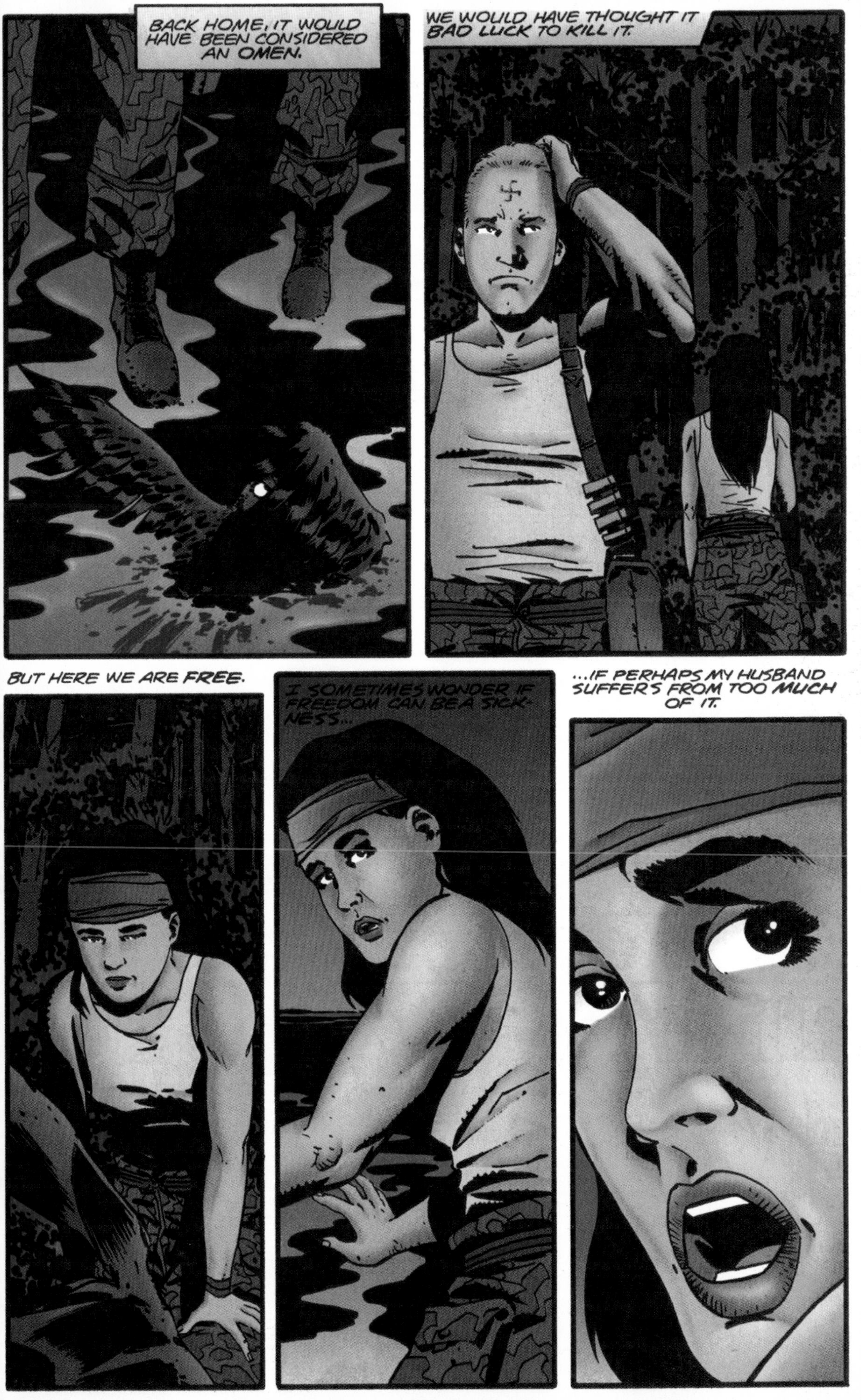
BACK HOME, IT WOULD HAVE BEEN CONSIDERED AN OMEN.
WE WOULD HAVE THOUGHT IT BAD LUCK TO KILL IT.
BUT HERE WE ARE FREE.
I SOMETIMES WONDER IF FREEDOM CAN BE A SICKNESS...
...IF PERHAPS MY HUSBAND SUFFERS FROM TOO MUCH OF IT.

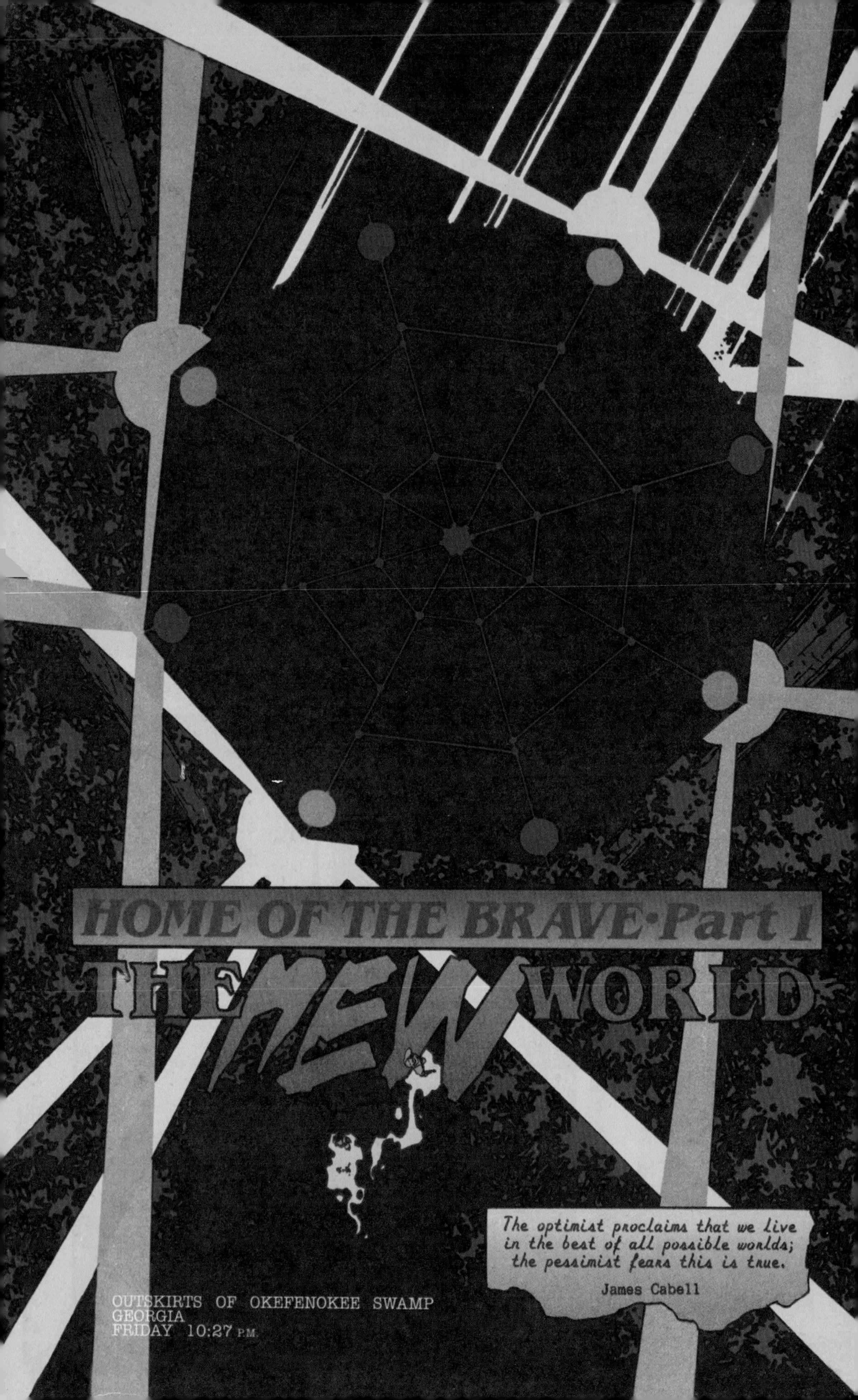

HOME OF THE BRAVE • Part 1
THE NEW WORLD
The optimist proclaims that we live in the best of all possible worlds; the pessimist fears this is true.
James Cabell
OUTSKIRTS OF OKEFENOKEE SWAMP
GEORGIA
FRIDAY 10:27 P.M.

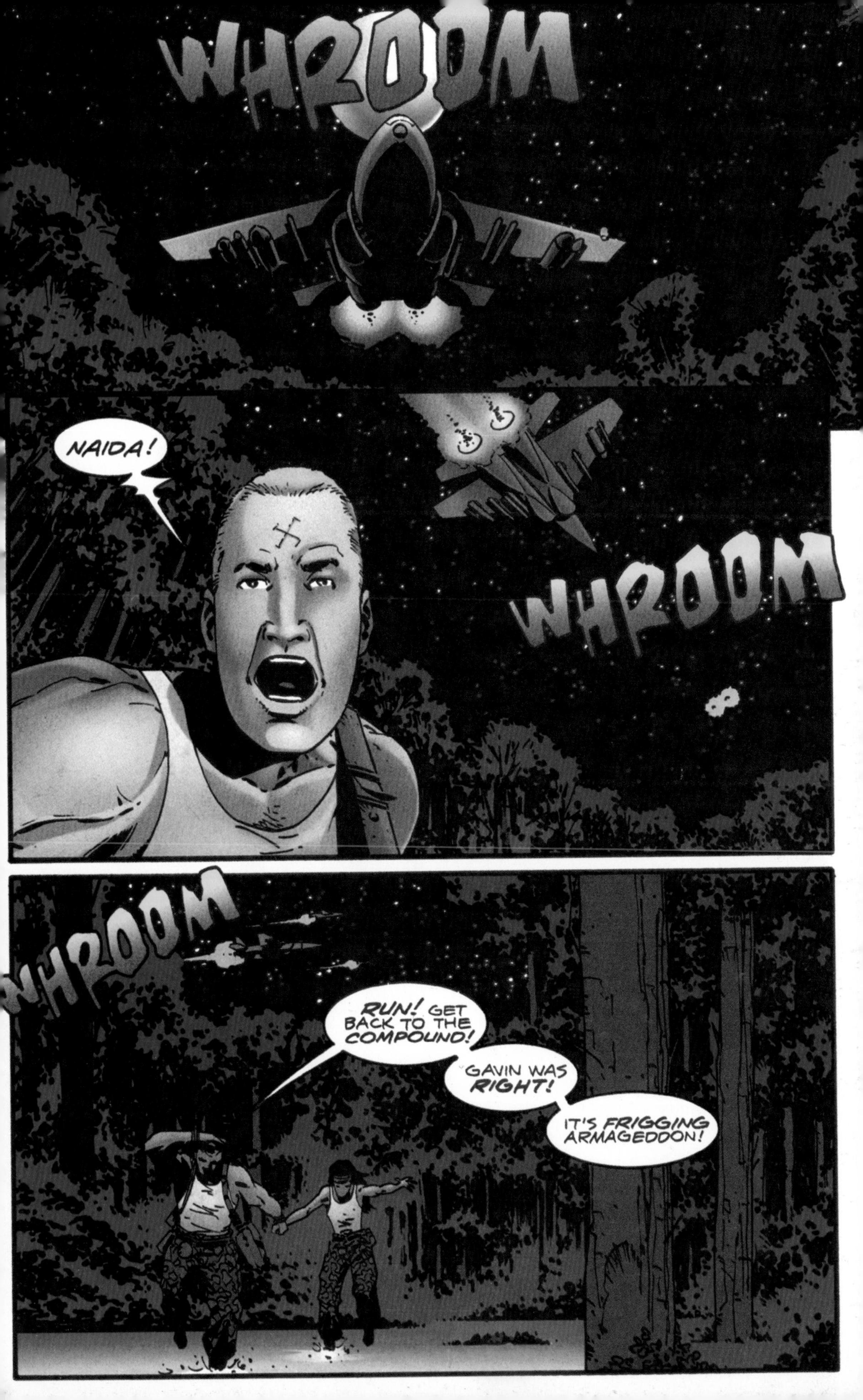
WHROOM
NAIDA!
WHROOM
WHROOM
RUN! GET BACK TO THE COMPOUND!
GAVIN WAS RIGHT!
IT'S FRIGGING ARMAGEDDON!

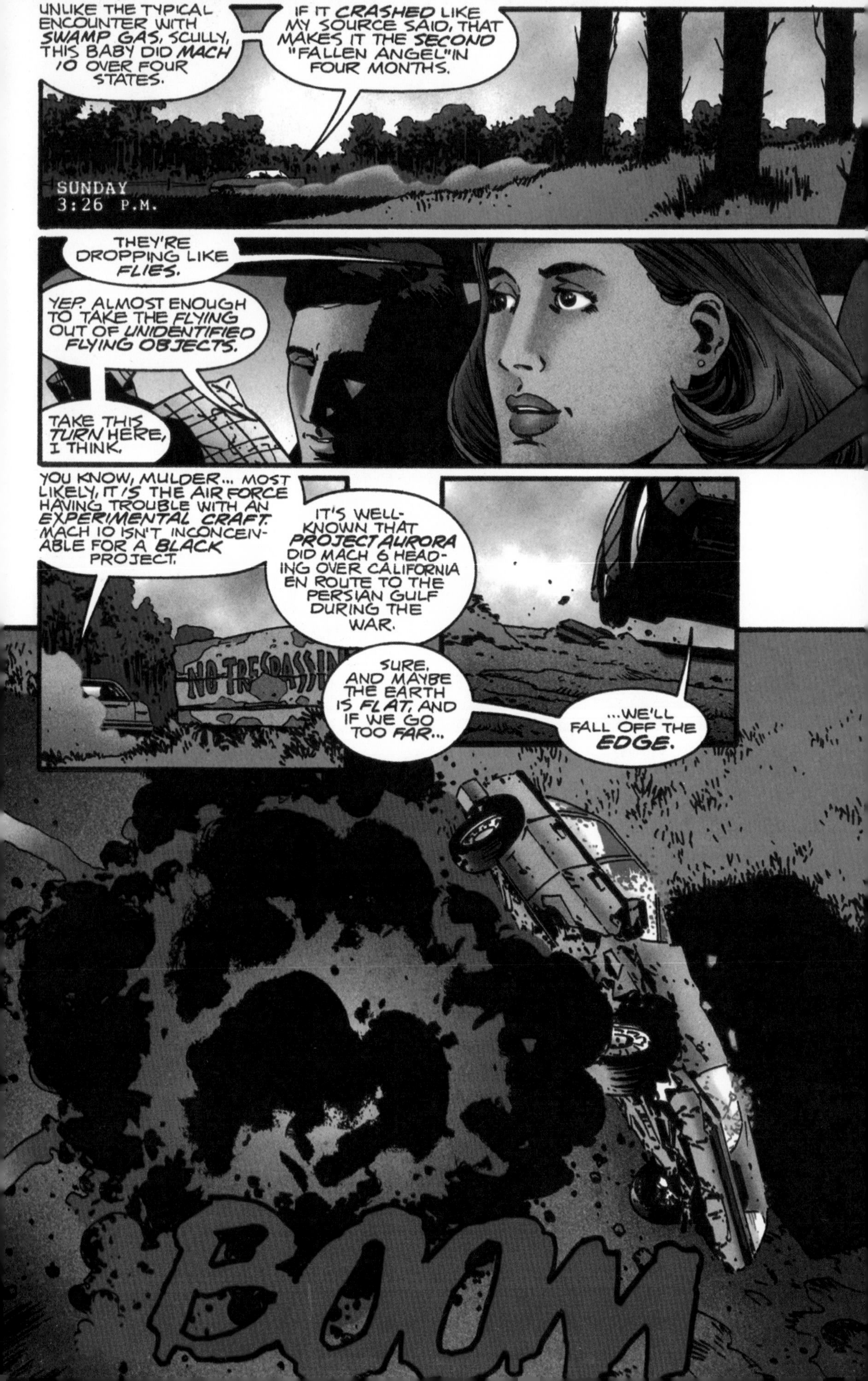
UNLIKE THE TYPICAL ENCOUNTER WITH SWAMP GAS, SCULLY, THIS BABY DID MACH 10 OVER FOUR STATES.
IF IT CRASHED LIKE MY SOURCE SAID, THAT MAKES IT THE SECOND "FALLEN ANGEL" IN FOUR MONTHS.
SUNDAY
3:26 P.M.
THEY'RE DROPPING LIKE FLIES.
YEP. ALMOST ENOUGH TO TAKE THE FLYING OUT OF UNIDENTIFIED FLYING OBJECTS.
TAKE THIS TURN HERE, I THINK.
YOU KNOW, MULDER... MOST LIKELY, IT'S THE AIR FORCE HAVING TROUBLE WITH AN EXPERIMENTAL CRAFT. MACH 10 ISN'T INCONCEIVABLE FOR A BLACK PROJECT.
IT'S WELL-KNOWN THAT PROJECT AURORA DID MACH 6 HEADING OVER CALIFORNIA EN ROUTE TO THE PERSIAN GULF DURING THE WAR.
SURE. AND MAYBE THE EARTH IS FLAT, AND IF WE GO TOO FAR...
...WE'LL FALL OFF THE EDGE.
BOOM

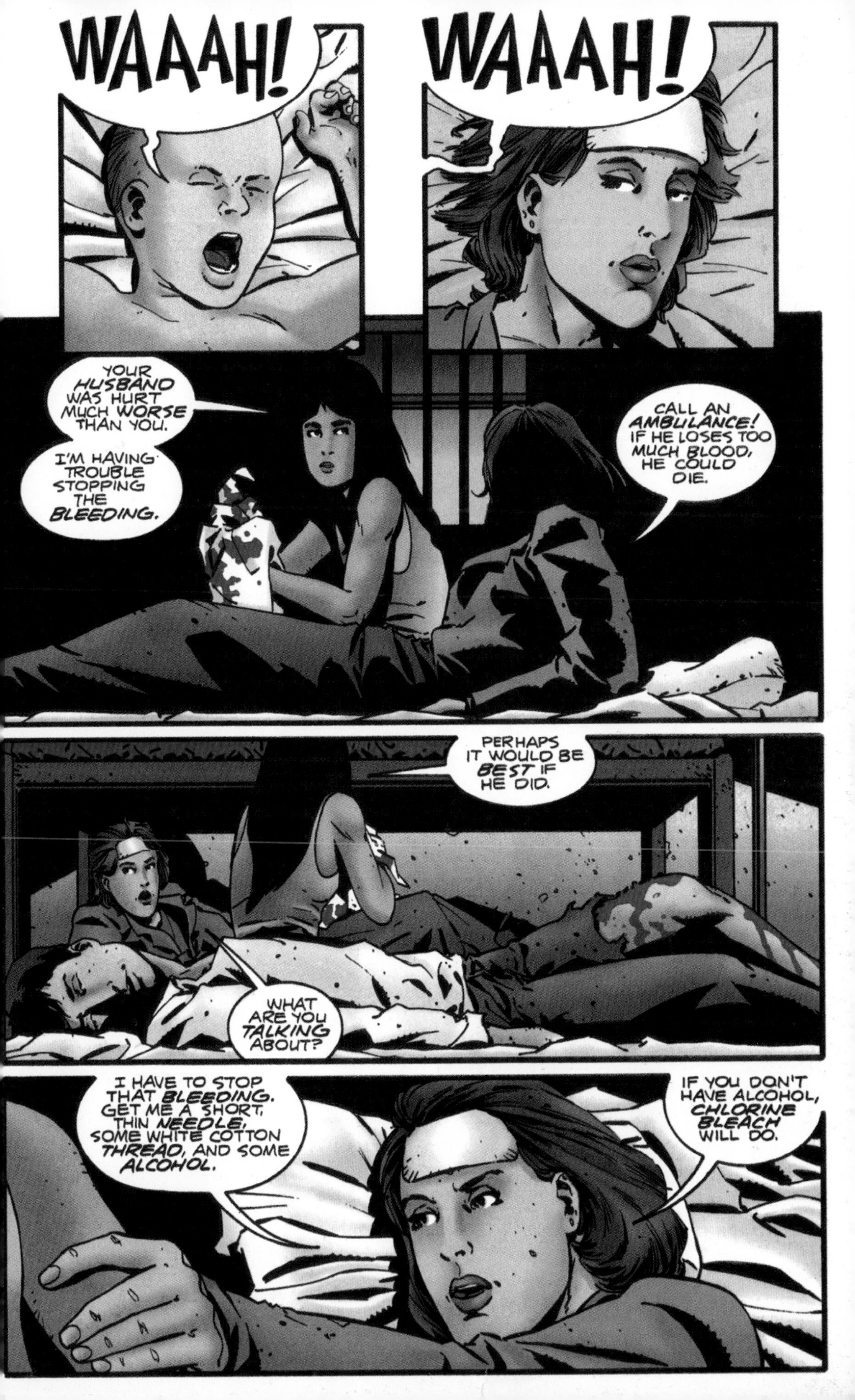
WAAAH!
WAAAH!
YOUR HUSBAND WAS HURT MUCH WORSE THAN YOU.
I'M HAVING TROUBLE STOPPING THE BLEEDING.
CALL AN AMBULANCE! IF HE LOSES TOO MUCH BLOOD, HE COULD DIE.
PERHAPS IT WOULD BE BEST IF HE DID.
WHAT ARE YOU TALKING ABOUT?
I HAVE TO STOP THAT BLEEDING. GET ME A SHORT, THIN NEEDLE, SOME WHITE COTTON THREAD, AND SOME ALCOHOL.
IF YOU DON'T HAVE ALCOHOL, CHLORINE BLEACH WILL DO.

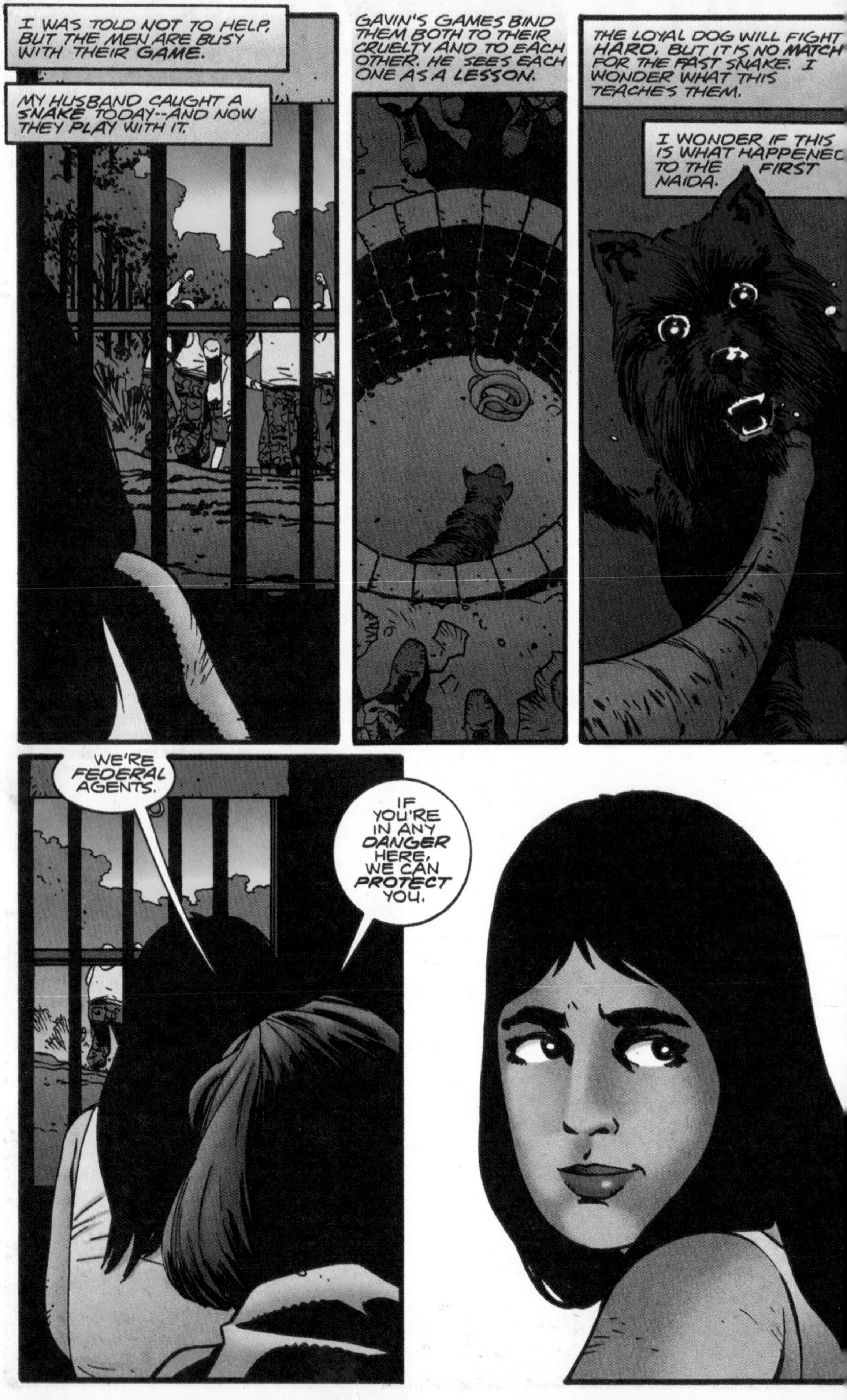

I WAS TOLD NOT TO HELP, BUT THE MEN ARE BUSY WITH THEIR GAME.
MY HUSBAND CAUGHT A SNAKE TODAY--AND NOW THEY PLAY WITH IT.
GAVIN'S GAMES BIND THEM BOTH TO THEIR CRUELTY AND TO EACH OTHER. HE SEES EACH ONE AS A LESSON.
THE LOYAL DOG WILL FIGHT HARD, BUT IT IS NO MATCH FOR THE FAST SNAKE. I WONDER WHAT THIS TEACHES THEM.
I WONDER IF THIS IS WHAT HAPPENED TO THE FIRST NAIDA.
WE'RE FEDERAL AGENTS.
IF YOU'RE IN ANY DANGER HERE, WE CAN PROTECT YOU.

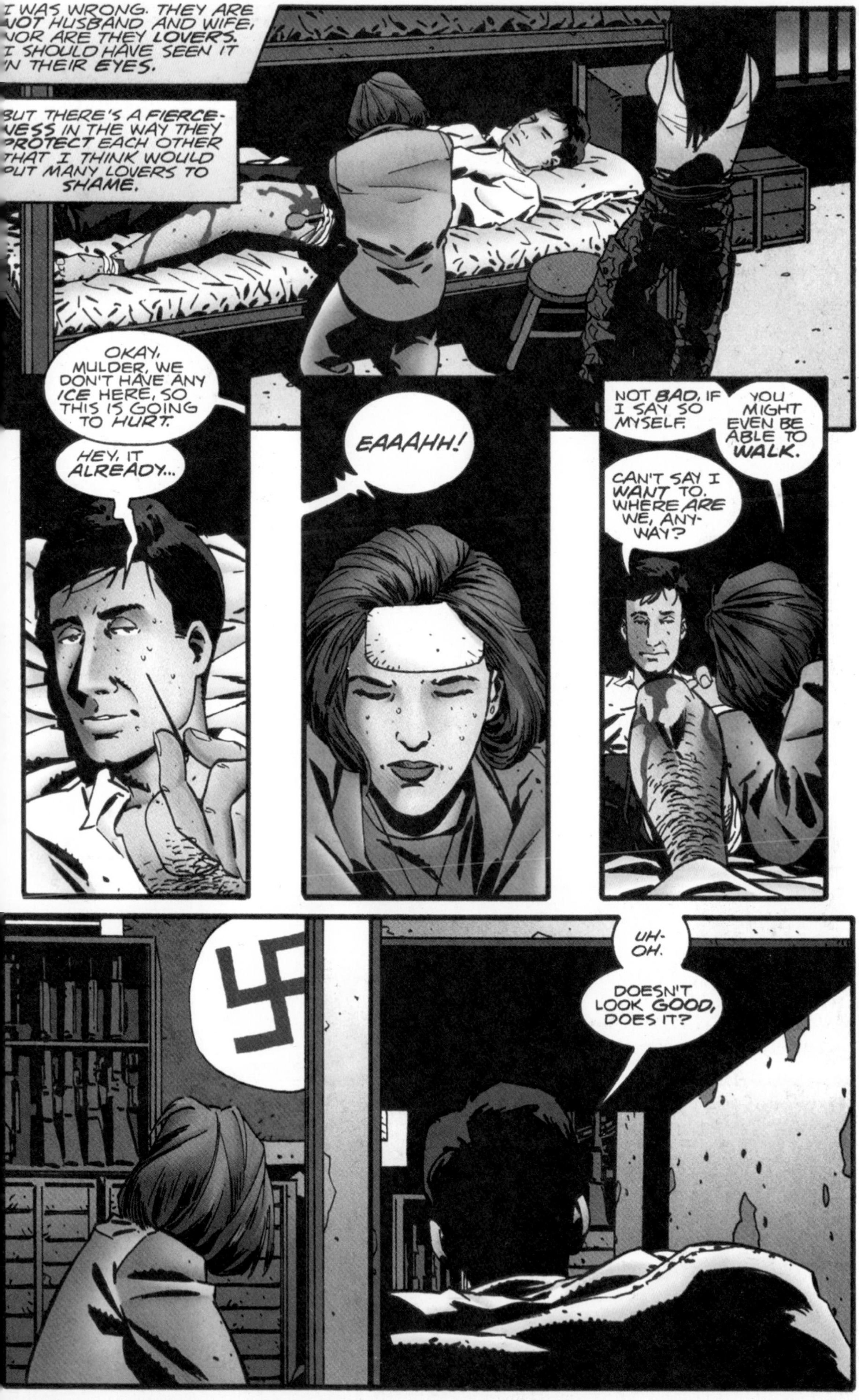
I WAS WRONG. THEY ARE NOT HUSBAND AND WIFE, NOR ARE THEY LOVERS. I SHOULD HAVE SEEN IT IN THEIR EYES.
BUT THERE'S A FIERCENESS IN THE WAY THEY PROTECT EACH OTHER THAT I THINK WOULD PUT MANY LOVERS TO SHAME.
OKAY, MULDER, WE DON'T HAVE ANY ICE HERE, SO THIS IS GOING TO HURT.
HEY, IT ALREADY...
EAAAHH!
NOT BAD, IF I SAY SO MYSELF.
YOU MIGHT EVEN BE ABLE TO WALK.
CAN'T SAY I WANT TO. WHERE ARE WE, ANYWAY?
UH-OH.
DOESN'T LOOK GOOD, DOES IT?

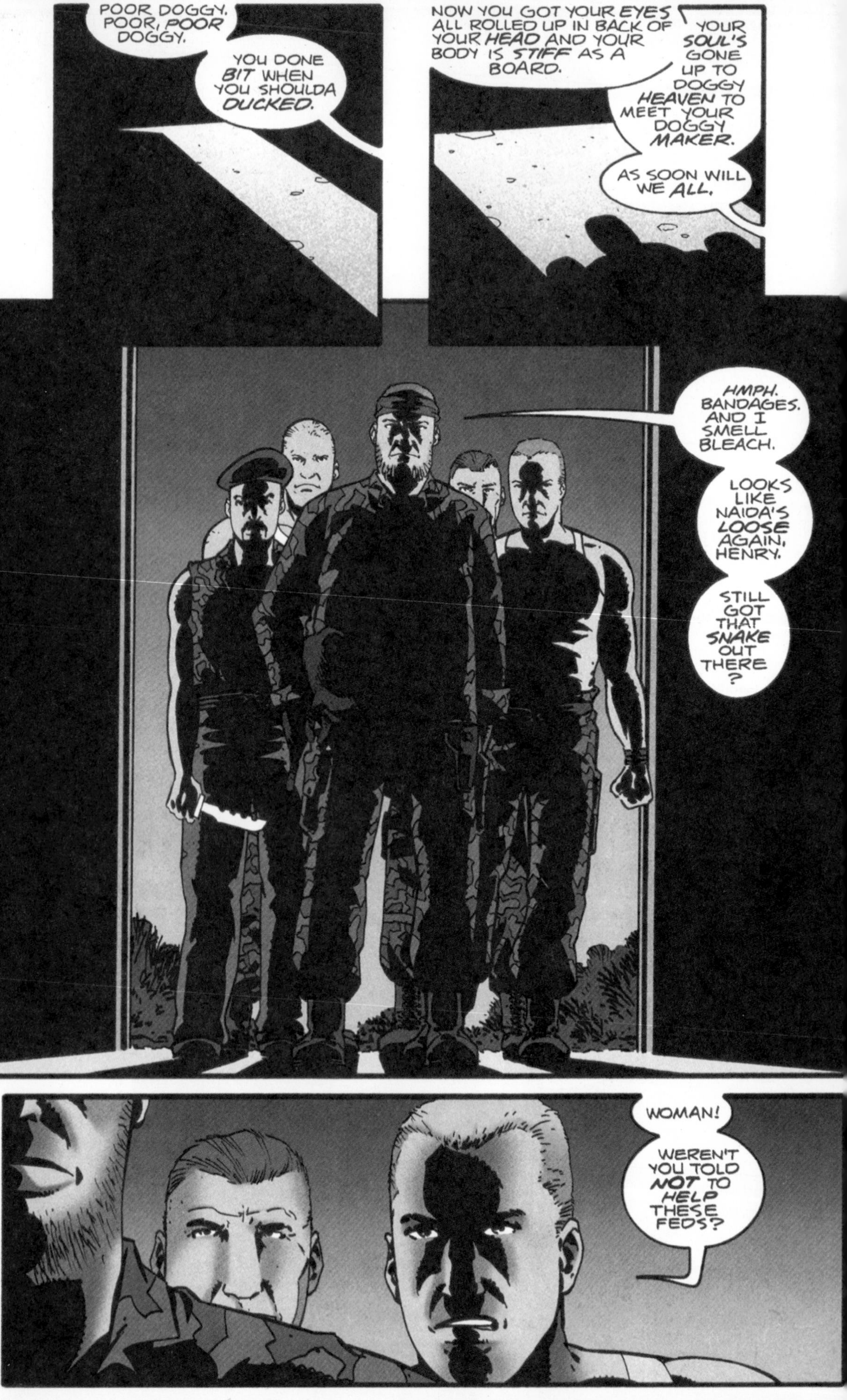
POOR DOGGY. POOR, POOR DOGGY.
YOU DONE BIT WHEN YOU SHOULDA DUCKED.
NOW YOU GOT YOUR EYES ALL ROLLED UP IN BACK OF YOUR HEAD AND YOUR BODY IS STIFF AS A BOARD.
YOUR SOUL'S GONE UP TO DOGGY HEAVEN TO MEET YOUR DOGGY MAKER.
AS SOON WILL WE ALL.
HMPH. BANDAGES. AND I SMELL BLEACH.
LOOKS LIKE NAIDA'S LOOSE AGAIN, HENRY.
STILL GOT THAT SNAKE OUT THERE?
WOMAN!
WEREN'T YOU TOLD NOT TO HELP THESE FEDS?

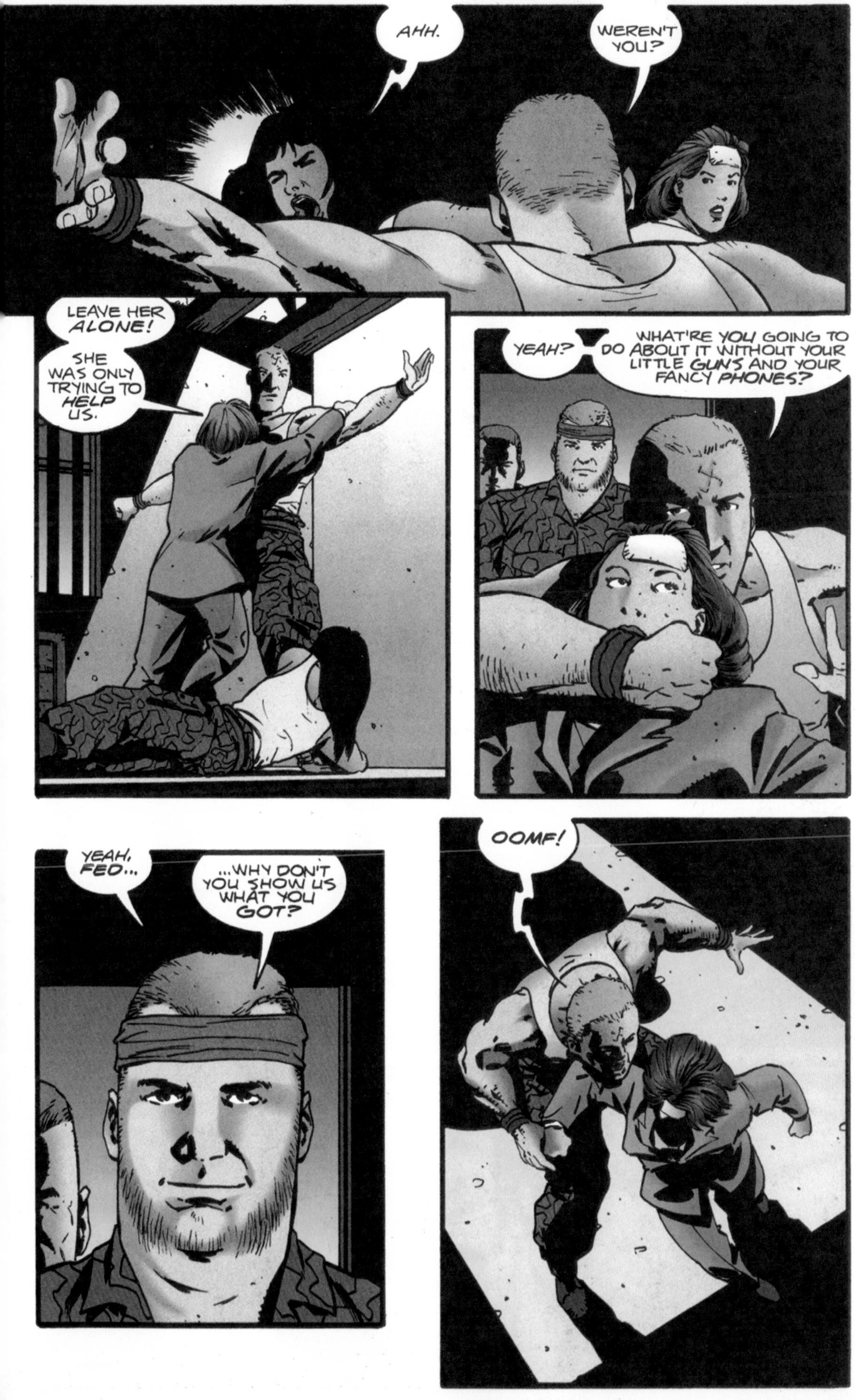
AHH.
WEREN'T YOU?
LEAVE HER ALONE!
SHE WAS ONLY TRYING TO HELP US.
YEAH?
WHAT'RE YOU GOING TO DO ABOUT IT WITHOUT YOUR LITTLE GUNS AND YOUR FANCY PHONES?
YEAH, FED...
...WHY DON'T YOU SHOW US WHAT YOU GOT?
OOMF!

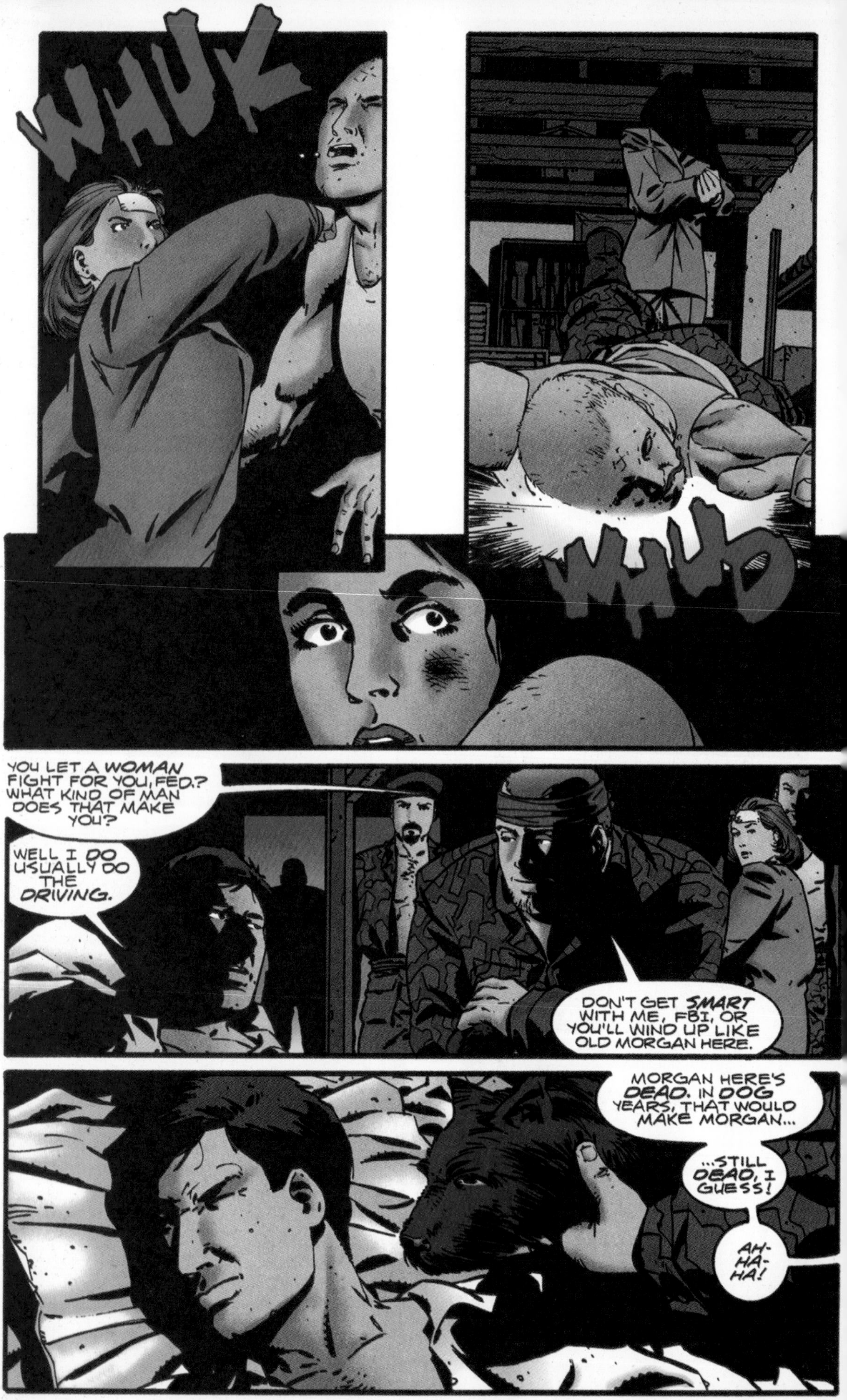
WHUK
WHUD
YOU LET A WOMAN FIGHT FOR YOU, FED.? WHAT KIND OF MAN DOES THAT MAKE YOU?
WELL I DO USUALLY DO THE DRIVING.
DON'T GET SMART WITH ME, FBI, OR YOU'LL WIND UP LIKE OLD MORGAN HERE.
MORGAN HERE'S DEAD. IN DOG YEARS, THAT WOULD MAKE MORGAN...
...STILL DEAD, I GUESS!
AH-HA-HA!

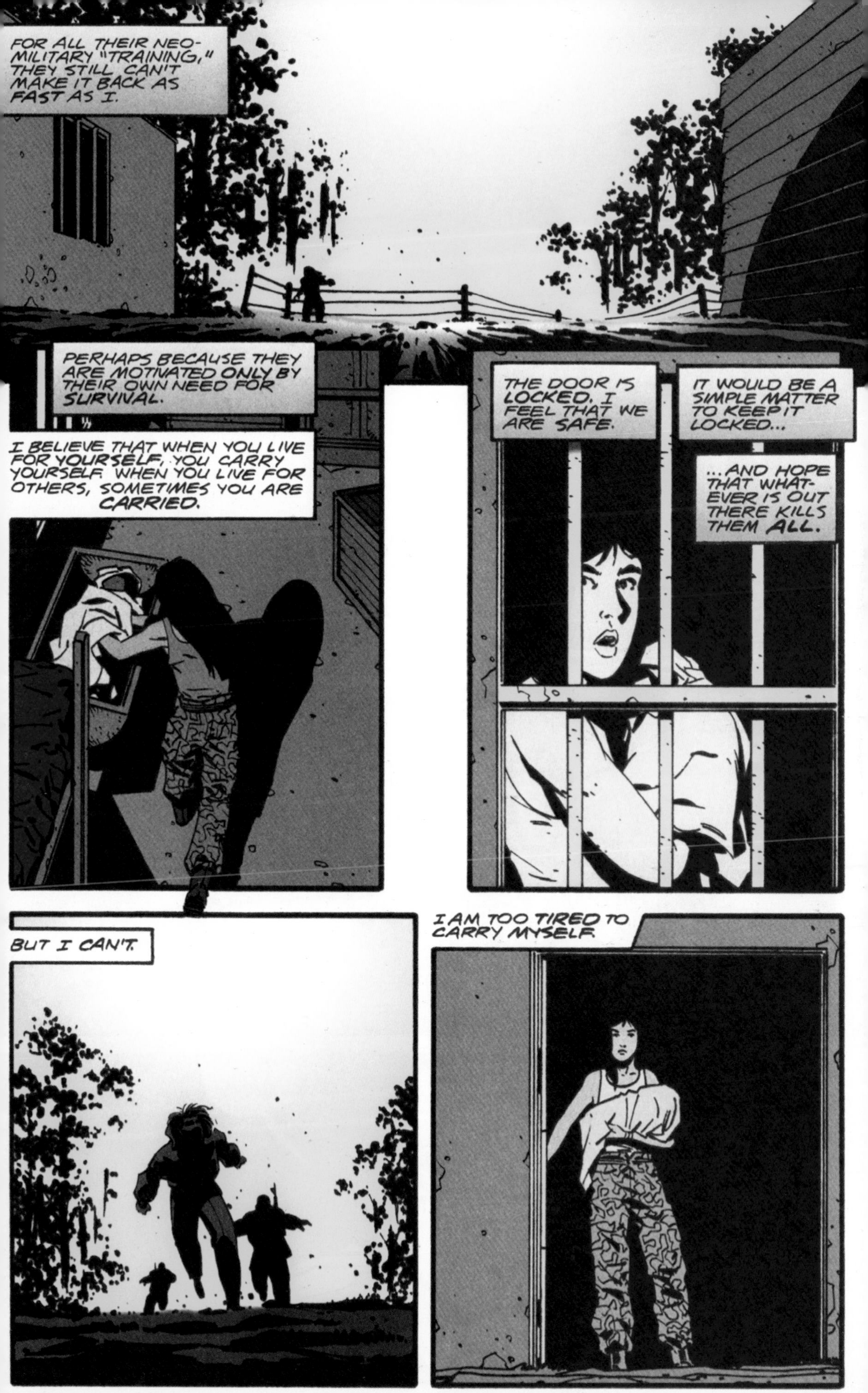
FOR ALL THEIR NEO-MILITARY "TRAINING," THEY STILL CAN'T MAKE IT BACK AS FAST AS I.
PERHAPS BECAUSE THEY ARE MOTIVATED ONLY BY THEIR OWN NEED FOR SURVIVAL.
I BELIEVE THAT WHEN YOU LIVE FOR YOURSELF, YOU CARRY YOURSELF. WHEN YOU LIVE FOR OTHERS, SOMETIMES YOU ARE CARRIED.
THE DOOR IS LOCKED. I FEEL THAT WE ARE SAFE.
IT WOULD BE A SIMPLE MATTER TO KEEP IT LOCKED...
...AND HOPE THAT WHATEVER IS OUT THERE KILLS THEM ALL.
BUT I CAN'T.
I AM TOO TIRED TO CARRY MYSELF.

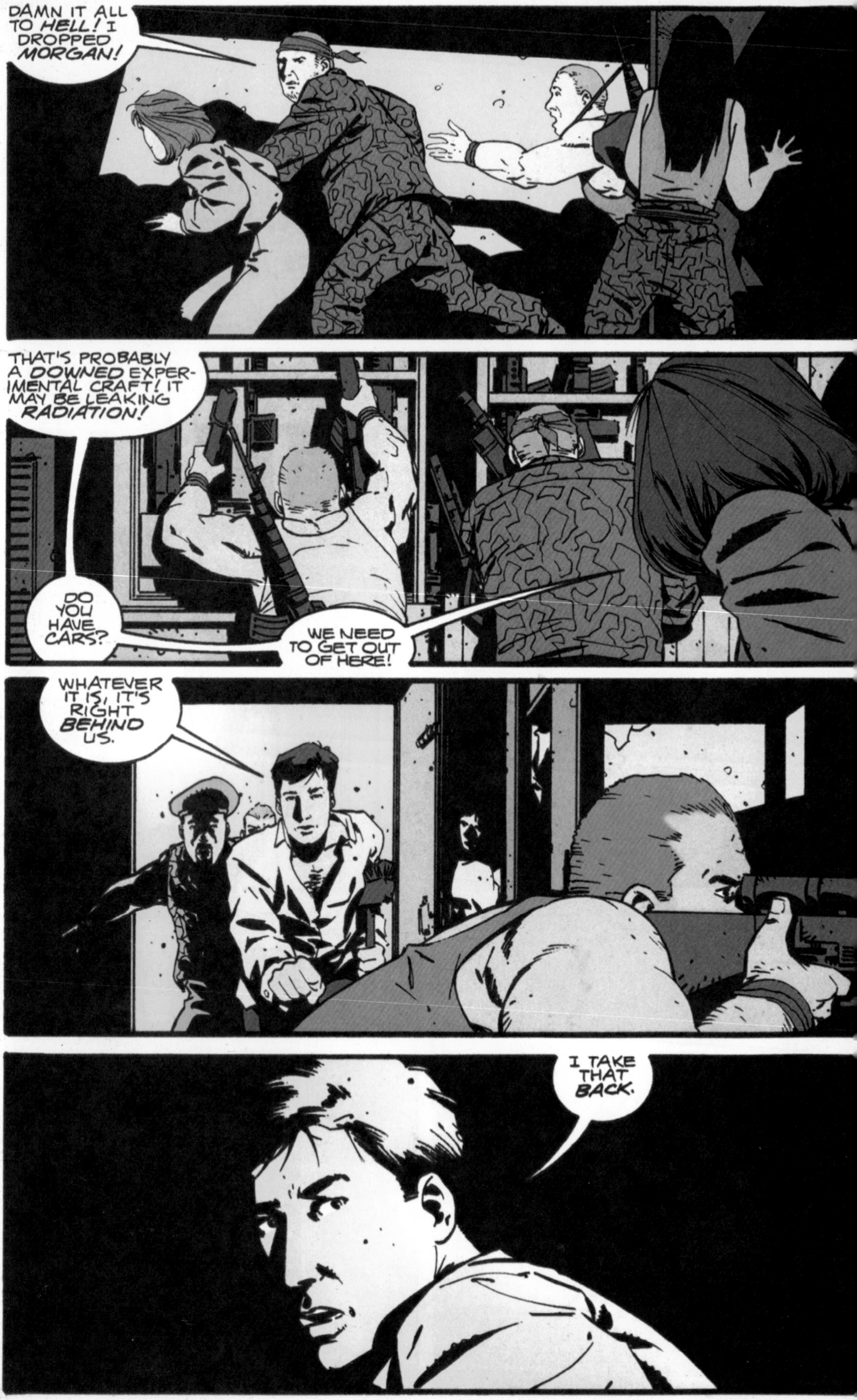
DAMN IT ALL TO HELL! I DROPPED MORGAN!
THAT'S PROBABLY A DOWNED EXPERIMENTAL CRAFT! IT MAY BE LEAKING RADIATION!
DO YOU HAVE CARS?
WE NEED TO GET OUT OF HERE!
WHATEVER IT IS, IT'S RIGHT BEHIND US.
I TAKE THAT BACK.

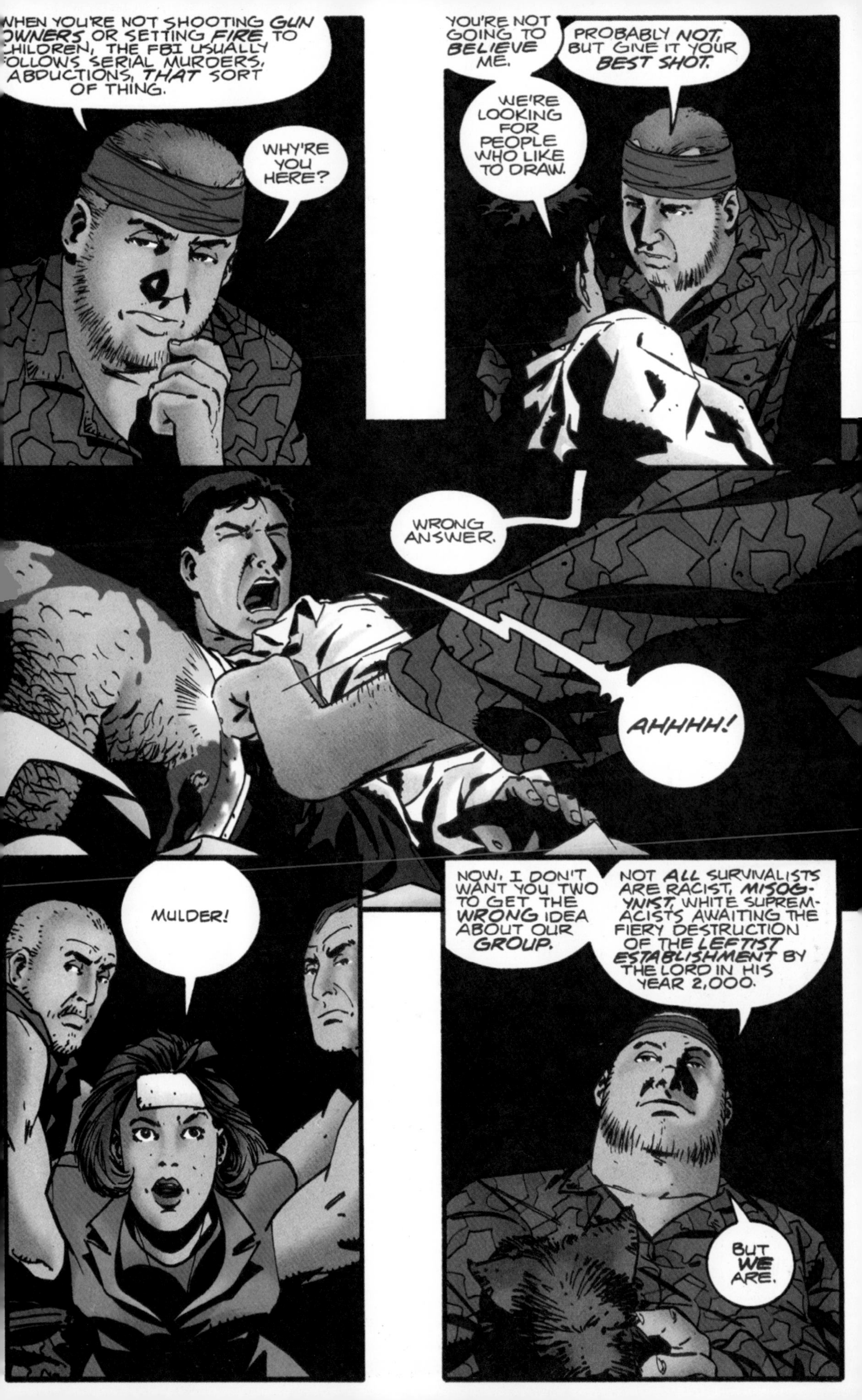
WHEN YOU'RE NOT SHOOTING GUN OWNERS OR SETTING FIRE TO CHILDREN, THE FBI USUALLY FOLLOWS SERIAL MURDERS, ABDUCTIONS, THAT SORT OF THING.
WHY'RE YOU HERE?
YOU'RE NOT GOING TO BELIEVE ME.
PROBABLY NOT, BUT GIVE IT YOUR BEST SHOT.
WE'RE LOOKING FOR PEOPLE WHO LIKE TO DRAW.
WRONG ANSWER.
AHHHH!
MULDER!
NOW, I DON'T WANT YOU TWO TO GET THE WRONG IDEA ABOUT OUR GROUP.
NOT ALL SURVIVALISTS ARE RACIST, MISOGYNIST, WHITE SUPREMACISTS AWAITING THE FIERY DESTRUCTION OF THE LEFTIST ESTABLISHMENT BY THE LORD IN HIS YEAR 2,000.
BUT WE ARE.

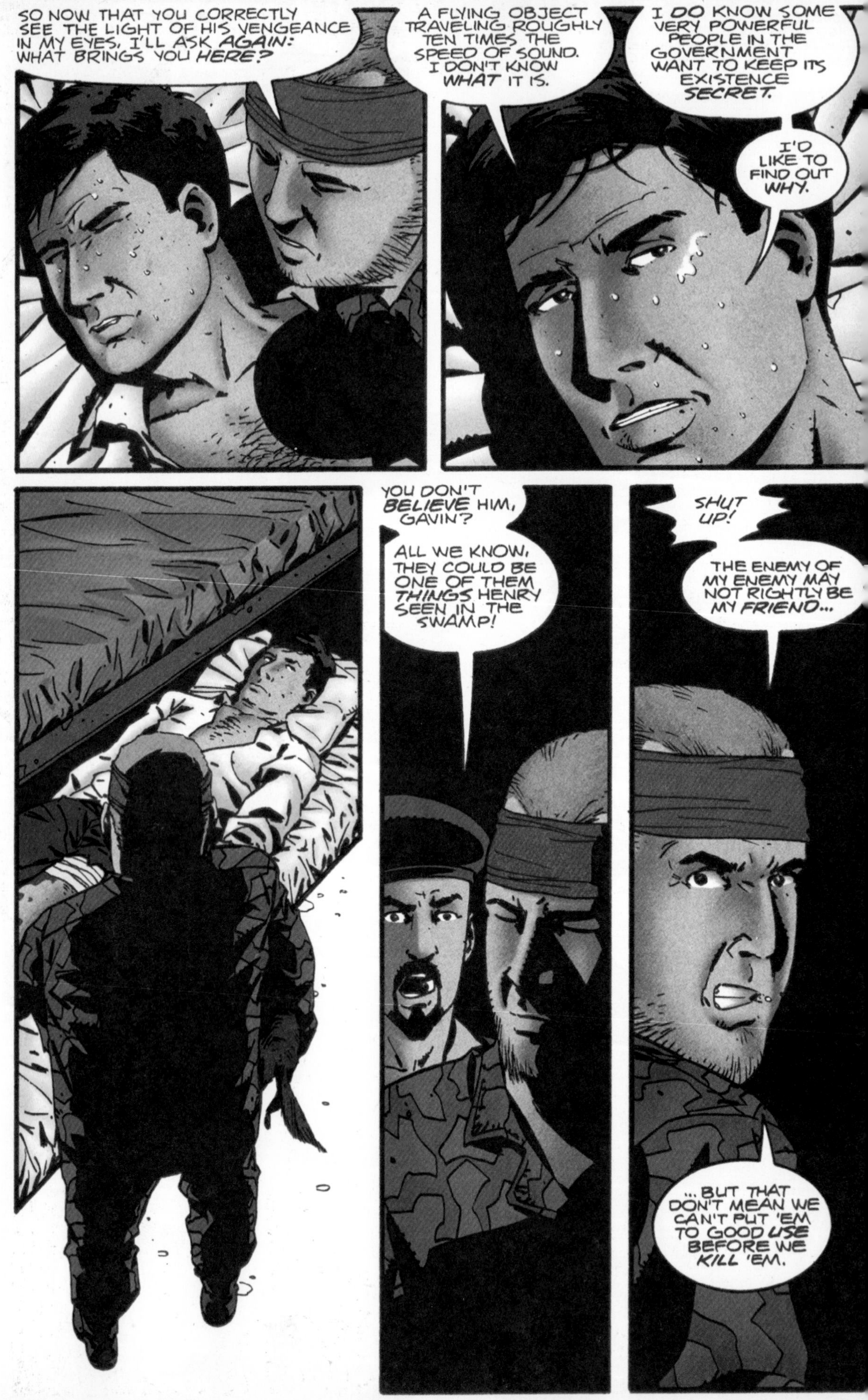
SO NOW THAT YOU CORRECTLY SEE THE LIGHT OF HIS VENGEANCE IN MY EYES, I'LL ASK AGAIN: WHAT BRINGS YOU HERE?
A FLYING OBJECT TRAVELING ROUGHLY TEN TIMES THE SPEED OF SOUND. I DON'T KNOW WHAT IT IS.
I DO KNOW SOME VERY POWERFUL PEOPLE IN THE GOVERNMENT WANT TO KEEP ITS EXISTENCE SECRET.
I'D LIKE TO FIND OUT WHY.
YOU DON'T BELIEVE HIM, GAVIN?
ALL WE KNOW, THEY COULD BE ONE OF THEM THINGS HENRY SEEN IN THE SWAMP!
SHUT UP!
THE ENEMY OF MY ENEMY MAY NOT RIGHTLY BE MY FRIEND...
...BUT THAT DON'T MEAN WE CAN'T PUT 'EM TO GOOD USE BEFORE WE KILL 'EM.

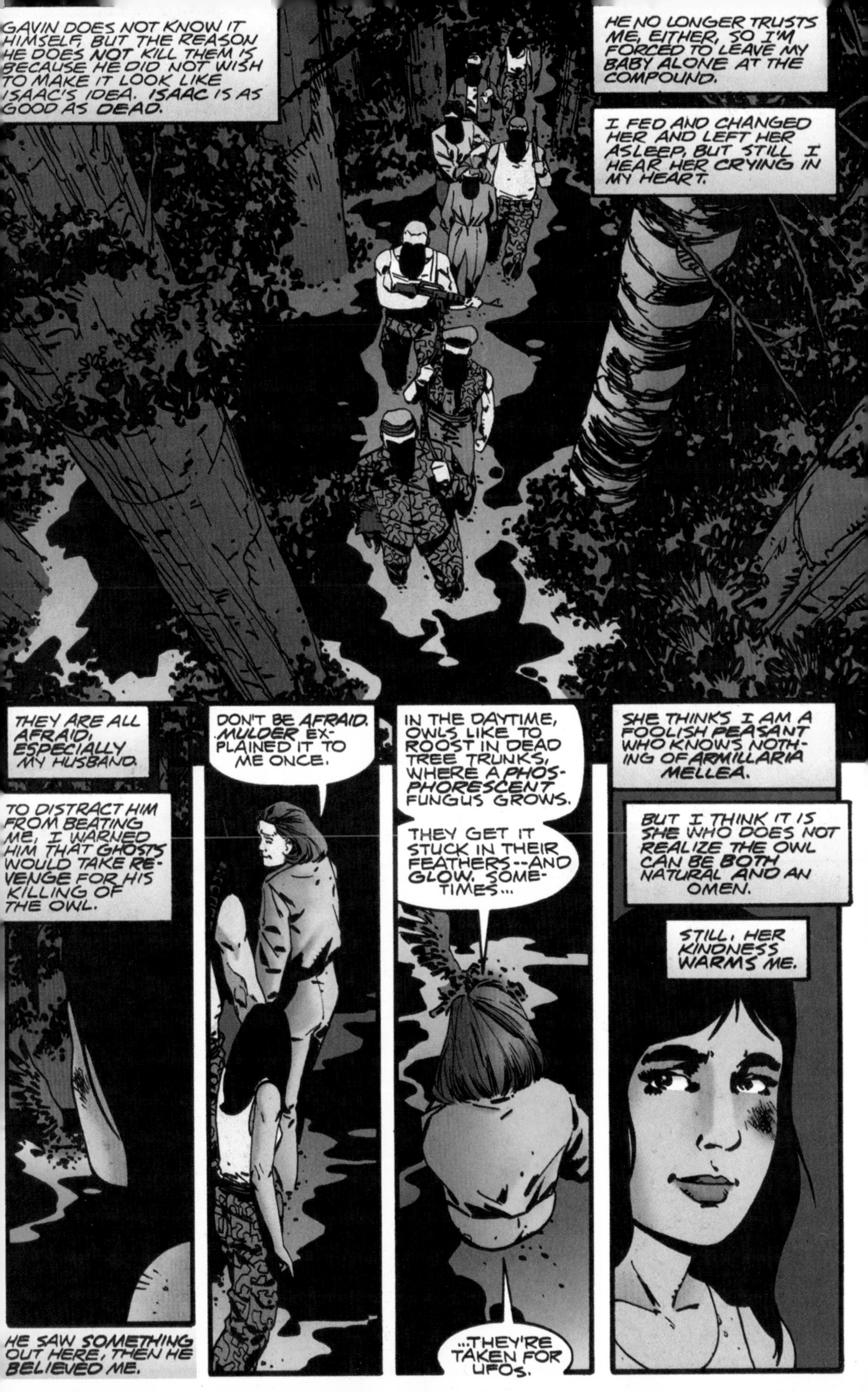
GAVIN DOES NOT KNOW IT HIMSELF, BUT THE REASON HE DOES NOT KILL THEM IS BECAUSE HE DID NOT WISH TO MAKE IT LOOK LIKE ISAAC'S IDEA. ISAAC IS AS GOOD AS DEAD.
HE NO LONGER TRUSTS ME, EITHER, SO I'M FORCED TO LEAVE MY BABY ALONE AT THE COMPOUND.
I FED AND CHANGED HER AND LEFT HER ASLEEP, BUT STILL I HEAR HER CRYING IN MY HEART.
THEY ARE ALL AFRAID, ESPECIALLY MY HUSBAND.
TO DISTRACT HIM FROM BEATING ME, I WARNED HIM THAT GHOSTS WOULD TAKE REVENGE FOR HIS KILLING OF THE OWL.
HE SAW SOMETHING OUT HERE, THEN HE BELIEVED ME.
DON'T BE AFRAID. MULDER EXPLAINED IT TO ME ONCE.
IN THE DAYTIME, OWLS LIKE TO ROOST IN DEAD TREE TRUNKS, WHERE A PHOSPHORESCENT FUNGUS GROWS.
THEY GET IT STUCK IN THEIR FEATHERS--AND GLOW. SOMETIMES...
...THEY'RE TAKEN FOR UFOs.
SHE THINKS I AM A FOOLISH PEASANT WHO KNOWS NOTHING OF ARMILLARIA MELLEA.
BUT I THINK IT IS SHE WHO DOES NOT REALIZE THE OWL CAN BE BOTH NATURAL AND AN OMEN.
STILL, HER KINDNESS WARMS ME.

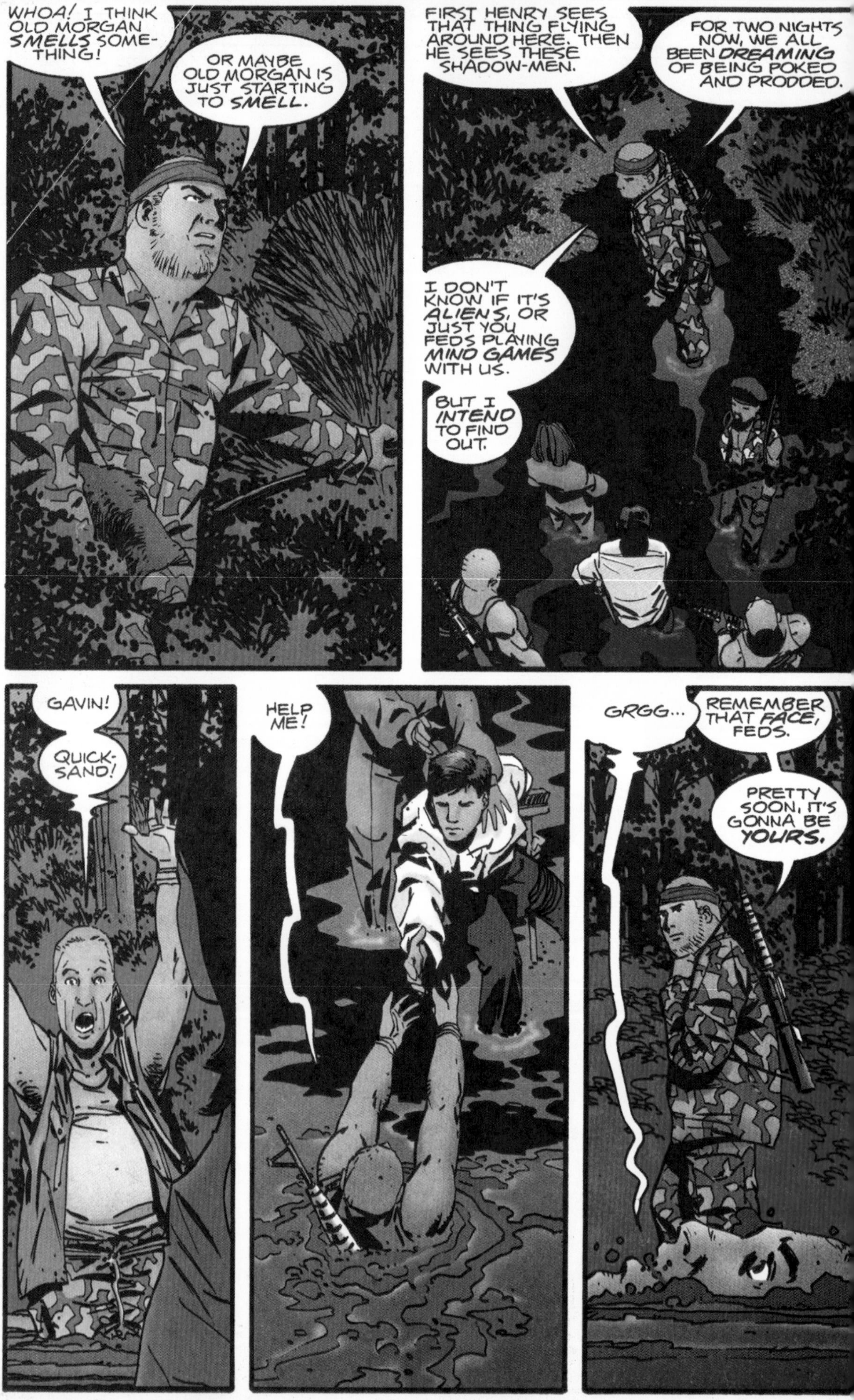
WHOA! I THINK OLD MORGAN SMELLS SOMETHING!
OR MAYBE OLD MORGAN IS JUST STARTING TO SMELL.
FIRST HENRY SEES THAT THING FLYING AROUND HERE. THEN HE SEES THESE SHADOW-MEN.
FOR TWO NIGHTS NOW, WE ALL BEEN DREAMING OF BEING POKED AND PRODDED.
I DON'T KNOW IF IT'S ALIENS, OR JUST YOU FEDS PLAYING MIND GAMES WITH US.
BUT I INTEND TO FIND OUT.
GAVIN!
QUICK-SAND!
HELP ME!
GRGG...
REMEMBER THAT FACE, FEDS.
PRETTY SOON, IT'S GONNA BE YOURS.

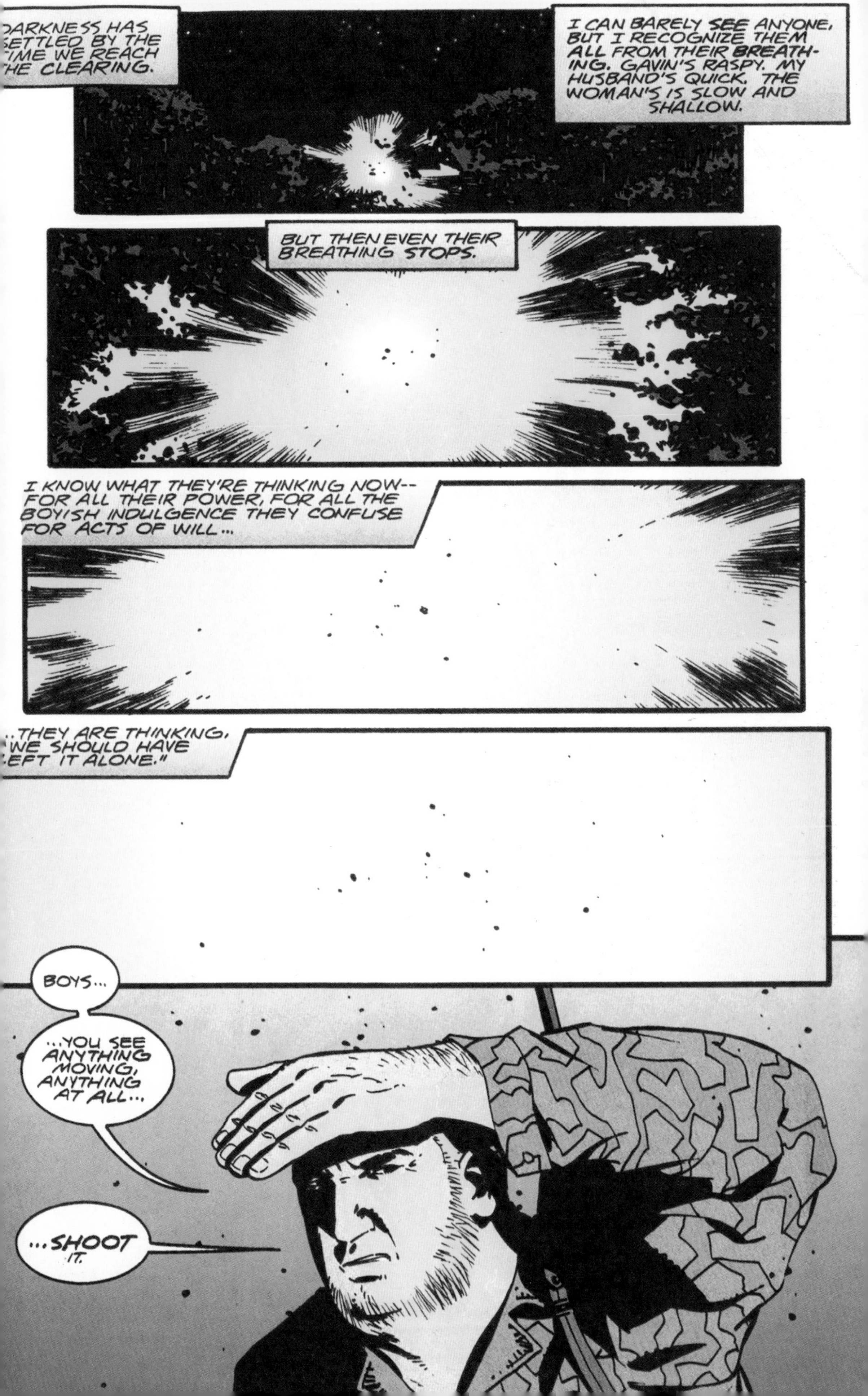
DARKNESS HAS SETTLED BY THE TIME WE REACH THE CLEARING.
I CAN BARELY SEE ANYONE, BUT I RECOGNIZE THEM ALL FROM THEIR BREATHING. GAVIN'S RASPY. MY HUSBAND'S QUICK. THE WOMAN'S IS SLOW AND SHALLOW.
BUT THEN EVEN THEIR BREATHING STOPS.
I KNOW WHAT THEY'RE THINKING NOW-- FOR ALL THEIR POWER, FOR ALL THE BOYISH INDULGENCE THEY CONFUSE FOR ACTS OF WILL...
..THEY ARE THINKING, "WE SHOULD HAVE LEFT IT ALONE."
BOYS...
...YOU SEE ANYTHING MOVING, ANYTHING AT ALL...
...SHOOT IT.

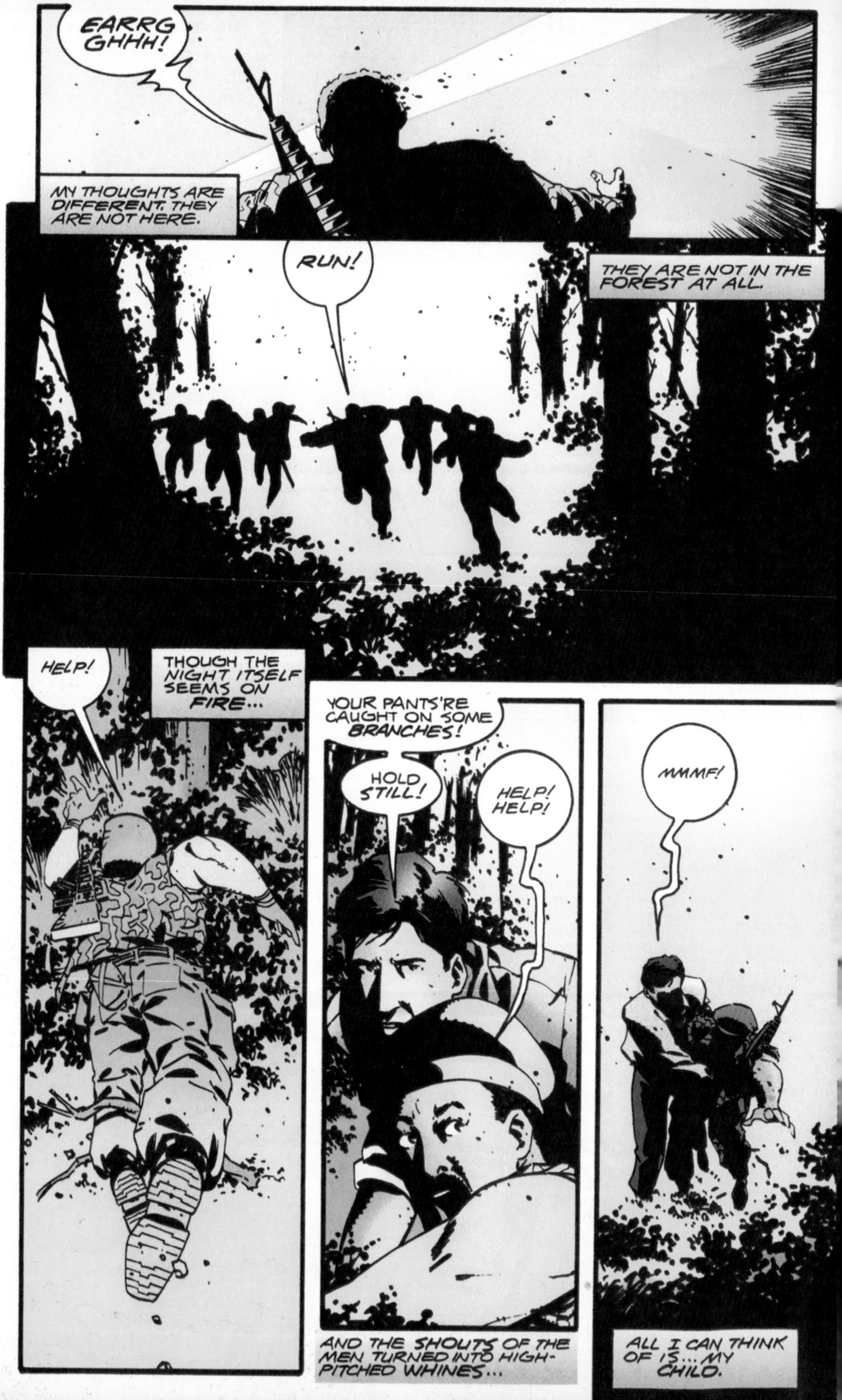
EARRG GHHH!
MY THOUGHTS ARE DIFFERENT. THEY ARE NOT HERE.
RUN!
THEY ARE NOT IN THE FOREST AT ALL.
HELP!
THOUGH THE NIGHT ITSELF SEEMS ON FIRE...
YOUR PANTS'RE CAUGHT ON SOME BRANCHES!
HOLD STILL!
HELP! HELP!
AND THE SHOUTS OF THE MEN TURNED INTO HIGH-PITCHED WHINES...
MMMF!
ALL I CAN THINK OF IS... MY CHILD.

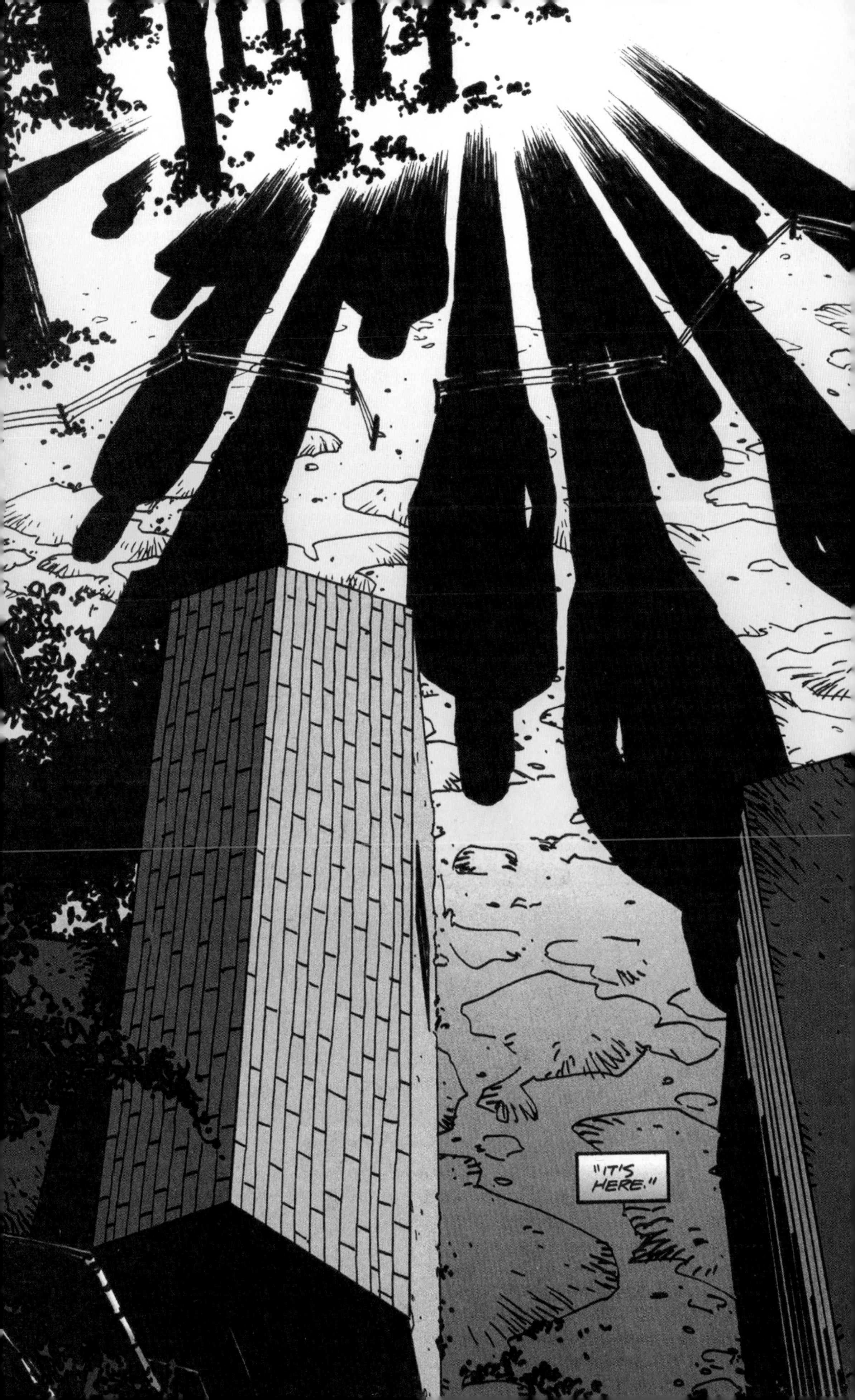
"IT'S HERE."

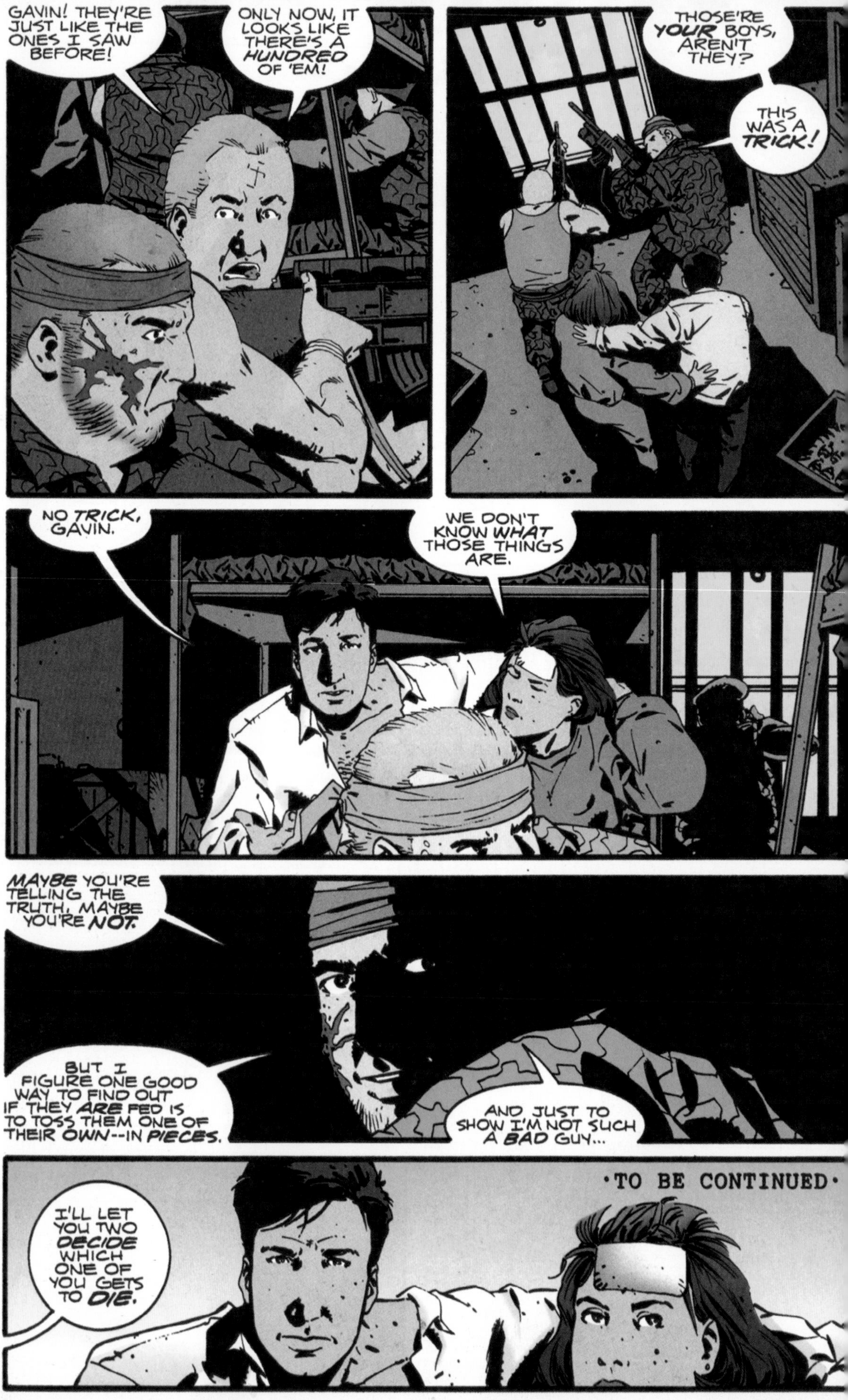
GAVIN! THEY'RE JUST LIKE THE ONES I SAW BEFORE!
ONLY NOW, IT LOOKS LIKE THERE'S A HUNDRED OF 'EM!
THOSE'RE YOUR BOYS, AREN'T THEY?
THIS WAS A TRICK!
NO TRICK, GAVIN.
WE DON'T KNOW WHAT THOSE THINGS ARE.
MAYBE YOU'RE TELLING THE TRUTH, MAYBE YOU'RE NOT.
BUT I FIGURE ONE GOOD WAY TO FIND OUT IF THEY ARE FED IS TO TOSS THEM ONE OF THEIR OWN--IN PIECES.
AND JUST TO SHOW I'M NOT SUCH A BAD GUY...
·TO BE CONTINUED·
I'LL LET YOU TWO DECIDE WHICH ONE OF YOU GETS TO DIE.

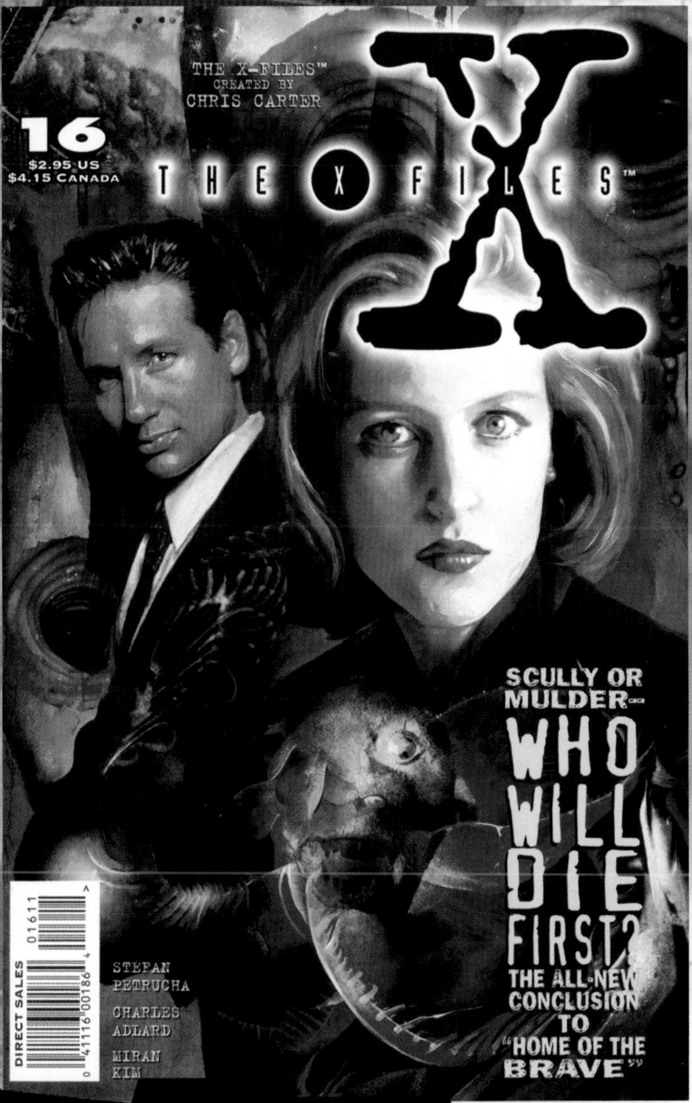
THE X-FILES™
CREATED BY
CHRIS CARTER
16
$2.95 US
$4.15 CANADA
THE X FILES™
SCULLY OR MULDER...
WHO WILL DIE FIRST?
THE ALL-NEW CONCLUSION TO "HOME OF THE BRAVE"
DIRECT SALES
STEFAN PETRUCHA
CHARLES ADLARD
MIRAN KIM

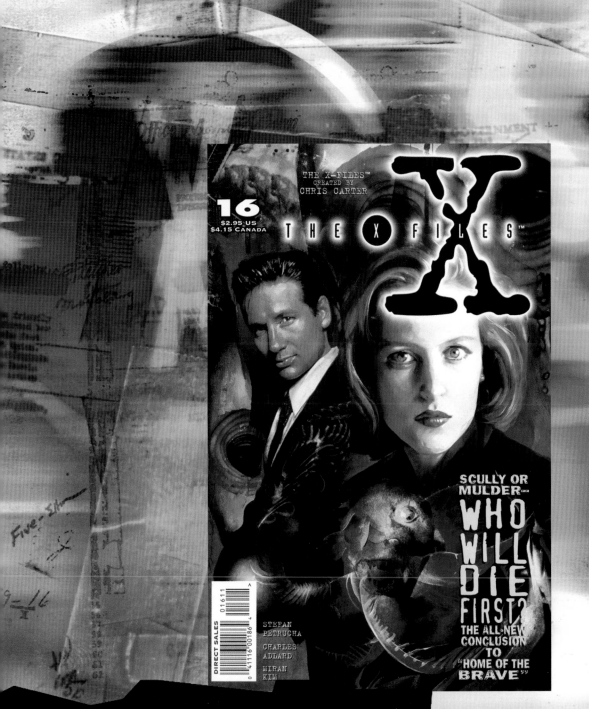

CHAPTER 4: HOME OF THE BRAVE

PART 2 (OF 2)

STORY: Author Name
ART: Artist Name

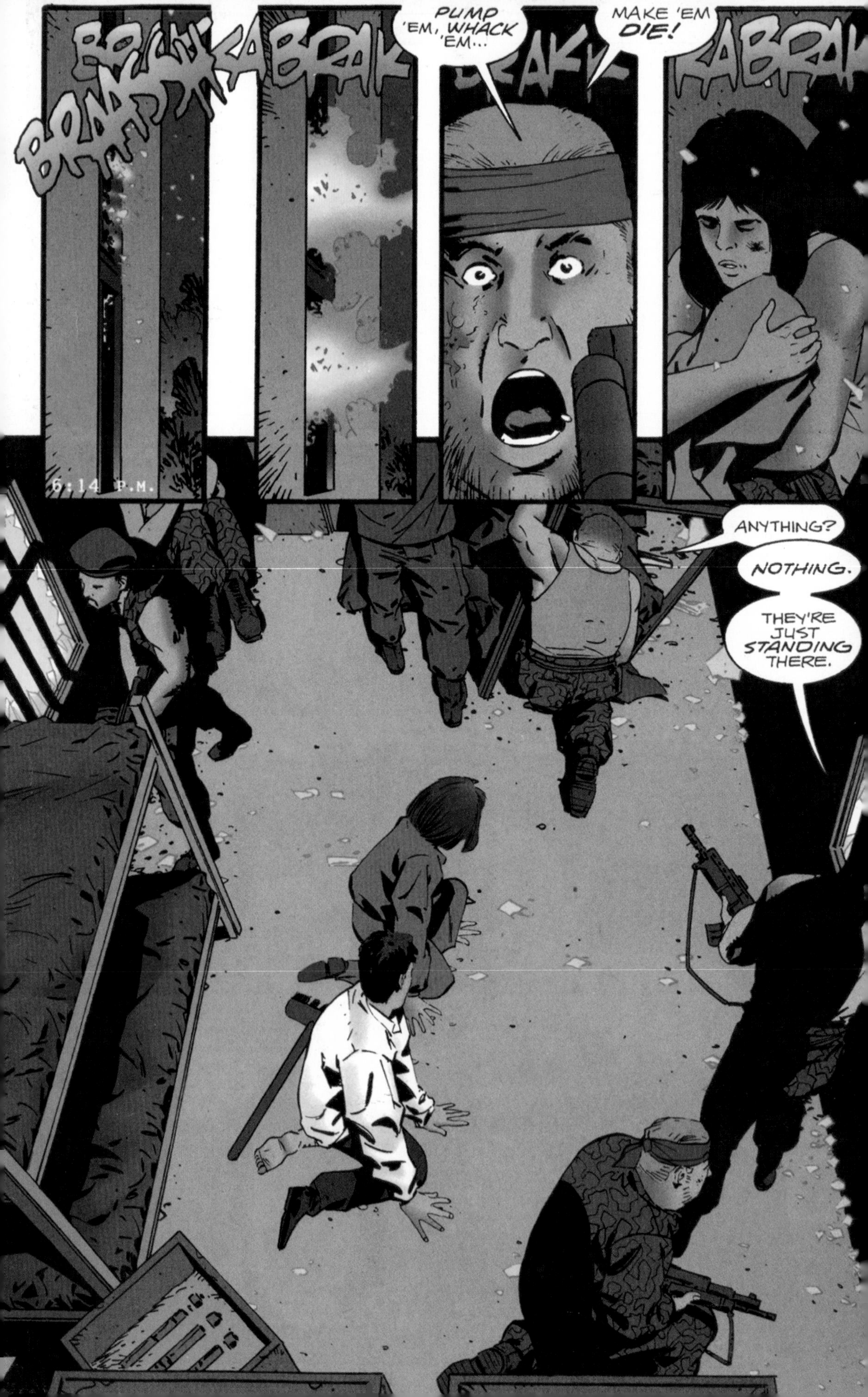
BOOM
BRAKKABRAK
PUMP 'EM, WHACK 'EM...
MAKE 'EM DIE!
KABRAK
6:14 P.M.
ANYTHING?
NOTHING.
THEY'RE JUST STANDING THERE.

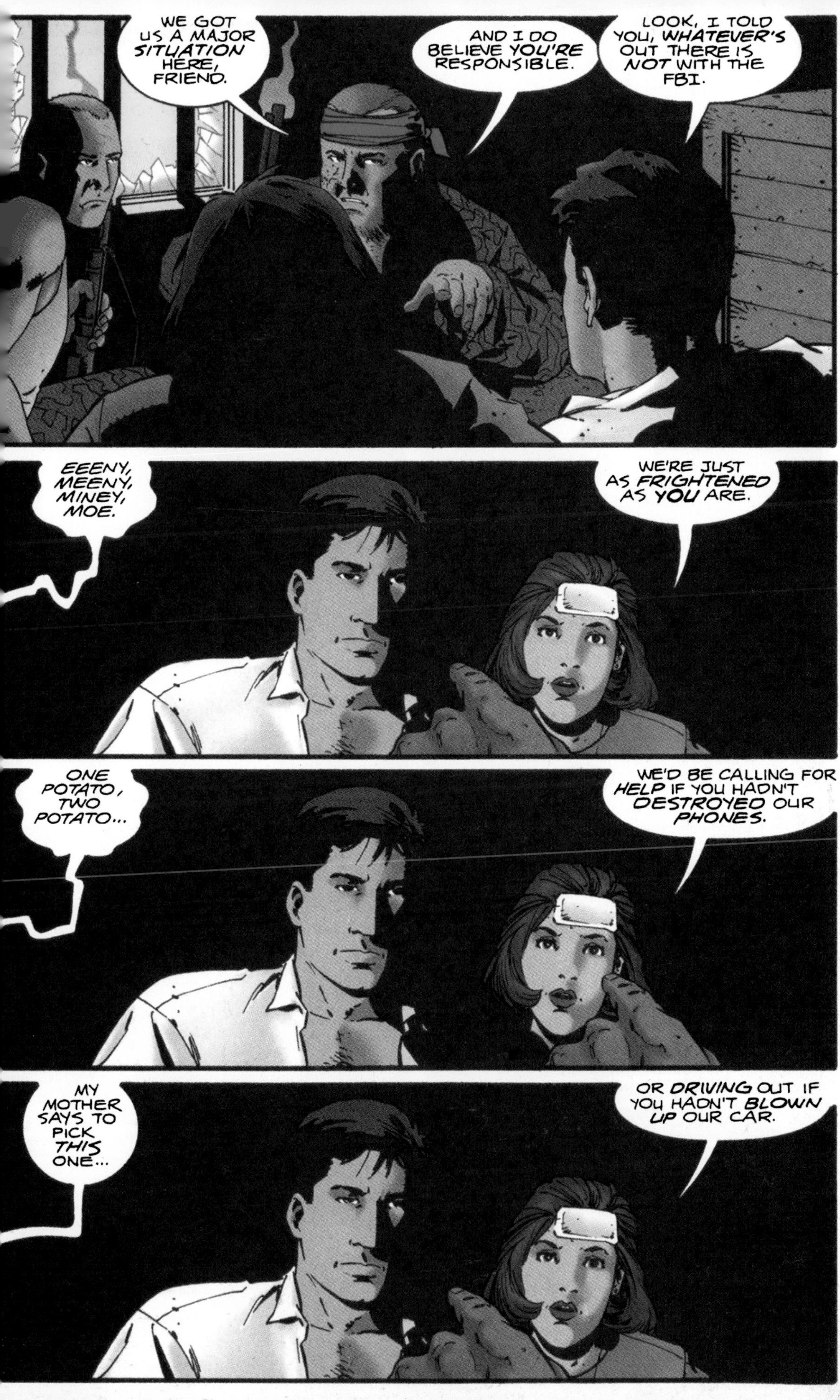
WE GOT US A MAJOR SITUATION HERE, FRIEND.
AND I DO BELIEVE YOU'RE RESPONSIBLE.
LOOK, I TOLD YOU, WHATEVER'S OUT THERE IS NOT WITH THE FBI.
EEENY, MEENY, MINEY, MOE.
WE'RE JUST AS FRIGHTENED AS YOU ARE.
ONE POTATO, TWO POTATO...
WE'D BE CALLING FOR HELP IF YOU HADN'T DESTROYED OUR PHONES.
MY MOTHER SAYS TO PICK THIS ONE...
OR DRIVING OUT IF YOU HADN'T BLOWN UP OUR CAR.

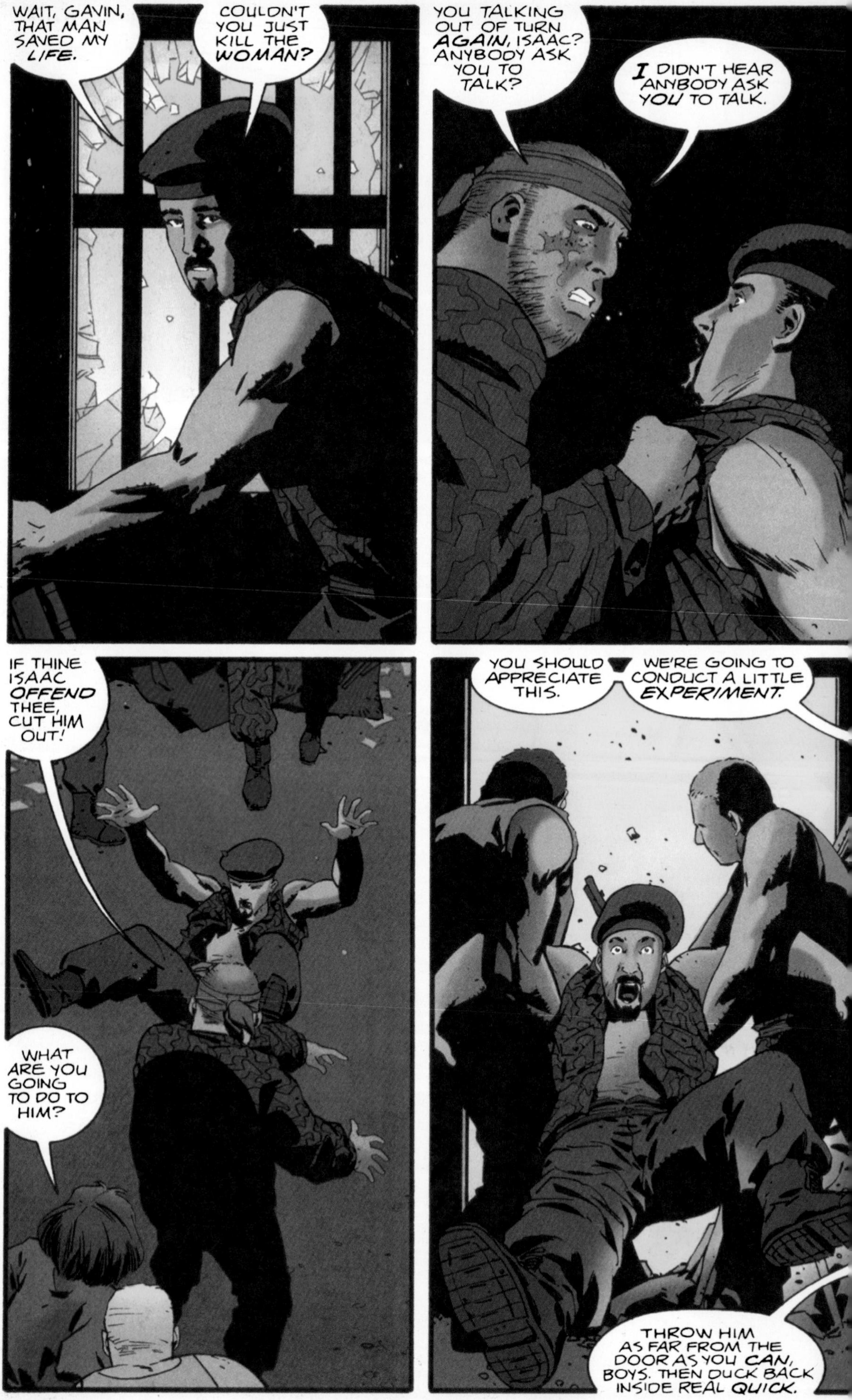
WAIT, GAVIN, THAT MAN SAVED MY LIFE.
COULDN'T YOU JUST KILL THE WOMAN?
YOU TALKING OUT OF TURN AGAIN, ISAAC? ANYBODY ASK YOU TO TALK?
I DIDN'T HEAR ANYBODY ASK YOU TO TALK.
IF THINE ISAAC OFFEND THEE, CUT HIM OUT!
WHAT ARE YOU GOING TO DO TO HIM?
YOU SHOULD APPRECIATE THIS.
WE'RE GOING TO CONDUCT A LITTLE EXPERIMENT.
THROW HIM AS FAR FROM THE DOOR AS YOU CAN, BOYS. THEN DUCK BACK INSIDE REAL QUICK.

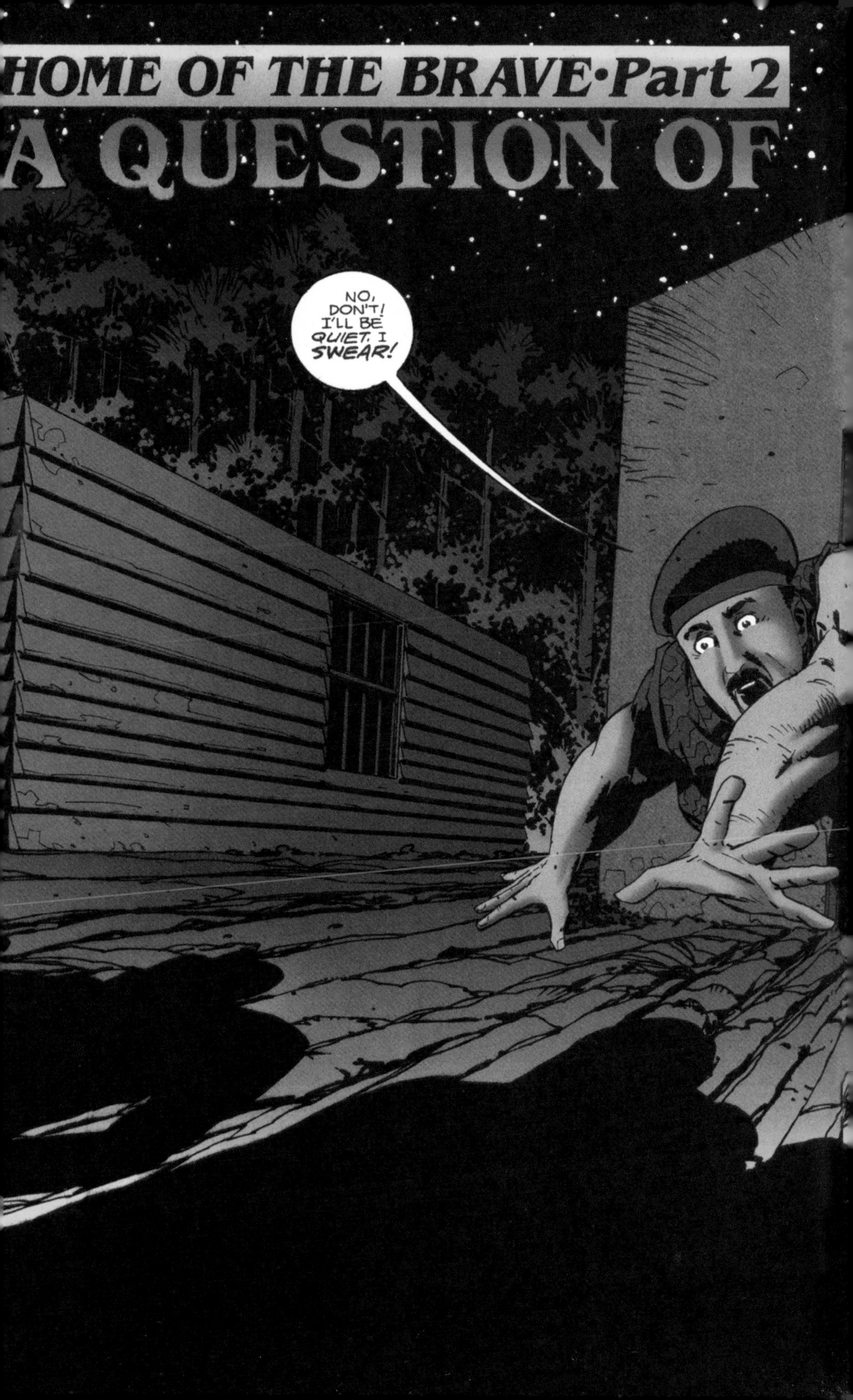
HOME OF THE BRAVE•Part 2
A QUESTION OF
NO, DON'T! I'LL BE QUIET. I SWEAR!

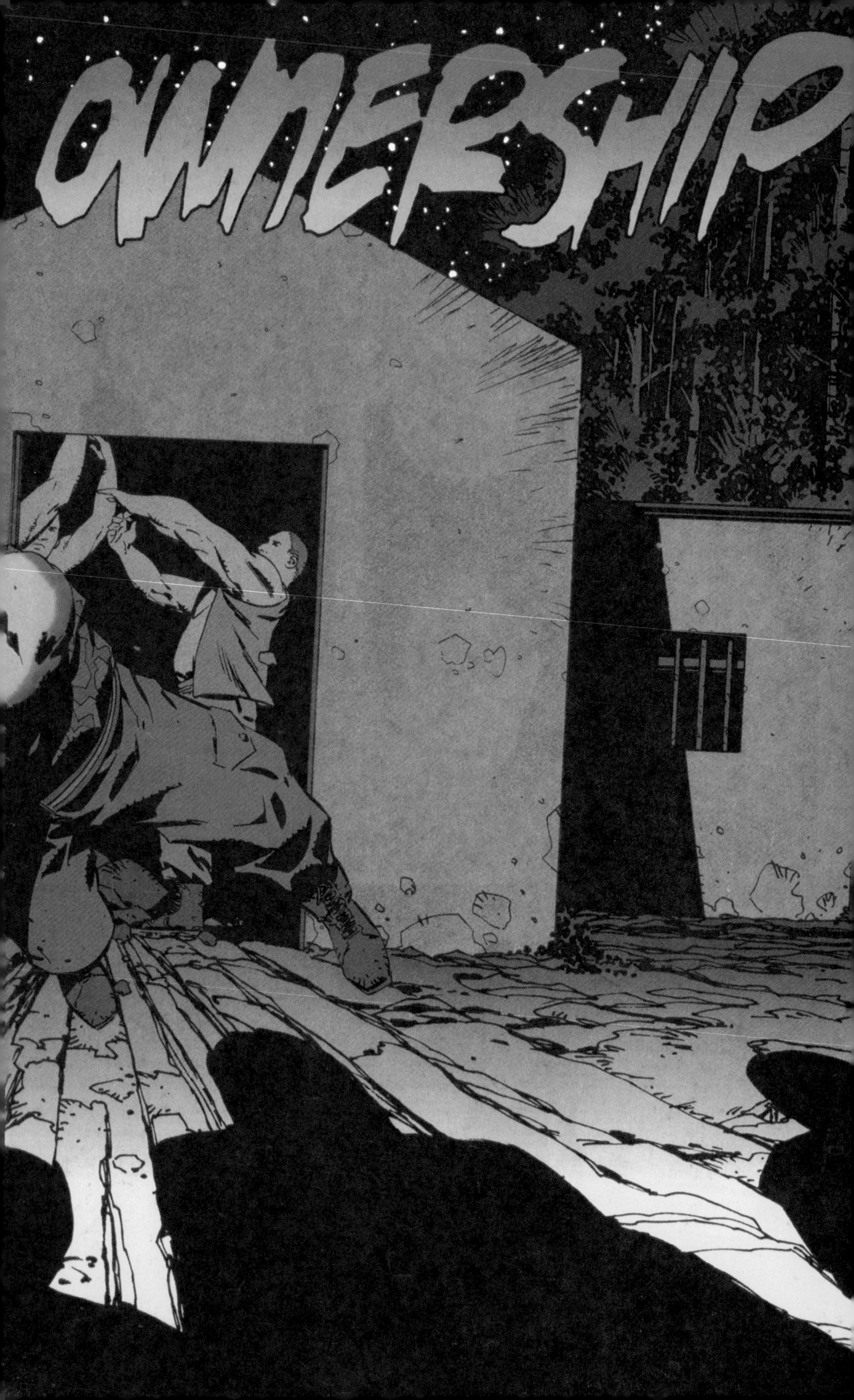
OWNERSHIP

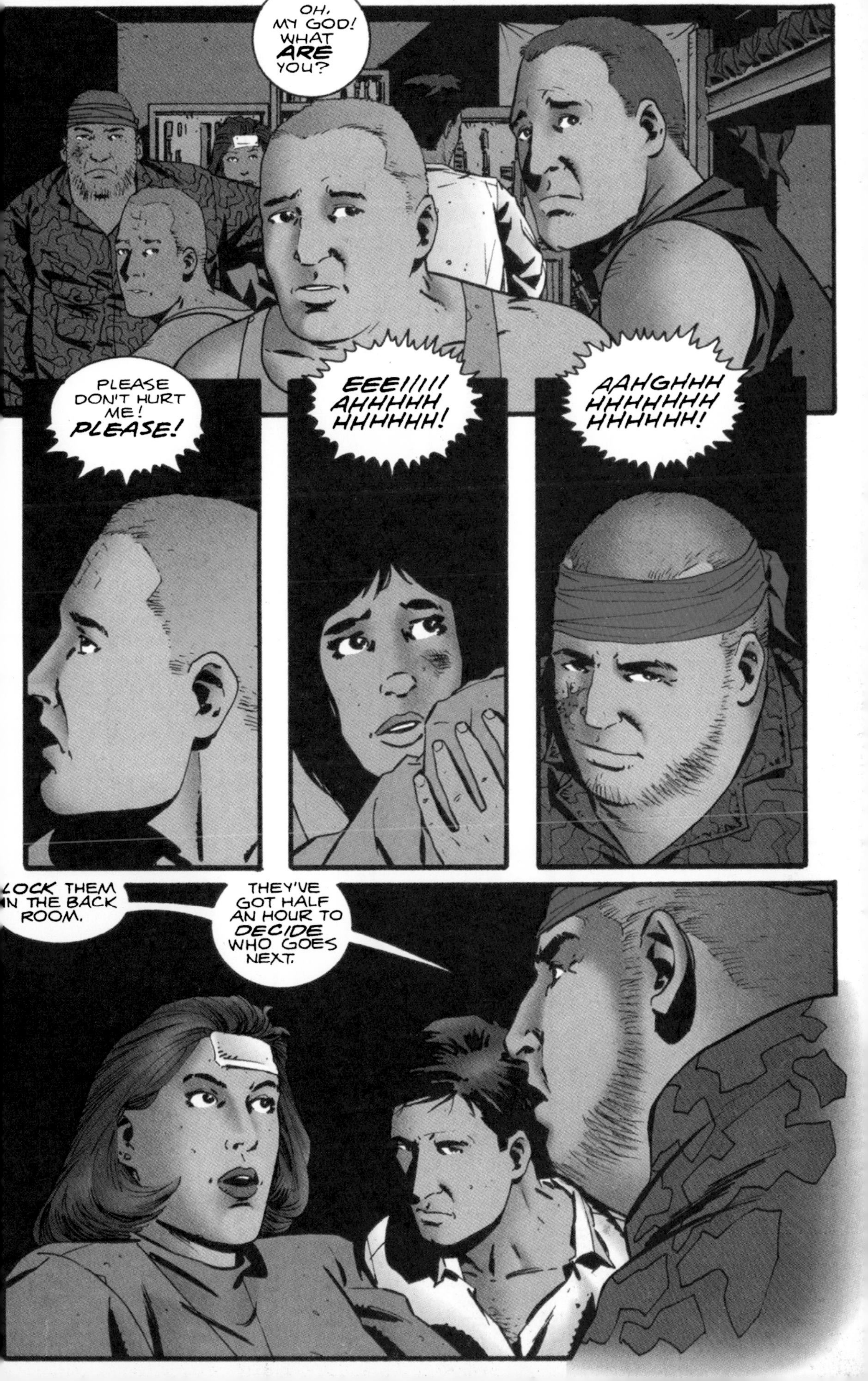
OH, MY GOD! WHAT ARE YOU?
PLEASE DON'T HURT ME! PLEASE!
EEE!!!!! AHHHHHH HHHHHH!
AAHGHHH HHHHHHH HHHHHH!
LOCK THEM IN THE BACK ROOM.
THEY'VE GOT HALF AN HOUR TO DECIDE WHO GOES NEXT.

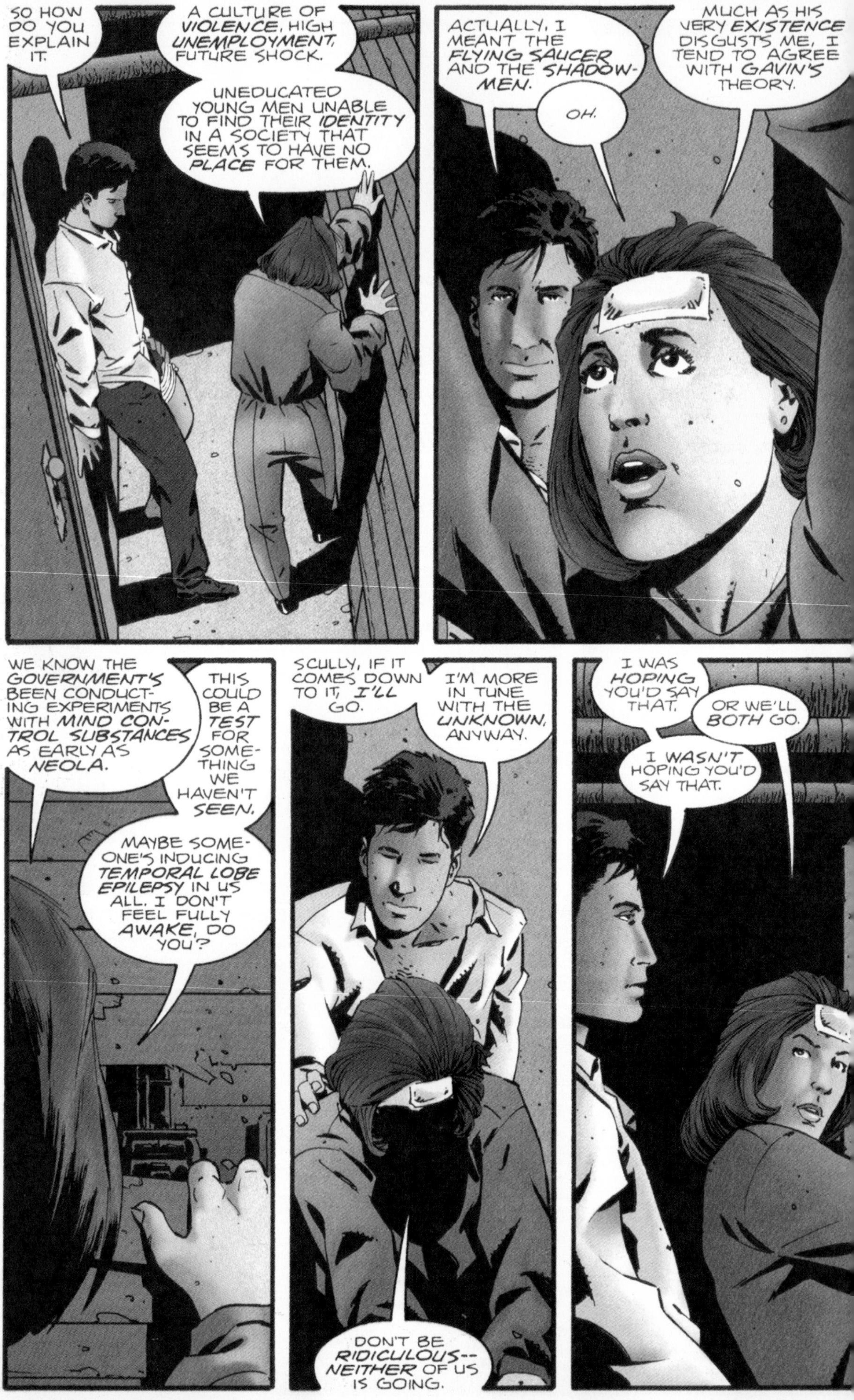
SO HOW DO YOU EXPLAIN IT.
A CULTURE OF VIOLENCE, HIGH UNEMPLOYMENT, FUTURE SHOCK.
UNEDUCATED YOUNG MEN UNABLE TO FIND THEIR IDENTITY IN A SOCIETY THAT SEEMS TO HAVE NO PLACE FOR THEM.
ACTUALLY, I MEANT THE FLYING SAUCER AND THE SHADOW-MEN.
OH.
MUCH AS HIS VERY EXISTENCE DISGUSTS ME, I TEND TO AGREE WITH GAVIN'S THEORY.
WE KNOW THE GOVERNMENT'S BEEN CONDUCTING EXPERIMENTS WITH MIND CONTROL SUBSTANCES AS EARLY AS NEOLA.
THIS COULD BE A TEST FOR SOMETHING WE HAVEN'T SEEN.
MAYBE SOMEONE'S INDUCING TEMPORAL LOBE EPILEPSY IN US ALL. I DON'T FEEL FULLY AWAKE, DO YOU?
SCULLY, IF IT COMES DOWN TO IT, I'LL GO.
I'M MORE IN TUNE WITH THE UNKNOWN, ANYWAY.
DON'T BE RIDICULOUS-- NEITHER OF US IS GOING.
I WAS HOPING YOU'D SAY THAT.
OR WE'LL BOTH GO.
I WASN'T HOPING YOU'D SAY THAT.

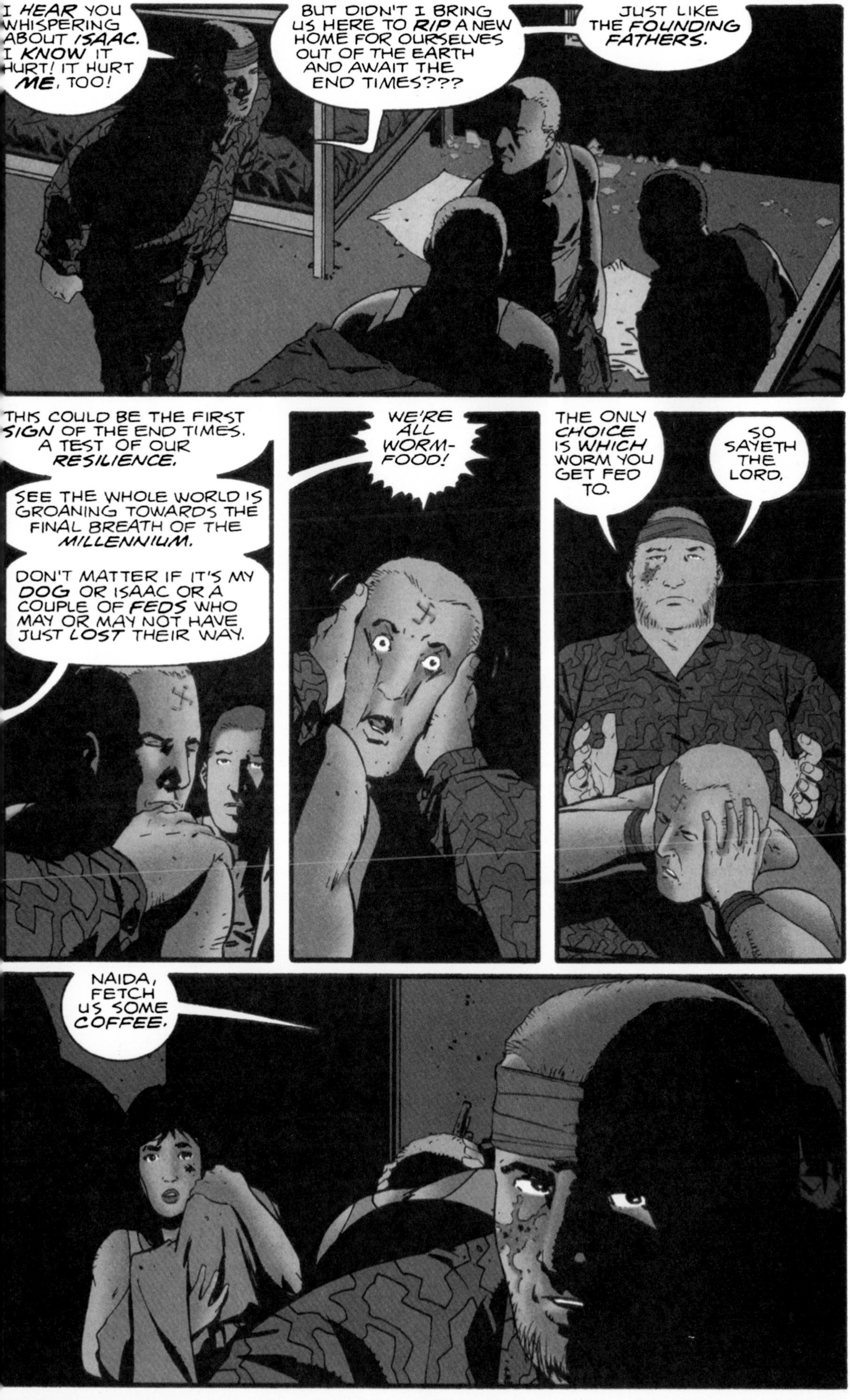
I HEAR YOU WHISPERING ABOUT ISAAC. I KNOW IT HURT! IT HURT ME, TOO!
BUT DIDN'T I BRING US HERE TO RIP A NEW HOME FOR OURSELVES OUT OF THE EARTH AND AWAIT THE END TIMES???
JUST LIKE THE FOUNDING FATHERS.
THIS COULD BE THE FIRST SIGN OF THE END TIMES. A TEST OF OUR RESILIENCE.
SEE THE WHOLE WORLD IS GROANING TOWARDS THE FINAL BREATH OF THE MILLENNIUM.
DON'T MATTER IF IT'S MY DOG OR ISAAC OR A COUPLE OF FEDS WHO MAY OR MAY NOT HAVE JUST LOST THEIR WAY.
WE'RE ALL WORM-FOOD!
THE ONLY CHOICE IS WHICH WORM YOU GET FED TO.
SO SAYETH THE LORD.
NAIDA, FETCH US SOME COFFEE.

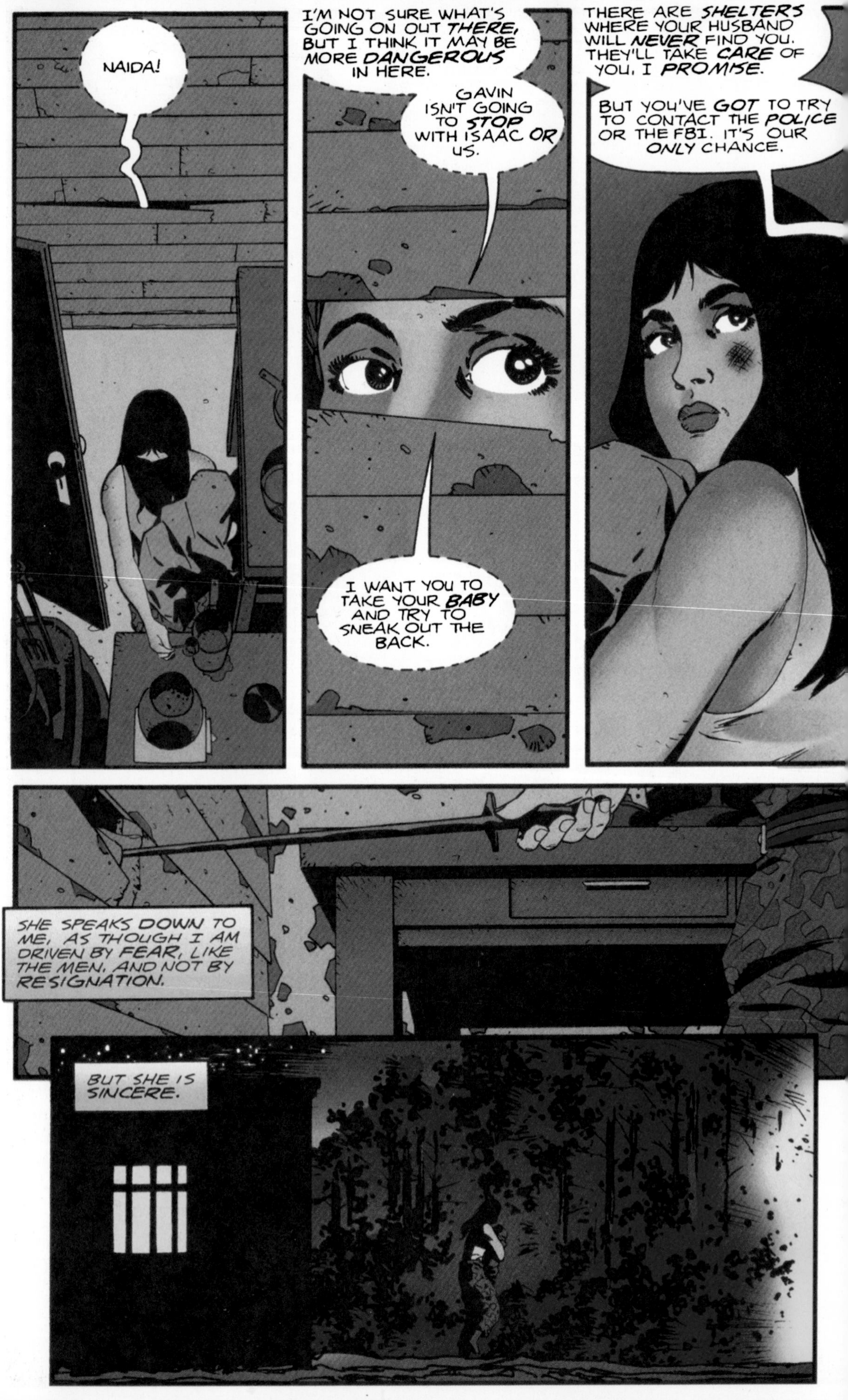
NAIDA!
I'M NOT SURE WHAT'S GOING ON OUT THERE, BUT I THINK IT MAY BE MORE DANGEROUS IN HERE.
GAVIN ISN'T GOING TO STOP WITH ISAAC OR US.
I WANT YOU TO TAKE YOUR BABY AND TRY TO SNEAK OUT THE BACK.
THERE ARE SHELTERS WHERE YOUR HUSBAND WILL NEVER FIND YOU. THEY'LL TAKE CARE OF YOU, I PROMISE.
BUT YOU'VE GOT TO TRY TO CONTACT THE POLICE OR THE FBI. IT'S OUR ONLY CHANCE.
SHE SPEAKS DOWN TO ME, AS THOUGH I AM DRIVEN BY FEAR, LIKE THE MEN, AND NOT BY RESIGNATION.
BUT SHE IS SINCERE.

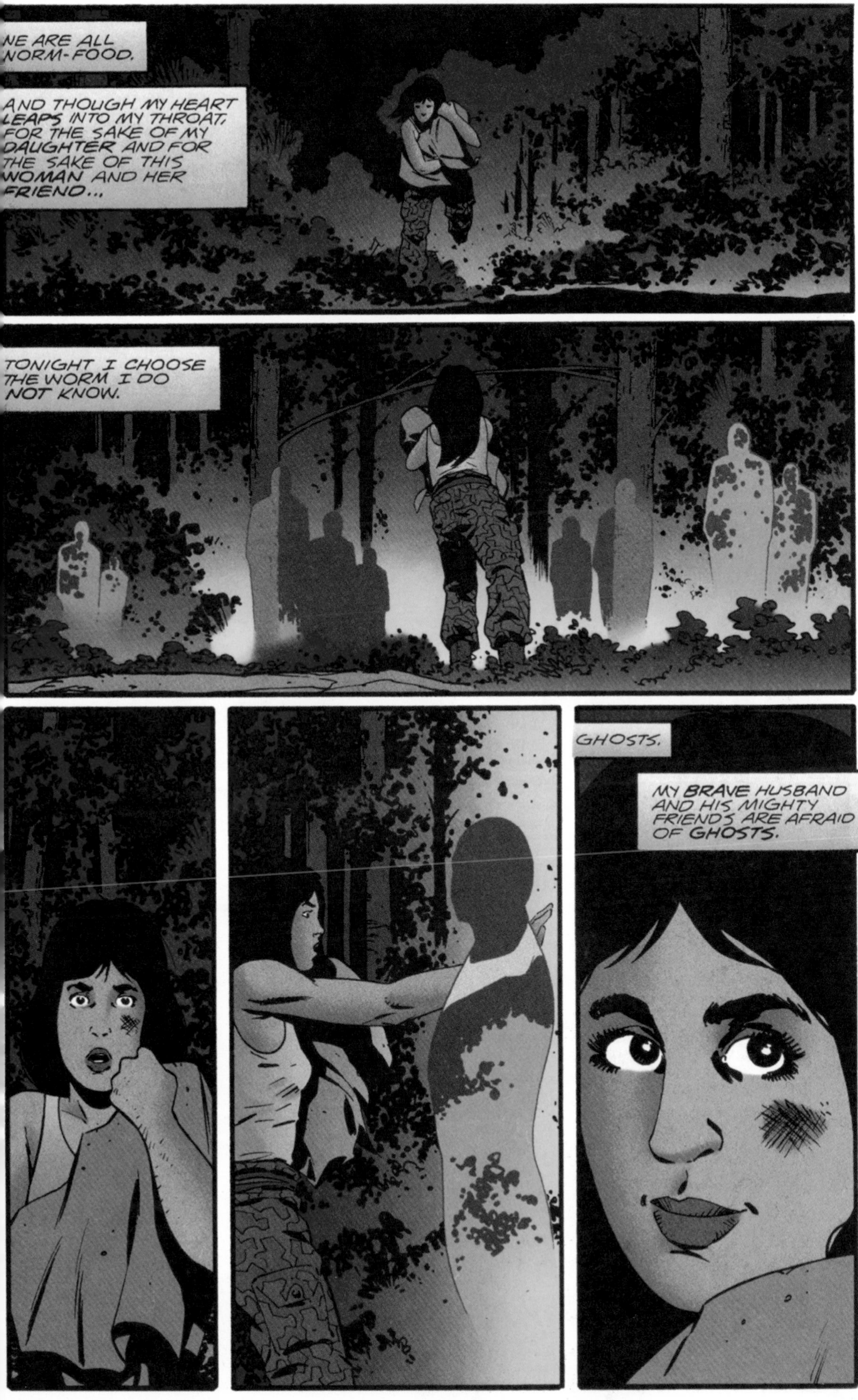
NE ARE ALL NORM-FOOD.
AND THOUGH MY HEART LEAPS INTO MY THROAT, FOR THE SAKE OF MY DAUGHTER AND FOR THE SAKE OF THIS WOMAN AND HER FRIEND...
TONIGHT I CHOOSE THE WORM I DO NOT KNOW.
GHOSTS.
MY BRAVE HUSBAND AND HIS MIGHTY FRIENDS ARE AFRAID OF GHOSTS.

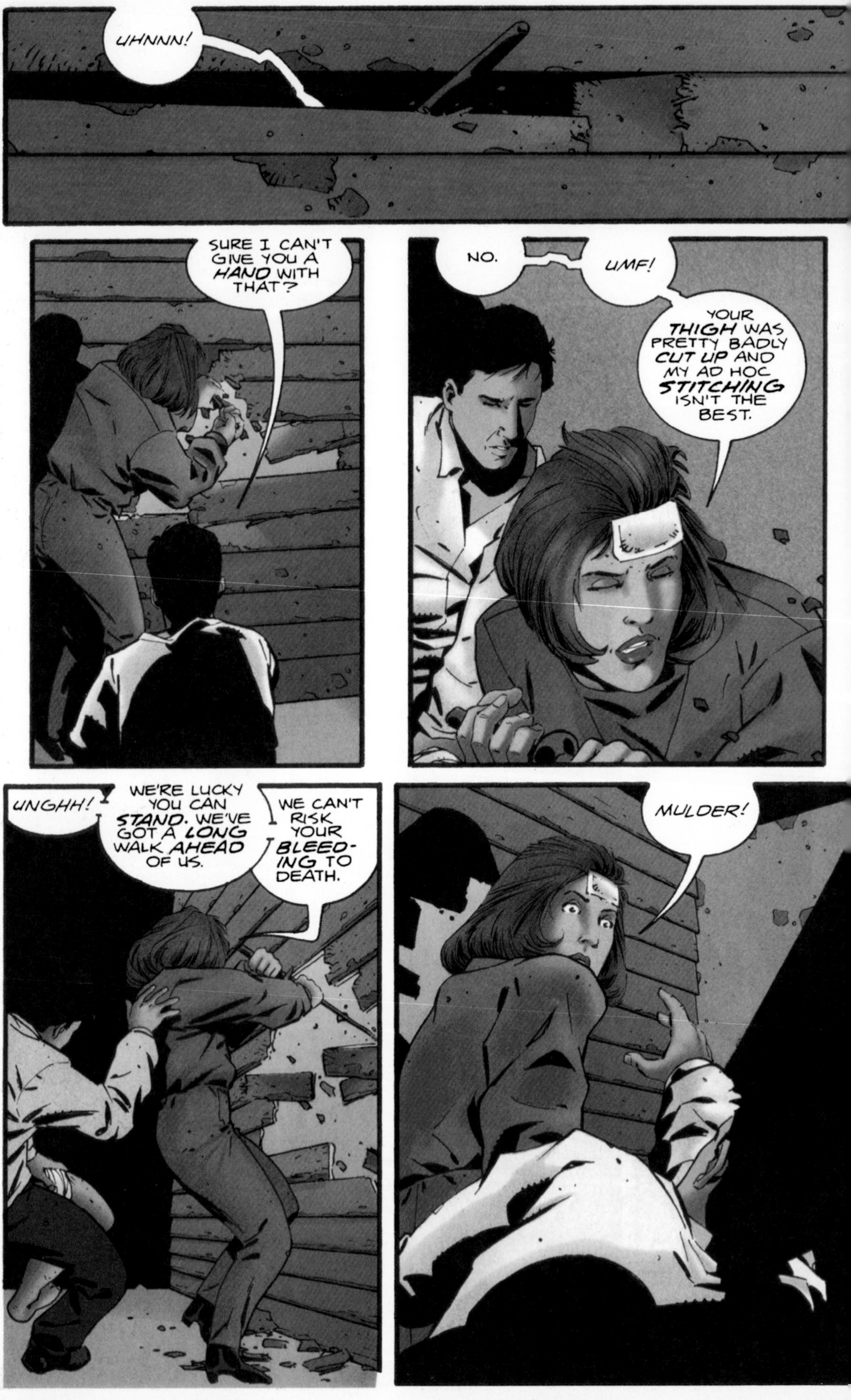
UHNNN!
SURE I CAN'T GIVE YOU A HAND WITH THAT?
NO.
UMF!
YOUR THIGH WAS PRETTY BADLY CUT UP AND MY AD HOC STITCHING ISN'T THE BEST.
UNGHH!
WE'RE LUCKY YOU CAN STAND. WE'VE GOT A LONG WALK AHEAD OF US.
WE CAN'T RISK YOUR BLEEDING TO DEATH.
MULDER!

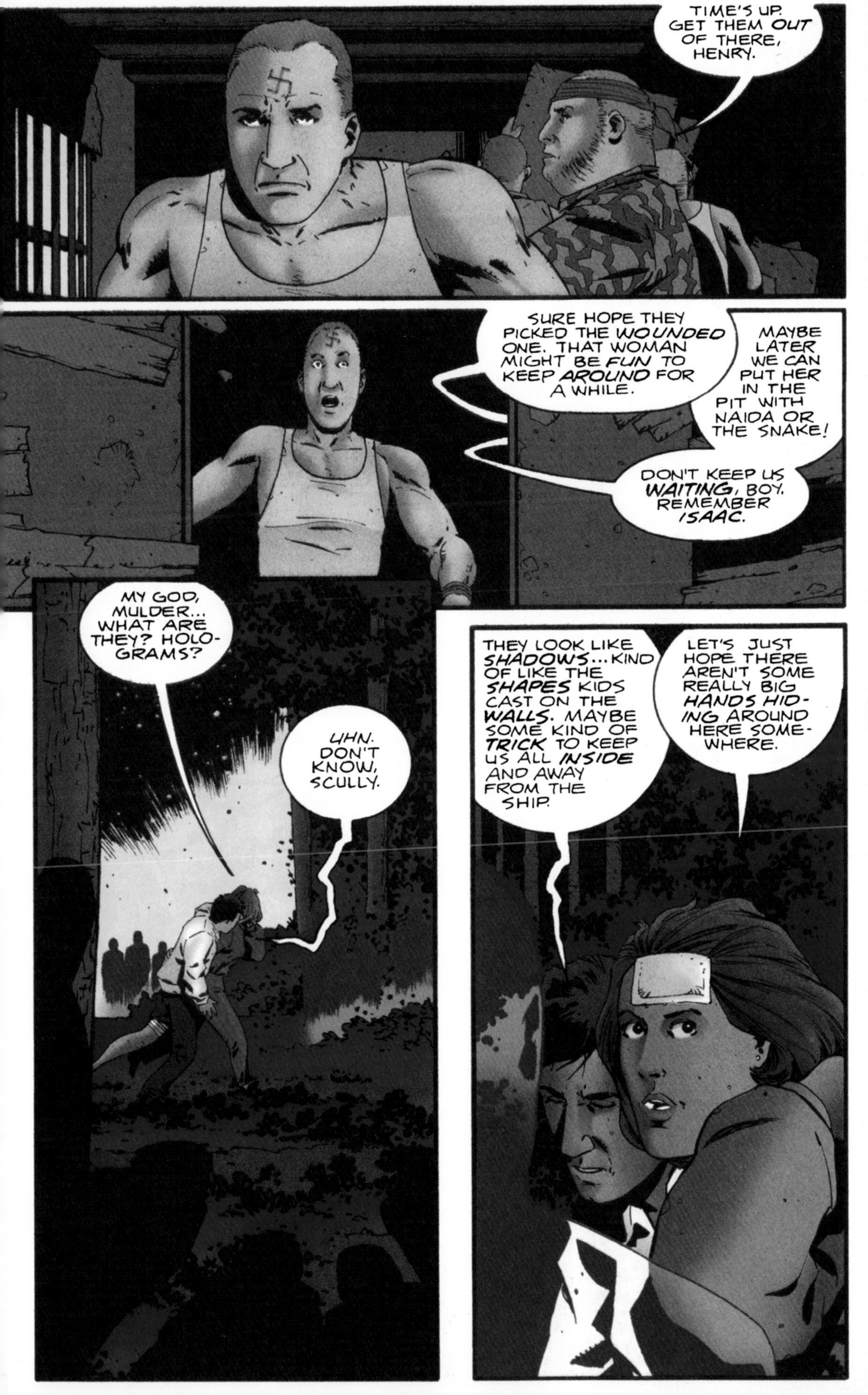
TIME'S UP. GET THEM OUT OF THERE, HENRY.
SURE HOPE THEY PICKED THE WOUNDED ONE. THAT WOMAN MIGHT BE FUN TO KEEP AROUND FOR A WHILE.
MAYBE LATER WE CAN PUT HER IN THE PIT WITH NAIDA OR THE SNAKE!
DON'T KEEP US WAITING, BOY. REMEMBER ISAAC.
MY GOD, MULDER... WHAT ARE THEY? HOLO-GRAMS?
UHN. DON'T KNOW, SCULLY.
THEY LOOK LIKE SHADOWS... KIND OF LIKE THE SHAPES KIDS CAST ON THE WALLS. MAYBE SOME KIND OF TRICK TO KEEP US ALL INSIDE AND AWAY FROM THE SHIP.
LET'S JUST HOPE THERE AREN'T SOME REALLY BIG HANDS HID-ING AROUND HERE SOME-WHERE.

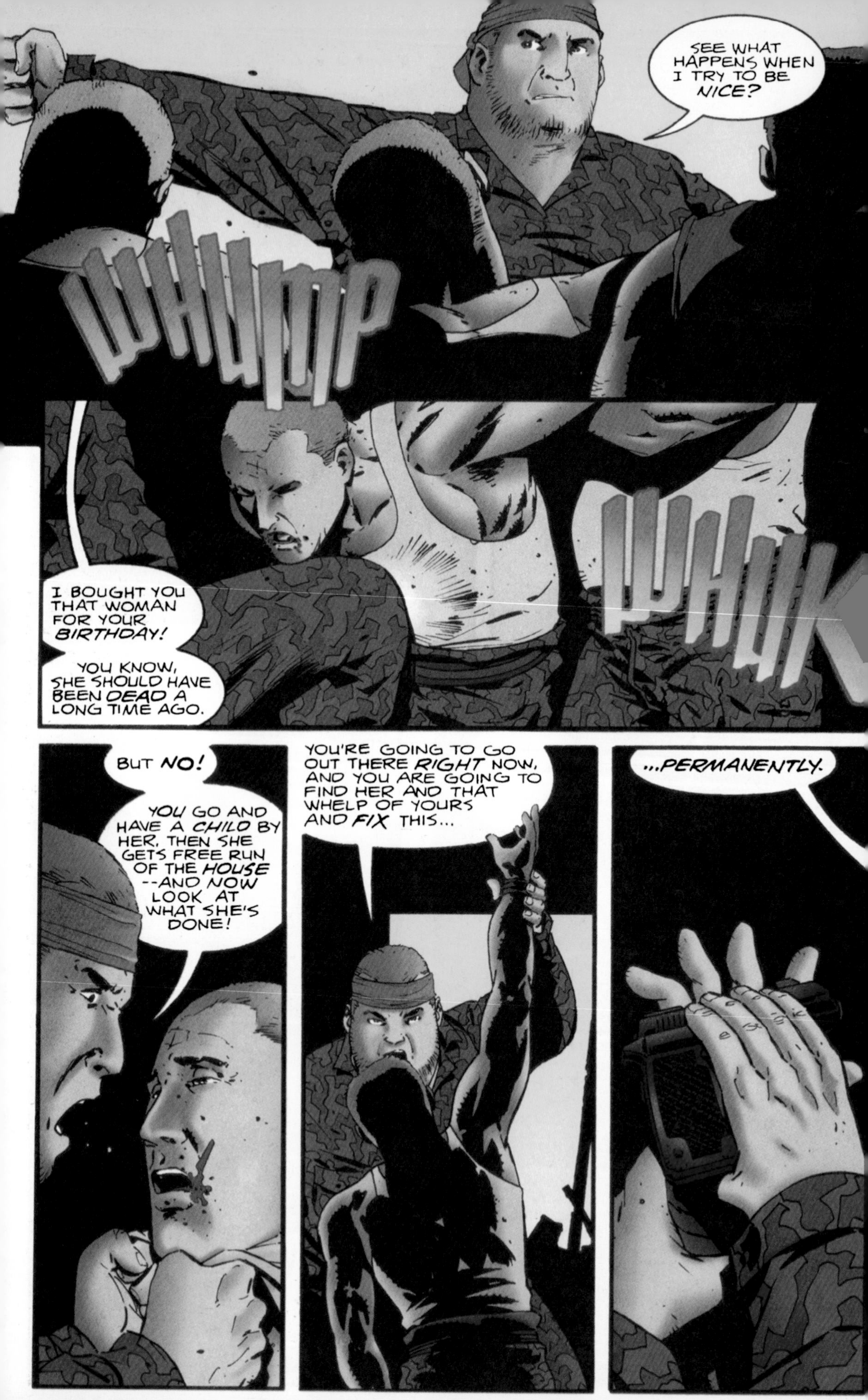
SEE WHAT HAPPENS WHEN I TRY TO BE NICE?
WHUMP
WHUK
I BOUGHT YOU THAT WOMAN FOR YOUR BIRTHDAY!
YOU KNOW, SHE SHOULD HAVE BEEN DEAD A LONG TIME AGO.
BUT NO!
YOU GO AND HAVE A CHILD BY HER, THEN SHE GETS FREE RUN OF THE HOUSE --AND NOW LOOK AT WHAT SHE'S DONE!
YOU'RE GOING TO GO OUT THERE RIGHT NOW, AND YOU ARE GOING TO FIND HER AND THAT WHELP OF YOURS AND FIX THIS...
...PERMANENTLY.

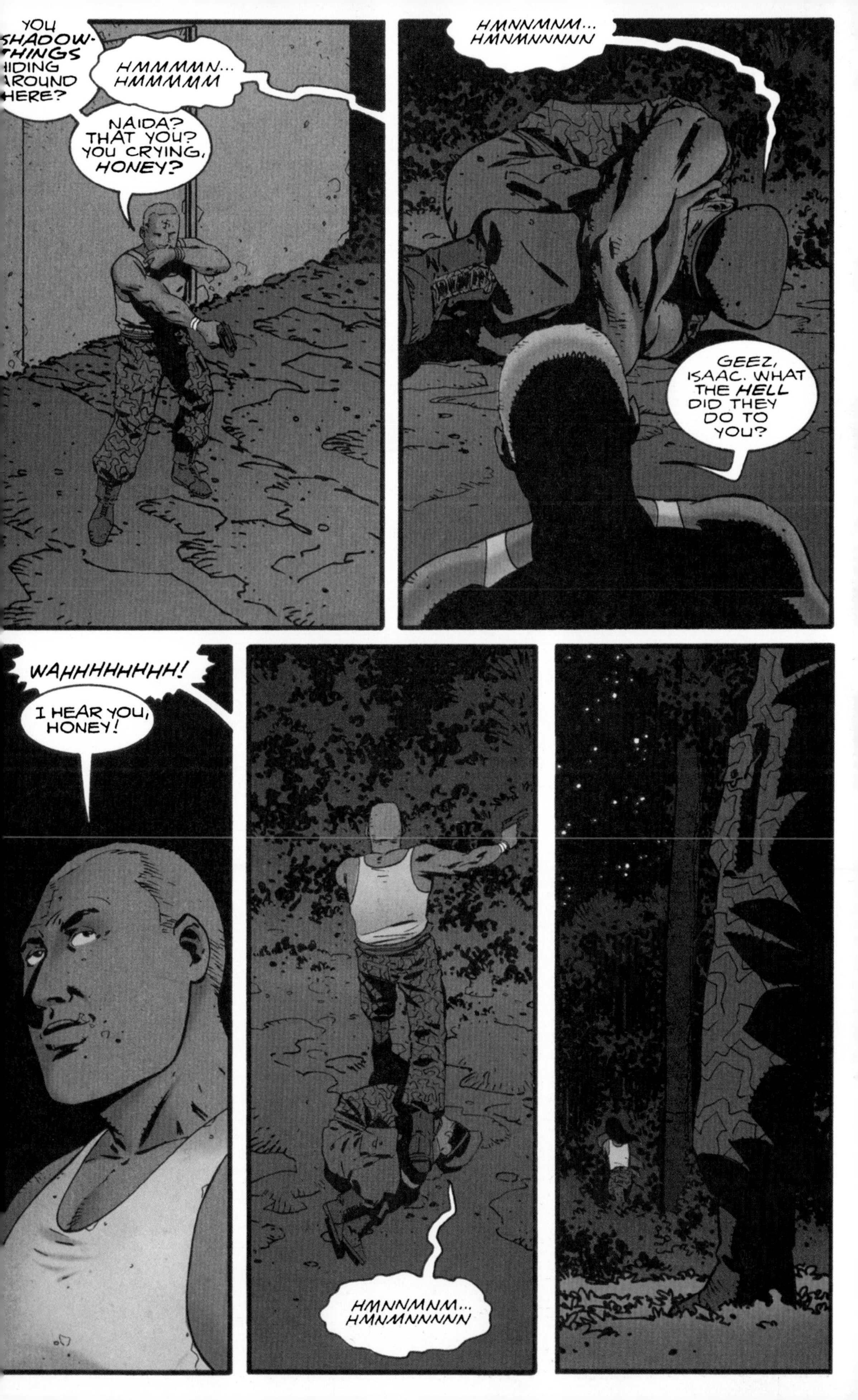
YOU SHADOW-THINGS HIDING AROUND HERE?
HMMMMMN... HMMMMMM
NAIDA? THAT YOU? YOU CRYING, HONEY?
HMNNMNM... HMNMNNNNN
GEEZ, ISAAC. WHAT THE HELL DID THEY DO TO YOU?
WAHHHHHHHH!
I HEAR YOU, HONEY!
HMNNMNM... HMNMNNNNN

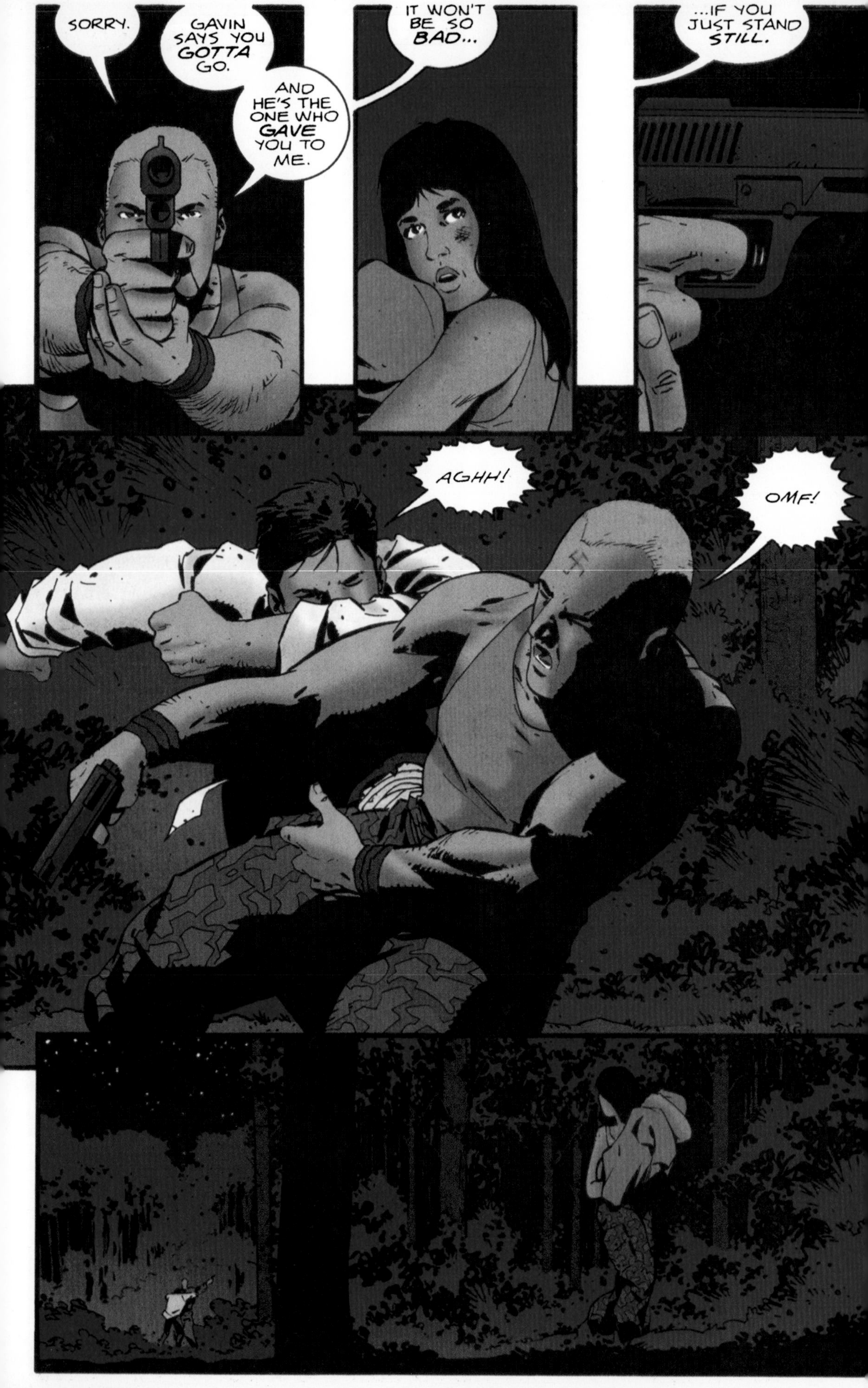
SORRY.
GAVIN SAYS YOU GOTTA GO.
AND HE'S THE ONE WHO GAVE YOU TO ME.
IT WON'T BE SO BAD...
...IF YOU JUST STAND STILL.
AGHH!
OMF!

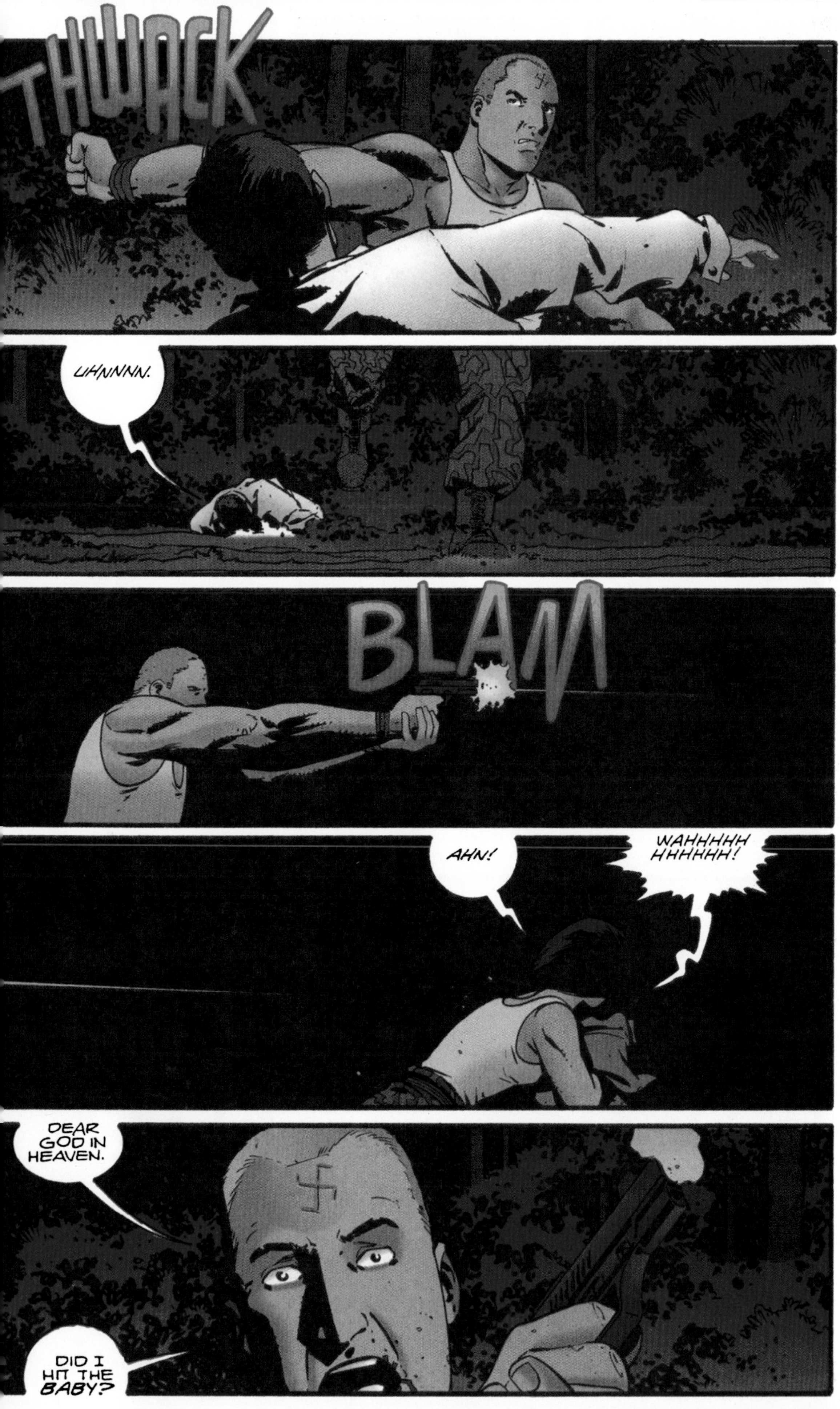
THWACK
UHNNNN.
BLAM
AHN!
WAHHHHH HHHHHH!
DEAR GOD IN HEAVEN.
DID I HIT THE *BABY*?

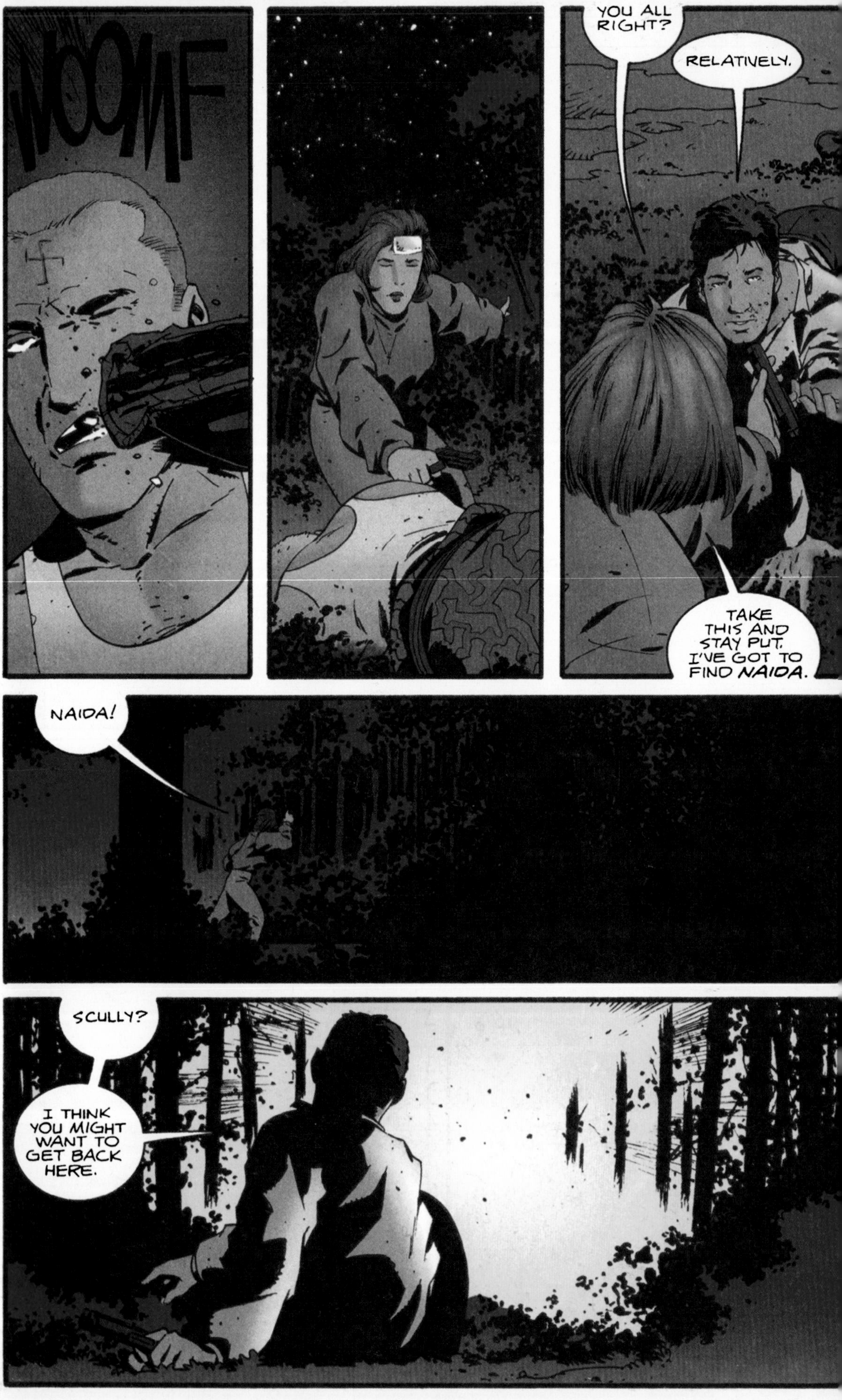
WOOMF
YOU ALL RIGHT?
RELATIVELY.
TAKE THIS AND STAY PUT. I'VE GOT TO FIND NAIDA.
NAIDA!
SCULLY?
I THINK YOU MIGHT WANT TO GET BACK HERE.

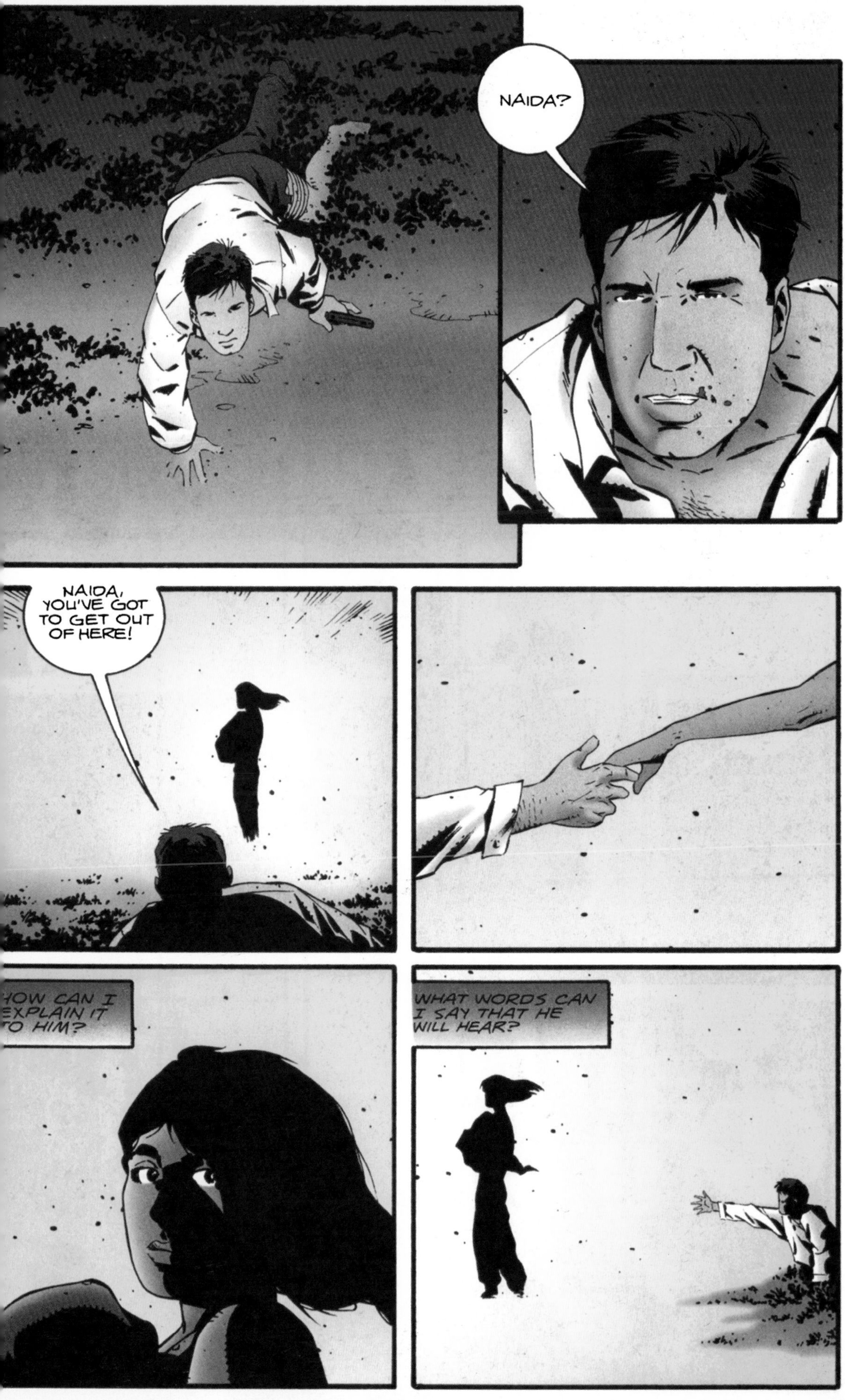
NAIDA?
NAIDA, YOU'VE GOT TO GET OUT OF HERE!
HOW CAN I EXPLAIN IT TO HIM?
WHAT WORDS CAN I SAY THAT HE WILL HEAR?

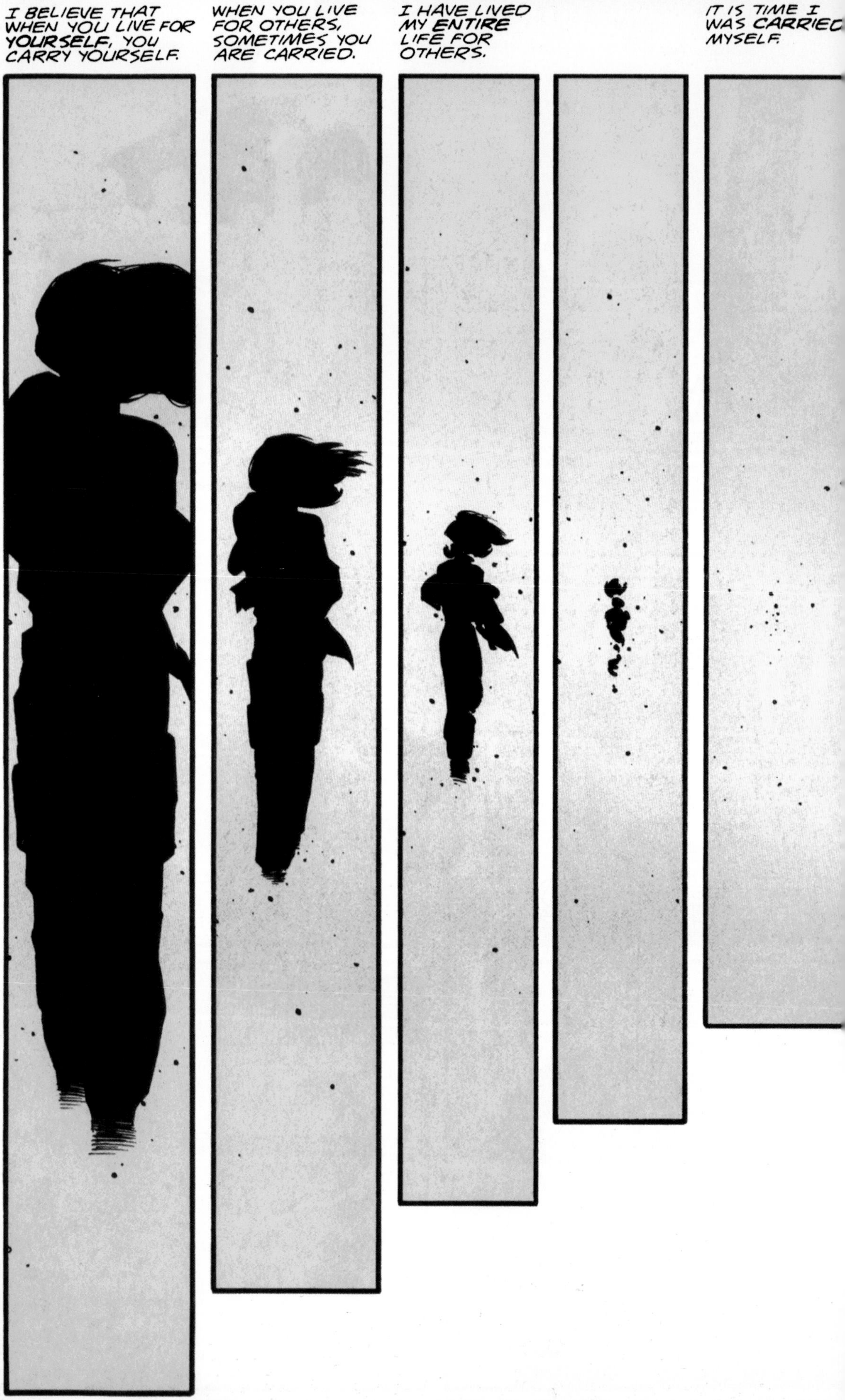
I BELIEVE THAT WHEN YOU LIVE FOR **YOURSELF**, YOU CARRY YOURSELF.
WHEN YOU LIVE FOR OTHERS, SOMETIMES YOU ARE CARRIED.
I HAVE LIVED MY **ENTIRE** LIFE FOR OTHERS.
IT IS TIME I WAS **CARRIED** MYSELF.

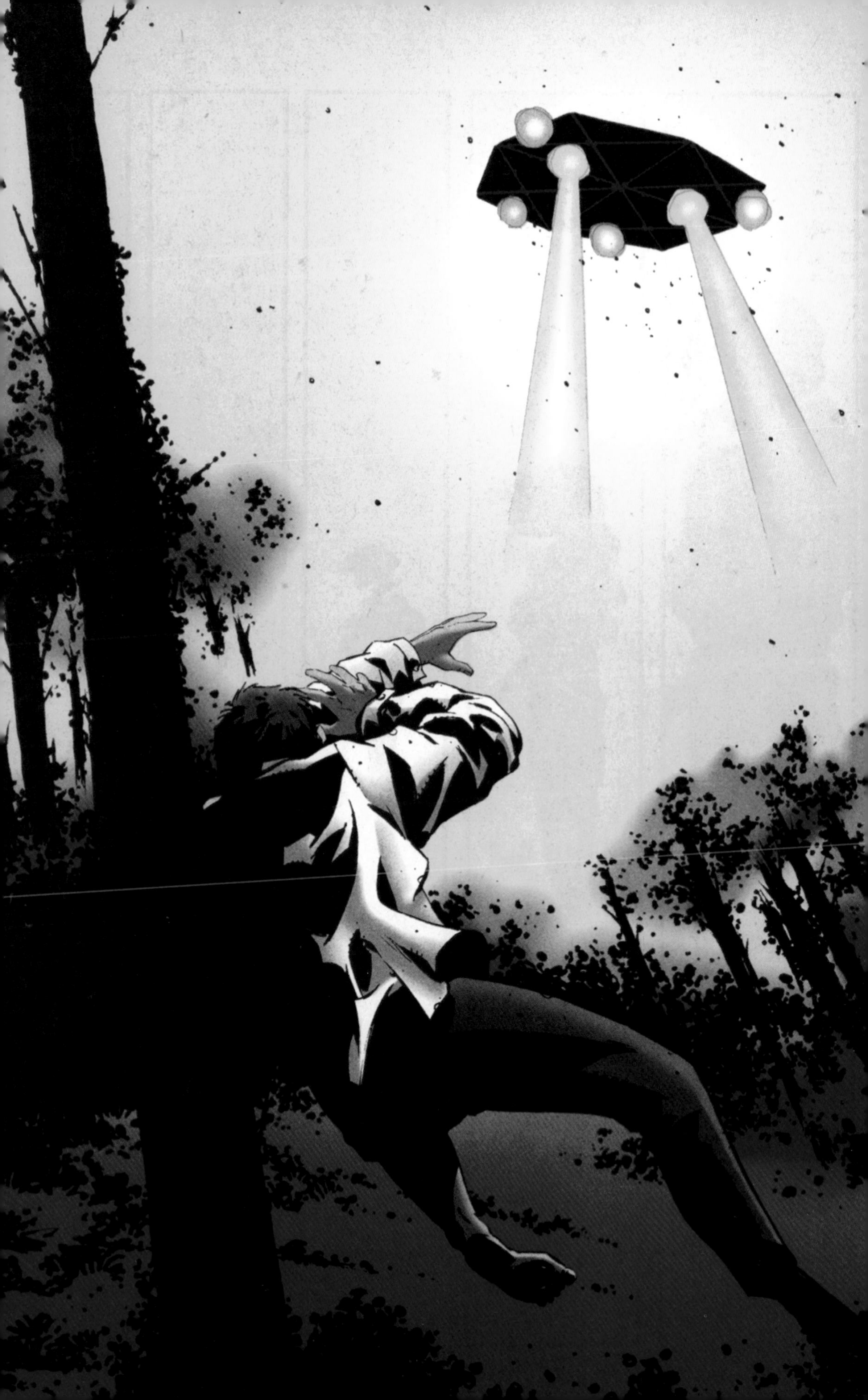

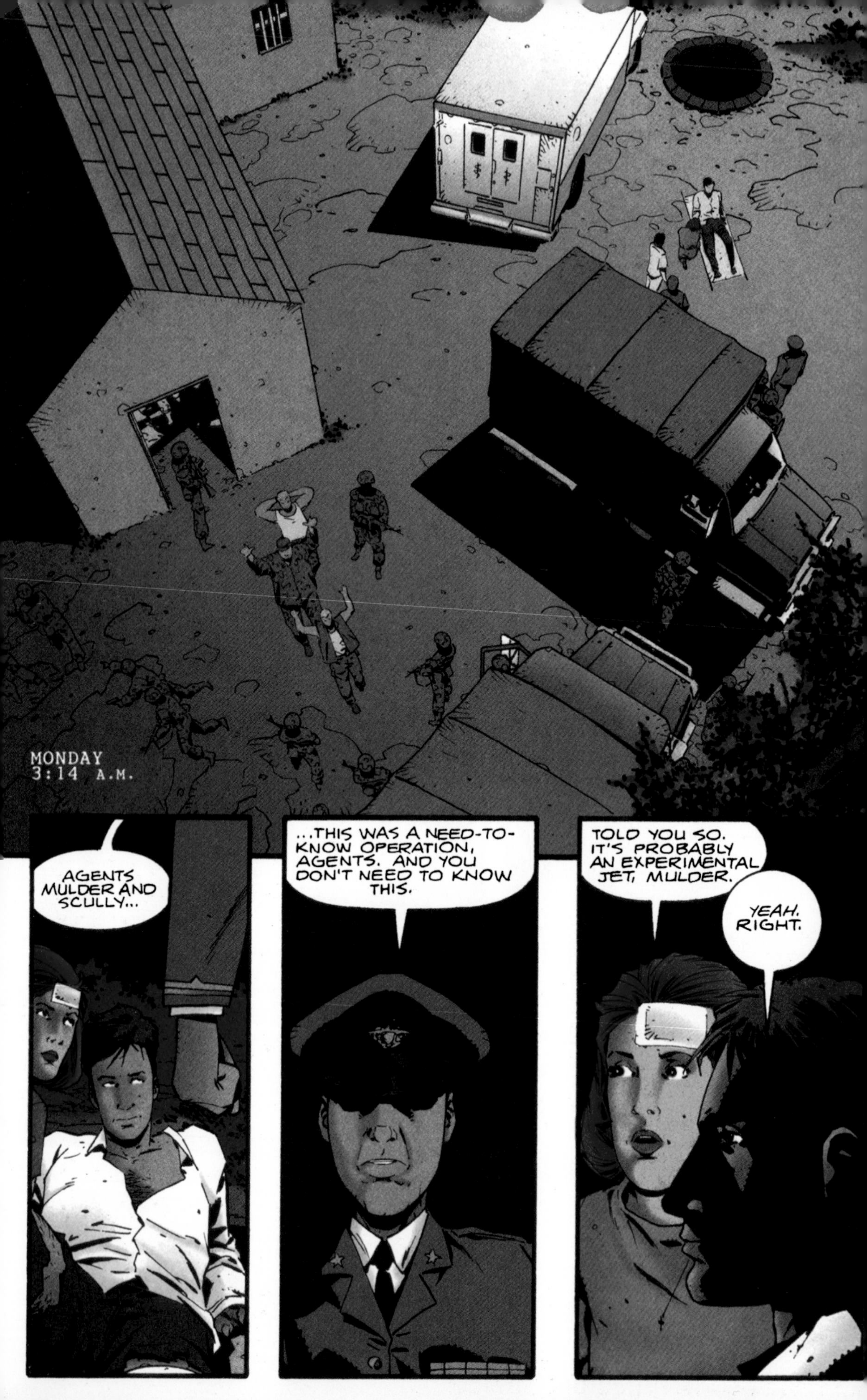
MONDAY
3:14 A.M.
AGENTS MULDER AND SCULLY...
...THIS WAS A NEED-TO-KNOW OPERATION, AGENTS. AND YOU DON'T NEED TO KNOW THIS.
TOLD YOU SO. IT'S PROBABLY AN EXPERIMENTAL JET, MULDER.
YEAH. RIGHT.

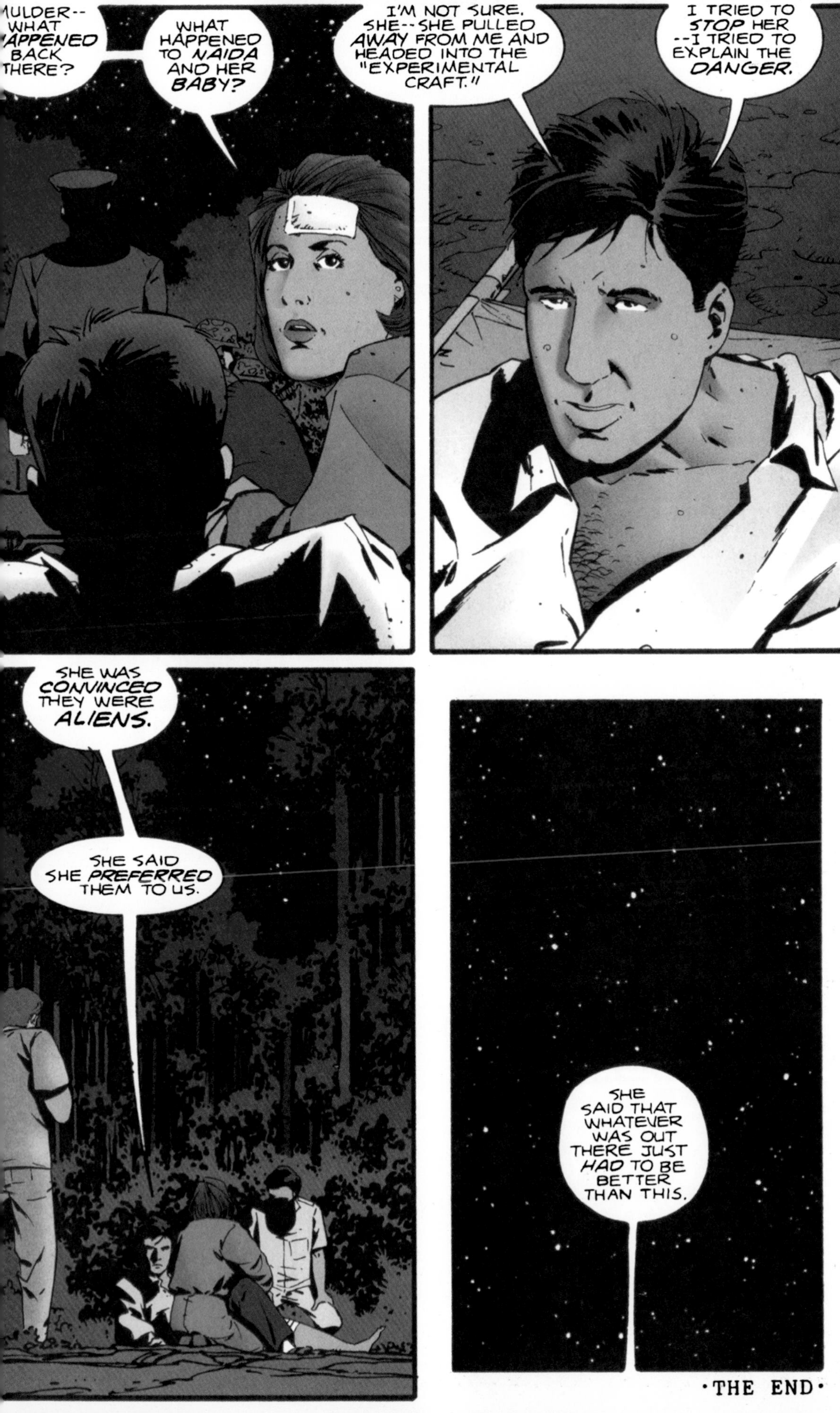
MULDER-- WHAT HAPPENED BACK THERE?
WHAT HAPPENED TO NAIDA AND HER BABY?
I'M NOT SURE. SHE--SHE PULLED AWAY FROM ME AND HEADED INTO THE "EXPERIMENTAL CRAFT."
I TRIED TO STOP HER --I TRIED TO EXPLAIN THE DANGER.
SHE WAS CONVINCED THEY WERE ALIENS.
SHE SAID SHE PREFERRED THEM TO US.
SHE SAID THAT WHATEVER WAS OUT THERE JUST HAD TO BE BETTER THAN THIS.

•THE END•

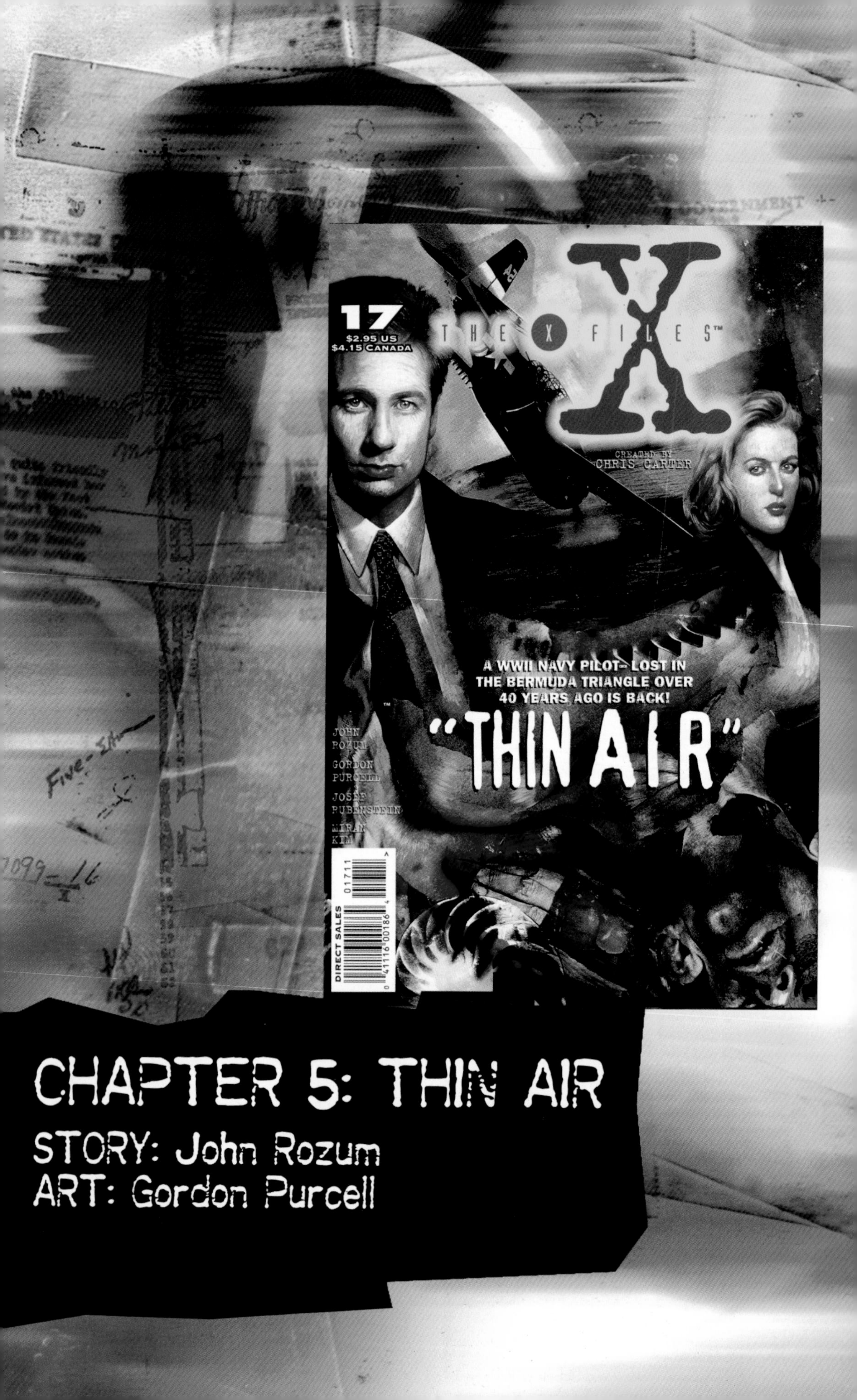
17
$2.95 US
$4.15 CANADA
THE X FILES
CREATED BY
CHRIS CARTER
A WWII NAVY PILOT– LOST IN THE BERMUDA TRIANGLE OVER 40 YEARS AGO IS BACK!
"THIN AIR"
JOHN ROZUM
GORDON PURCELL
JOSEF RUBENSTEIN
MIRAN KIM
DIRECT SALES

CHAPTER 5: THIN AIR

STORY: John Rozum
ART: Gordon Purcell

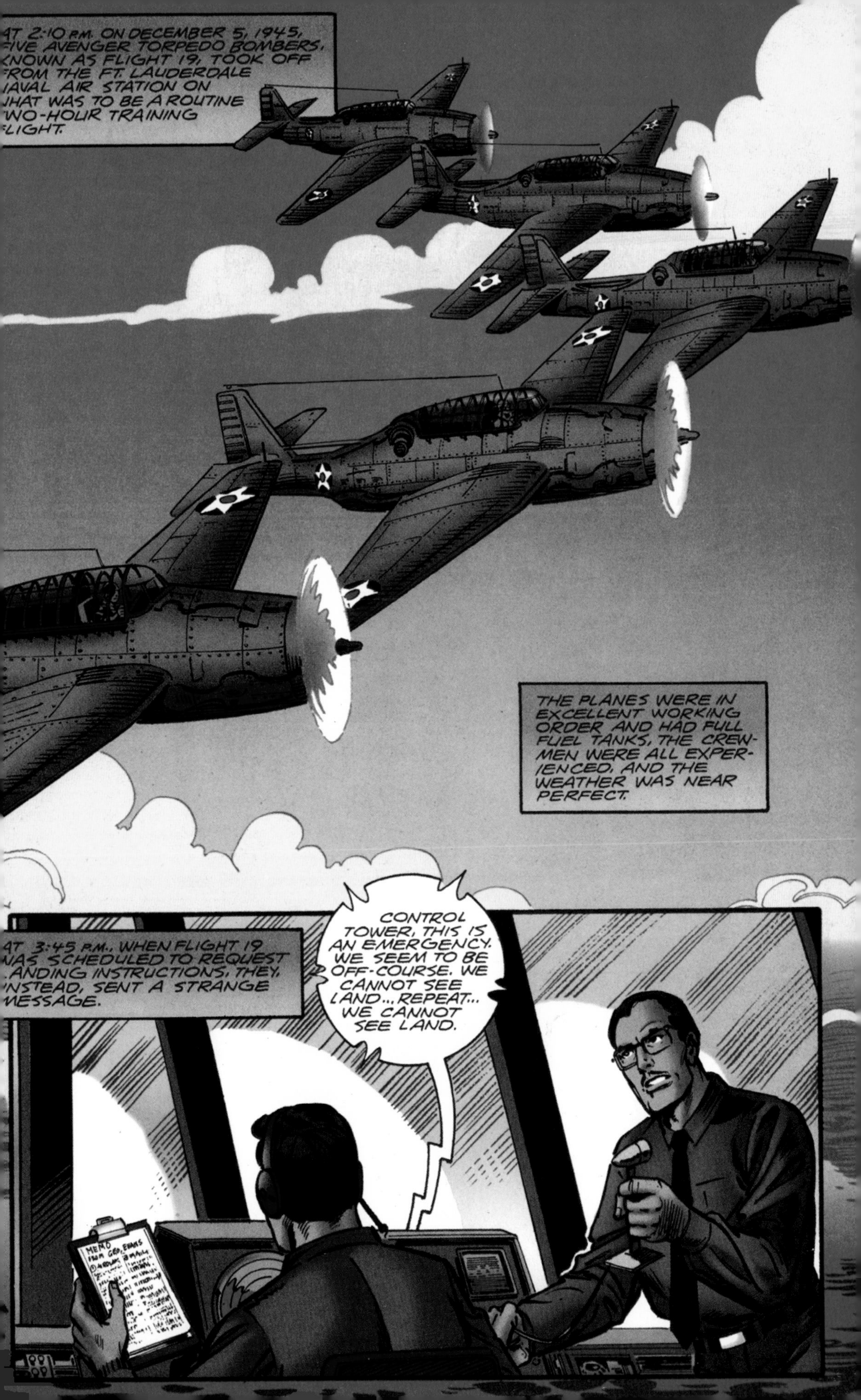
AT 2:10 P.M. ON DECEMBER 5, 1945, FIVE AVENGER TORPEDO BOMBERS, KNOWN AS FLIGHT 19, TOOK OFF FROM THE FT. LAUDERDALE NAVAL AIR STATION ON WHAT WAS TO BE A ROUTINE TWO-HOUR TRAINING FLIGHT.
THE PLANES WERE IN EXCELLENT WORKING ORDER AND HAD FULL FUEL TANKS, THE CREWMEN WERE ALL EXPERIENCED, AND THE WEATHER WAS NEAR PERFECT.
AT 3:45 P.M., WHEN FLIGHT 19 WAS SCHEDULED TO REQUEST LANDING INSTRUCTIONS, THEY, INSTEAD, SENT A STRANGE MESSAGE.
CONTROL TOWER, THIS IS AN EMERGENCY. WE SEEM TO BE OFF-COURSE. WE CANNOT SEE LAND... REPEAT... WE CANNOT SEE LAND.
MEMO
FROM GEO. EVANS

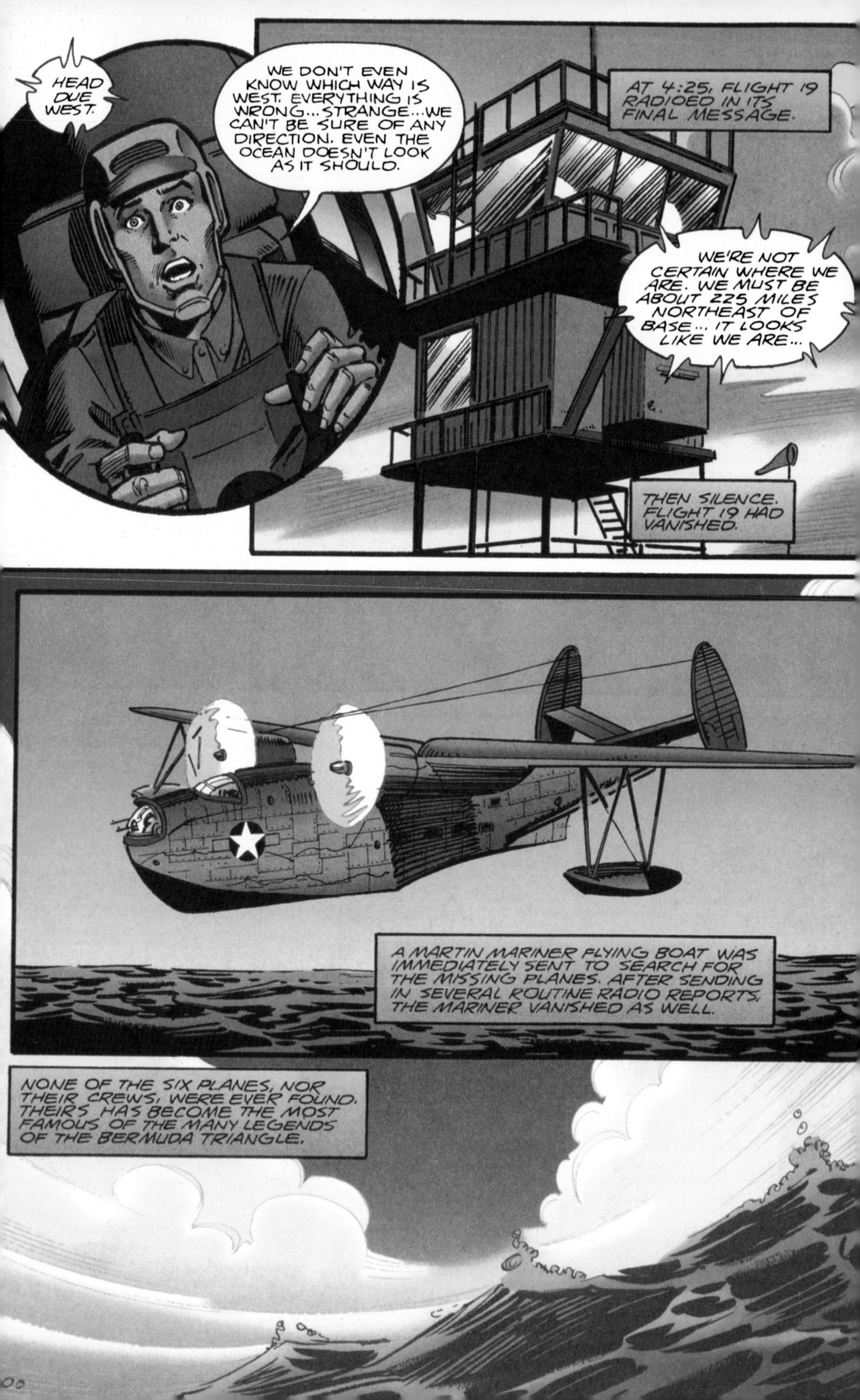
HEAD DUE WEST.
WE DON'T EVEN KNOW WHICH WAY IS WEST. EVERYTHING IS WRONG... STRANGE... WE CAN'T BE SURE OF ANY DIRECTION. EVEN THE OCEAN DOESN'T LOOK AS IT SHOULD.
AT 4:25, FLIGHT 19 RADIOED IN ITS FINAL MESSAGE.
WE'RE NOT CERTAIN WHERE WE ARE. WE MUST BE ABOUT 225 MILES NORTHEAST OF BASE... IT LOOKS LIKE WE ARE...
THEN SILENCE. FLIGHT 19 HAD VANISHED.
A MARTIN MARINER FLYING BOAT WAS IMMEDIATELY SENT TO SEARCH FOR THE MISSING PLANES. AFTER SENDING IN SEVERAL ROUTINE RADIO REPORTS, THE MARINER VANISHED AS WELL.
NONE OF THE SIX PLANES, NOR THEIR CREWS, WERE EVER FOUND. THEIRS HAS BECOME THE MOST FAMOUS OF THE MANY LEGENDS OF THE BERMUDA TRIANGLE.

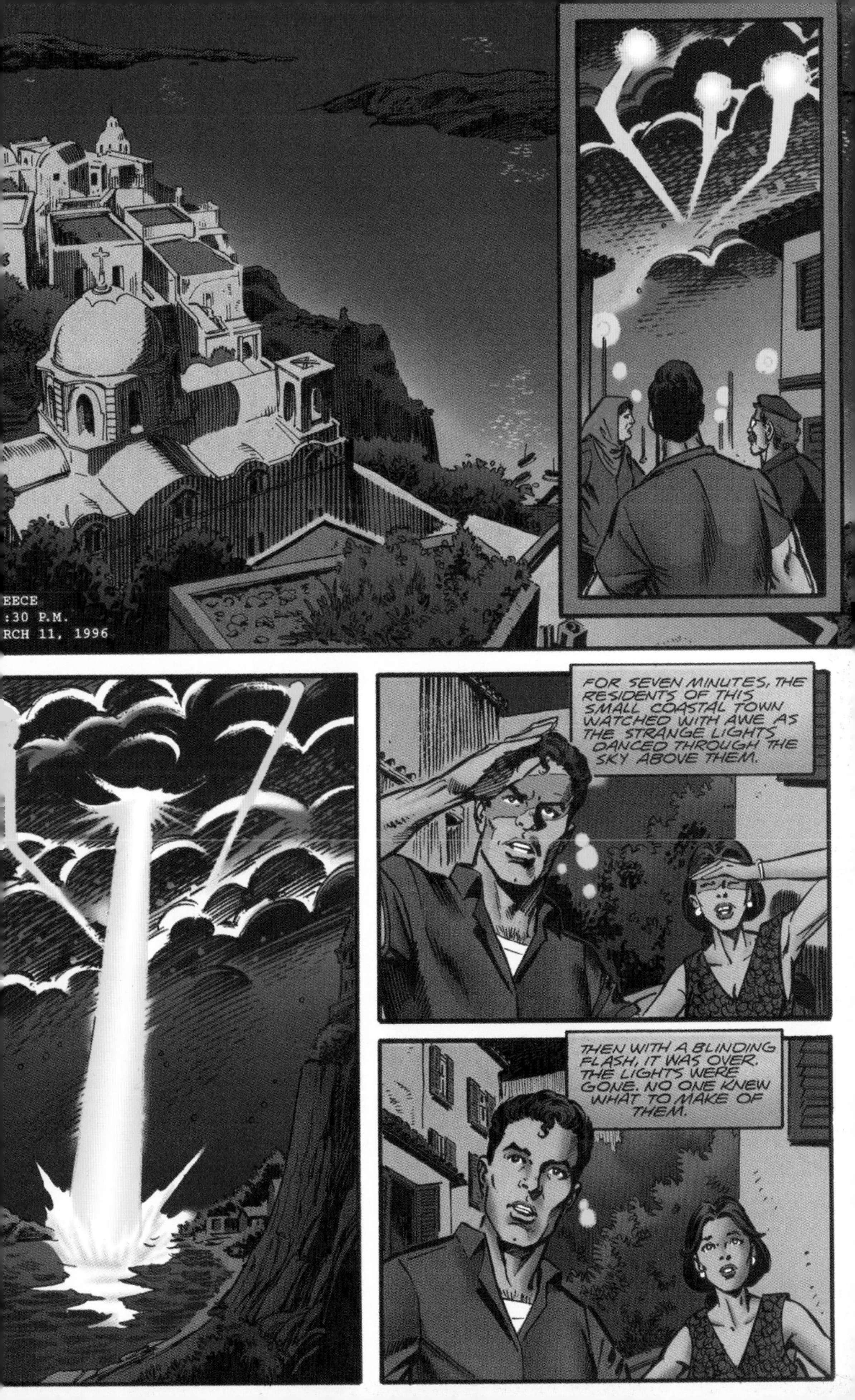
EECE
:30 P.M.
RCH 11, 1996
FOR SEVEN MINUTES, THE RESIDENTS OF THIS SMALL COASTAL TOWN WATCHED WITH AWE AS THE STRANGE LIGHTS DANCED THROUGH THE SKY ABOVE THEM.
THEN WITH A BLINDING FLASH, IT WAS OVER. THE LIGHTS WERE GONE. NO ONE KNEW WHAT TO MAKE OF THEM.

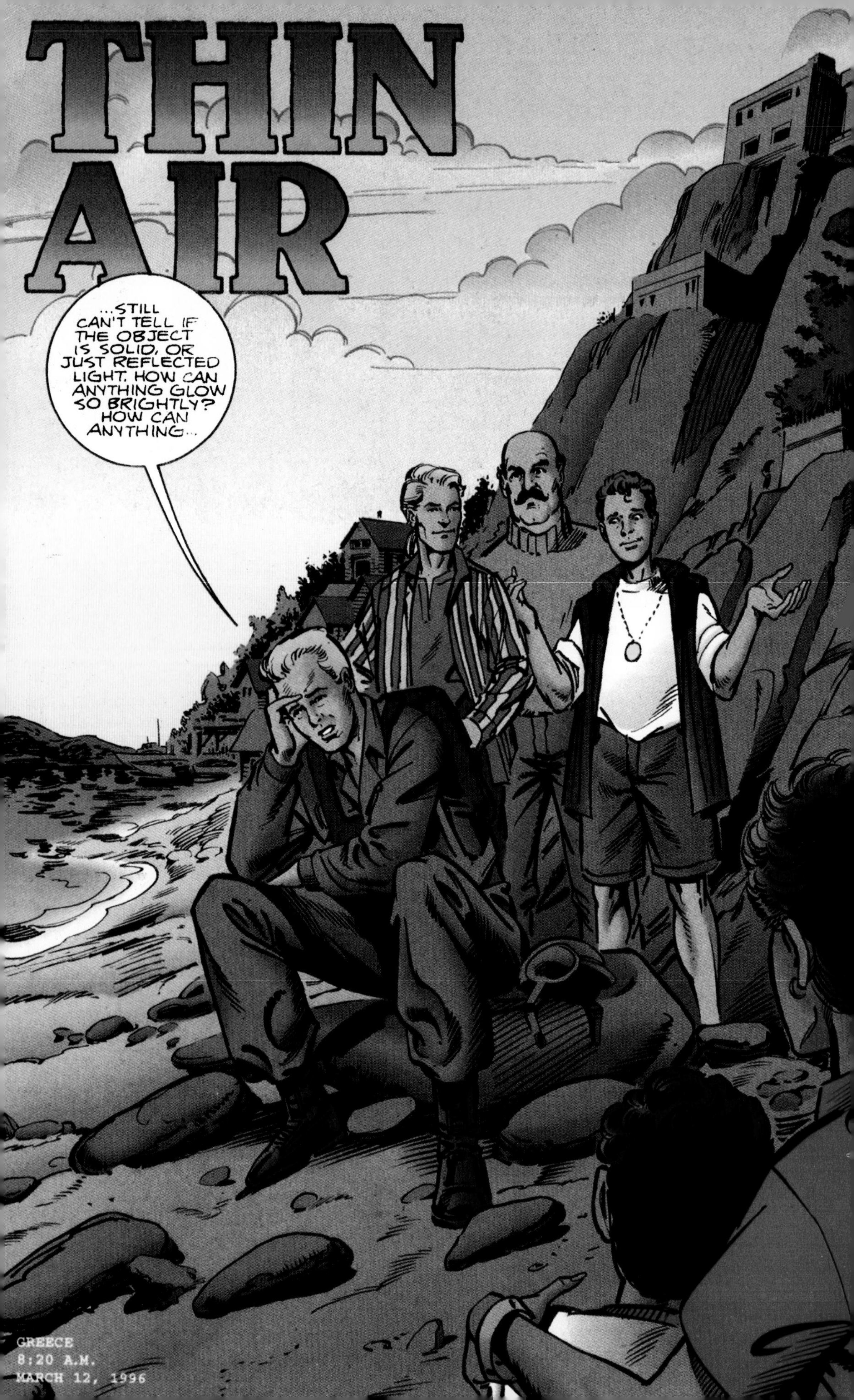
THIN AIR
...STILL CAN'T TELL IF THE OBJECT IS SOLID, OR JUST REFLECTED LIGHT. HOW CAN ANYTHING GLOW SO BRIGHTLY? HOW CAN ANYTHING...
GREECE
8:20 A.M.
MARCH 12, 1996

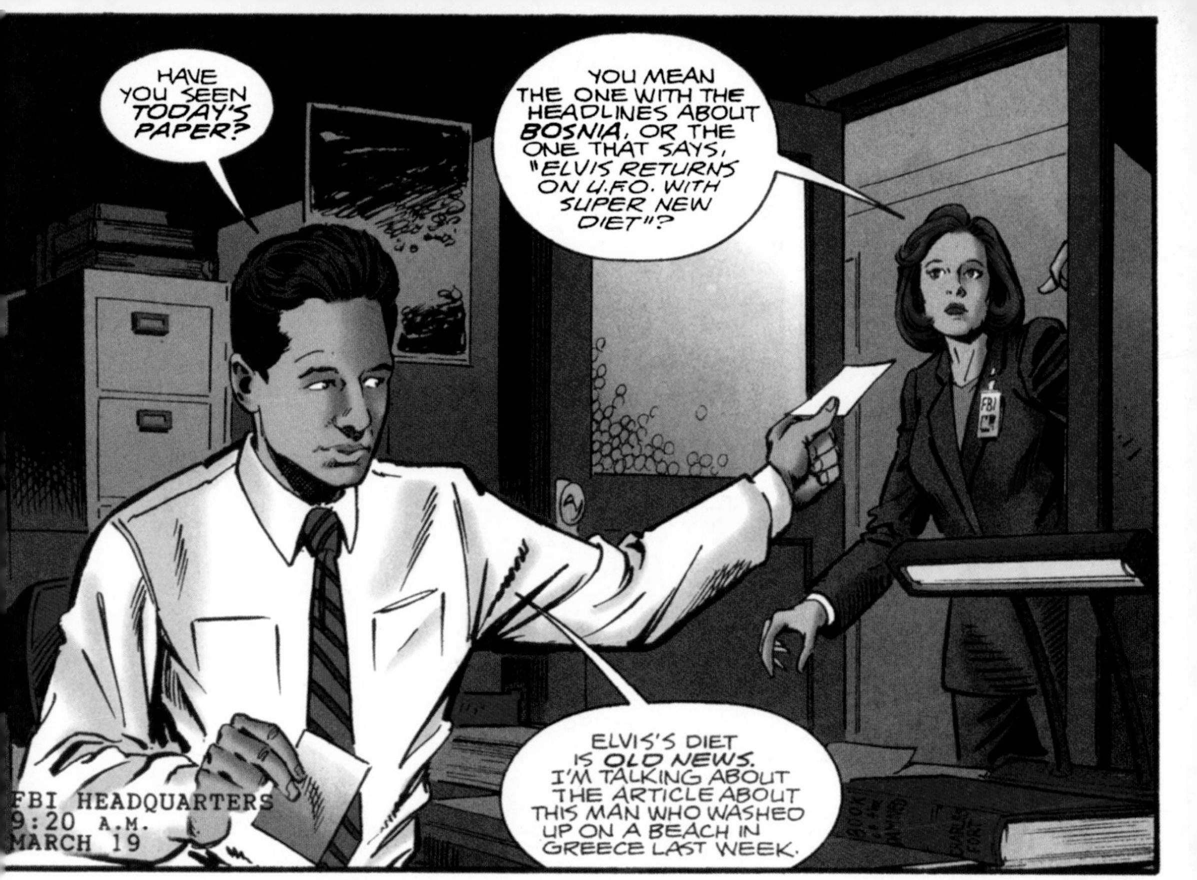
HAVE YOU SEEN TODAY'S PAPER?
YOU MEAN THE ONE WITH THE HEADLINES ABOUT BOSNIA, OR THE ONE THAT SAYS, "ELVIS RETURNS ON U.F.O. WITH SUPER NEW DIET"?
ELVIS'S DIET IS OLD NEWS. I'M TALKING ABOUT THE ARTICLE ABOUT THIS MAN WHO WASHED UP ON A BEACH IN GREECE LAST WEEK.
FBI HEADQUARTERS
9:20 A.M.
MARCH 19
CHARLES FORT

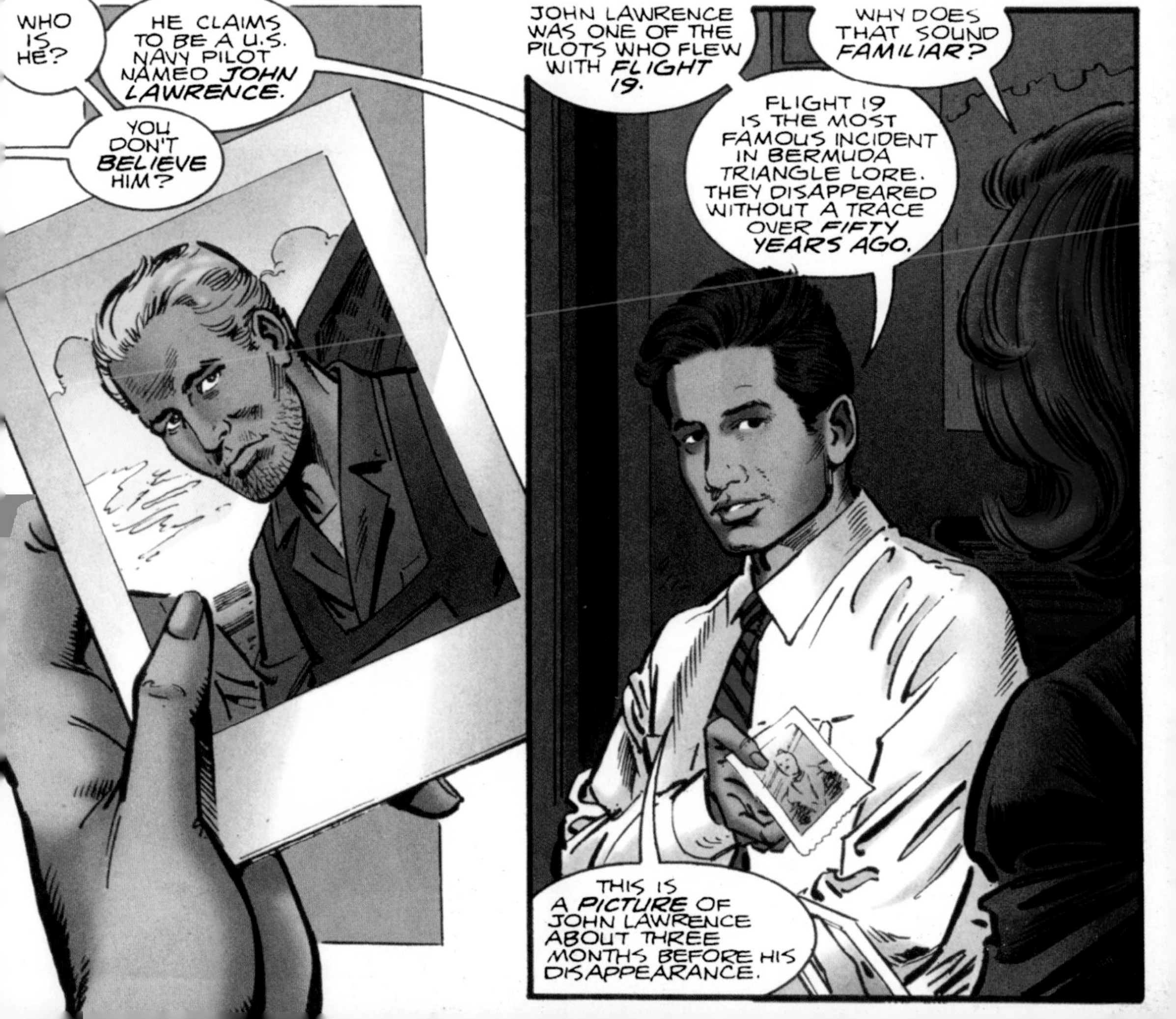
WHO IS HE?
HE CLAIMS TO BE A U.S. NAVY PILOT NAMED JOHN LAWRENCE.
YOU DON'T BELIEVE HIM?
JOHN LAWRENCE WAS ONE OF THE PILOTS WHO FLEW WITH FLIGHT 19.
WHY DOES THAT SOUND FAMILIAR?
FLIGHT 19 IS THE MOST FAMOUS INCIDENT IN BERMUDA TRIANGLE LORE. THEY DISAPPEARED WITHOUT A TRACE OVER FIFTY YEARS AGO.
THIS IS A PICTURE OF JOHN LAWRENCE ABOUT THREE MONTHS BEFORE HIS DISAPPEARANCE.

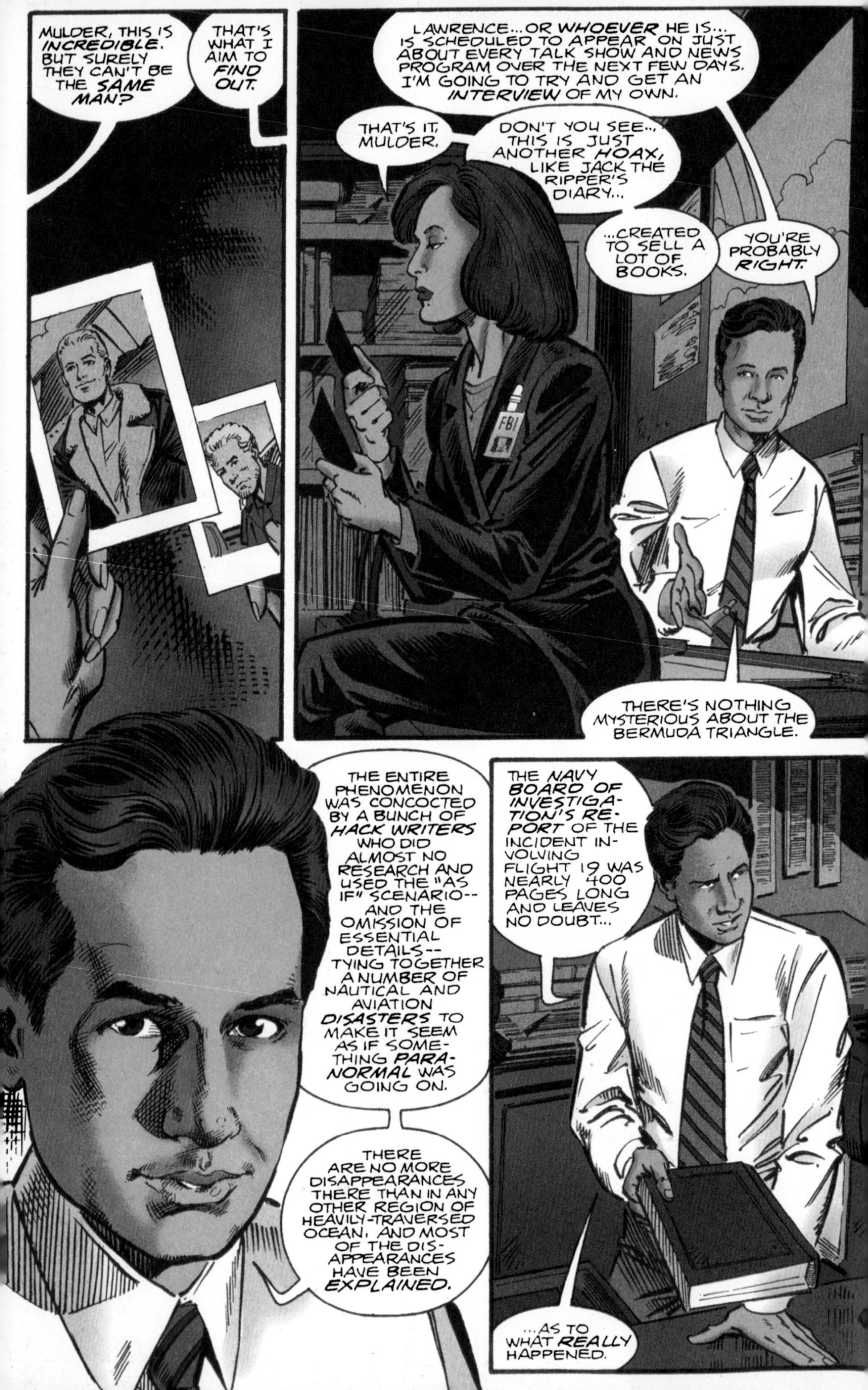
MULDER, THIS IS INCREDIBLE. BUT SURELY THEY CAN'T BE THE SAME MAN?
THAT'S WHAT I AIM TO FIND OUT.
LAWRENCE...OR WHOEVER HE IS... IS SCHEDULED TO APPEAR ON JUST ABOUT EVERY TALK SHOW AND NEWS PROGRAM OVER THE NEXT FEW DAYS. I'M GOING TO TRY AND GET AN INTERVIEW OF MY OWN.
THAT'S IT, MULDER.
DON'T YOU SEE... THIS IS JUST ANOTHER HOAX, LIKE JACK THE RIPPER'S DIARY...
...CREATED TO SELL A LOT OF BOOKS.
YOU'RE PROBABLY RIGHT.
THERE'S NOTHING MYSTERIOUS ABOUT THE BERMUDA TRIANGLE.
THE ENTIRE PHENOMENON WAS CONCOCTED BY A BUNCH OF HACK WRITERS WHO DID ALMOST NO RESEARCH AND USED THE "AS IF" SCENARIO-- AND THE OMISSION OF ESSENTIAL DETAILS-- TYING TOGETHER A NUMBER OF NAUTICAL AND AVIATION DISASTERS TO MAKE IT SEEM AS IF SOMETHING PARANORMAL WAS GOING ON.
THERE ARE NO MORE DISAPPEARANCES THERE THAN IN ANY OTHER REGION OF HEAVILY-TRAVERSED OCEAN, AND MOST OF THE DISAPPEARANCES HAVE BEEN EXPLAINED.
THE NAVY BOARD OF INVESTIGATION'S REPORT OF THE INCIDENT INVOLVING FLIGHT 19 WAS NEARLY 400 PAGES LONG AND LEAVES NO DOUBT...
...AS TO WHAT REALLY HAPPENED.

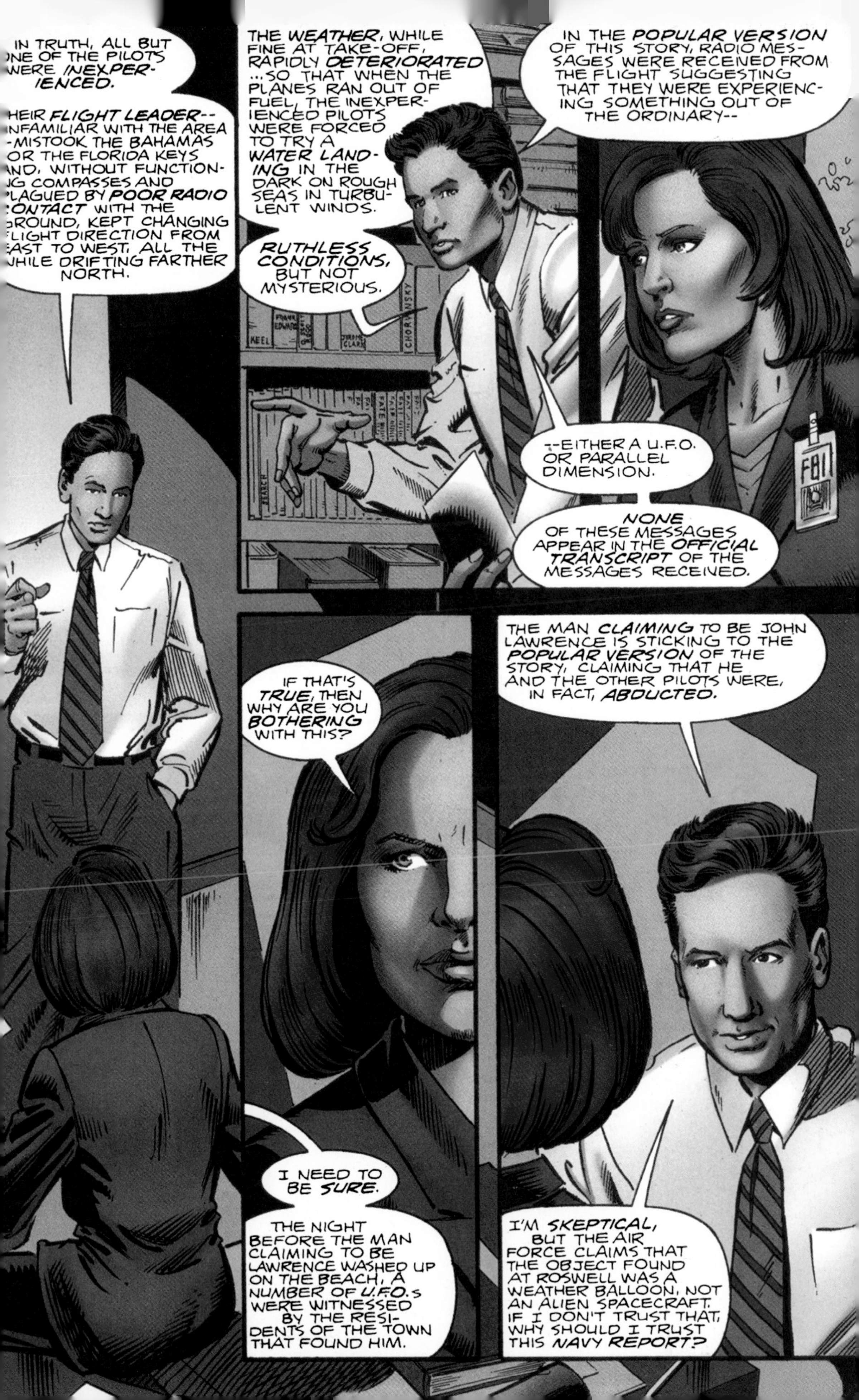
IN TRUTH, ALL BUT NE OF THE PILOTS VERE INEXPERIENCED.
HEIR FLIGHT LEADER-- NFAMILIAR WITH THE AREA -MISTOOK THE BAHAMAS OR THE FLORIDA KEYS AND, WITHOUT FUNCTION- NG COMPASSES AND PLAGUED BY POOR RADIO CONTACT WITH THE GROUND, KEPT CHANGING FLIGHT DIRECTION FROM EAST TO WEST, ALL THE WHILE DRIFTING FARTHER NORTH.
THE WEATHER, WHILE FINE AT TAKE-OFF, RAPIDLY DETERIORATED ...SO THAT WHEN THE PLANES RAN OUT OF FUEL, THE INEXPERIENCED PILOTS WERE FORCED TO TRY A WATER LANDING IN THE DARK ON ROUGH SEAS IN TURBULENT WINDS.
RUTHLESS CONDITIONS, BUT NOT MYSTERIOUS.
IN THE POPULAR VERSION OF THIS STORY, RADIO MESSAGES WERE RECEIVED FROM THE FLIGHT SUGGESTING THAT THEY WERE EXPERIENCING SOMETHING OUT OF THE ORDINARY--
--EITHER A U.F.O. OR PARALLEL DIMENSION.
NONE OF THESE MESSAGES APPEAR IN THE OFFICIAL TRANSCRIPT OF THE MESSAGES RECEIVED.
FBI
IF THAT'S TRUE, THEN WHY ARE YOU BOTHERING WITH THIS?
THE MAN CLAIMING TO BE JOHN LAWRENCE IS STICKING TO THE POPULAR VERSION OF THE STORY, CLAIMING THAT HE AND THE OTHER PILOTS WERE, IN FACT, ABDUCTED.
I NEED TO BE SURE.
THE NIGHT BEFORE THE MAN CLAIMING TO BE LAWRENCE WASHED UP ON THE BEACH, A NUMBER OF U.F.O.s WERE WITNESSED BY THE RESIDENTS OF THE TOWN THAT FOUND HIM.
I'M SKEPTICAL, BUT THE AIR FORCE CLAIMS THAT THE OBJECT FOUND AT ROSWELL WAS A WEATHER BALLOON, NOT AN ALIEN SPACECRAFT. IF I DON'T TRUST THAT, WHY SHOULD I TRUST THIS NAVY REPORT?

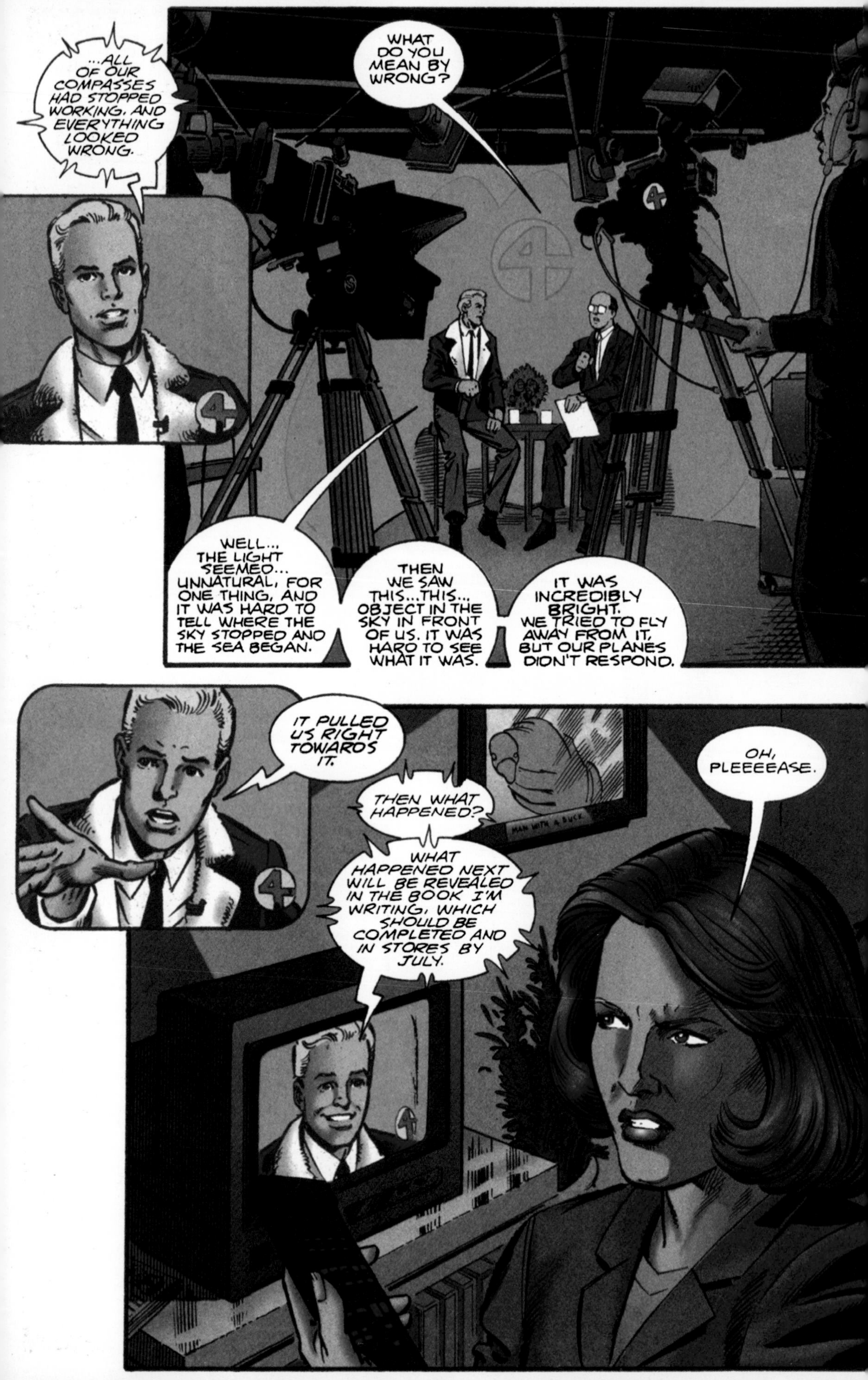
...ALL OF OUR COMPASSES HAD STOPPED WORKING, AND EVERYTHING LOOKED WRONG.
WHAT DO YOU MEAN BY WRONG?
WELL... THE LIGHT SEEMED... UNNATURAL, FOR ONE THING, AND IT WAS HARD TO TELL WHERE THE SKY STOPPED AND THE SEA BEGAN.
THEN WE SAW THIS...THIS... OBJECT IN THE SKY IN FRONT OF US. IT WAS HARD TO SEE WHAT IT WAS.
IT WAS INCREDIBLY BRIGHT. WE TRIED TO FLY AWAY FROM IT, BUT OUR PLANES DIDN'T RESPOND.
IT PULLED US RIGHT TOWARDS IT.
THEN WHAT HAPPENED?
WHAT HAPPENED NEXT WILL BE REVEALED IN THE BOOK I'M WRITING, WHICH SHOULD BE COMPLETED AND IN STORES BY JULY.
OH, PLEEEEASE.

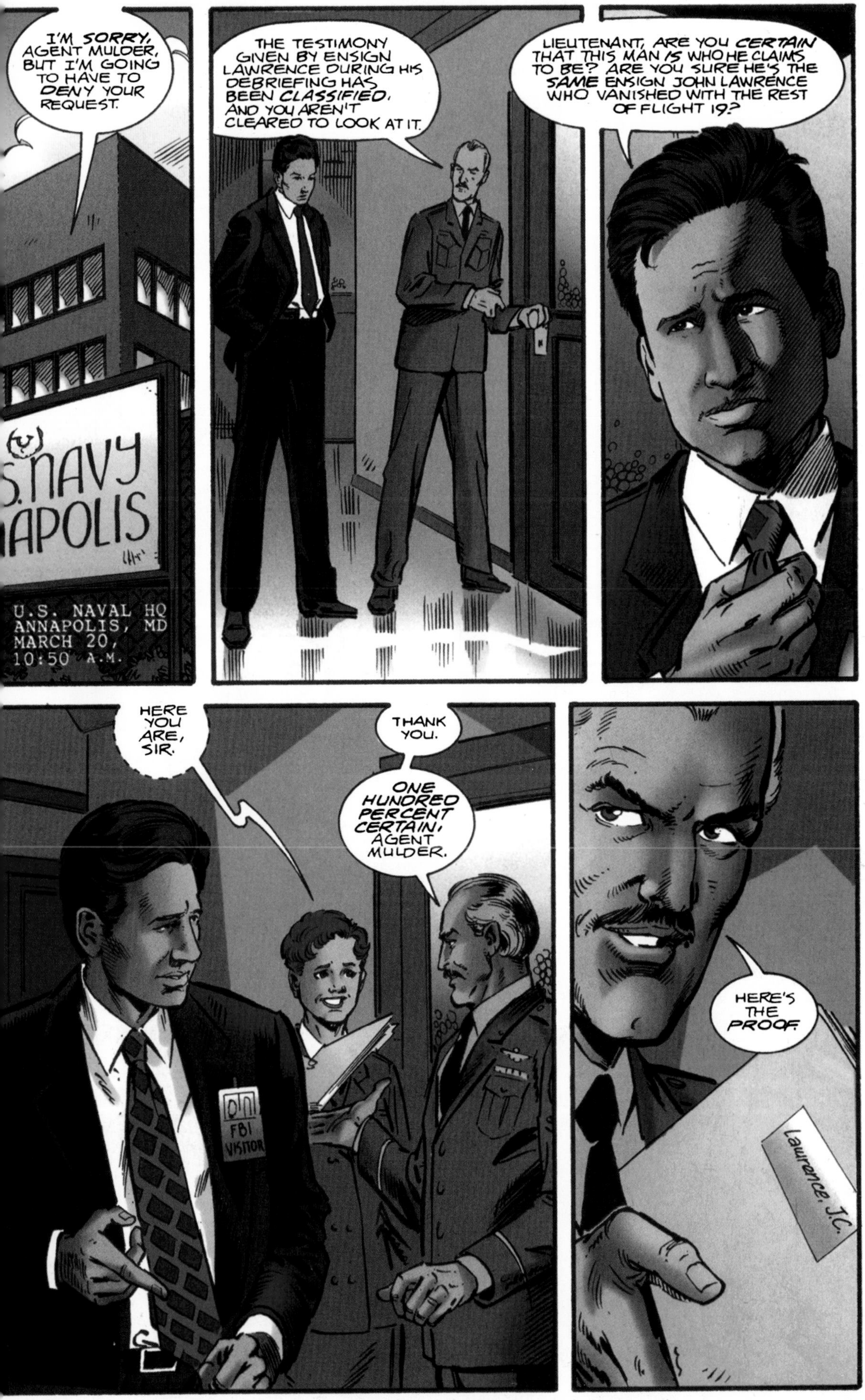
I'M SORRY, AGENT MULDER, BUT I'M GOING TO HAVE TO DENY YOUR REQUEST.
S. NAVY
APOLIS
U.S. NAVAL HQ ANNAPOLIS, MD MARCH 20, 10:50 A.M.
THE TESTIMONY GIVEN BY ENSIGN LAWRENCE DURING HIS DEBRIEFING HAS BEEN CLASSIFIED, AND YOU AREN'T CLEARED TO LOOK AT IT.
LIEUTENANT, ARE YOU CERTAIN THAT THIS MAN IS WHO HE CLAIMS TO BE? ARE YOU SURE HE'S THE SAME ENSIGN JOHN LAWRENCE WHO VANISHED WITH THE REST OF FLIGHT 19?
HERE YOU ARE, SIR.
THANK YOU.
ONE HUNDRED PERCENT CERTAIN, AGENT MULDER.
FBI VISITOR
HERE'S THE PROOF.
Laurence. J.C.

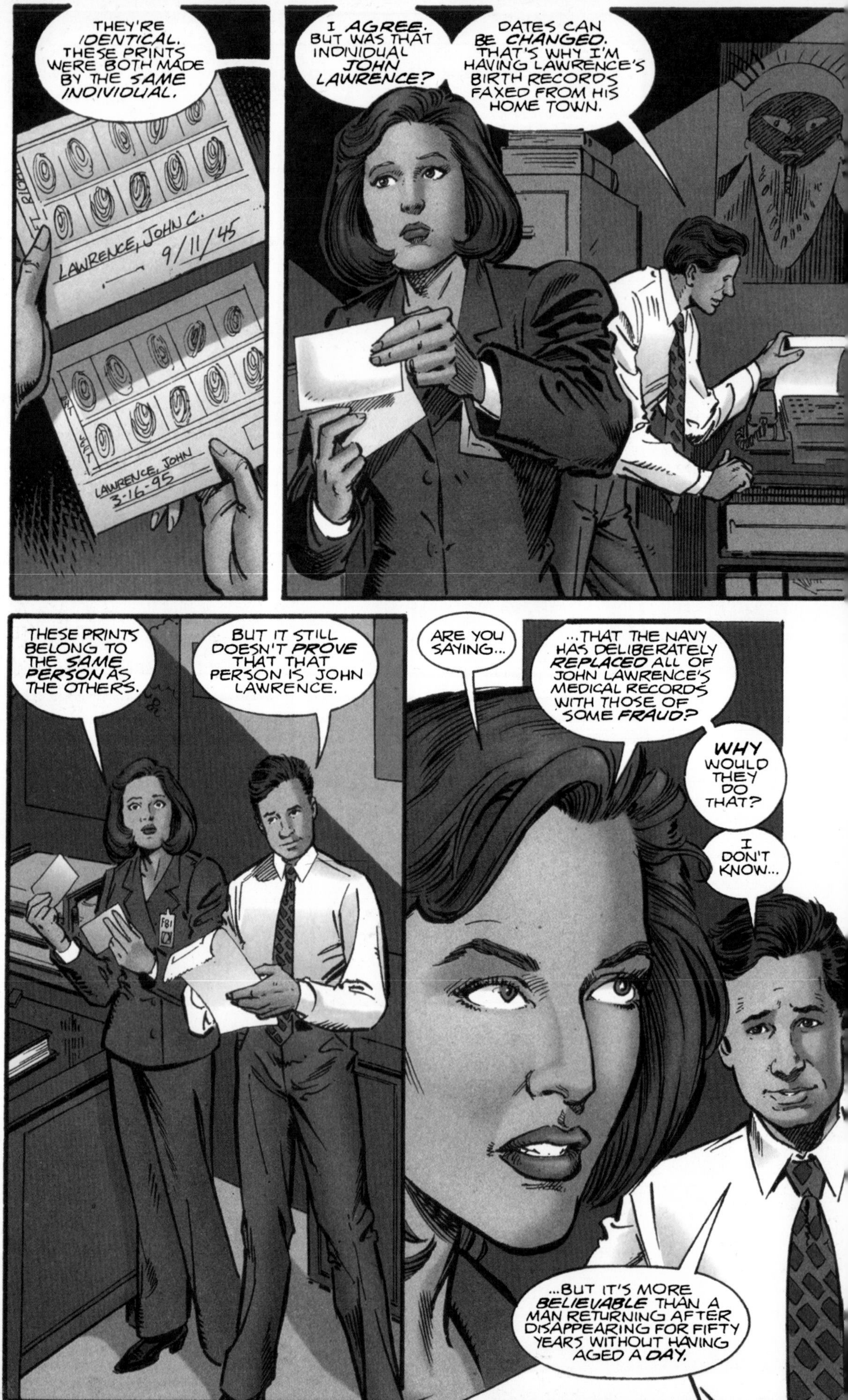

THEY'RE IDENTICAL. THESE PRINTS WERE BOTH MADE BY THE SAME INDIVIDUAL.
LAWRENCE, JOHN C. 9/11/45
LAWRENCE, JOHN 3-16-95
I AGREE. BUT WAS THAT INDIVIDUAL JOHN LAWRENCE?
DATES CAN BE CHANGED. THAT'S WHY I'M HAVING LAWRENCE'S BIRTH RECORDS FAXED FROM HIS HOME TOWN.
THESE PRINTS BELONG TO THE SAME PERSON AS THE OTHERS.
BUT IT STILL DOESN'T PROVE THAT THAT PERSON IS JOHN LAWRENCE.
ARE YOU SAYING...
...THAT THE NAVY HAS DELIBERATELY REPLACED ALL OF JOHN LAWRENCE'S MEDICAL RECORDS WITH THOSE OF SOME FRAUD?
WHY WOULD THEY DO THAT?
I DON'T KNOW...
...BUT IT'S MORE BELIEVABLE THAN A MAN RETURNING AFTER DISAPPEARING FOR FIFTY YEARS WITHOUT HAVING AGED A DAY.

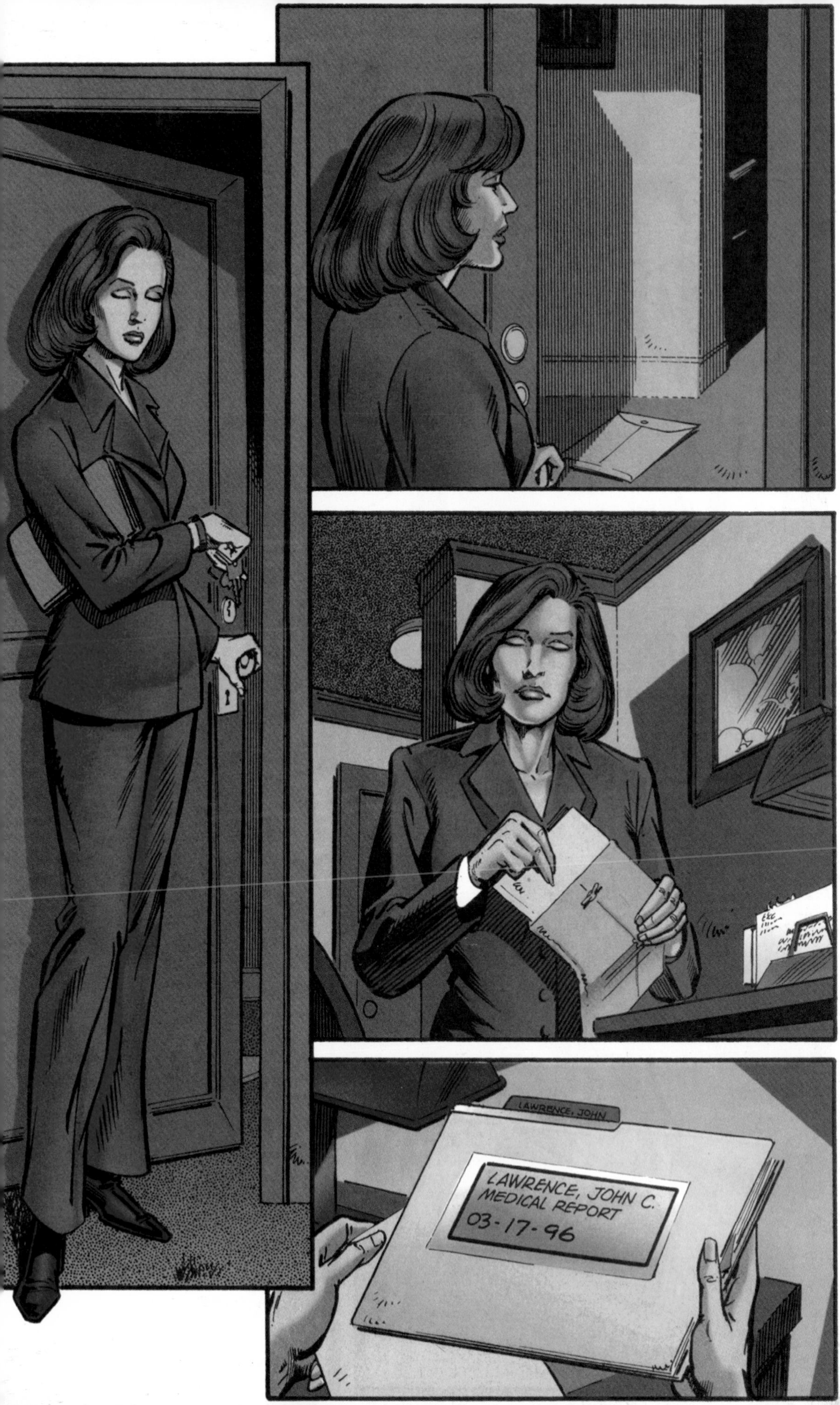

LAWRENCE, JOHN
LAWRENCE, JOHN C.
MEDICAL REPORT
03-17-96

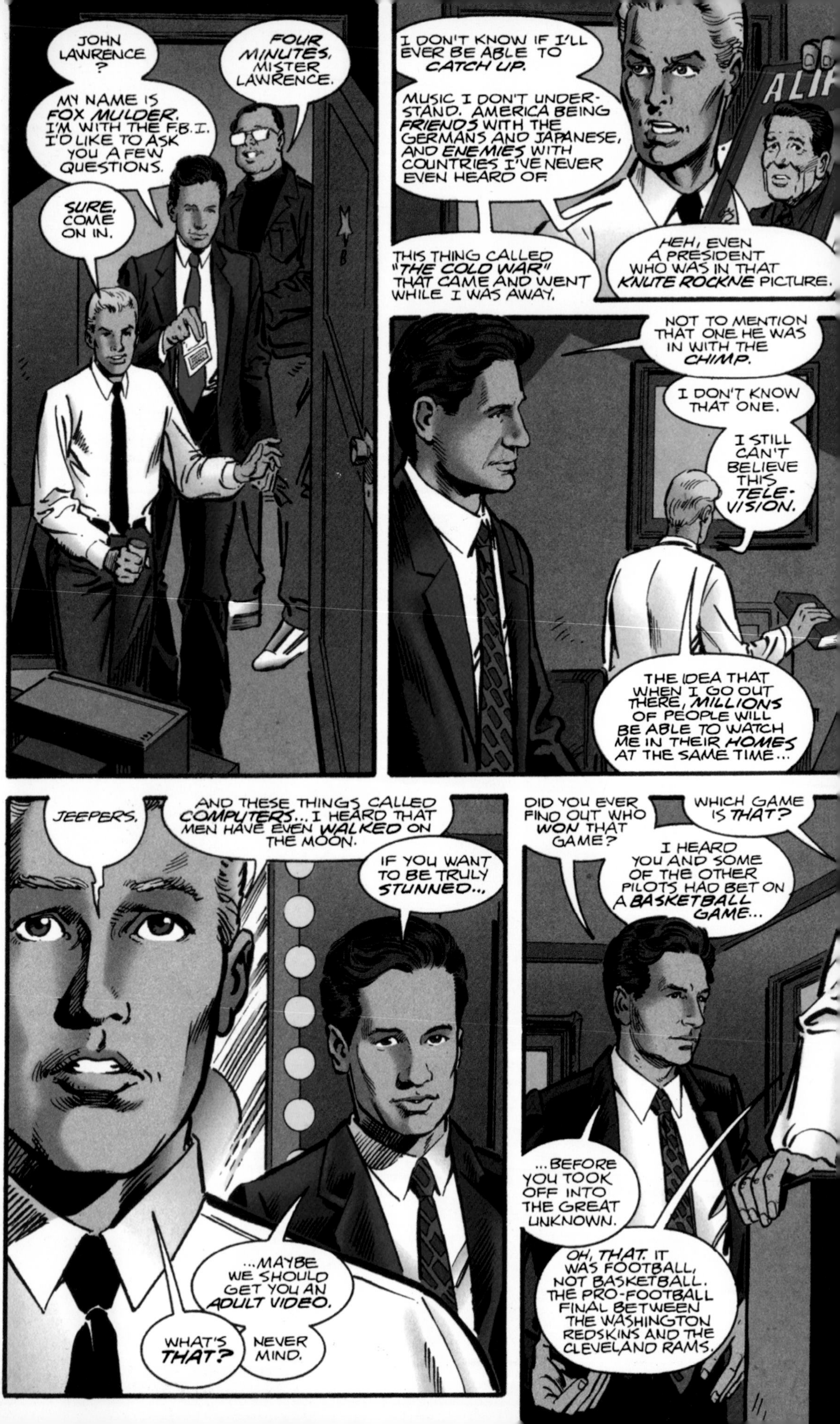
JOHN LAWRENCE?
MY NAME IS FOX MULDER. I'M WITH THE F.B.I. I'D LIKE TO ASK YOU A FEW QUESTIONS.
FOUR MINUTES, MISTER LAWRENCE.
SURE, COME ON IN.
I DON'T KNOW IF I'LL EVER BE ABLE TO CATCH UP.
MUSIC I DON'T UNDERSTAND. AMERICA BEING FRIENDS WITH THE GERMANS AND JAPANESE, AND ENEMIES WITH COUNTRIES I'VE NEVER EVEN HEARD OF.
THIS THING CALLED "THE COLD WAR" THAT CAME AND WENT WHILE I WAS AWAY.
HEH, EVEN A PRESIDENT WHO WAS IN THAT KNUTE ROCKNE PICTURE.
NOT TO MENTION THAT ONE HE WAS IN WITH THE CHIMP.
I DON'T KNOW THAT ONE.
I STILL CAN'T BELIEVE THIS TELE-VISION.
THE IDEA THAT WHEN I GO OUT THERE, MILLIONS OF PEOPLE WILL BE ABLE TO WATCH ME IN THEIR HOMES AT THE SAME TIME...
JEEPERS.
AND THESE THINGS CALLED COMPUTERS... I HEARD THAT MEN HAVE EVEN WALKED ON THE MOON.
IF YOU WANT TO BE TRULY STUNNED...
...MAYBE WE SHOULD GET YOU AN ADULT VIDEO.
WHAT'S THAT?
NEVER MIND.
DID YOU EVER FIND OUT WHO WON THAT GAME?
WHICH GAME IS THAT?
I HEARD YOU AND SOME OF THE OTHER PILOTS HAD BET ON A BASKETBALL GAME...
...BEFORE YOU TOOK OFF INTO THE GREAT UNKNOWN.
OH, THAT. IT WAS FOOTBALL, NOT BASKETBALL. THE PRO-FOOTBALL FINAL BETWEEN THE WASHINGTON REDSKINS AND THE CLEVELAND RAMS.

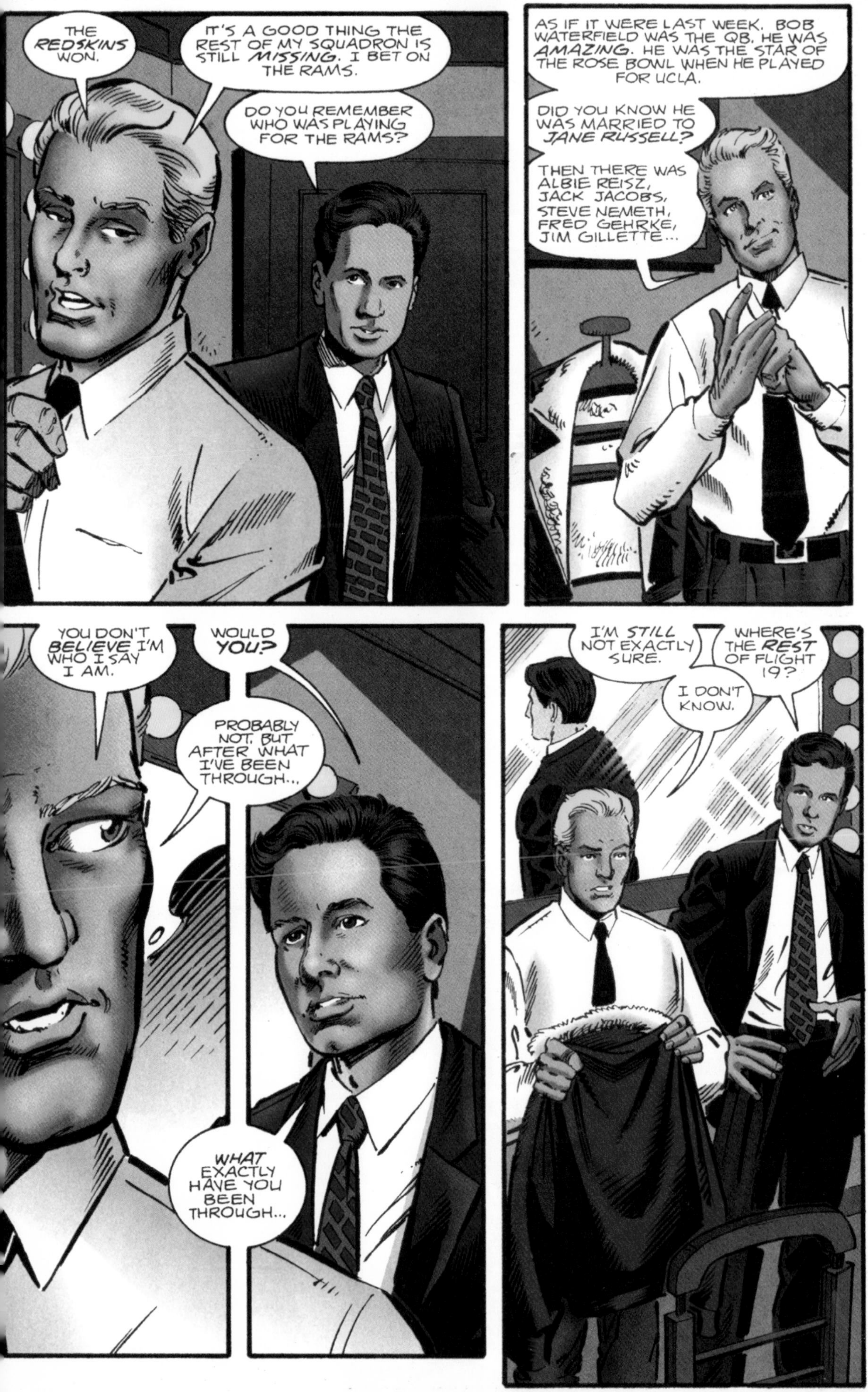
THE REDSKINS WON.
IT'S A GOOD THING THE REST OF MY SQUADRON IS STILL MISSING. I BET ON THE RAMS.
DO YOU REMEMBER WHO WAS PLAYING FOR THE RAMS?
AS IF IT WERE LAST WEEK. BOB WATERFIELD WAS THE QB. HE WAS AMAZING. HE WAS THE STAR OF THE ROSE BOWL WHEN HE PLAYED FOR UCLA.
DID YOU KNOW HE WAS MARRIED TO JANE RUSSELL?
THEN THERE WAS ALBIE REISZ, JACK JACOBS, STEVE NEMETH, FRED GEHRKE, JIM GILLETTE...
YOU DON'T BELIEVE I'M WHO I SAY I AM.
WOULD YOU?
PROBABLY NOT. BUT AFTER WHAT I'VE BEEN THROUGH...
WHAT EXACTLY HAVE YOU BEEN THROUGH...
I'M STILL NOT EXACTLY SURE.
WHERE'S THE REST OF FLIGHT 19?
I DON'T KNOW.

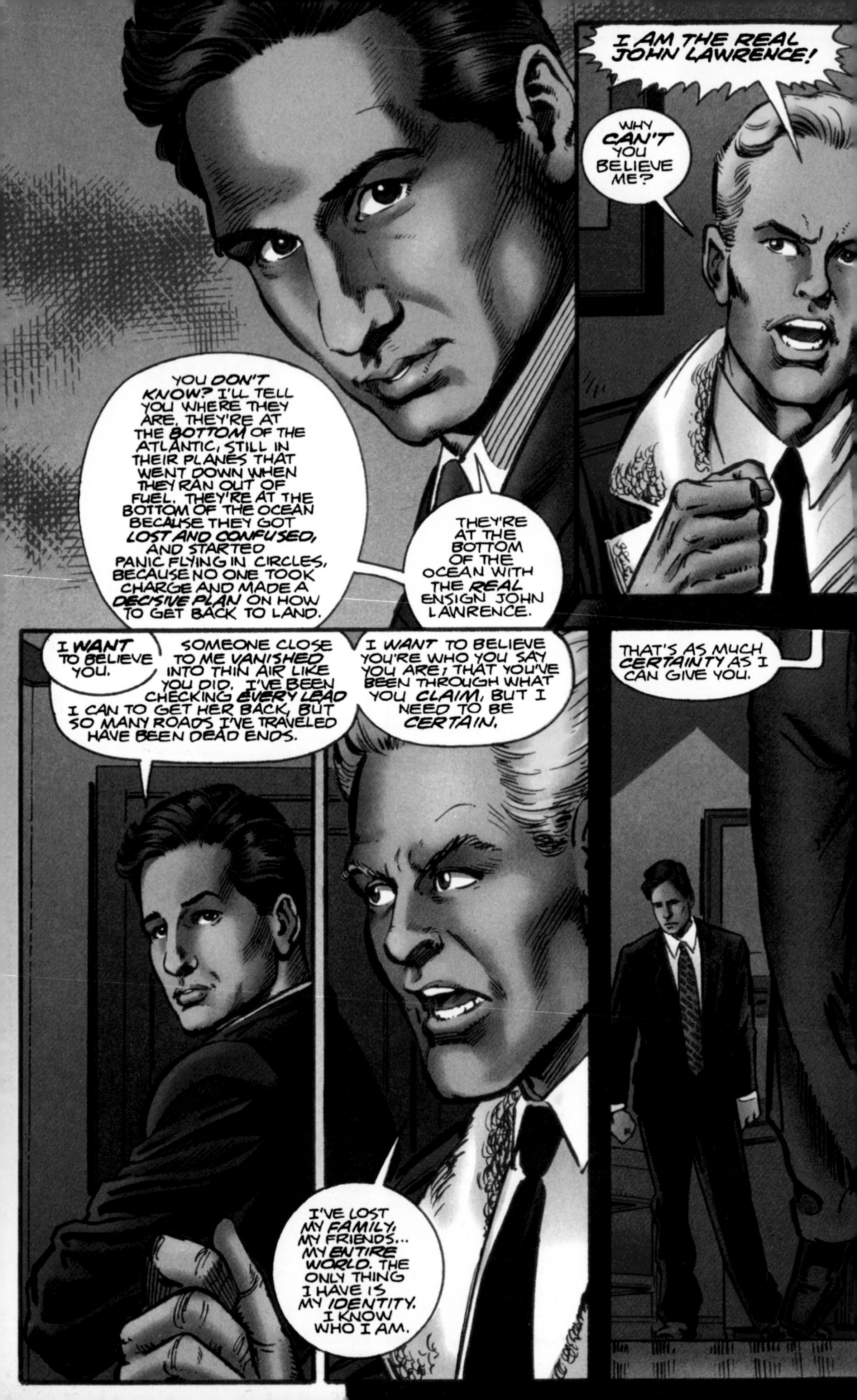
I AM THE REAL JOHN LAWRENCE!
WHY CAN'T YOU BELIEVE ME?
YOU DON'T KNOW? I'LL TELL YOU WHERE THEY ARE. THEY'RE AT THE BOTTOM OF THE ATLANTIC, STILL IN THEIR PLANES THAT WENT DOWN WHEN THEY RAN OUT OF FUEL. THEY'RE AT THE BOTTOM OF THE OCEAN BECAUSE THEY GOT LOST AND CONFUSED, AND STARTED PANIC FLYING IN CIRCLES, BECAUSE NO ONE TOOK CHARGE AND MADE A DECISIVE PLAN ON HOW TO GET BACK TO LAND.
THEY'RE AT THE BOTTOM OF THE OCEAN WITH THE REAL ENSIGN JOHN LAWRENCE.
I WANT TO BELIEVE YOU.
SOMEONE CLOSE TO ME VANISHED INTO THIN AIR LIKE YOU DID. I'VE BEEN CHECKING EVERY LEAD I CAN TO GET HER BACK, BUT SO MANY ROADS I'VE TRAVELED HAVE BEEN DEAD ENDS.
I WANT TO BELIEVE YOU'RE WHO YOU SAY YOU ARE; THAT YOU'VE BEEN THROUGH WHAT YOU CLAIM, BUT I NEED TO BE CERTAIN.
I'VE LOST MY FAMILY, MY FRIENDS... MY ENTIRE WORLD. THE ONLY THING I HAVE IS MY IDENTITY. I KNOW WHO I AM.
THAT'S AS MUCH CERTAINTY AS I CAN GIVE YOU.

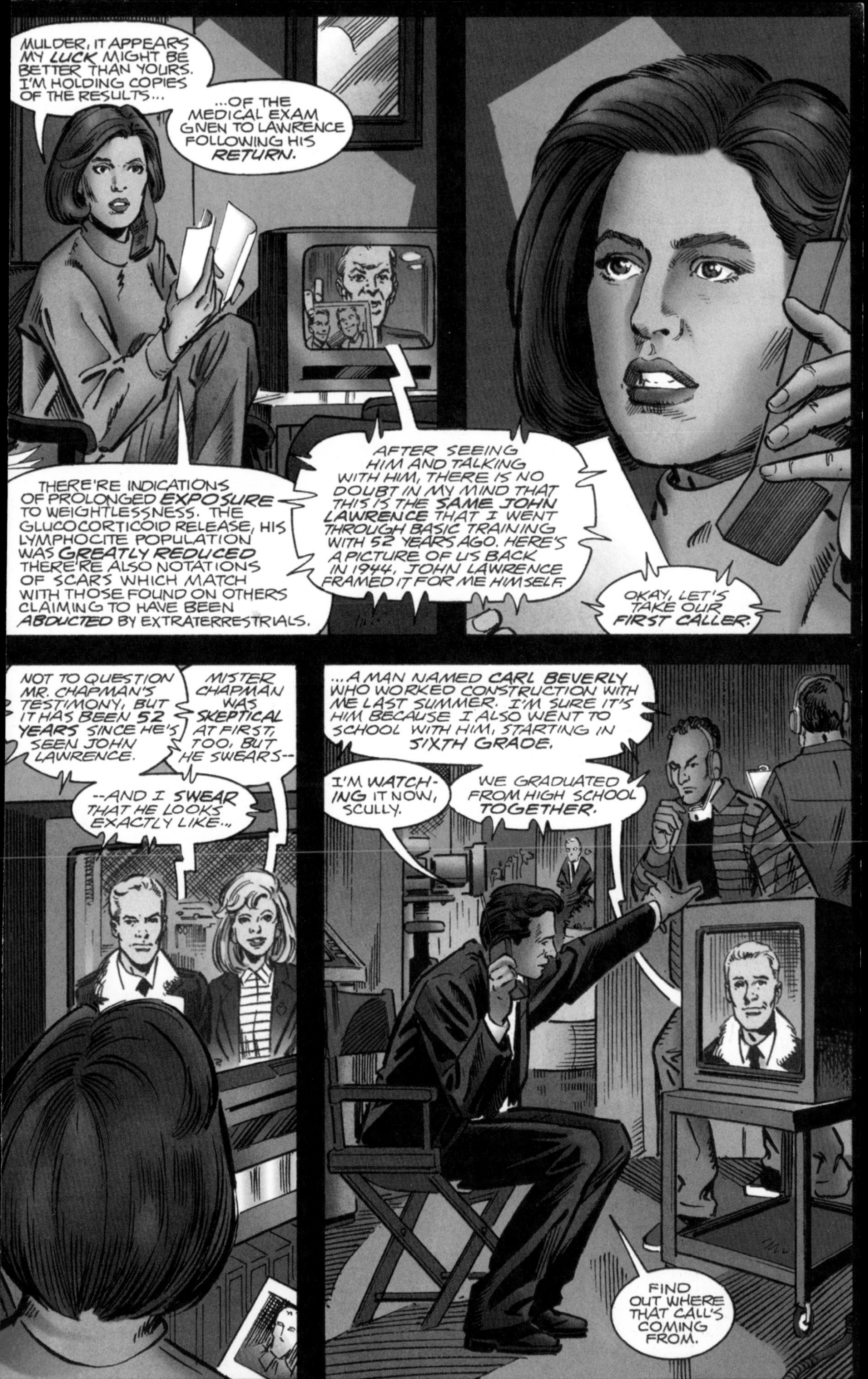
MULDER, IT APPEARS MY LUCK MIGHT BE BETTER THAN YOURS. I'M HOLDING COPIES OF THE RESULTS...
...OF THE MEDICAL EXAM GIVEN TO LAWRENCE FOLLOWING HIS RETURN.
THERE'RE INDICATIONS OF PROLONGED EXPOSURE TO WEIGHTLESSNESS. THE GLUCOCORTICOID RELEASE, HIS LYMPHOCITE POPULATION WAS GREATLY REDUCED THERE'RE ALSO NOTATIONS OF SCARS WHICH MATCH WITH THOSE FOUND ON OTHERS CLAIMING TO HAVE BEEN ABDUCTED BY EXTRATERRESTRIALS.
AFTER SEEING HIM AND TALKING WITH HIM, THERE IS NO DOUBT IN MY MIND THAT THIS IS THE SAME JOHN LAWRENCE THAT I WENT THROUGH BASIC TRAINING WITH 52 YEARS AGO. HERE'S A PICTURE OF US BACK IN 1944. JOHN LAWRENCE FRAMED IT FOR ME HIMSELF.
OKAY, LET'S TAKE OUR FIRST CALLER.
NOT TO QUESTION MR. CHAPMAN'S TESTIMONY, BUT IT HAS BEEN 52 YEARS SINCE HE'S SEEN JOHN LAWRENCE.
MISTER CHAPMAN WAS SKEPTICAL AT FIRST, TOO, BUT HE SWEARS--
--AND I SWEAR THAT HE LOOKS EXACTLY LIKE...
...A MAN NAMED CARL BEVERLY WHO WORKED CONSTRUCTION WITH ME LAST SUMMER. I'M SURE IT'S HIM BECAUSE I ALSO WENT TO SCHOOL WITH HIM, STARTING IN SIXTH GRADE.
I'M WATCHING IT NOW, SCULLY.
WE GRADUATED FROM HIGH SCHOOL TOGETHER.
FIND OUT WHERE THAT CALL'S COMING FROM.

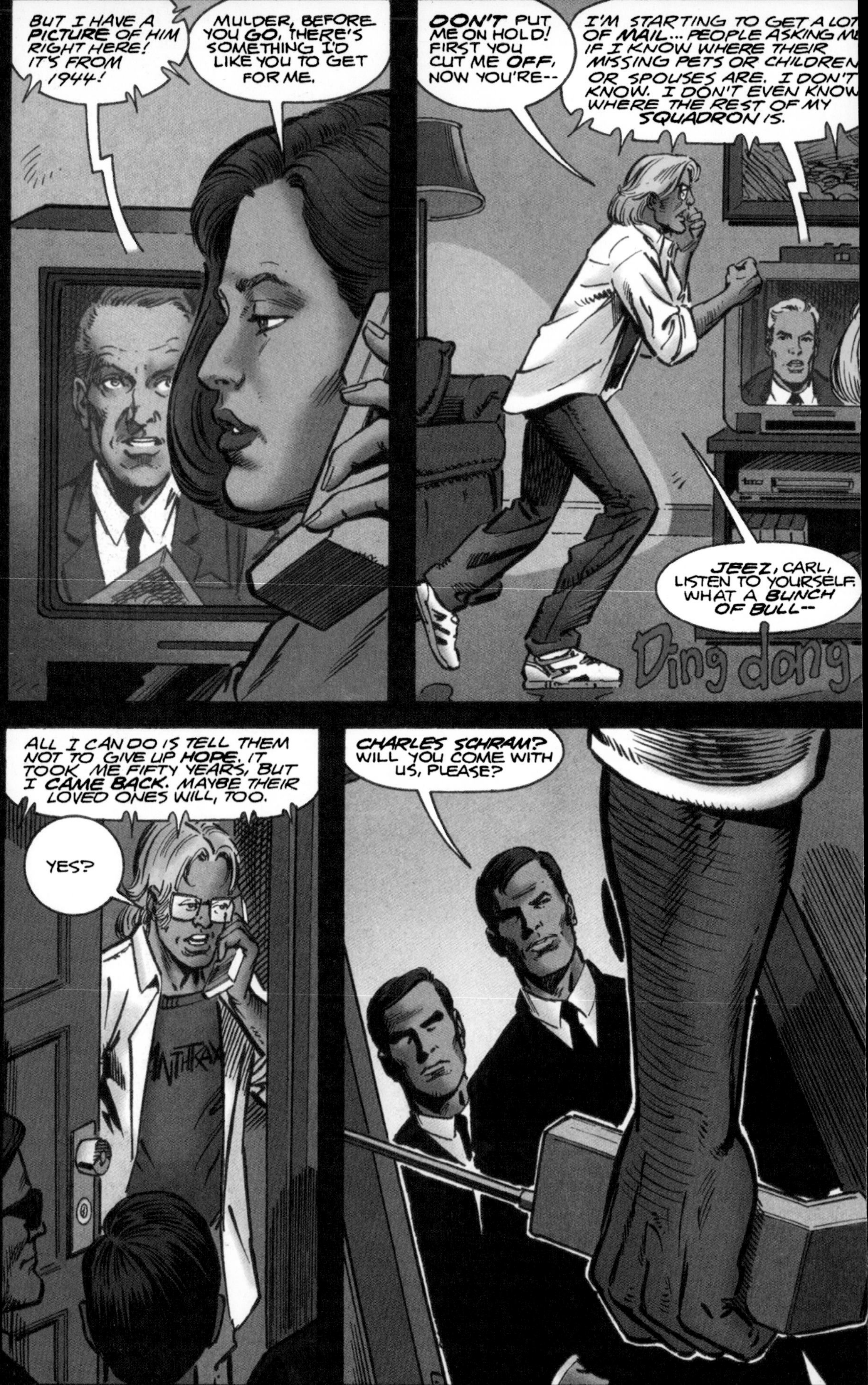
BUT I HAVE A PICTURE OF HIM RIGHT HERE! IT'S FROM 1944!
MULDER, BEFORE YOU GO, THERE'S SOMETHING I'D LIKE YOU TO GET FOR ME.
DON'T PUT ME ON HOLD! FIRST YOU CUT ME OFF, NOW YOU'RE--
I'M STARTING TO GET A LOT OF MAIL... PEOPLE ASKING M IF I KNOW WHERE THEIR MISSING PETS OR CHILDREN OR SPOUSES ARE. I DON'T KNOW. I DON'T EVEN KNOW WHERE THE REST OF MY SQUADRON IS.
JEEZ, CARL, LISTEN TO YOURSELF. WHAT A BUNCH OF BULL--
Ding dong
ALL I CAN DO IS TELL THEM NOT TO GIVE UP HOPE. IT TOOK ME FIFTY YEARS, BUT I CAME BACK. MAYBE THEIR LOVED ONES WILL, TOO.
YES?
CHARLES SCHRAM? WILL YOU COME WITH US, PLEASE?

AT *FIRST GLANCE*, THE SIGNATURE'S LOOK AS IF THEY COULD BE WRITTEN BY THE *SAME HAND*.

THE ONE IN THE PHOTOGRAPH IS MORE *CONTROLLED*, AS IF THE WRITER WERE PURPOSE-FULLY TRYING TO KEEP IT *LEGIBLE*.

THE MORE *RECENT* SIGNATURE LOOKS LIKE IT WAS WRITTEN IN A *HURRY*, BUT THERE ARE DEFINITE PLACES WHERE THE WRITER HESITATED AND WAS UNSURE OF HIMSELF.

THIS WOULD INDICATE THAT THE PERSON HAD BEEN PRACTICING TRYING TO *REPLICATE* THE ORIGINAL SIGNATURE AND WAS ABLE TO APPROXIMATE IT WELL ENOUGH TO FOOL THE *CASUAL OBSERVER*, BUT WAS NOT COM-FORTABLE ENOUGH TO DO IT WITHOUT THINKING ABOUT IT.

IF THIS GUY *REALLY* SPENT THE LAST FIFTY YEARS IN A UFO LIKE HE CLAIMS, THEN THERE MIGHT NOT HAVE BEEN...

...MUCH NEED FOR HIM TO SIGN HIS NAME. HE MAY HAVE JUST *FORGOTTEN*.

THE *ORIGINALS* ARE IN THIS ENVELOPE.

THANKS, MARTHA.

SIGN HERE X *John Law...*

SIGN HERE *John...*

X *John Lawre...*

John Lawren...

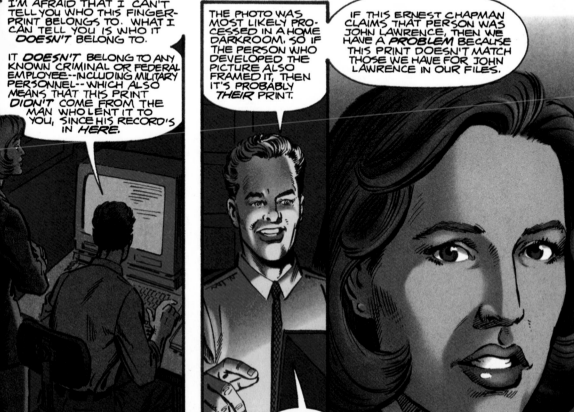

I'M AFRAID THAT I CAN'T TELL YOU WHO THIS FINGER-PRINT BELONGS TO. WHAT I CAN TELL YOU IS WHO IT *DOESN'T* BELONG TO.

IT *DOESN'T* BELONG TO ANY KNOWN CRIMINAL OR FEDERAL EMPLOYEE--INCLUDING MILITARY PERSONNEL--WHICH ALSO MEANS THAT THIS PRINT *DIDN'T* COME FROM THE MAN WHO LENT IT TO YOU, SINCE HIS RECORD'S IN *HERE*.

THE PHOTO WAS MOST LIKELY PRO-CESSED IN A HOME DARKROOM, SO IF THE PERSON WHO DEVELOPED THE PICTURE ALSO FRAMED IT, THEN IT'S PROBABLY *THEIR* PRINT.

IF THIS ERNEST CHAPMAN CLAIMS THAT PERSON WAS JOHN LAWRENCE, THEN WE HAVE A *PROBLEM* BECAUSE THIS PRINT DOESN'T MATCH THOSE WE HAVE FOR JOHN LAWRENCE IN OUR FILES.

I'M *SORRY* I COULDN'T BE MORE HELPFUL.

NO. ACTUALLY, YOU'VE BEEN *VERY CAREFUL*.

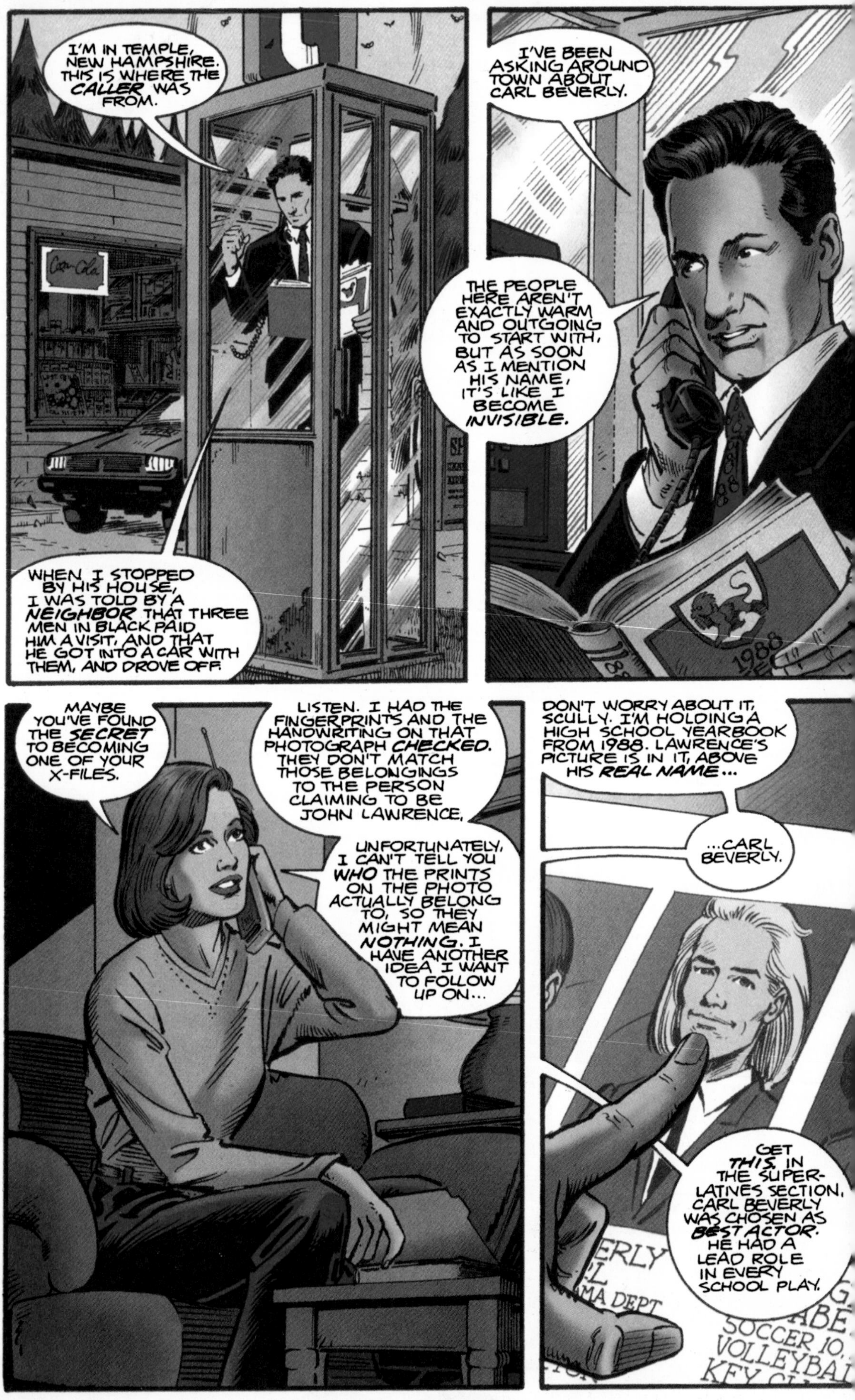
I'M IN TEMPLE, NEW HAMPSHIRE. THIS IS WHERE THE *CALLER* WAS FROM.
WHEN I STOPPED BY HIS HOUSE, I WAS TOLD BY A *NEIGHBOR* THAT THREE MEN IN BLACK PAID HIM A VISIT, AND THAT HE GOT INTO A CAR WITH THEM, AND DROVE OFF.
I'VE BEEN ASKING AROUND TOWN ABOUT CARL BEVERLY.
THE PEOPLE HERE AREN'T EXACTLY WARM AND OUTGOING TO START WITH, BUT AS SOON AS I MENTION HIS NAME, IT'S LIKE I BECOME *INVISIBLE*.
1988
MAYBE YOU'VE FOUND THE *SECRET* TO BECOMING ONE OF YOUR X-FILES.
LISTEN. I HAD THE FINGERPRINTS AND THE HANDWRITING ON THAT PHOTOGRAPH *CHECKED*. THEY DON'T MATCH THOSE BELONGINGS TO THE PERSON CLAIMING TO BE JOHN LAWRENCE.
UNFORTUNATELY, I CAN'T TELL YOU *WHO* THE PRINTS ON THE PHOTO ACTUALLY BELONG TO, SO THEY MIGHT MEAN *NOTHING*. I HAVE ANOTHER IDEA I WANT TO FOLLOW UP ON...
DON'T WORRY ABOUT IT, SCULLY. I'M HOLDING A HIGH SCHOOL YEARBOOK FROM 1988. LAWRENCE'S PICTURE IS IN IT, ABOVE HIS *REAL NAME*...
...CARL BEVERLY.
GET *THIS*. IN THE SUPER-LATIVES SECTION, CARL BEVERLY WAS CHOSEN AS *BEST ACTOR*. HE HAD A LEAD ROLE IN EVERY SCHOOL PLAY.

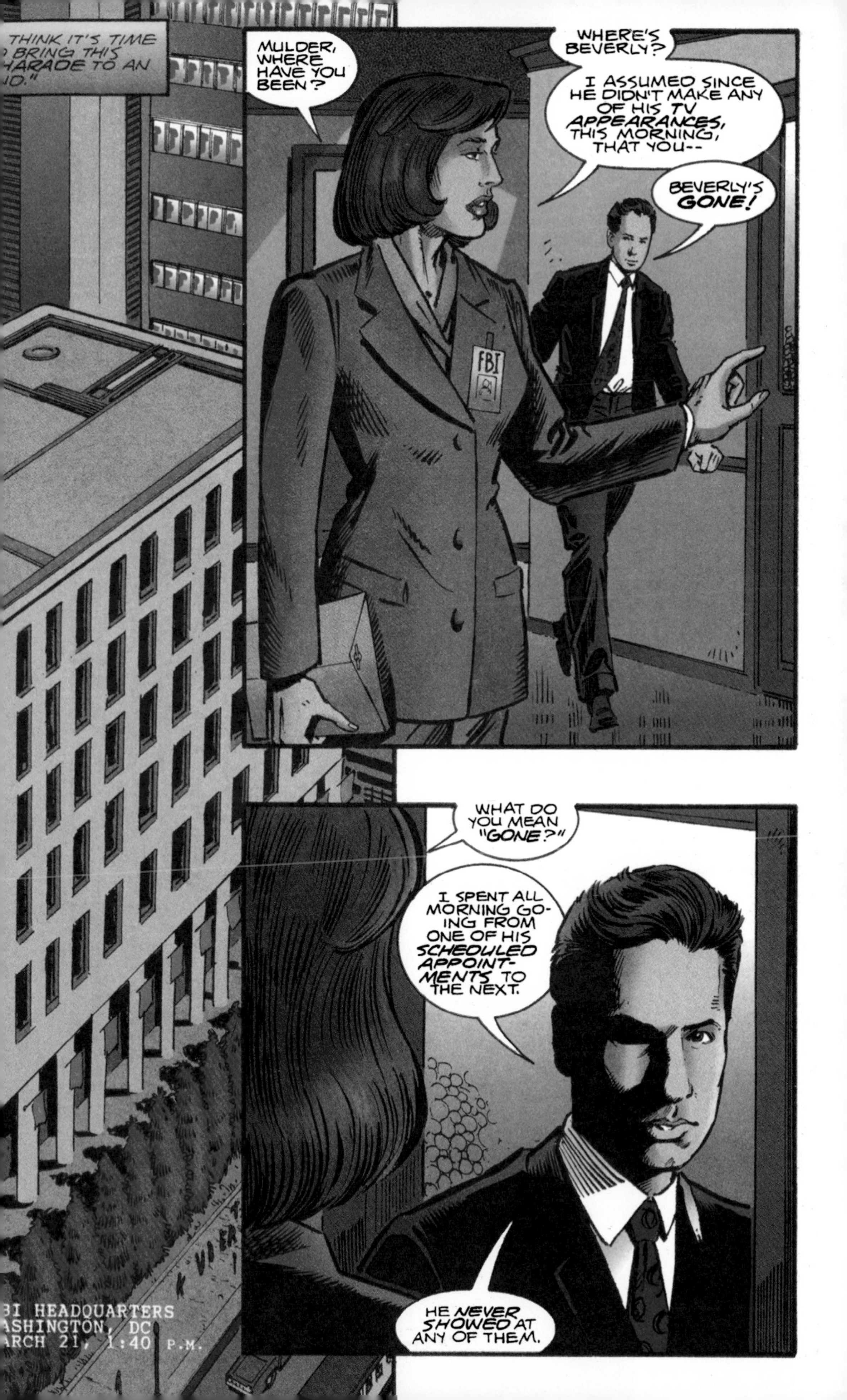
THINK IT'S TIME
BRING THIS
HARADE TO AN
ND."
BI HEADQUARTERS
ASHINGTON, DC
ARCH 21, 1:40 P.M.
MULDER, WHERE HAVE YOU BEEN?
WHERE'S BEVERLY?
I ASSUMED SINCE HE DIDN'T MAKE ANY OF HIS TV APPEARANCES, THIS MORNING, THAT YOU--
BEVERLY'S GONE!
WHAT DO YOU MEAN "GONE?"
I SPENT ALL MORNING GOING FROM ONE OF HIS SCHEDULED APPOINTMENTS TO THE NEXT.
HE NEVER SHOWED AT ANY OF THEM.

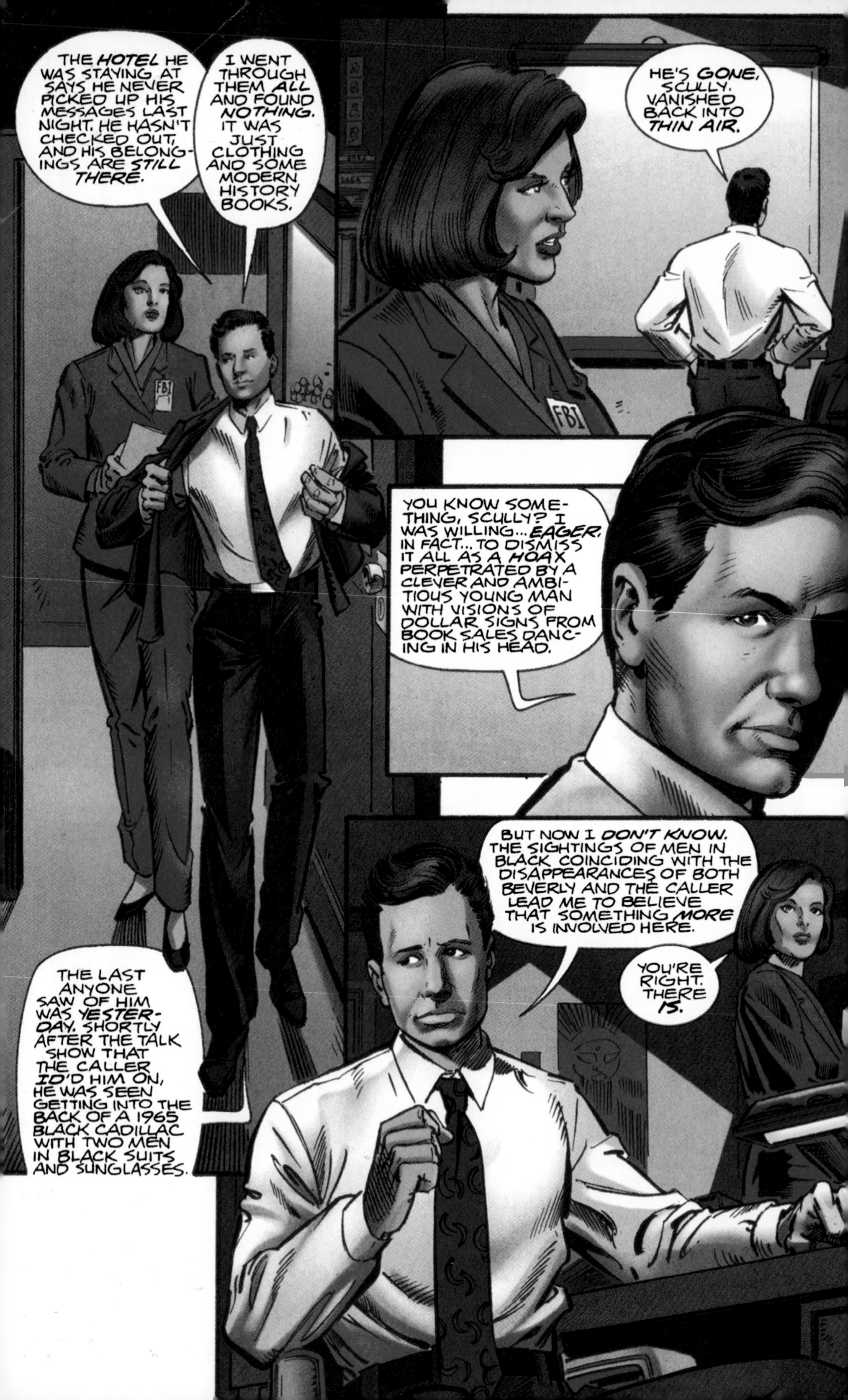
THE HOTEL HE WAS STAYING AT SAYS HE NEVER PICKED UP HIS MESSAGES LAST NIGHT. HE HASN'T CHECKED OUT, AND HIS BELONGINGS ARE STILL THERE.
I WENT THROUGH THEM ALL AND FOUND NOTHING. IT WAS JUST CLOTHING AND SOME MODERN HISTORY BOOKS.
THE LAST ANYONE SAW OF HIM WAS YESTERDAY. SHORTLY AFTER THE TALK SHOW THAT THE CALLER ID'D HIM ON, HE WAS SEEN GETTING INTO THE BACK OF A 1965 BLACK CADILLAC WITH TWO MEN IN BLACK SUITS AND SUNGLASSES.
HE'S GONE, SCULLY. VANISHED BACK INTO THIN AIR.
YOU KNOW SOMETHING, SCULLY? I WAS WILLING... EAGER, IN FACT... TO DISMISS IT ALL AS A HOAX PERPETRATED BY A CLEVER AND AMBITIOUS YOUNG MAN WITH VISIONS OF DOLLAR SIGNS FROM BOOK SALES DANCING IN HIS HEAD.
BUT NOW I DON'T KNOW. THE SIGHTINGS OF MEN IN BLACK COINCIDING WITH THE DISAPPEARANCES OF BOTH BEVERLY AND THE CALLER LEAD ME TO BELIEVE THAT SOMETHING MORE IS INVOLVED HERE.
YOU'RE RIGHT. THERE IS.

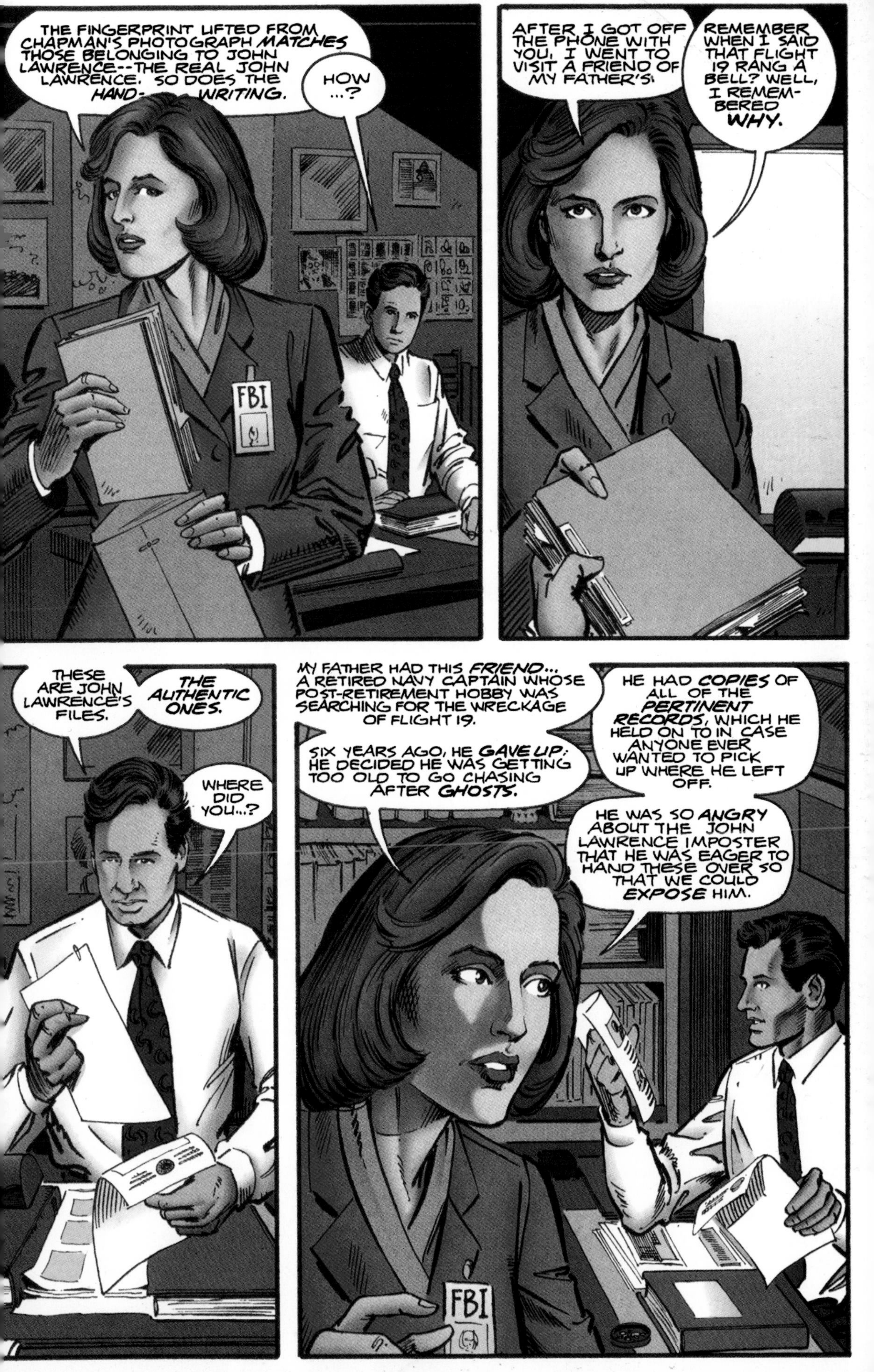
THE FINGERPRINT LIFTED FROM CHAPMAN'S PHOTOGRAPH *MATCHES* THOSE BELONGING TO JOHN LAWRENCE--THE REAL JOHN LAWRENCE. SO DOES THE *HAND-WRITING.*
HOW ...?
AFTER I GOT OFF THE PHONE WITH YOU, I WENT TO VISIT A FRIEND OF MY FATHER'S.
REMEMBER WHEN I SAID THAT FLIGHT 19 RANG A BELL? WELL, I REMEMBERED **WHY.**
THESE ARE JOHN LAWRENCE'S FILES.
THE AUTHENTIC ONES.
WHERE DID YOU...?
MY FATHER HAD THIS *FRIEND*... A RETIRED NAVY CAPTAIN WHOSE POST-RETIREMENT HOBBY WAS SEARCHING FOR THE WRECKAGE OF FLIGHT 19.
SIX YEARS AGO, HE *GAVE UP*: HE DECIDED HE WAS GETTING TOO OLD TO GO CHASING AFTER *GHOSTS.*
HE HAD *COPIES* OF ALL OF THE *PERTINENT RECORDS*, WHICH HE HELD ON TO IN CASE ANYONE EVER WANTED TO PICK UP WHERE HE LEFT OFF.
HE WAS SO *ANGRY* ABOUT THE JOHN LAWRENCE IMPOSTER THAT HE WAS EAGER TO HAND THESE OVER SO THAT WE COULD *EXPOSE* HIM.

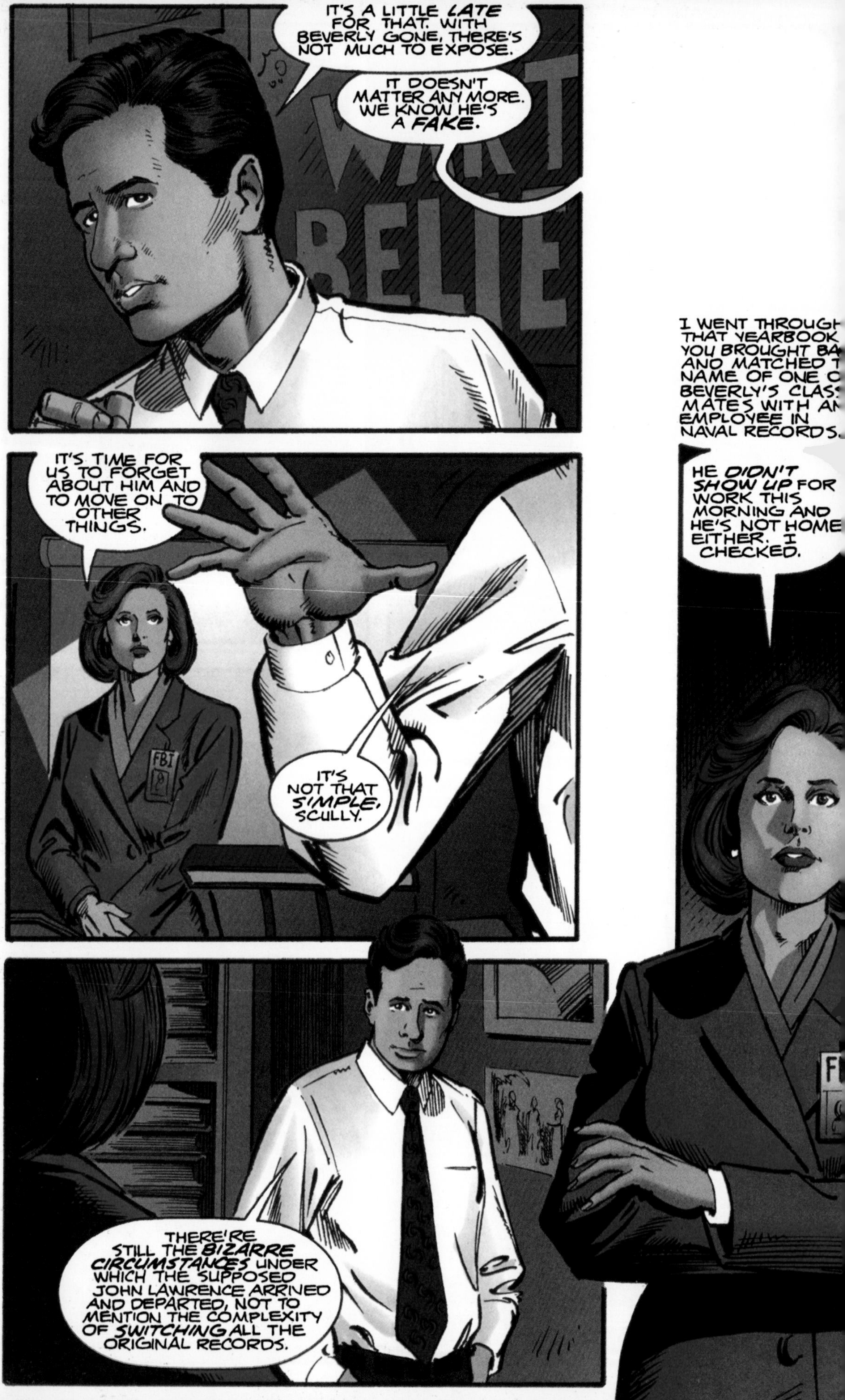
IT'S A LITTLE LATE FOR THAT. WITH BEVERLY GONE, THERE'S NOT MUCH TO EXPOSE.
IT DOESN'T MATTER ANY MORE. WE KNOW HE'S A FAKE.
IT'S TIME FOR US TO FORGET ABOUT HIM AND TO MOVE ON TO OTHER THINGS.
IT'S NOT THAT SIMPLE, SCULLY.
THERE'RE STILL THE BIZARRE CIRCUMSTANCES UNDER WHICH THE SUPPOSED JOHN LAWRENCE ARRIVED AND DEPARTED, NOT TO MENTION THE COMPLEXITY OF SWITCHING ALL THE ORIGINAL RECORDS.
I WENT THROUGH THAT YEARBOOK YOU BROUGHT BA AND MATCHED T NAME OF ONE O BEVERLY'S CLAS MATES WITH AN EMPLOYEE IN NAVAL RECORDS.
HE DIDN'T SHOW UP FOR WORK THIS MORNING AND HE'S NOT HOME EITHER. I CHECKED.

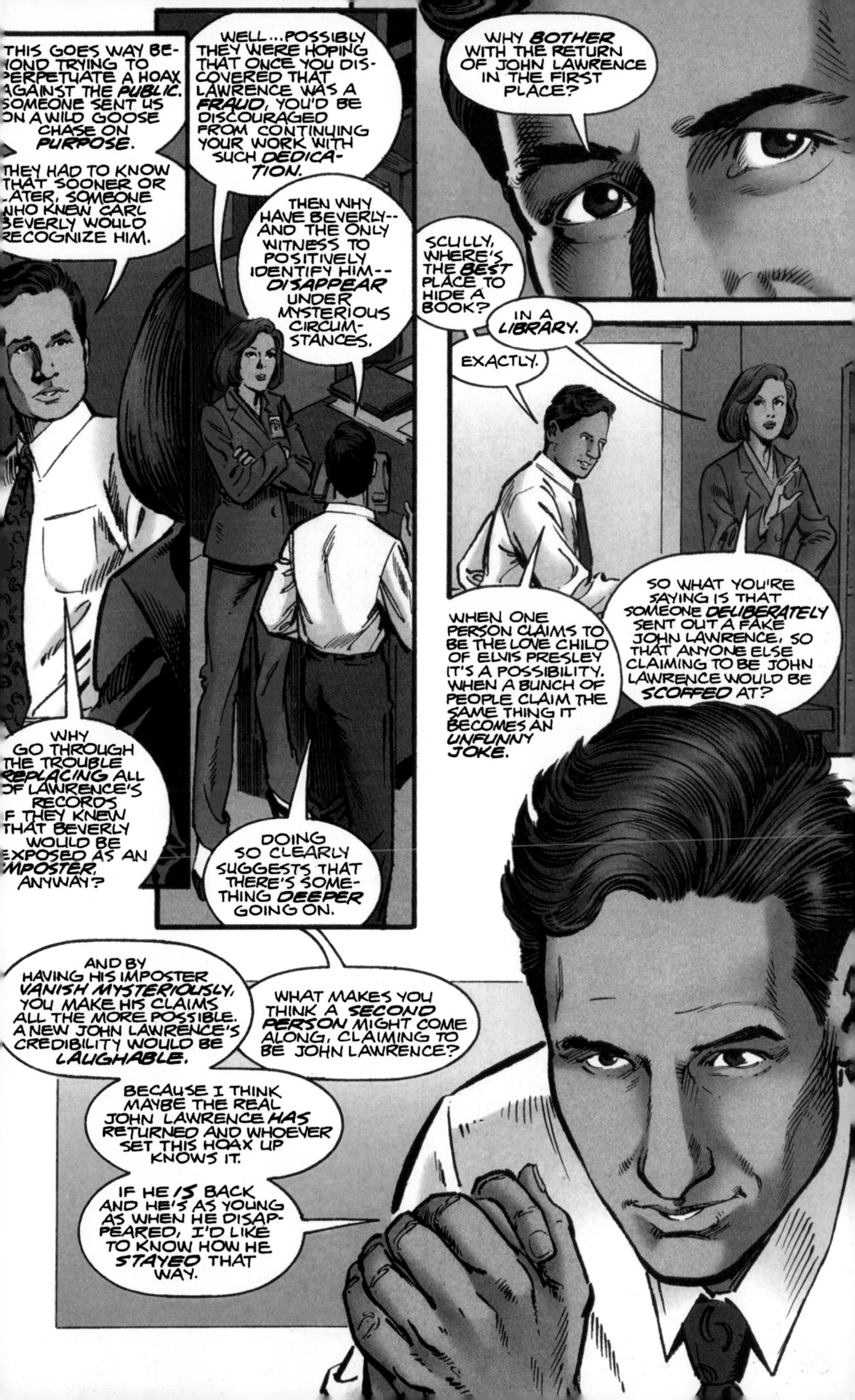

THIS GOES WAY BEYOND TRYING TO PERPETUATE A HOAX AGAINST THE PUBLIC. SOMEONE SENT US ON A WILD GOOSE CHASE ON PURPOSE.
THEY HAD TO KNOW THAT SOONER OR LATER, SOMEONE WHO KNEW CARL BEVERLY WOULD RECOGNIZE HIM.
WELL...POSSIBLY THEY WERE HOPING THAT ONCE YOU DISCOVERED THAT LAWRENCE WAS A FRAUD, YOU'D BE DISCOURAGED FROM CONTINUING YOUR WORK WITH SUCH DEDICATION.
THEN WHY HAVE BEVERLY-- AND THE ONLY WITNESS TO POSITIVELY IDENTIFY HIM-- DISAPPEAR UNDER MYSTERIOUS CIRCUMSTANCES.
WHY GO THROUGH THE TROUBLE REPLACING ALL OF LAWRENCE'S RECORDS IF THEY KNEW THAT BEVERLY WOULD BE EXPOSED AS AN IMPOSTER, ANYWAY?
DOING SO CLEARLY SUGGESTS THAT THERE'S SOMETHING DEEPER GOING ON.
WHY BOTHER WITH THE RETURN OF JOHN LAWRENCE IN THE FIRST PLACE?
SCULLY, WHERE'S THE BEST PLACE TO HIDE A BOOK?
IN A LIBRARY.
EXACTLY.
WHEN ONE PERSON CLAIMS TO BE THE LOVE CHILD OF ELVIS PRESLEY IT'S A POSSIBILITY. WHEN A BUNCH OF PEOPLE CLAIM THE SAME THING IT BECOMES AN UNFUNNY JOKE.
SO WHAT YOU'RE SAYING IS THAT SOMEONE DELIBERATELY SENT OUT A FAKE JOHN LAWRENCE, SO THAT ANYONE ELSE CLAIMING TO BE JOHN LAWRENCE WOULD BE SCOFFED AT?
AND BY HAVING HIS IMPOSTER VANISH MYSTERIOUSLY, YOU MAKE HIS CLAIMS ALL THE MORE POSSIBLE. A NEW JOHN LAWRENCE'S CREDIBILITY WOULD BE LAUGHABLE.
WHAT MAKES YOU THINK A SECOND PERSON MIGHT COME ALONG, CLAIMING TO BE JOHN LAWRENCE?
BECAUSE I THINK MAYBE THE REAL JOHN LAWRENCE HAS RETURNED AND WHOEVER SET THIS HOAX UP KNOWS IT.
IF HE IS BACK AND HE'S AS YOUNG AS WHEN HE DISAPPEARED, I'D LIKE TO KNOW HOW HE STAYED THAT WAY.

IT WASN'T UNTIL THAT POINT THAT I TRULY UNDERSTOOD MULDER'S UNFLAGGING INTEREST IN THE JOHN LAWRENCE MYSTERY. IT GAVE HIM HOPE. DURING HIS SEARCH FOR HIS MISSING SISTER, MULDER HAD BEEN FEELING THE CONSTANT PRESSURE OF A TICKING CLOCK. HE WAS RACING AGAINST TIME.

IF LAWRENCE HAD REALLY BEEN ABDUCTED AND RE-TURNED UNAGED AFTER HAVING BEEN MISSING FOR 51 YEARS, THEN WHY WOULDN'T THE SAME HOLD FOR SAMANTHA WHO'S ONLY BEEN MISSING FOR THIRTEEN?

IF SHE RETURNED AS A NINE-YEAR-OLD GIRL, SHE'D FINALLY GET TO EXPERIENCE THE CHILDHOOD OF WHICH SHE WAS ROBBED. SHE'D RETURN AS THE SISTER MULDER REMEMBERED LOSING.

I LEAVE MY SKEPTICIS[M] UNSPOKEN. MULDER NEEDS HIS FAITH.

BUT IF LAWRENCE HAS TRULY RETURNED, THERE'S BEEN NO SIGN, AND NEITHER OF US HAS ANY IDEA WHERE TO LOOK.

...UNDERSTAND YOUR DESIRES TO RETURN HOME AND TO SEE YOUR FAMILIES. I MUST ASK YOU TO CONTINUE YOUR PATIENCE. THERE IS STILL MUCH YOU MUST LEARN AND PREPARE FOR BEFORE YOU ARE RETURNED TO THE WORLD. DISMISSED.

EVERY ONE OF THEM IS ACCOUNTED FOR. THE ENTIRE FLIGHT.

SO HOW LONG DO YOU THINK BEFORE THEY CAN GO HOME?

HOME?

THEY CAN NEVER BE ALLOWED TO LEAVE.

FROM NOW ON, THIS IS THEIR HOME.

Taylor,
Powers, Edward J.
Gerber, For[rest] J.
Stivers
Lawrenc[e]
Bossi, J[o]
Swan

THE END

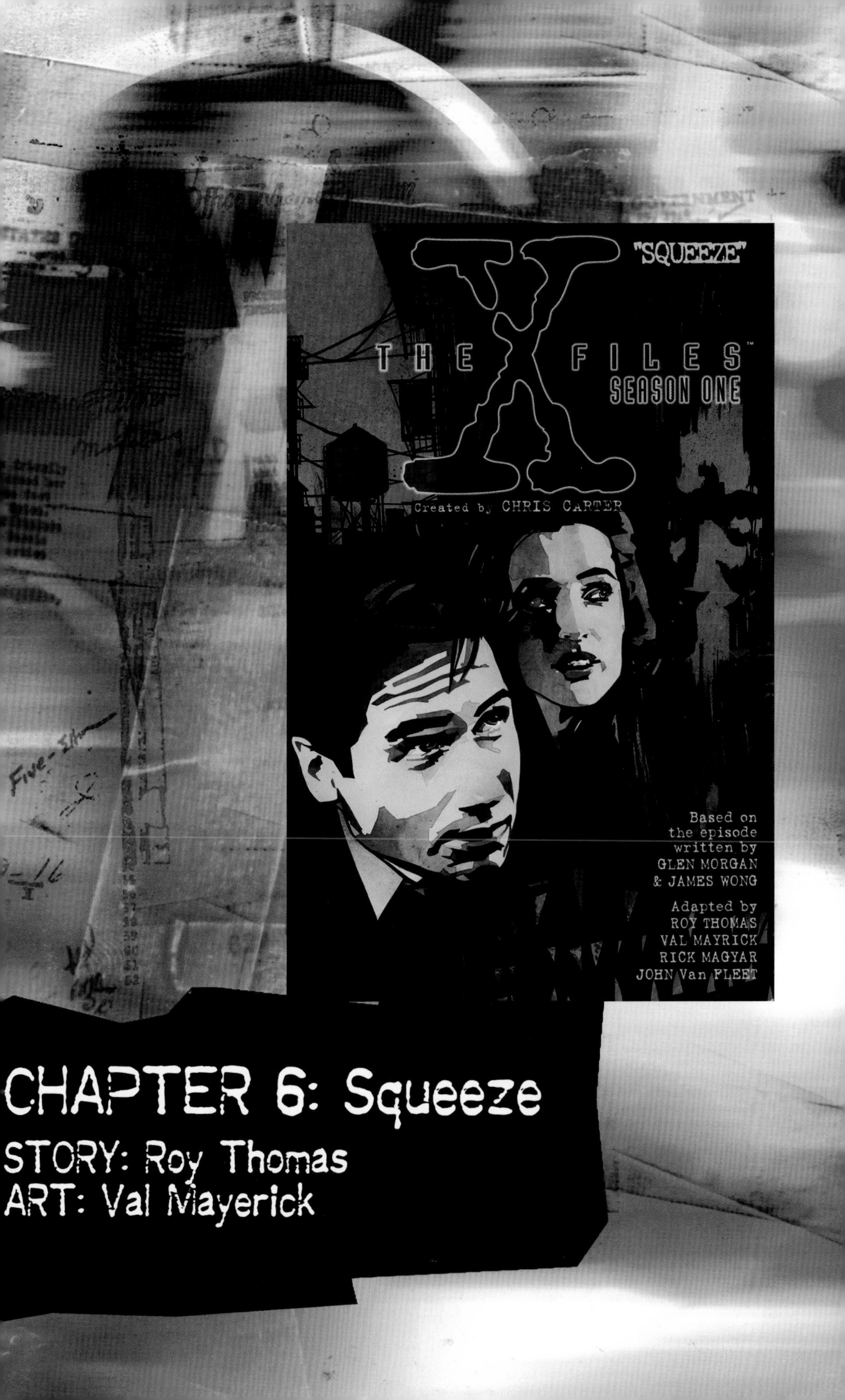
"SQUEEZE"
THE X FILES™
SEASON ONE
Created by CHRIS CARTER
Based on the episode written by GLEN MORGAN & JAMES WONG
Adapted by ROY THOMAS VAL MAYRICK RICK MAGYAR JOHN Van FLEET

CHAPTER 6: Squeeze

STORY: Roy Thomas
ART: Val Mayerick

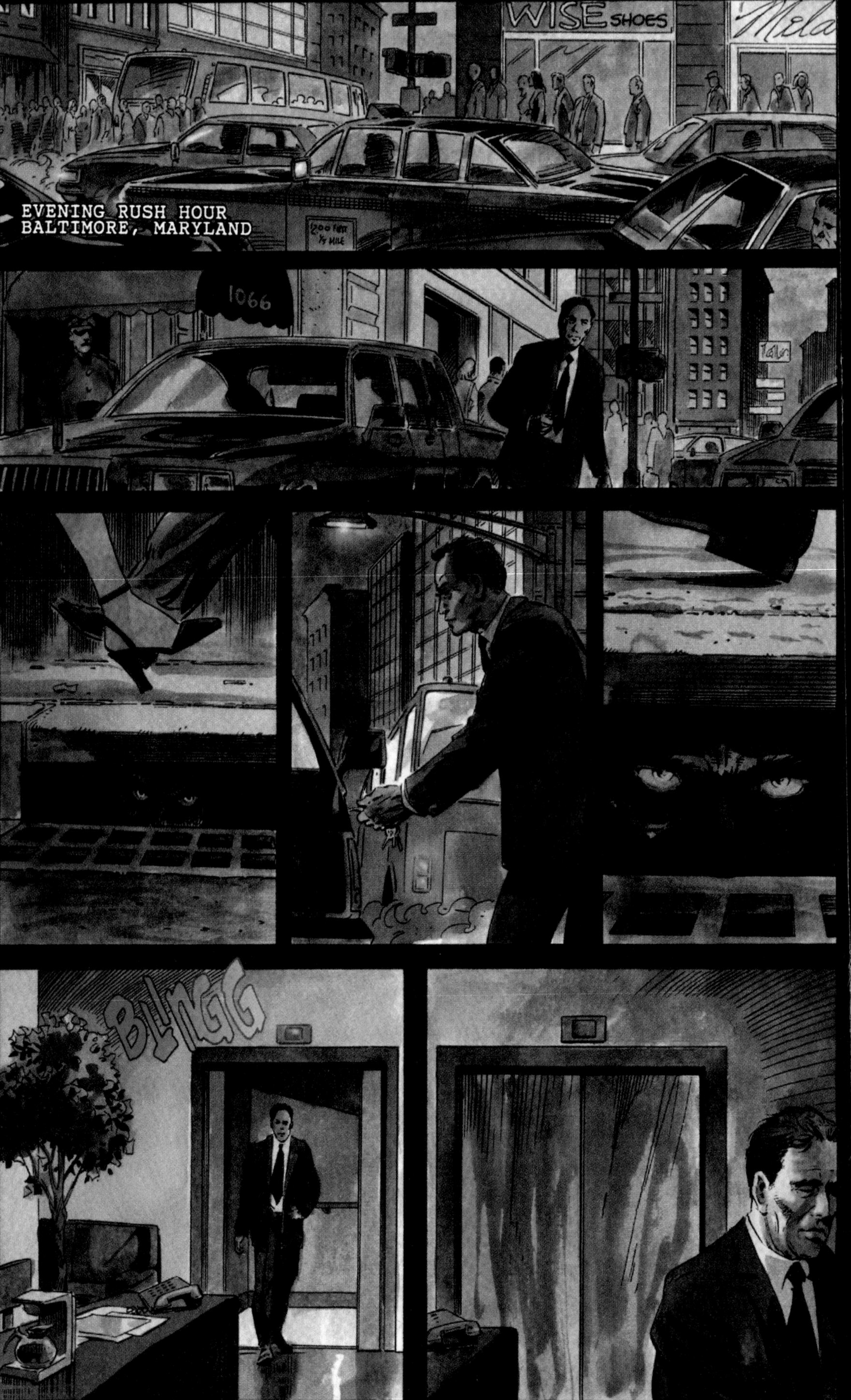
EVENING RUSH HOUR
BALTIMORE, MARYLAND
WISE SHOES
1066
BLNGG

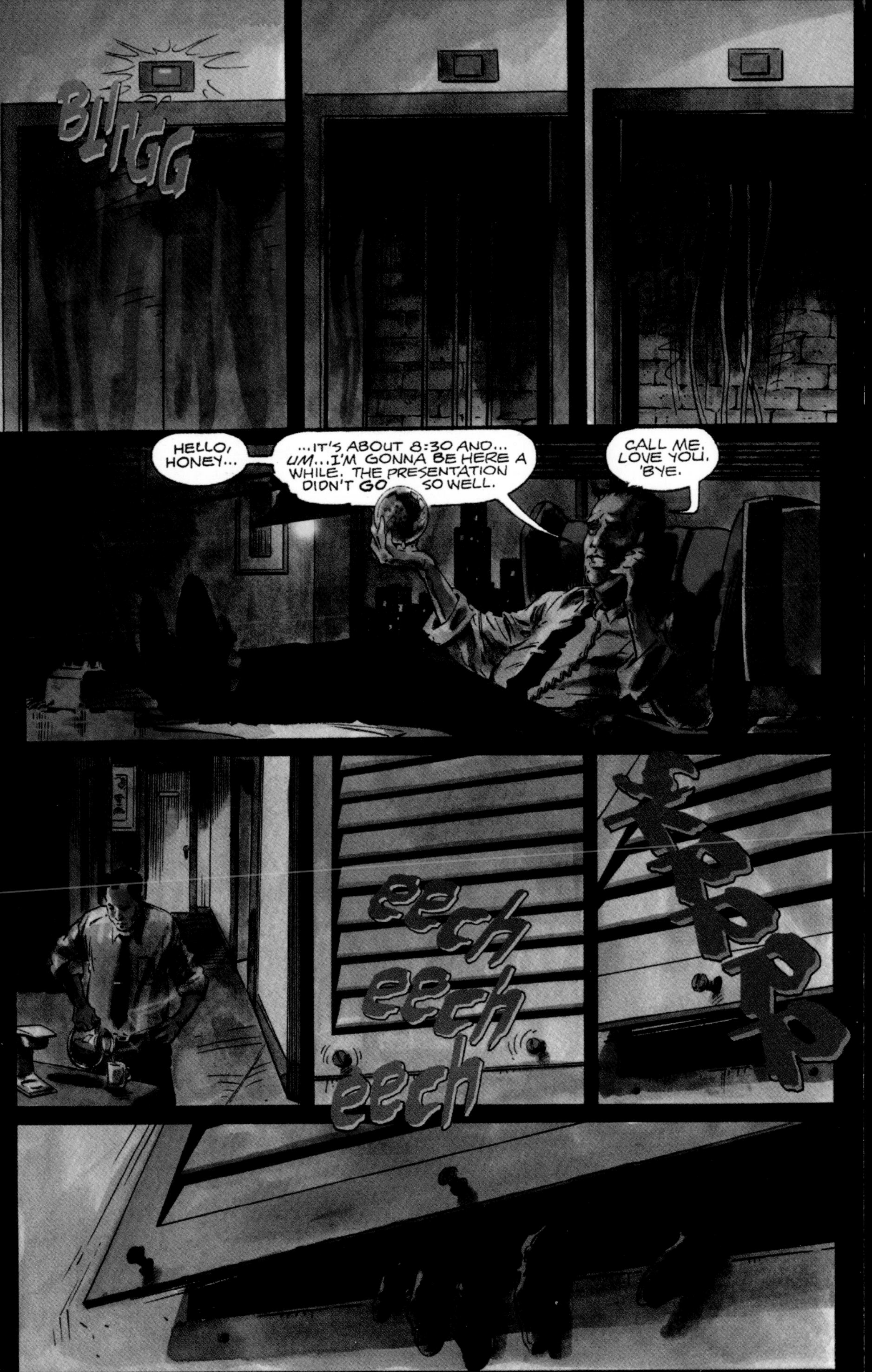
BLIIGG
HELLO, HONEY...
...IT'S ABOUT 8:30 AND... UM...I'M GONNA BE HERE A WHILE. THE PRESENTATION DIDN'T GO SO WELL.
CALL ME. LOVE YOU. 'BYE.
eech eech eech

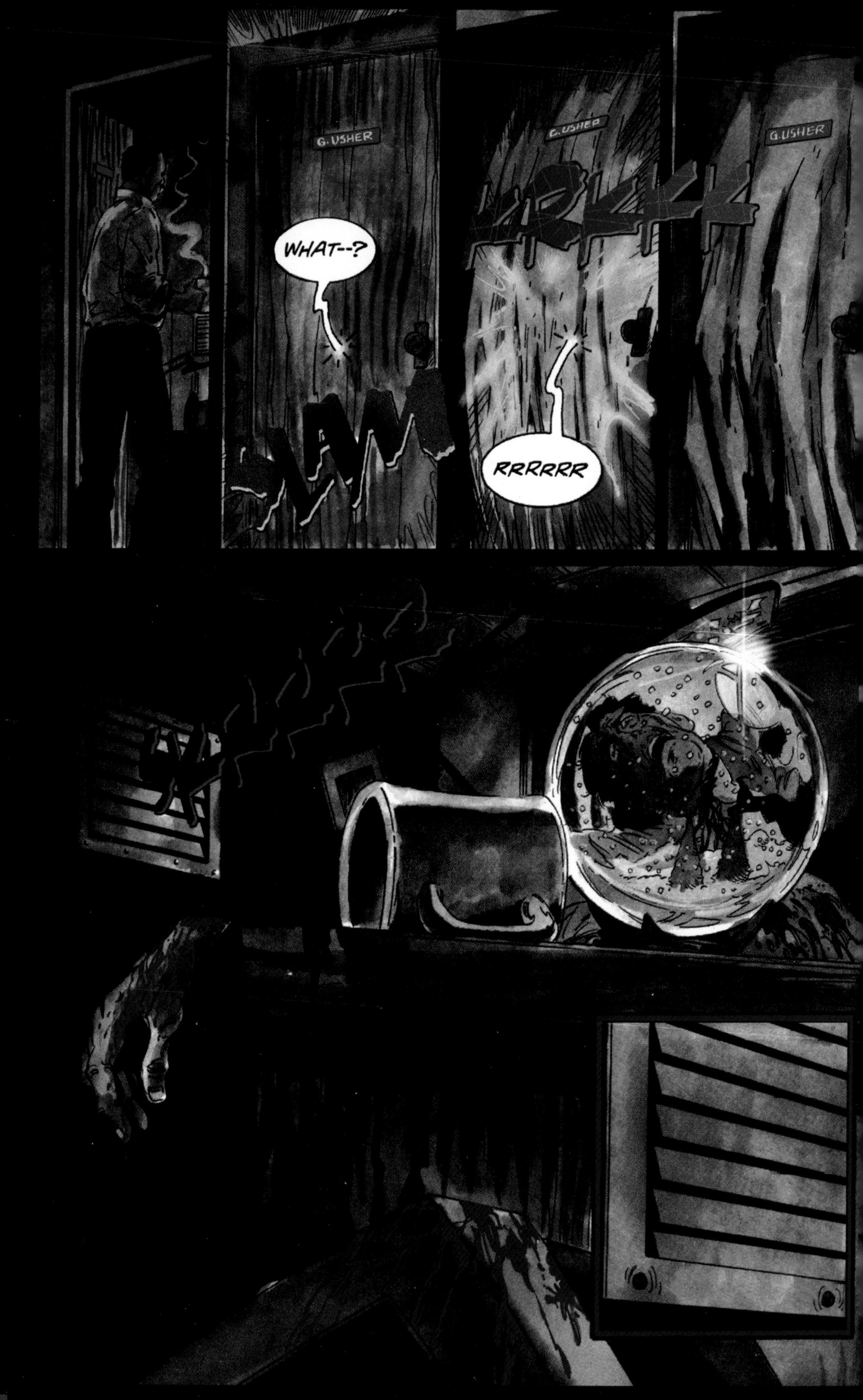
G. USHER
WHAT--?
G. USHER
RRRRRR
G. USHER

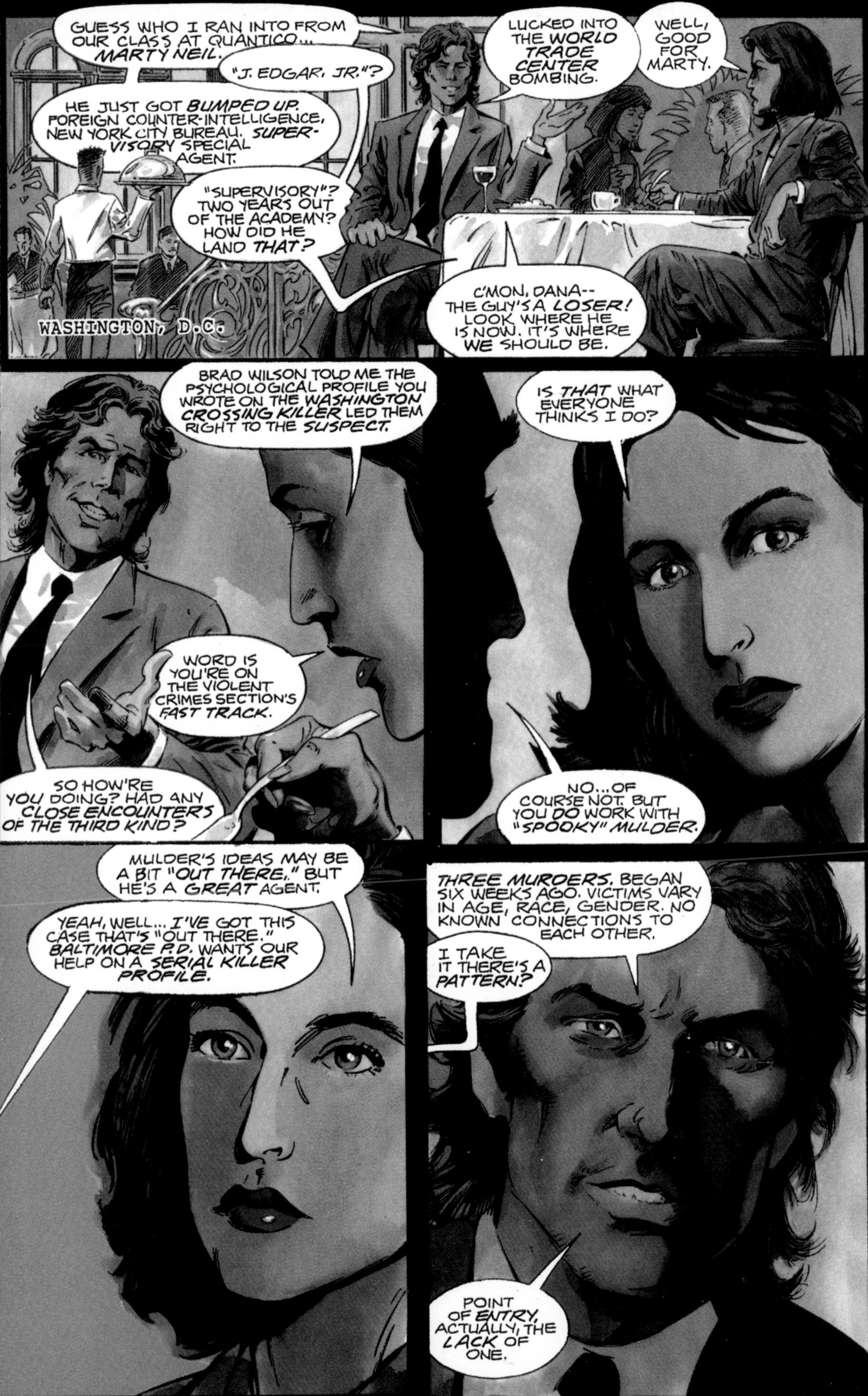
GUESS WHO I RAN INTO FROM OUR CLASS AT QUANTICO... MARTY NEIL.
"J. EDGAR, JR."?
HE JUST GOT BUMPED UP. FOREIGN COUNTER-INTELLIGENCE, NEW YORK CITY BUREAU. SUPER-VISORY SPECIAL AGENT.
LUCKED INTO THE WORLD TRADE CENTER BOMBING.
WELL, GOOD FOR MARTY.
"SUPERVISORY"? TWO YEARS OUT OF THE ACADEMY? HOW DID HE LAND THAT?
C'MON, DANA-- THE GUY'S A LOSER! LOOK WHERE HE IS NOW. IT'S WHERE WE SHOULD BE.
WASHINGTON, D.C.
BRAD WILSON TOLD ME THE PSYCHOLOGICAL PROFILE YOU WROTE ON THE WASHINGTON CROSSING KILLER LED THEM RIGHT TO THE SUSPECT.
WORD IS YOU'RE ON THE VIOLENT CRIMES SECTION'S FAST TRACK.
SO HOW'RE YOU DOING? HAD ANY CLOSE ENCOUNTERS OF THE THIRD KIND?
IS THAT WHAT EVERYONE THINKS I DO?
NO... OF COURSE NOT. BUT YOU DO WORK WITH "SPOOKY" MULDER.
MULDER'S IDEAS MAY BE A BIT "OUT THERE," BUT HE'S A GREAT AGENT.
YEAH, WELL... I'VE GOT THIS CASE THAT'S "OUT THERE." BALTIMORE P.D. WANTS OUR HELP ON A SERIAL KILLER PROFILE.
THREE MURDERS. BEGAN SIX WEEKS AGO. VICTIMS VARY IN AGE, RACE, GENDER. NO KNOWN CONNECTIONS TO EACH OTHER.
I TAKE IT THERE'S A PATTERN?
POINT OF ENTRY. ACTUALLY, THE LACK OF ONE.

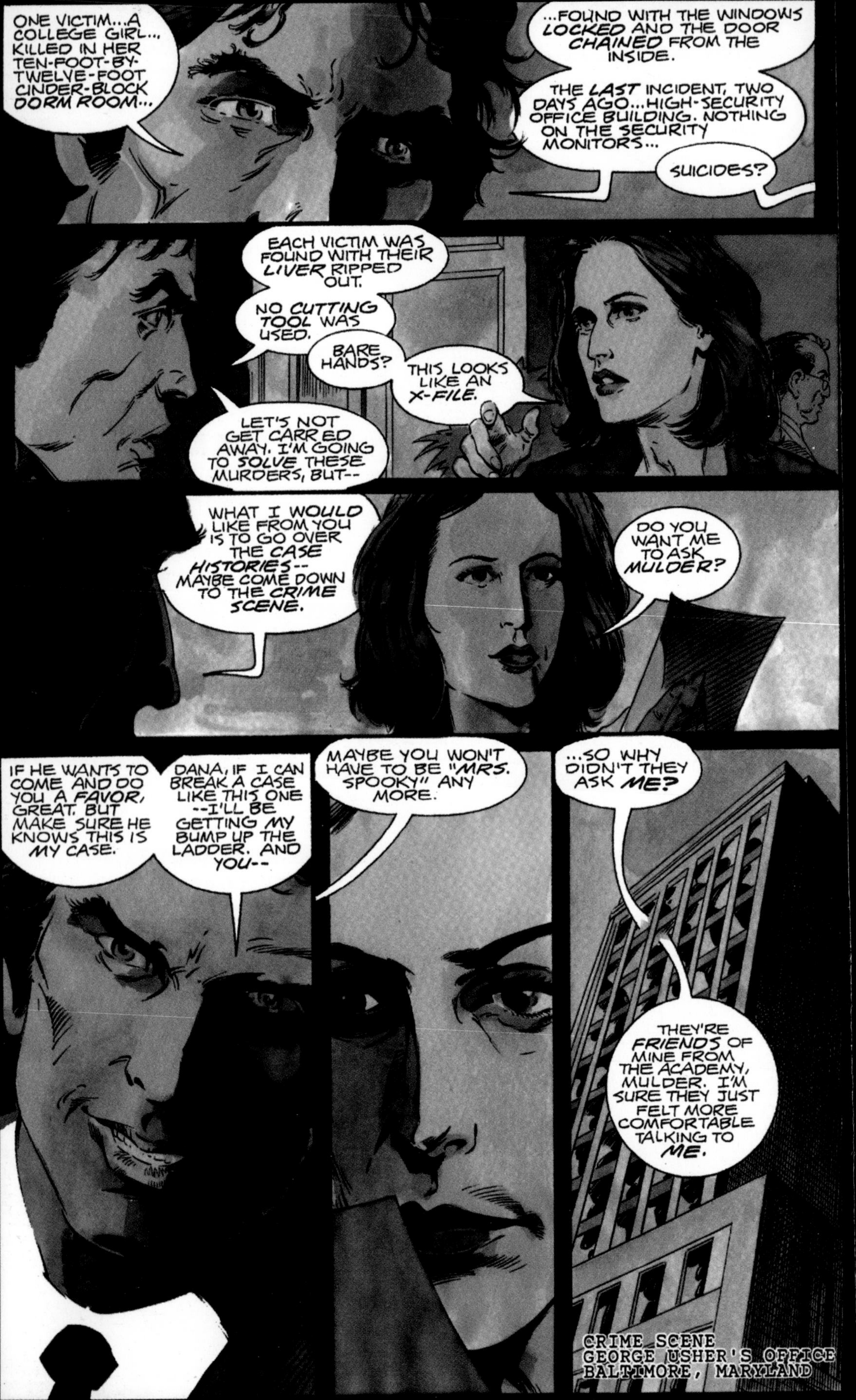
ONE VICTIM...A COLLEGE GIRL... KILLED IN HER TEN-FOOT-BY-TWELVE-FOOT CINDER-BLOCK DORM ROOM...
...FOUND WITH THE WINDOWS LOCKED AND THE DOOR CHAINED FROM THE INSIDE.
THE LAST INCIDENT, TWO DAYS AGO...HIGH-SECURITY OFFICE BUILDING. NOTHING ON THE SECURITY MONITORS...
SUICIDES?
EACH VICTIM WAS FOUND WITH THEIR LIVER RIPPED OUT.
NO CUTTING TOOL WAS USED.
BARE HANDS?
THIS LOOKS LIKE AN X-FILE.
LET'S NOT GET CARR ED AWAY. I'M GOING TO SOLVE THESE MURDERS, BUT--
WHAT I WOULD LIKE FROM YOU IS TO GO OVER THE CASE HISTORIES-- MAYBE COME DOWN TO THE CRIME SCENE.
DO YOU WANT ME TO ASK MULDER?
IF HE WANTS TO COME AND DO YOU A FAVOR, GREAT. BUT MAKE SURE HE KNOWS THIS IS MY CASE.
DANA, IF I CAN BREAK A CASE LIKE THIS ONE --I'LL BE GETTING MY BUMP UP THE LADDER. AND YOU--
MAYBE YOU WON'T HAVE TO BE "MRS. SPOOKY" ANY MORE.
...SO WHY DIDN'T THEY ASK ME?
THEY'RE FRIENDS OF MINE FROM THE ACADEMY, MULDER. I'M SURE THEY JUST FELT MORE COMFORTABLE TALKING TO ME.
CRIME SCENE
GEORGE USHER'S OFFICE
BALTIMORE, MARYLAND

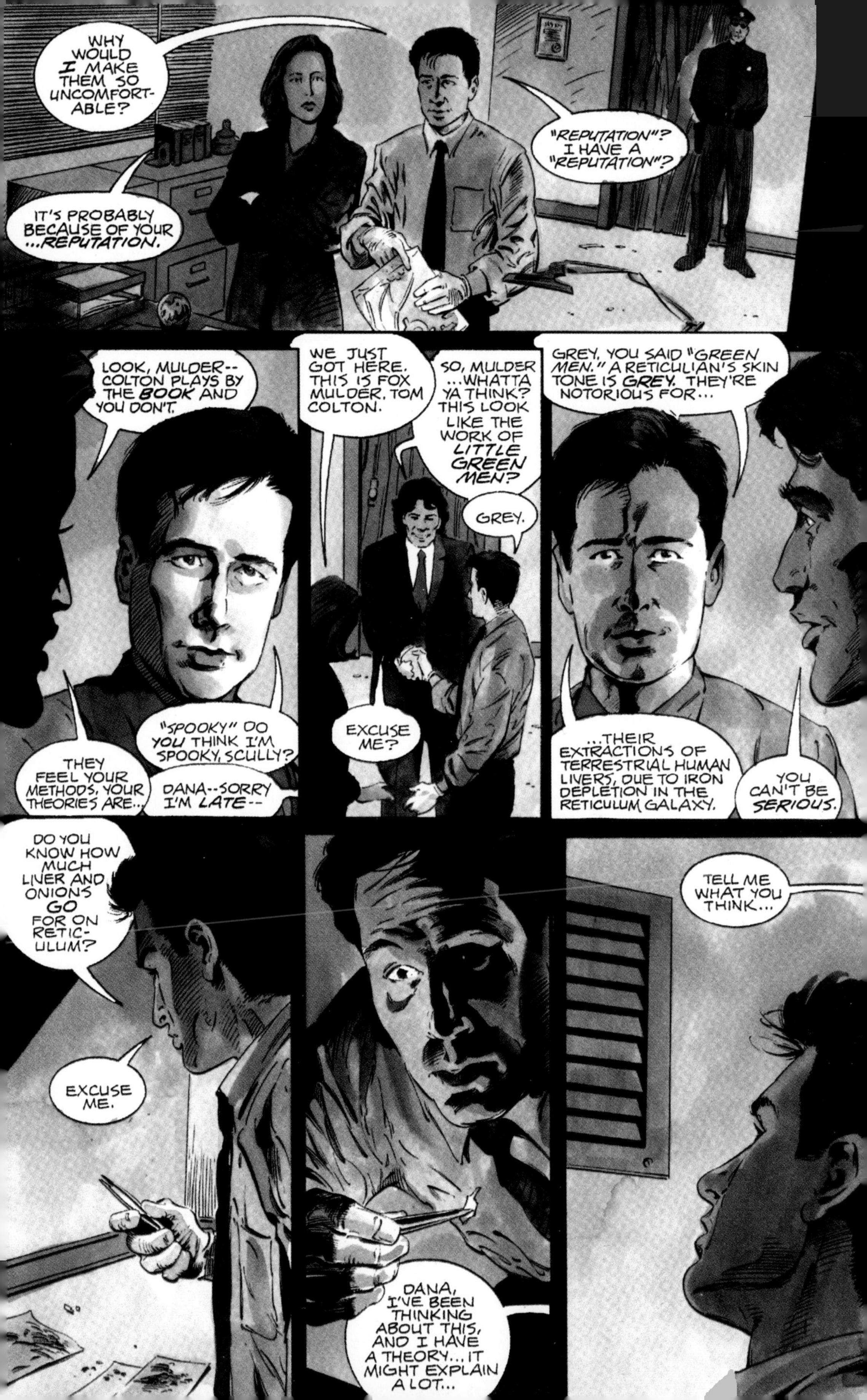
WHY WOULD I MAKE THEM SO UNCOMFORTABLE?
IT'S PROBABLY BECAUSE OF YOUR ...REPUTATION.
"REPUTATION"? I HAVE A "REPUTATION"?
LOOK, MULDER-- COLTON PLAYS BY THE BOOK AND YOU DON'T.
THEY FEEL YOUR METHODS, YOUR THEORIES ARE...
"SPOOKY" DO YOU THINK I'M SPOOKY, SCULLY?
DANA--SORRY I'M LATE--
WE JUST GOT HERE. THIS IS FOX MULDER. TOM COLTON.
SO, MULDER ...WHATTA YA THINK? THIS LOOK LIKE THE WORK OF LITTLE GREEN MEN?
GREY.
EXCUSE ME?
GREY. YOU SAID "GREEN MEN." A RETICULIAN'S SKIN TONE IS GREY. THEY'RE NOTORIOUS FOR...
...THEIR EXTRACTIONS OF TERRESTRIAL HUMAN LIVERS, DUE TO IRON DEPLETION IN THE RETICULUM GALAXY.
YOU CAN'T BE SERIOUS.
DO YOU KNOW HOW MUCH LIVER AND ONIONS GO FOR ON RETIC-ULUM?
EXCUSE ME.
DANA, I'VE BEEN THINKING ABOUT THIS, AND I HAVE A THEORY... IT MIGHT EXPLAIN A LOT...
TELL ME WHAT YOU THINK...

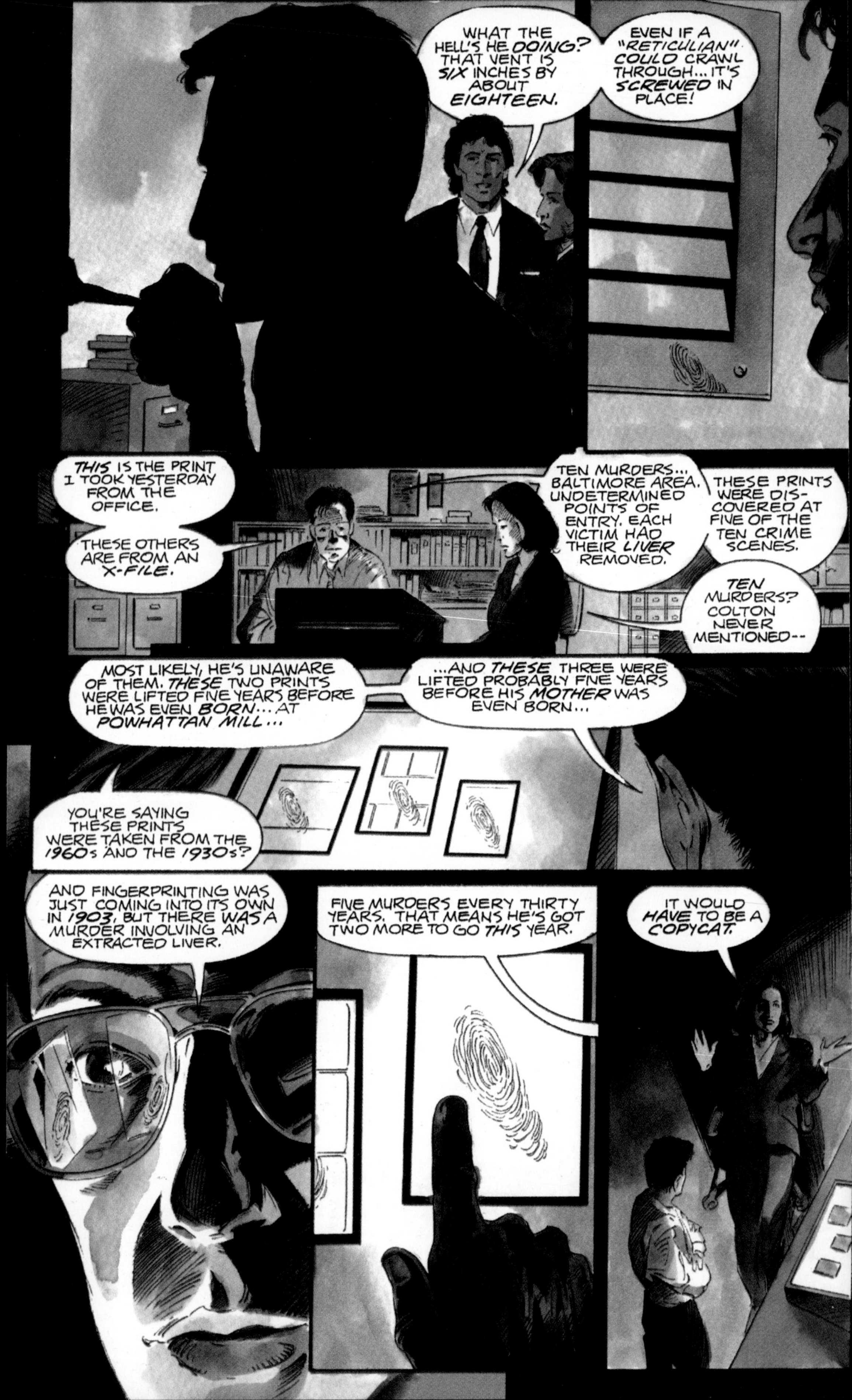
WHAT THE HELL'S HE DOING? THAT VENT IS SIX INCHES BY ABOUT EIGHTEEN.
EVEN IF A "RETICULIAN" COULD CRAWL THROUGH... IT'S SCREWED IN PLACE!
THIS IS THE PRINT I TOOK YESTERDAY FROM THE OFFICE.
THESE OTHERS ARE FROM AN X-FILE.
TEN MURDERS... BALTIMORE AREA. UNDETERMINED POINTS OF ENTRY. EACH VICTIM HAD THEIR LIVER REMOVED.
THESE PRINTS WERE DISCOVERED AT FIVE OF THE TEN CRIME SCENES.
TEN MURDERS? COLTON NEVER MENTIONED--
MOST LIKELY, HE'S UNAWARE OF THEM. THESE TWO PRINTS WERE LIFTED FIVE YEARS BEFORE HE WAS EVEN BORN... AT POWHATTAN MILL...
...AND THESE THREE WERE LIFTED PROBABLY FIVE YEARS BEFORE HIS MOTHER WAS EVEN BORN...
YOU'RE SAYING THESE PRINTS WERE TAKEN FROM THE 1960s AND THE 1930s?
AND FINGERPRINTING WAS JUST COMING INTO ITS OWN IN 1903, BUT THERE WAS A MURDER INVOLVING AN EXTRACTED LIVER.
FIVE MURDERS EVERY THIRTY YEARS. THAT MEANS HE'S GOT TWO MORE TO GO THIS YEAR.
IT WOULD HAVE TO BE A COPYCAT.

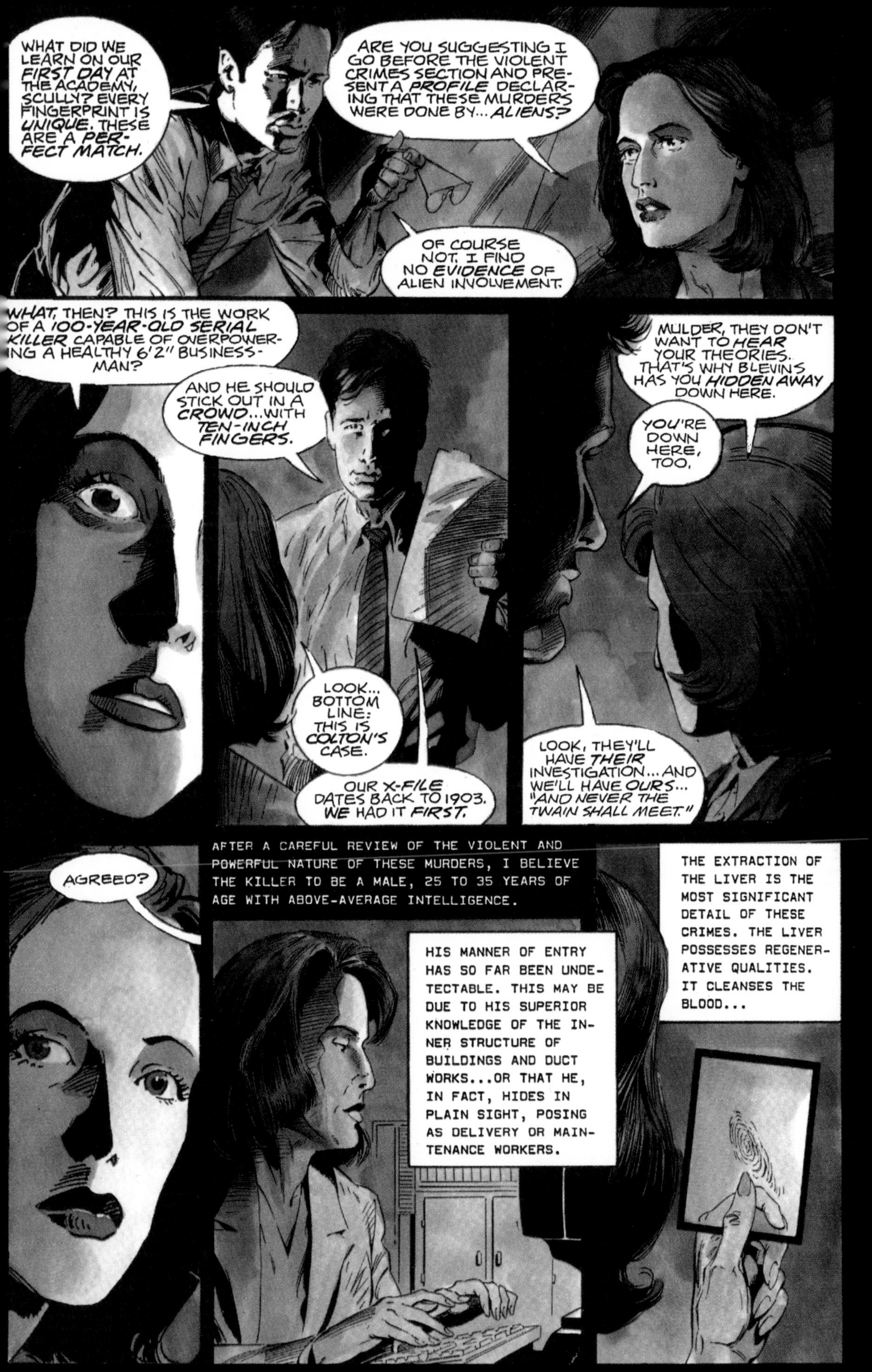
WHAT DID WE LEARN ON OUR FIRST DAY AT THE ACADEMY, SCULLY? EVERY FINGERPRINT IS UNIQUE. THESE ARE A PERFECT MATCH.
ARE YOU SUGGESTING I GO BEFORE THE VIOLENT CRIMES SECTION AND PRESENT A PROFILE DECLARING THAT THESE MURDERS WERE DONE BY... ALIENS?
OF COURSE NOT. I FIND NO EVIDENCE OF ALIEN INVOLVEMENT.
WHAT, THEN? THIS IS THE WORK OF A 100-YEAR-OLD SERIAL KILLER CAPABLE OF OVERPOWERING A HEALTHY 6'2" BUSINESSMAN?
AND HE SHOULD STICK OUT IN A CROWD... WITH TEN-INCH FINGERS.
LOOK... BOTTOM LINE: THIS IS COLTON'S CASE.
OUR X-FILE DATES BACK TO 1903. WE HAD IT FIRST.
MULDER, THEY DON'T WANT TO HEAR YOUR THEORIES. THAT'S WHY BLEVINS HAS YOU HIDDEN AWAY DOWN HERE.
YOU'RE DOWN HERE, TOO.
LOOK, THEY'LL HAVE THEIR INVESTIGATION... AND WE'LL HAVE OURS... "AND NEVER THE TWAIN SHALL MEET."
AGREED?
AFTER A CAREFUL REVIEW OF THE VIOLENT AND POWERFUL NATURE OF THESE MURDERS, I BELIEVE THE KILLER TO BE A MALE, 25 TO 35 YEARS OF AGE WITH ABOVE-AVERAGE INTELLIGENCE.
HIS MANNER OF ENTRY HAS SO FAR BEEN UNDETECTABLE. THIS MAY BE DUE TO HIS SUPERIOR KNOWLEDGE OF THE INNER STRUCTURE OF BUILDINGS AND DUCT WORKS...OR THAT HE, IN FACT, HIDES IN PLAIN SIGHT, POSING AS DELIVERY OR MAINTENANCE WORKERS.
THE EXTRACTION OF THE LIVER IS THE MOST SIGNIFICANT DETAIL OF THESE CRIMES. THE LIVER POSSESSES REGENERATIVE QUALITIES. IT CLEANSES THE BLOOD...

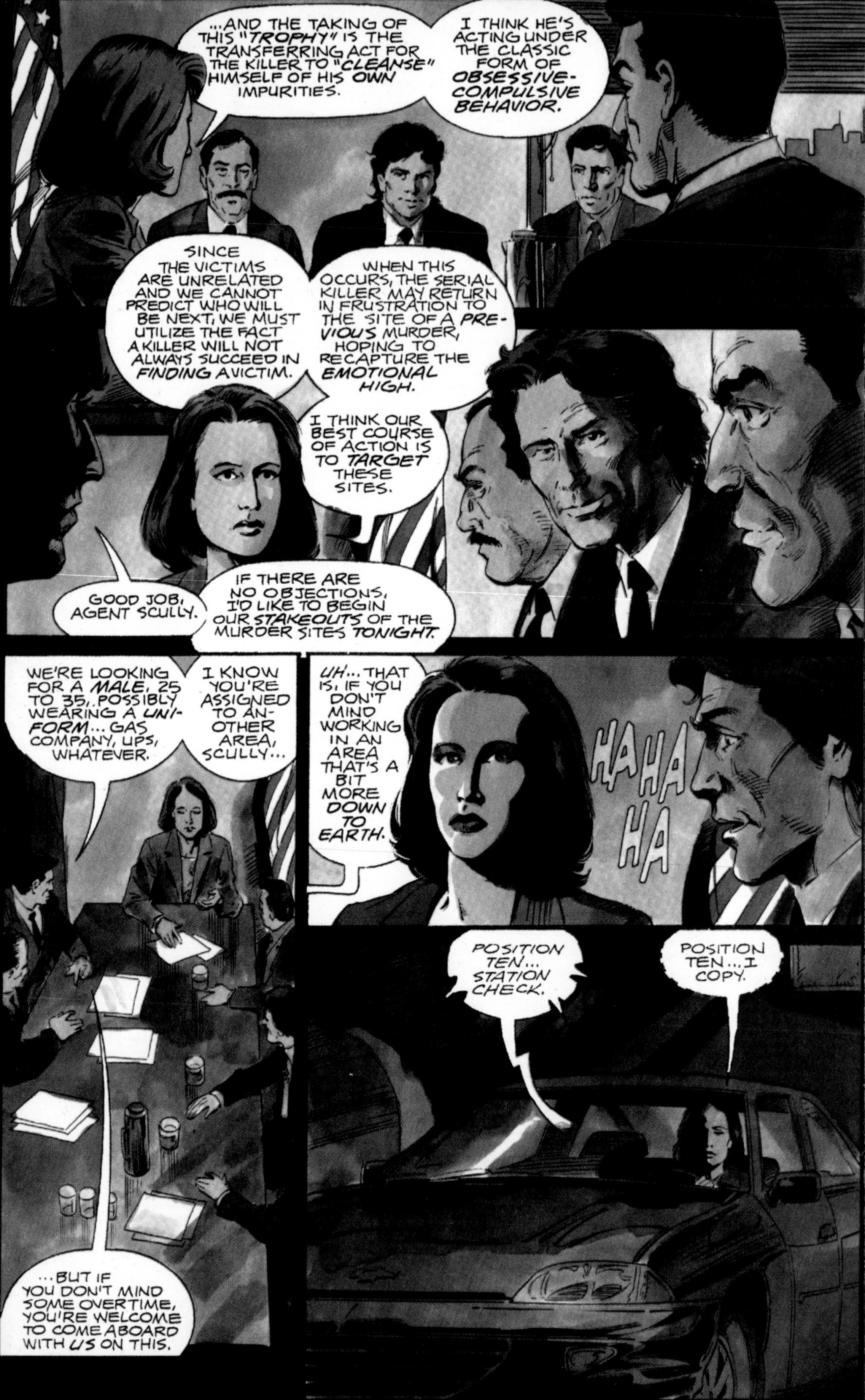
...AND THE TAKING OF THIS "TROPHY" IS THE TRANSFERRING ACT FOR THE KILLER TO "CLEANSE" HIMSELF OF HIS OWN IMPURITIES.
I THINK HE'S ACTING UNDER THE CLASSIC FORM OF OBSESSIVE-COMPULSIVE BEHAVIOR.
SINCE THE VICTIMS ARE UNRELATED AND WE CANNOT PREDICT WHO WILL BE NEXT, WE MUST UTILIZE THE FACT A KILLER WILL NOT ALWAYS SUCCEED IN FINDING A VICTIM.
WHEN THIS OCCURS, THE SERIAL KILLER MAY RETURN IN FRUSTRATION TO THE SITE OF A PREVIOUS MURDER, HOPING TO RECAPTURE THE EMOTIONAL HIGH.
I THINK OUR BEST COURSE OF ACTION IS TO TARGET THESE SITES.
GOOD JOB, AGENT SCULLY.
IF THERE ARE NO OBJECTIONS, I'D LIKE TO BEGIN OUR STAKEOUTS OF THE MURDER SITES TONIGHT.
WE'RE LOOKING FOR A MALE, 25 TO 35, POSSIBLY WEARING A UNIFORM... GAS COMPANY, UPS, WHATEVER.
I KNOW YOU'RE ASSIGNED TO ANOTHER AREA, SCULLY...
...BUT IF YOU DON'T MIND SOME OVERTIME, YOU'RE WELCOME TO COME ABOARD WITH US ON THIS.
UH... THAT IS, IF YOU DON'T MIND WORKING IN AN AREA THAT'S A BIT MORE DOWN TO EARTH.
HAHAHA HA
POSITION TEN... STATION CHECK.
POSITION TEN... I COPY.

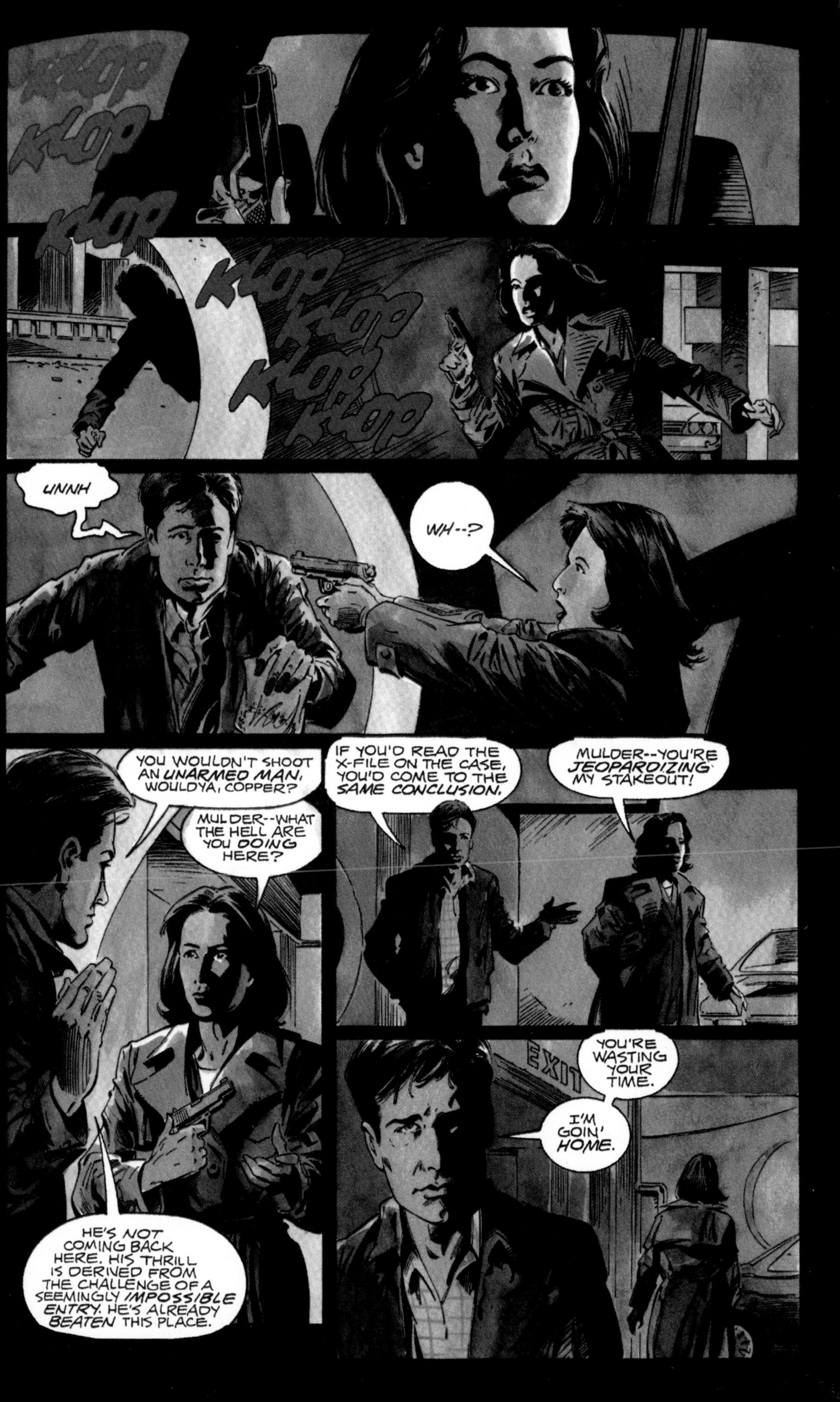
KLOP
KLOP
KLOP
KLOP KLOP KLOP KLOP KLOP
UNNH
WH--?
YOU WOULDN'T SHOOT AN UNARMED MAN, WOULDYA, COPPER?
MULDER--WHAT THE HELL ARE YOU DOING HERE?
HE'S NOT COMING BACK HERE. HIS THRILL IS DERIVED FROM THE CHALLENGE OF A SEEMINGLY IMPOSSIBLE ENTRY. HE'S ALREADY BEATEN THIS PLACE.
IF YOU'D READ THE X-FILE ON THE CASE, YOU'D COME TO THE SAME CONCLUSION.
MULDER--YOU'RE JEOPARDIZING MY STAKEOUT!
EXIT
YOU'RE WASTING YOUR TIME.
I'M GOIN' HOME.

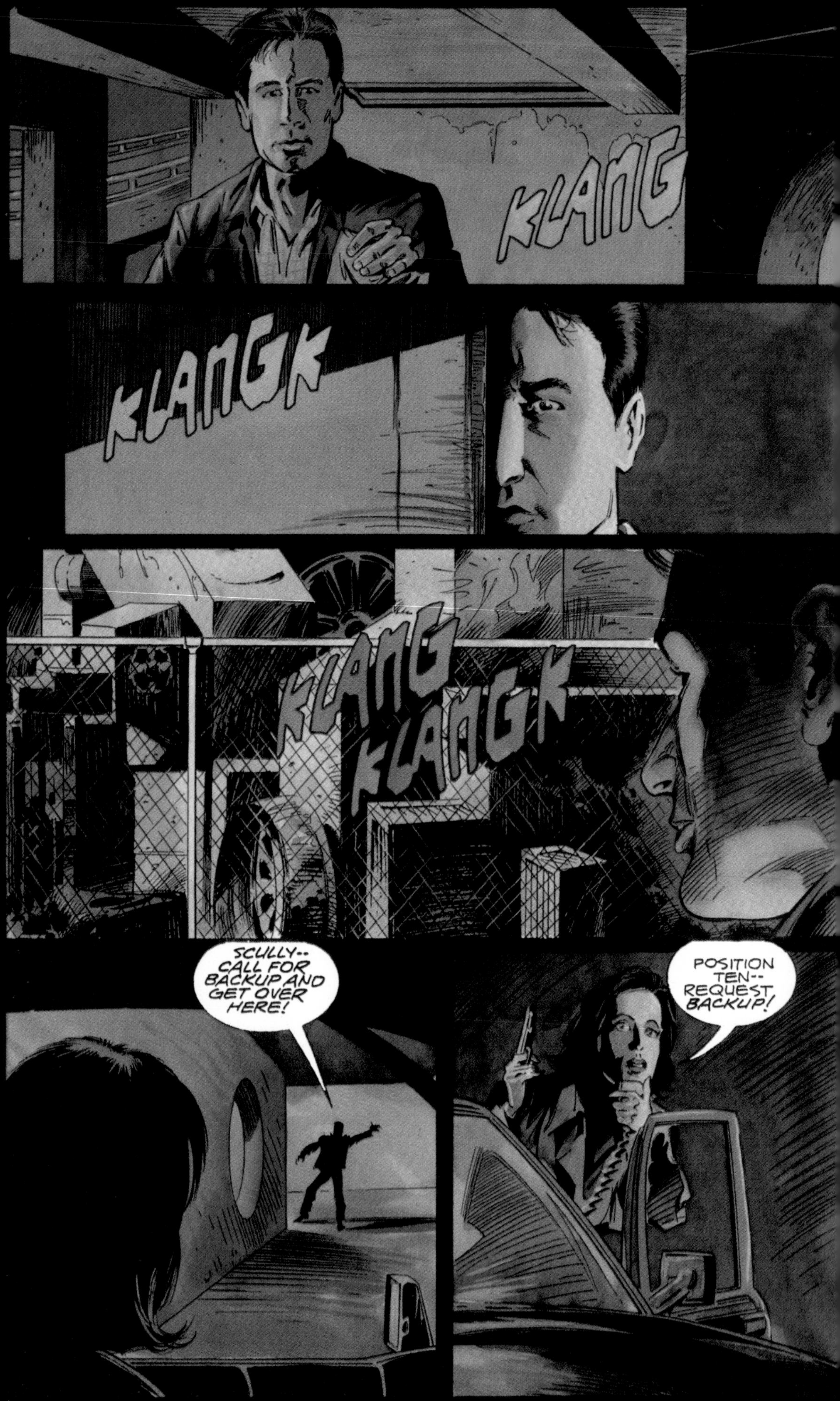
KLANG
KLANGK
KLANG
KLANGK
SCULLY-- CALL FOR BACKUP AND GET OVER HERE!
POSITION TEN-- REQUEST BACKUP!

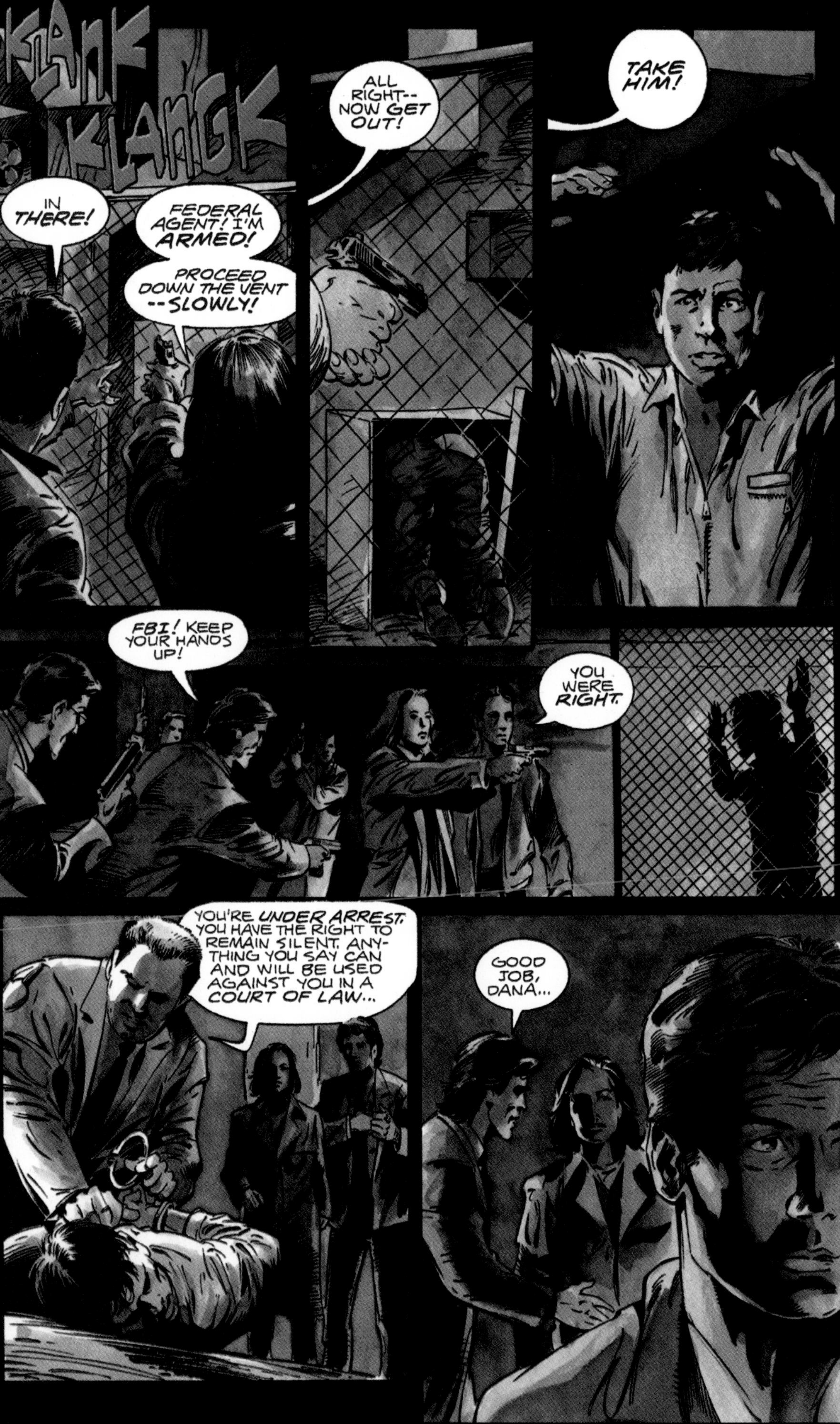
KLANK
KLANGK
IN THERE!
FEDERAL AGENT! I'M ARMED!
PROCEED DOWN THE VENT --SLOWLY!
ALL RIGHT-- NOW GET OUT!
TAKE HIM!
FBI! KEEP YOUR HANDS UP!
YOU WERE RIGHT.
YOU'RE UNDER ARREST. YOU HAVE THE RIGHT TO REMAIN SILENT. ANYTHING YOU SAY CAN AND WILL BE USED AGAINST YOU IN A COURT OF LAW...
GOOD JOB, DANA...

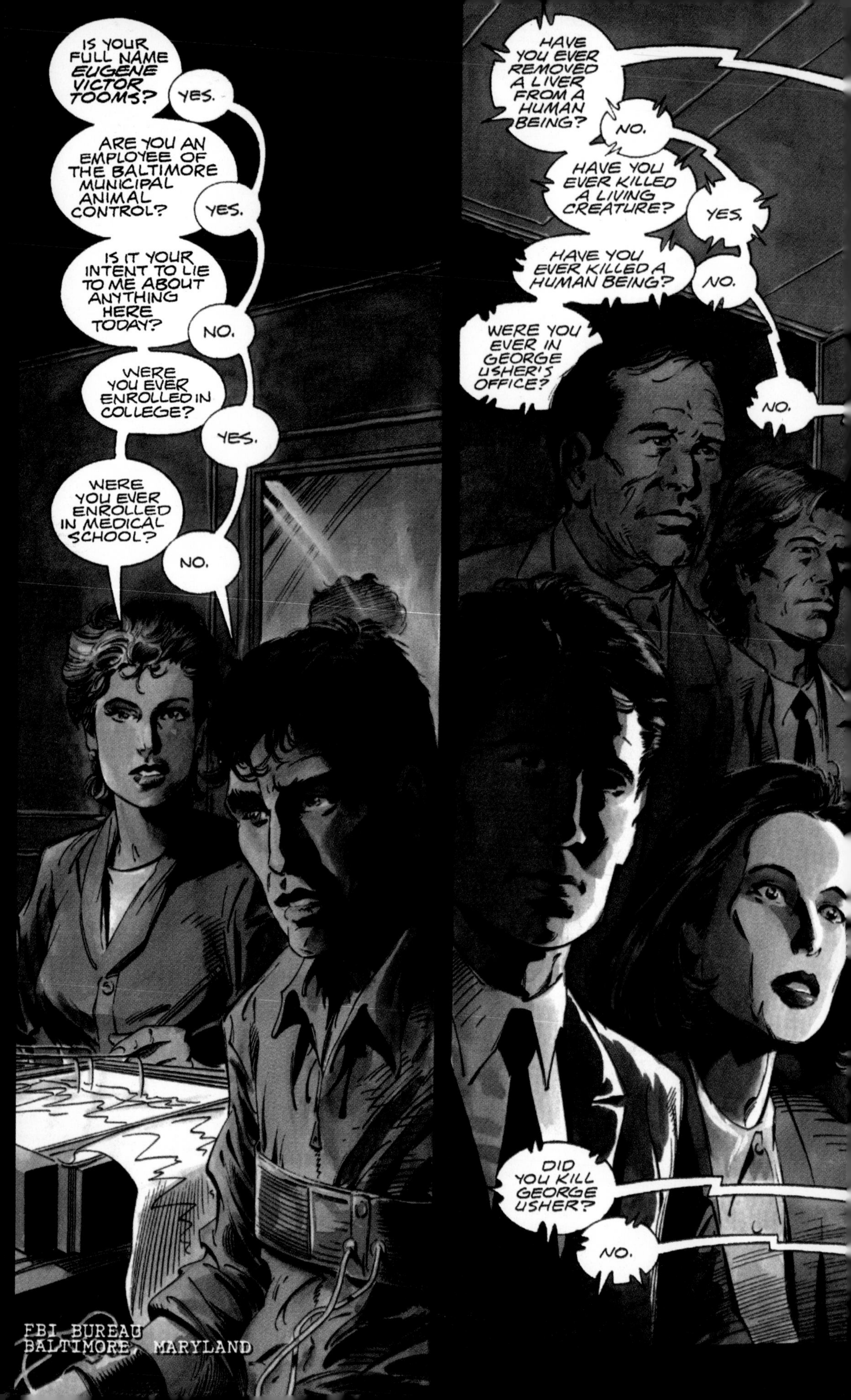
IS YOUR FULL NAME EUGENE VICTOR TOOMS?
YES.
ARE YOU AN EMPLOYEE OF THE BALTIMORE MUNICIPAL ANIMAL CONTROL?
YES.
IS IT YOUR INTENT TO LIE TO ME ABOUT ANYTHING HERE TODAY?
NO.
WERE YOU EVER ENROLLED IN COLLEGE?
YES.
WERE YOU EVER ENROLLED IN MEDICAL SCHOOL?
NO.
FBI BUREAU
BALTIMORE, MARYLAND
HAVE YOU EVER REMOVED A LIVER FROM A HUMAN BEING?
NO.
HAVE YOU EVER KILLED A LIVING CREATURE?
YES.
HAVE YOU EVER KILLED A HUMAN BEING?
NO.
WERE YOU EVER IN GEORGE USHER'S OFFICE?
NO.
DID YOU KILL GEORGE USHER?
NO.

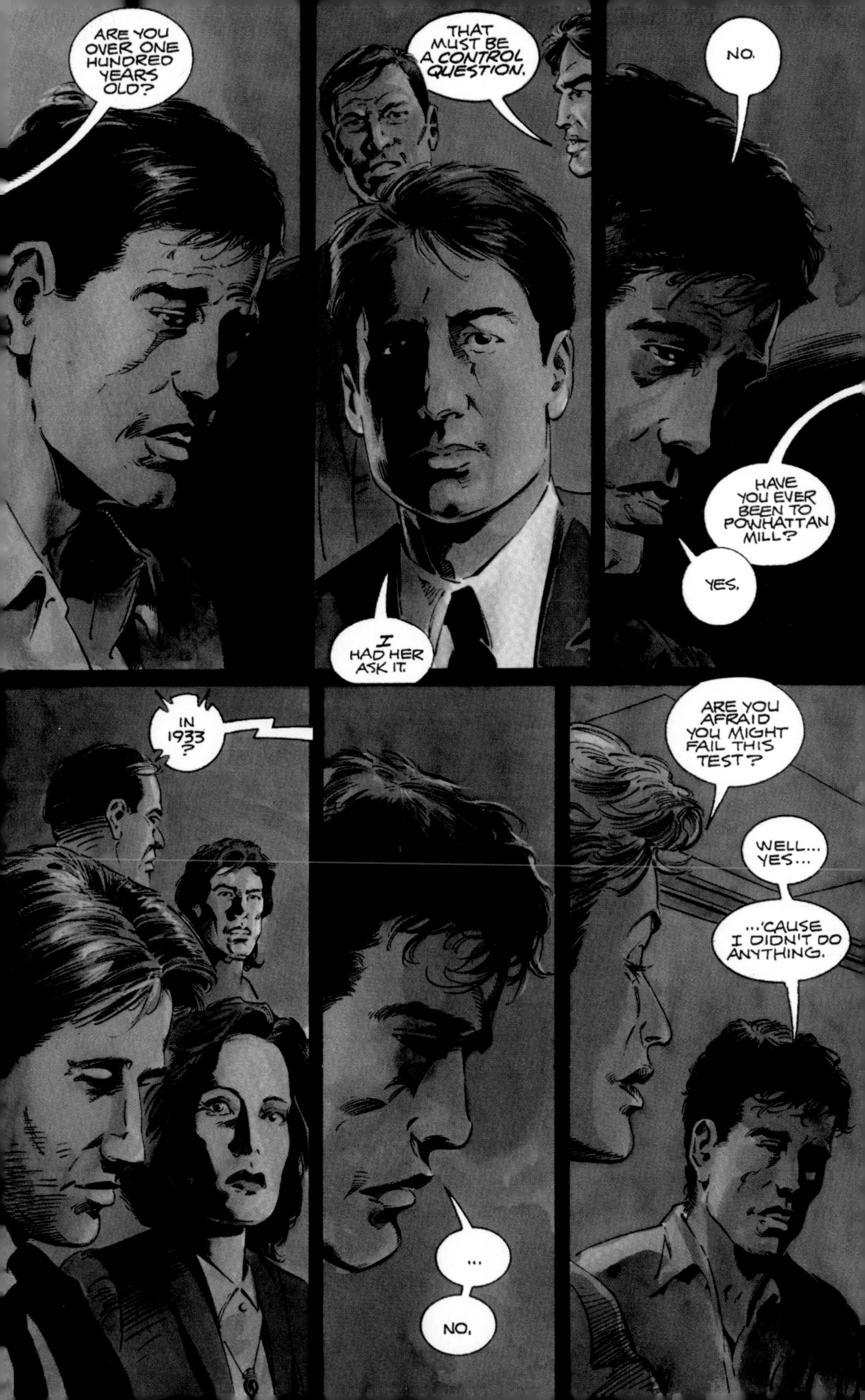
ARE YOU OVER ONE HUNDRED YEARS OLD?
THAT MUST BE A CONTROL QUESTION.
I HAD HER ASK IT.
NO.
HAVE YOU EVER BEEN TO POWHATTAN MILL?
YES.
IN 1933?
...
NO.
ARE YOU AFRAID YOU MIGHT FAIL THIS TEST?
WELL... YES...
...'CAUSE I DIDN'T DO ANYTHING.

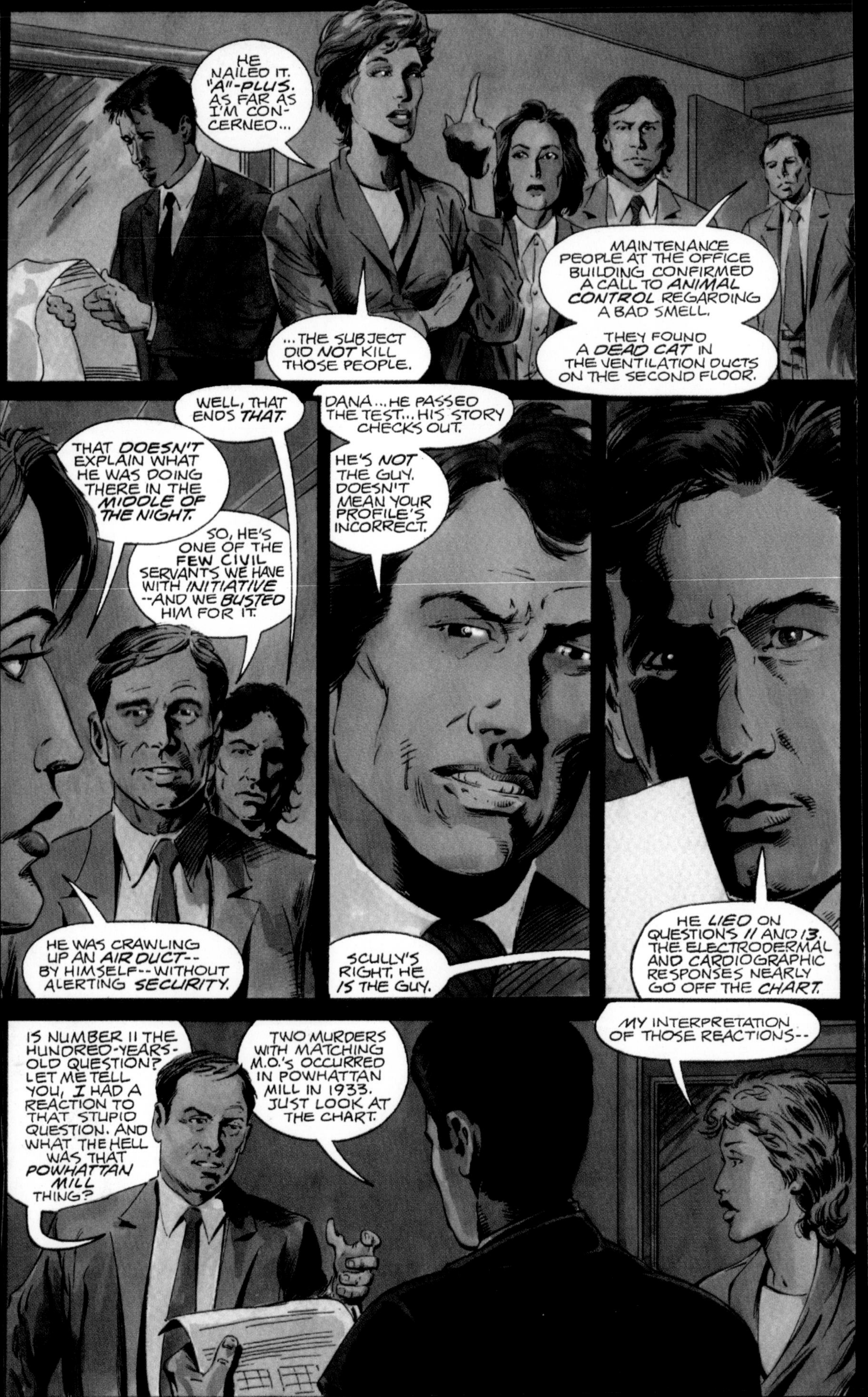

HE NAILED IT. "A"-PLUS. AS FAR AS I'M CONCERNED...
...THE SUBJECT DID NOT KILL THOSE PEOPLE.
MAINTENANCE PEOPLE AT THE OFFICE BUILDING CONFIRMED A CALL TO ANIMAL CONTROL REGARDING A BAD SMELL.
THEY FOUND A DEAD CAT IN THE VENTILATION DUCTS ON THE SECOND FLOOR.
WELL, THAT ENDS THAT.
THAT DOESN'T EXPLAIN WHAT HE WAS DOING THERE IN THE MIDDLE OF THE NIGHT.
SO, HE'S ONE OF THE FEW CIVIL SERVANTS WE HAVE WITH INITIATIVE --AND WE BUSTED HIM FOR IT.
HE WAS CRAWLING UP AN AIR DUCT-- BY HIMSELF-- WITHOUT ALERTING SECURITY.
DANA...HE PASSED THE TEST...HIS STORY CHECKS OUT.
HE'S NOT THE GUY. DOESN'T MEAN YOUR PROFILE'S INCORRECT.
SCULLY'S RIGHT. HE IS THE GUY.
HE LIED ON QUESTIONS 11 AND 13. THE ELECTRODERMAL AND CARDIOGRAPHIC RESPONSES NEARLY GO OFF THE CHART.
IS NUMBER 11 THE HUNDRED-YEARS-OLD QUESTION? LET ME TELL YOU, I HAD A REACTION TO THAT STUPID QUESTION. AND WHAT THE HELL WAS THAT POWHATTAN MILL THING?
TWO MURDERS WITH MATCHING M.O.'S OCCURRED IN POWHATTAN MILL IN 1933. JUST LOOK AT THE CHART.
MY INTERPRETATION OF THOSE REACTIONS--

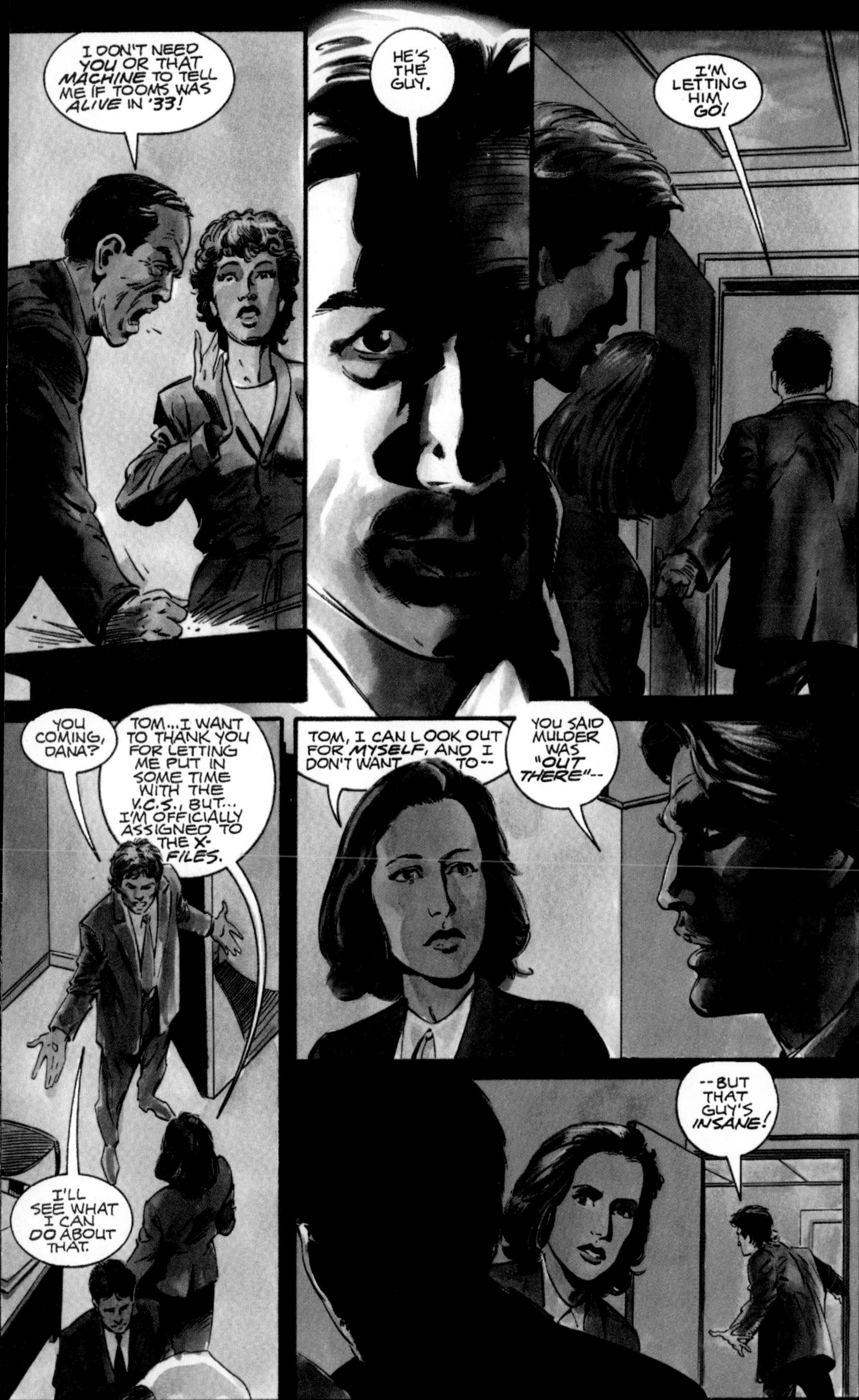
I DON'T NEED YOU OR THAT MACHINE TO TELL ME IF TOOMS WAS ALIVE IN '33!
HE'S THE GUY.
I'M LETTING HIM GO!
YOU COMING, DANA?
TOM... I WANT TO THANK YOU FOR LETTING ME PUT IN SOME TIME WITH THE V.C.S., BUT... I'M OFFICIALLY ASSIGNED TO THE X-FILES.
I'LL SEE WHAT I CAN DO ABOUT THAT.
TOM, I CAN LOOK OUT FOR MYSELF, AND I DON'T WANT TO--
YOU SAID MULDER WAS "OUT THERE"--
--BUT THAT GUY'S INSANE!

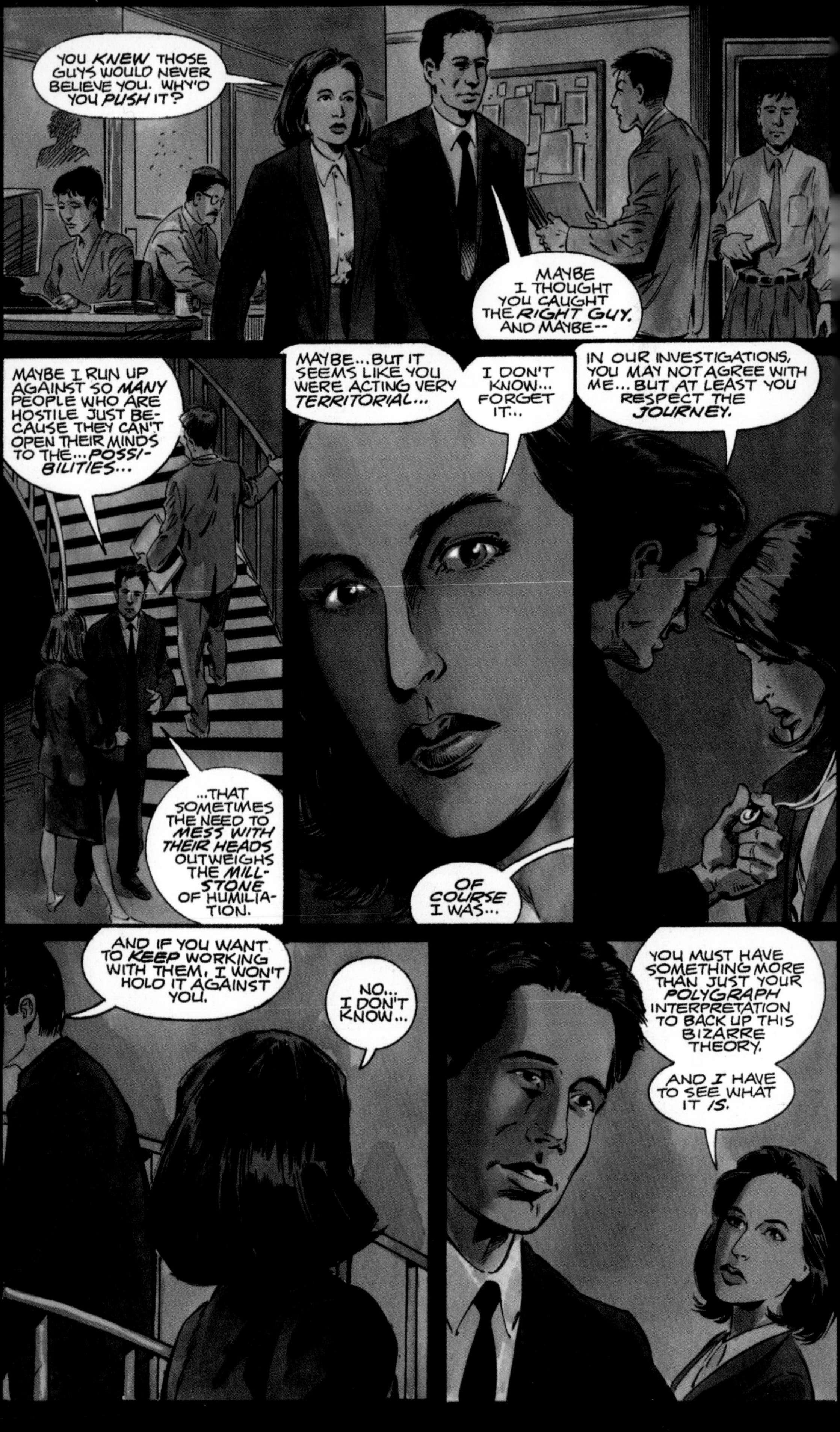
YOU KNEW THOSE GUYS WOULD NEVER BELIEVE YOU. WHY'D YOU PUSH IT?
MAYBE I THOUGHT YOU CAUGHT THE RIGHT GUY. AND MAYBE--
MAYBE I RUN UP AGAINST SO MANY PEOPLE WHO ARE HOSTILE JUST BECAUSE THEY CAN'T OPEN THEIR MINDS TO THE...POSSIBILITIES...
...THAT SOMETIMES THE NEED TO MESS WITH THEIR HEADS OUTWEIGHS THE MILLSTONE OF HUMILIATION.
MAYBE...BUT IT SEEMS LIKE YOU WERE ACTING VERY TERRITORIAL...
I DON'T KNOW... FORGET IT...
OF COURSE I WAS...
IN OUR INVESTIGATIONS, YOU MAY NOT AGREE WITH ME...BUT AT LEAST YOU RESPECT THE JOURNEY.
AND IF YOU WANT TO KEEP WORKING WITH THEM, I WON'T HOLD IT AGAINST YOU.
NO... I DON'T KNOW...
YOU MUST HAVE SOMETHING MORE THAN JUST YOUR POLYGRAPH INTERPRETATION TO BACK UP THIS BIZARRE THEORY.
AND I HAVE TO SEE WHAT IT IS.

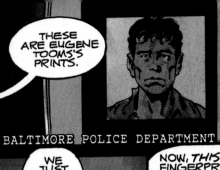

THESE ARE EUGENE TOOMS'S PRINTS.
ARREST REPORT
NAME
ADDRESS
CITY/ST/ZIP
ARRESTING OFFICER
SHIELD NUMBER
BALTIMORE POLICE DEPARTMENT
WE JUST NEED THIS ONE.
NOW, THIS IS THE FINGERPRINT THEY TOOK FROM USHER'S OFFICE. IT MATCHES THE OLD ONES FROM THE X-FILES.
OBVIOUSLY, NO MATCH. BUT WHAT IF ...SOMEHOW...
...WE STRETCH TOOMS'S PRINT ONE WAY...
...AND ..COMPRESS IT ANOTHER.
BEEP BEEP
MATCH - 100%
HOW COULD IT BE...?
THE ONLY THING I KNOW FOR CERTAIN IS...
...THEY LET HIM GO.

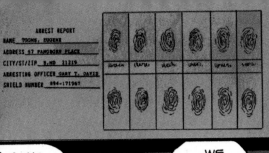

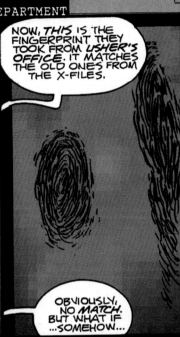

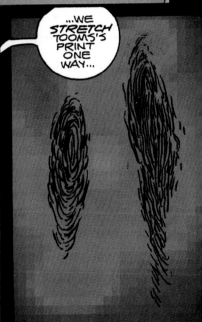

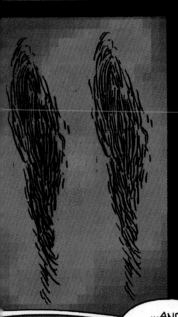

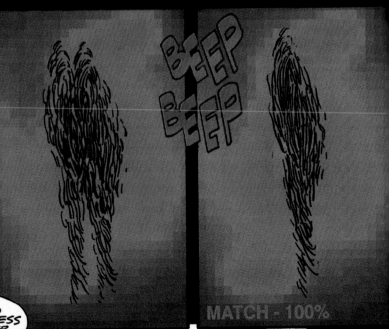

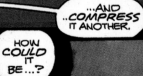

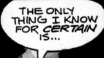

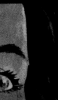

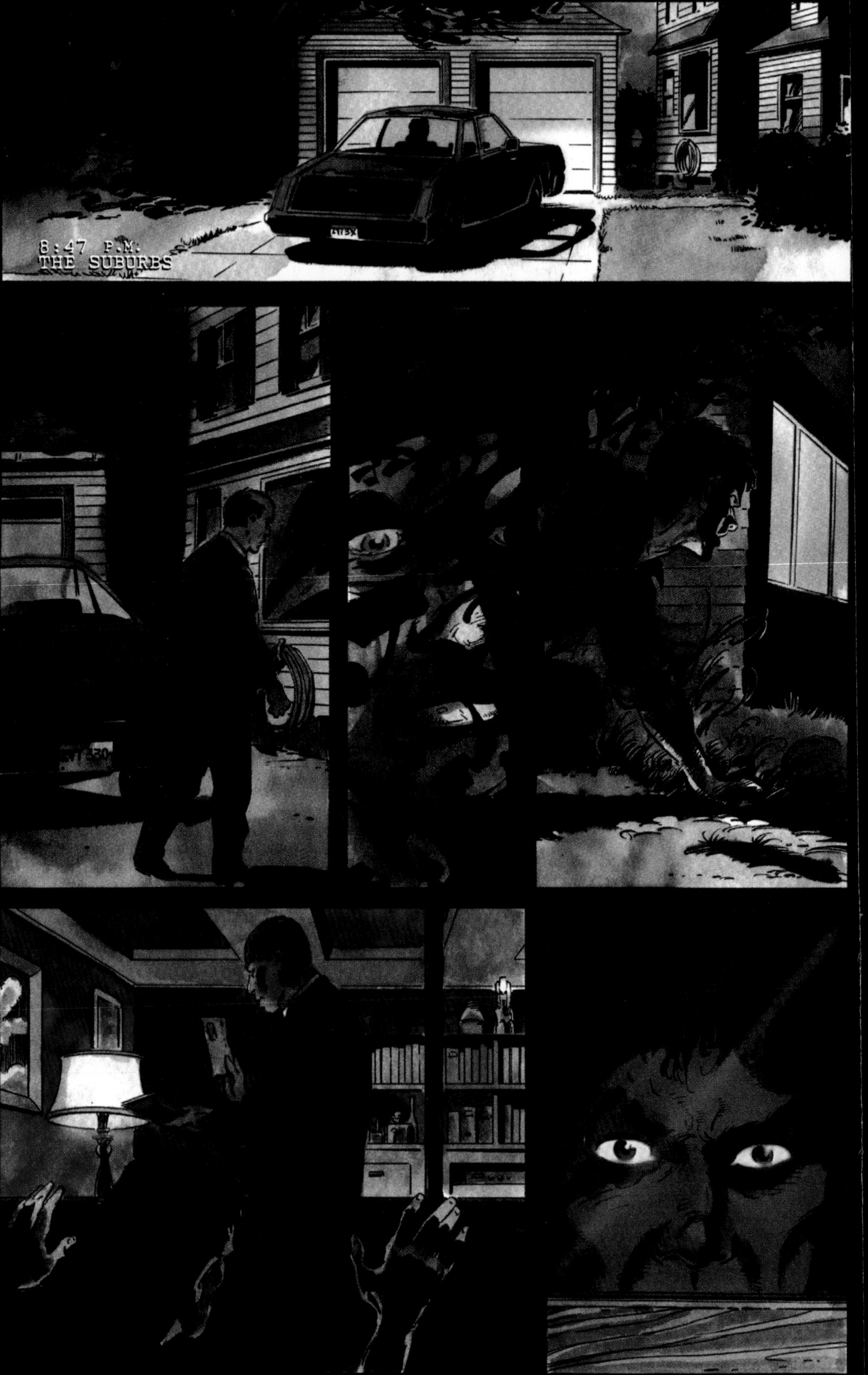
8:47 P.M.
THE SUBURBS

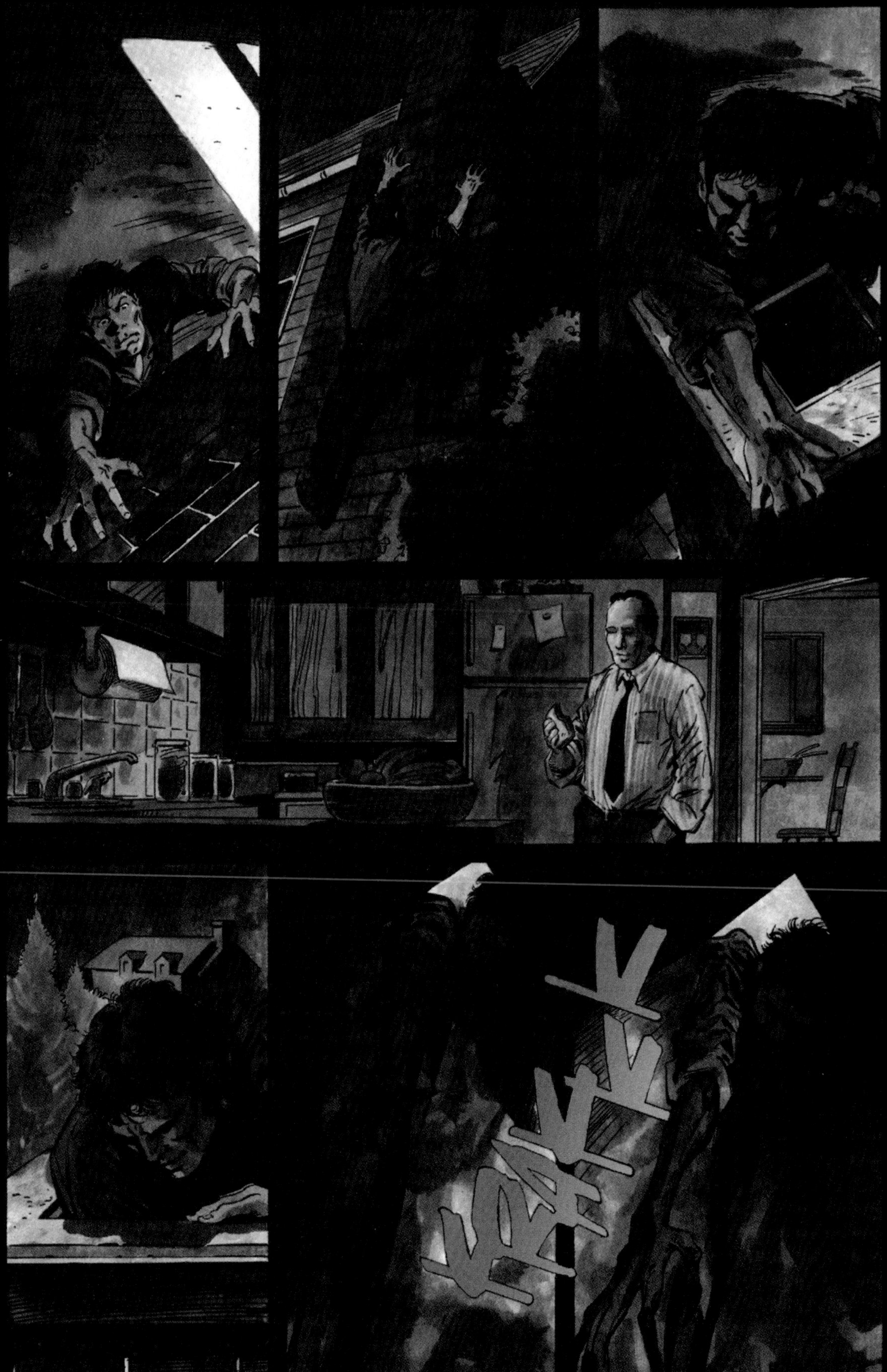

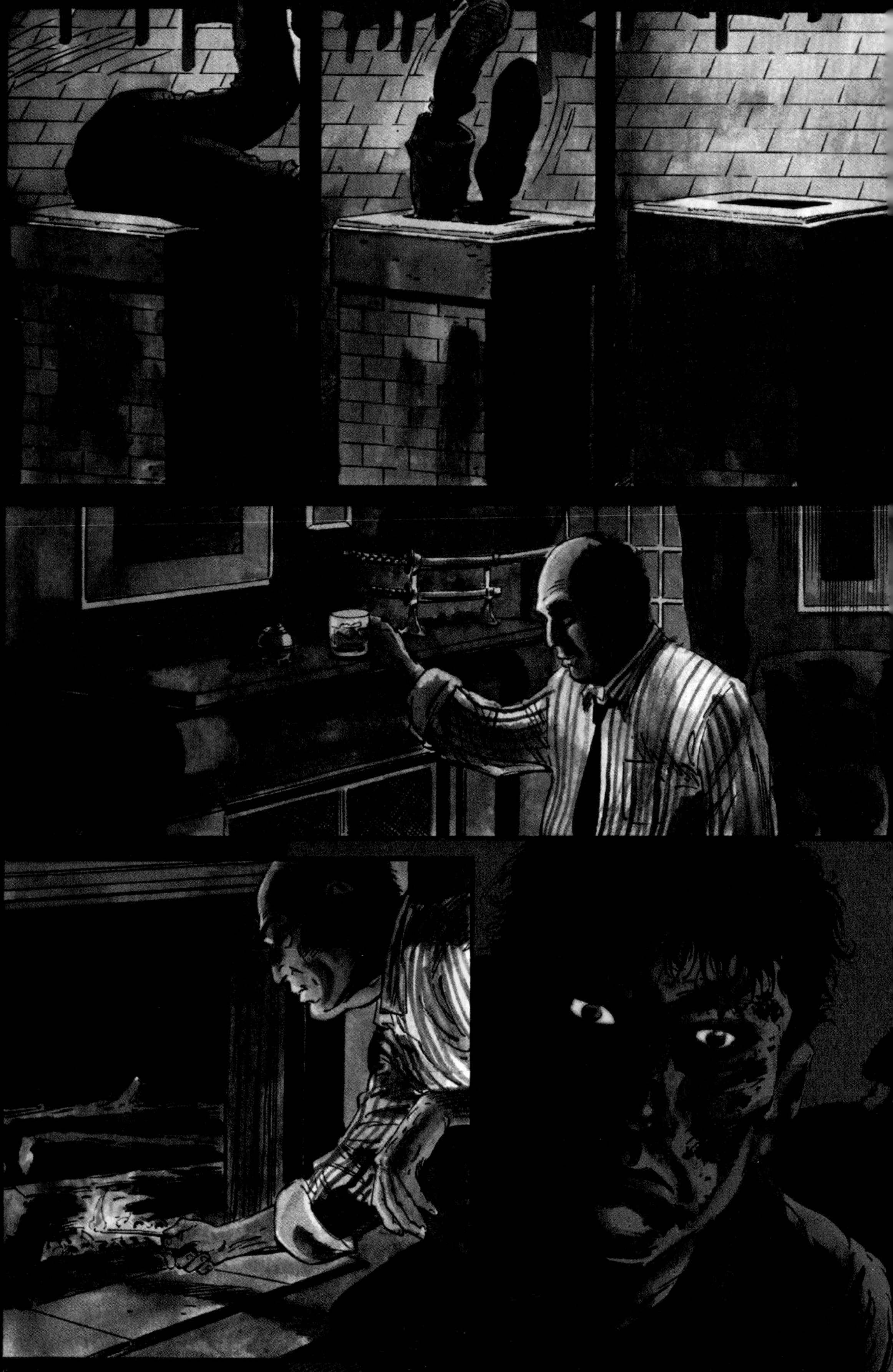

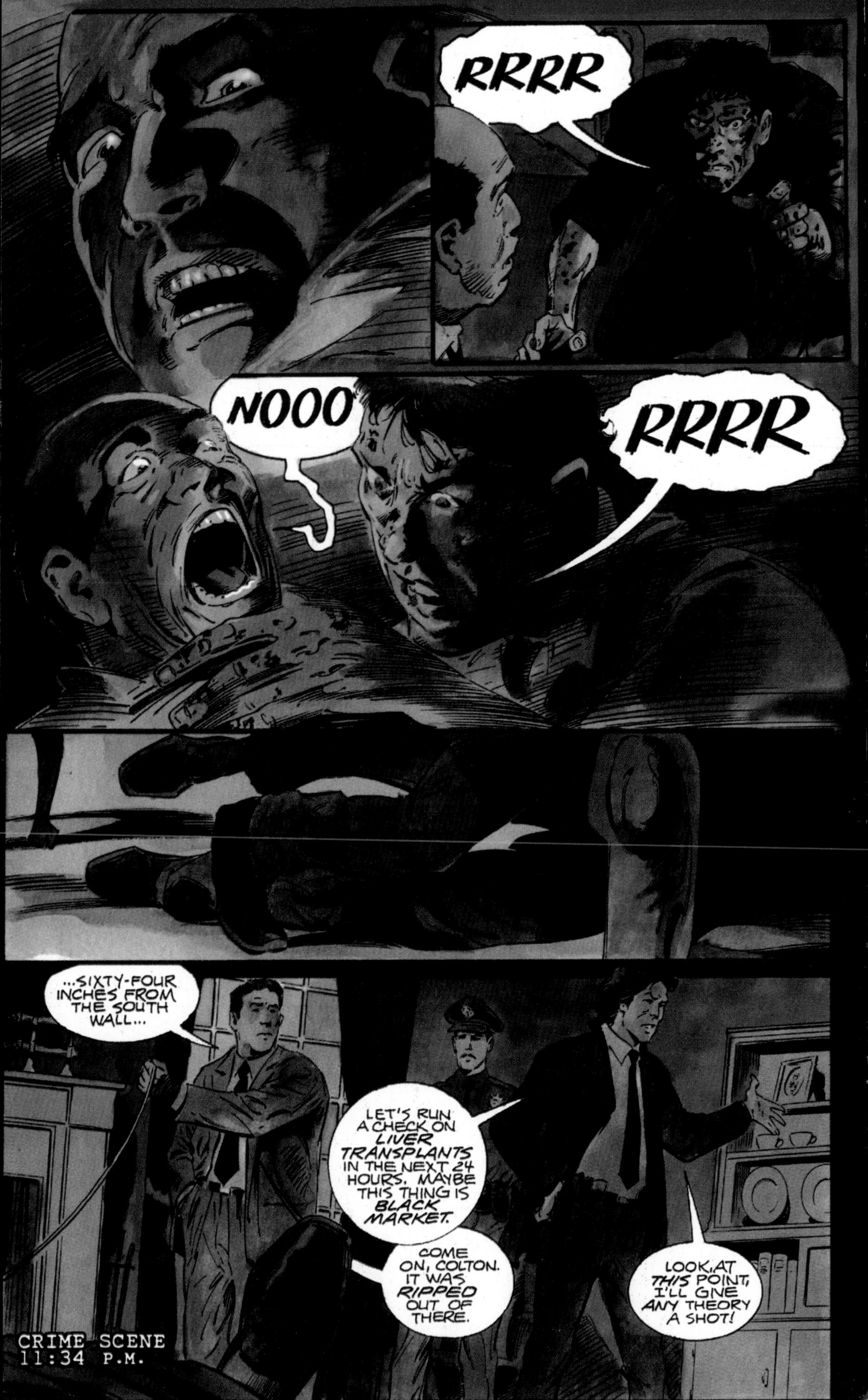
RRRR
NOOO
RRRR
...SIXTY-FOUR INCHES FROM THE SOUTH WALL...
LET'S RUN A CHECK ON LIVER TRANSPLANTS IN THE NEXT 24 HOURS. MAYBE THIS THING IS BLACK MARKET.
COME ON, COLTON. IT WAS RIPPED OUT OF THERE.
LOOK, AT THIS POINT, I'LL GIVE ANY THEORY A SHOT!
CRIME SCENE
11:34 P.M.

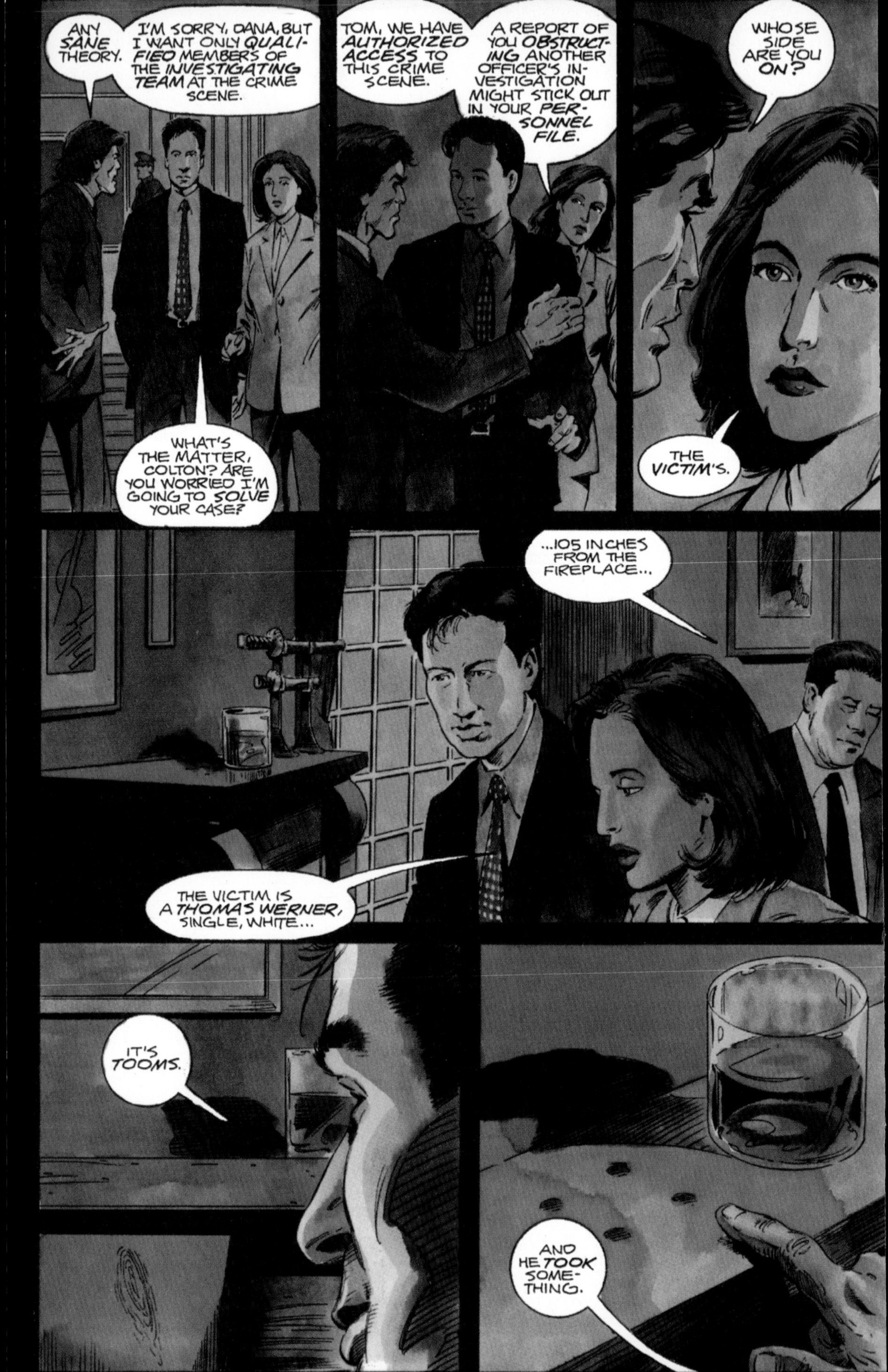
ANY SANE THEORY.
I'M SORRY, DANA, BUT I WANT ONLY QUALIFIED MEMBERS OF THE INVESTIGATING TEAM AT THE CRIME SCENE.
WHAT'S THE MATTER, COLTON? ARE YOU WORRIED I'M GOING TO SOLVE YOUR CASE?
TOM, WE HAVE AUTHORIZED ACCESS TO THIS CRIME SCENE.
A REPORT OF YOU OBSTRUCTING ANOTHER OFFICER'S INVESTIGATION MIGHT STICK OUT IN YOUR PERSONNEL FILE.
WHOSE SIDE ARE YOU ON?
THE VICTIM'S.
...105 INCHES FROM THE FIREPLACE...
THE VICTIM IS A THOMAS WERNER, SINGLE, WHITE...
IT'S TOOMS.
AND HE TOOK SOMETHING.

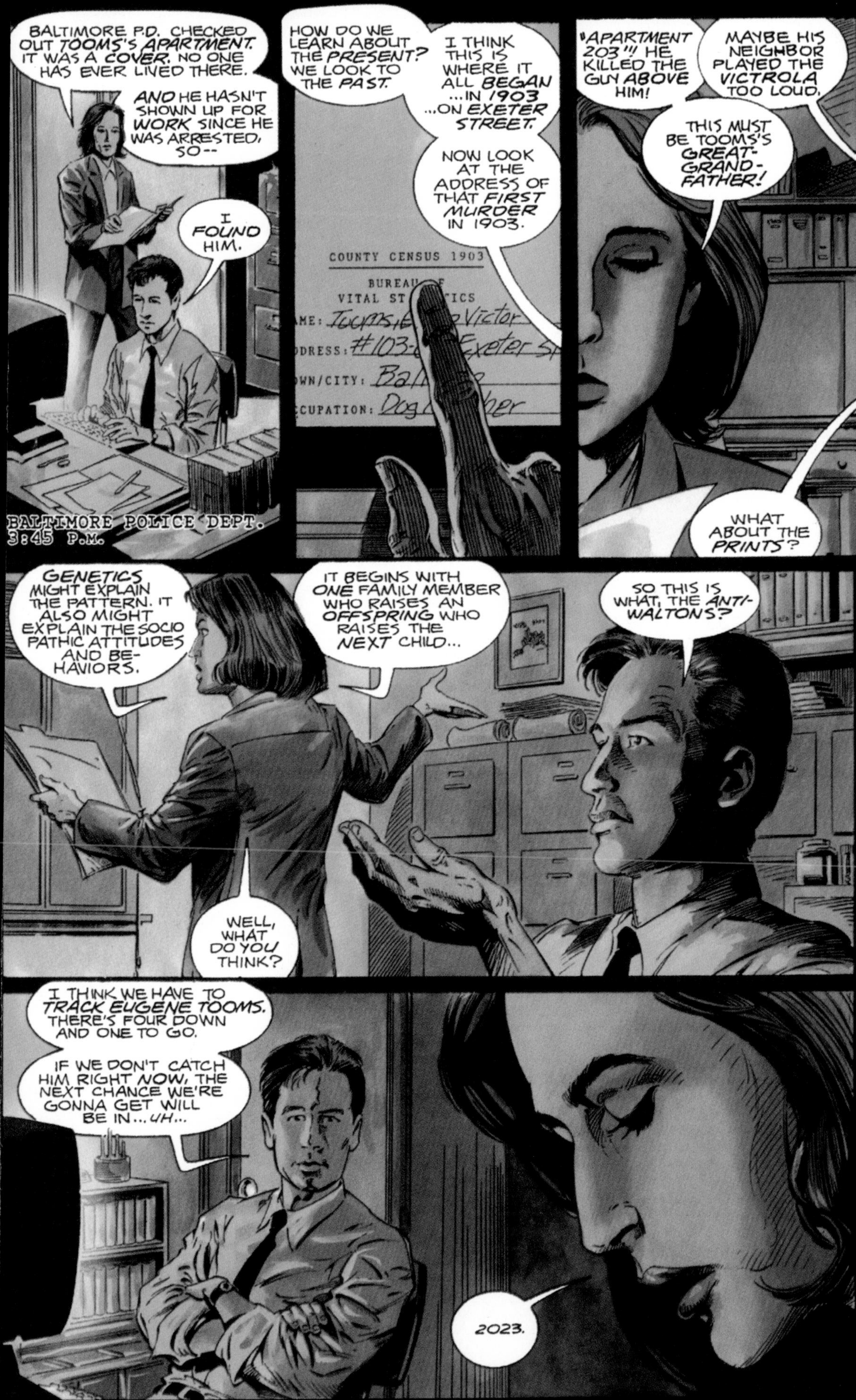
BALTIMORE P.D. CHECKED OUT TOOMS'S APARTMENT. IT WAS A COVER. NO ONE HAS EVER LIVED THERE.
AND HE HASN'T SHOWN UP FOR WORK SINCE HE WAS ARRESTED, SO--
I FOUND HIM.
BALTIMORE POLICE DEPT. 3:45 P.M.
HOW DO WE LEARN ABOUT THE PRESENT? WE LOOK TO THE PAST.
I THINK THIS IS WHERE IT ALL BEGAN ...IN 1903 ...ON EXETER STREET.
NOW LOOK AT THE ADDRESS OF THAT FIRST MURDER IN 1903.
COUNTY CENSUS 1903
"APARTMENT 203"!! HE KILLED THE GUY ABOVE HIM!
MAYBE HIS NEIGHBOR PLAYED THE VICTROLA TOO LOUD.
THIS MUST BE TOOMS'S GREAT-GRAND-FATHER!
WHAT ABOUT THE PRINTS?
GENETICS MIGHT EXPLAIN THE PATTERN. IT ALSO MIGHT EXPLAIN THE SOCIO PATHIC ATTITUDES AND BE-HAVIORS.
IT BEGINS WITH ONE FAMILY MEMBER WHO RAISES AN OFFSPRING WHO RAISES THE NEXT CHILD...
SO THIS IS WHAT, THE ANTI-WALTONS?
WELL, WHAT DO YOU THINK?
I THINK WE HAVE TO TRACK EUGENE TOOMS. THERE'S FOUR DOWN AND ONE TO GO.
IF WE DON'T CATCH HIM RIGHT NOW, THE NEXT CHANCE WE'RE GONNA GET WILL BE IN...UH...
2023.

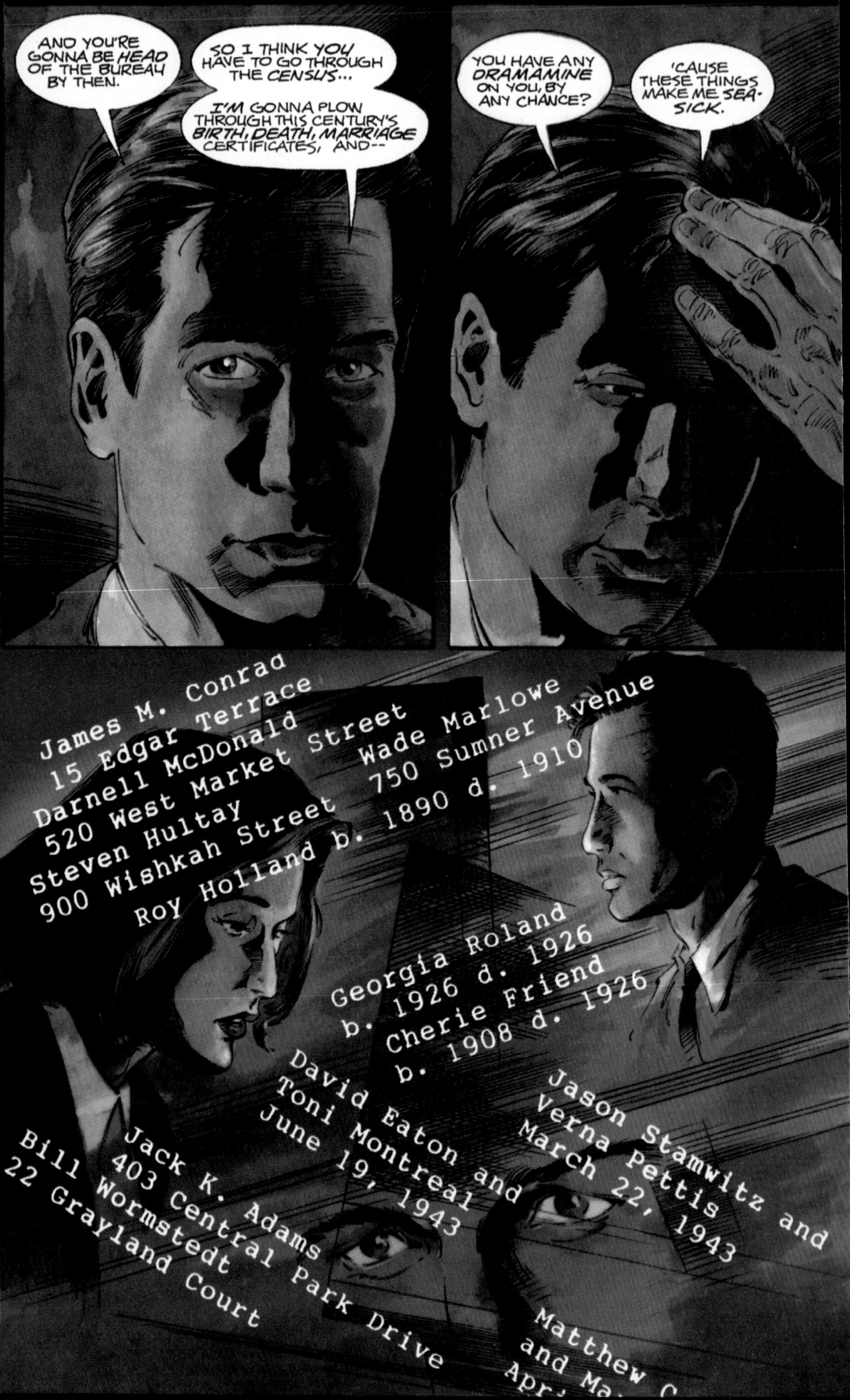
AND YOU'RE GONNA BE HEAD OF THE BUREAU BY THEN.
SO I THINK YOU HAVE TO GO THROUGH THE CENSUS...
I'M GONNA PLOW THROUGH THIS CENTURY'S BIRTH, DEATH, MARRIAGE CERTIFICATES, AND--
YOU HAVE ANY DRAMAMINE ON YOU, BY ANY CHANCE?
'CAUSE THESE THINGS MAKE ME SEA-SICK.
James M. Conrad
15 Edgar Terrace
Darnell McDonald
520 West Market Street
Wade Marlowe
Steven Hultay
750 Sumner Avenue
900 Wishkah Street
Roy Holland b. 1890 d. 1910
Georgia Roland
b. 1926 d. 1926
Cherie Friend
b. 1908 d. 1926
David Eaton and
Toni Montreal
June 19, 1943
Jason Stamwitz and
Verna Pettis
March 22, 1943
Jack K. Adams
403 Central Park Drive
Bill Wormstedt
22 Grayland Court
Matthew
and

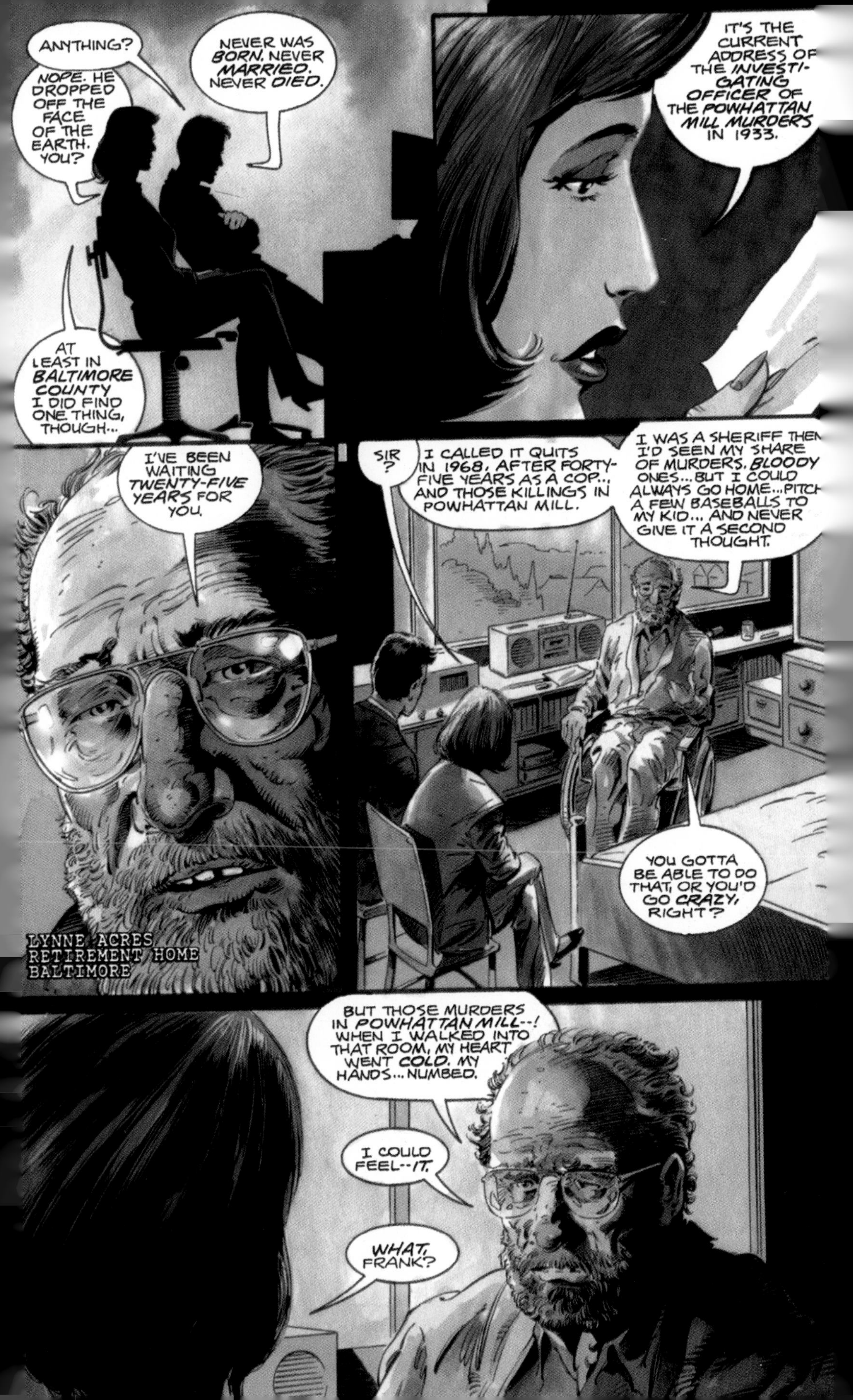
ANYTHING?
NEVER WAS BORN. NEVER MARRIED. NEVER DIED.
NOPE. HE DROPPED OFF THE FACE OF THE EARTH. YOU?
AT LEAST IN BALTIMORE COUNTY. I DID FIND ONE THING, THOUGH...
IT'S THE CURRENT ADDRESS OF THE INVESTIGATING OFFICER OF THE POWHATTAN MILL MURDERS IN 1933.
LYNNE ACRES RETIREMENT HOME BALTIMORE
I'VE BEEN WAITING TWENTY-FIVE YEARS FOR YOU.
SIR?
I CALLED IT QUITS IN 1968, AFTER FORTY-FIVE YEARS AS A COP... AND THOSE KILLINGS IN POWHATTAN MILL.
I WAS A SHERIFF THEN. I'D SEEN MY SHARE OF MURDERS. BLOODY ONES... BUT I COULD ALWAYS GO HOME... PITCH A FEW BASEBALLS TO MY KID... AND NEVER GIVE IT A SECOND THOUGHT.
YOU GOTTA BE ABLE TO DO THAT, OR YOU'D GO CRAZY, RIGHT?
BUT THOSE MURDERS IN POWHATTAN MILL--! WHEN I WALKED INTO THAT ROOM, MY HEART WENT COLD. MY HANDS... NUMBED.
I COULD FEEL--IT.
WHAT, FRANK?

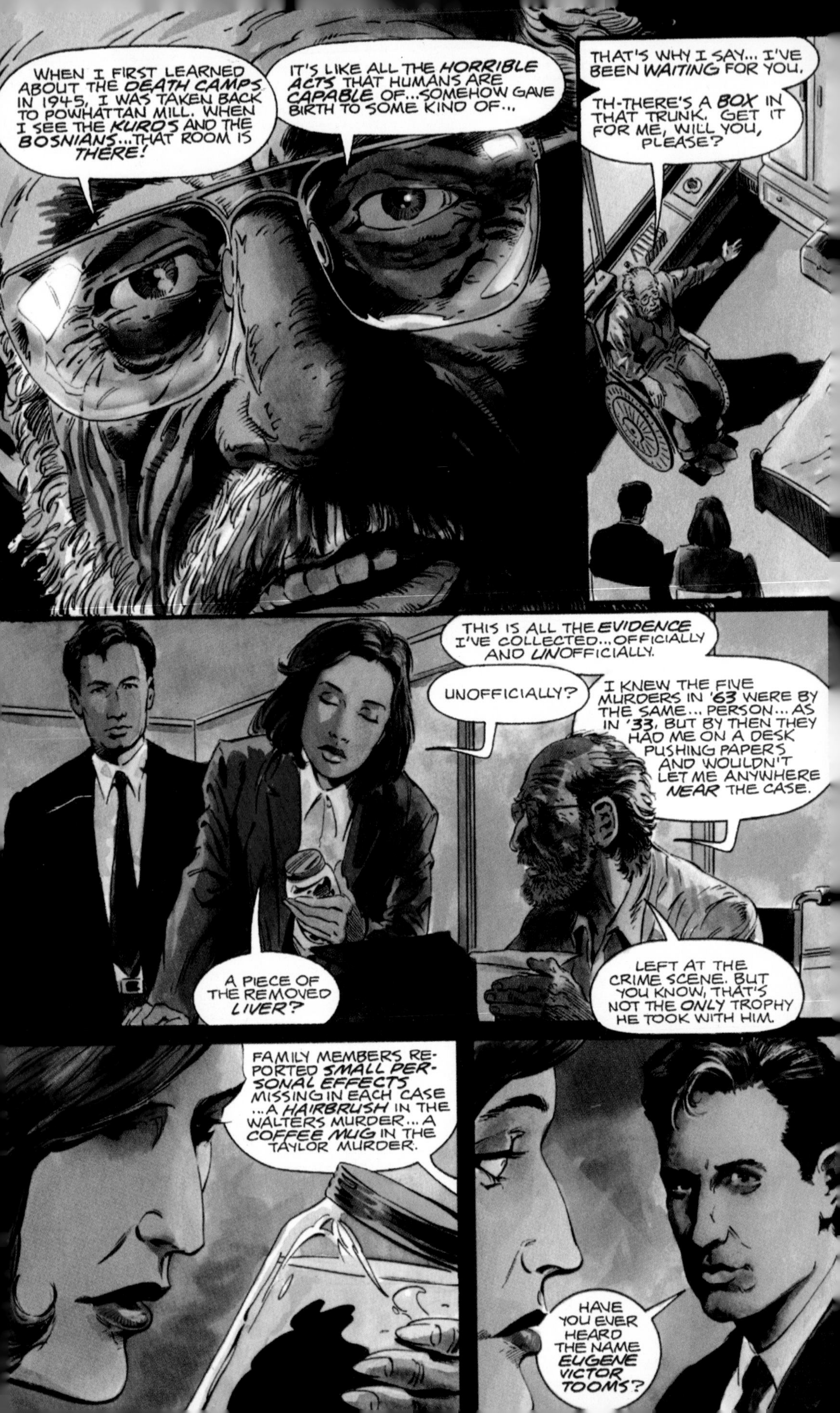
WHEN I FIRST LEARNED ABOUT THE DEATH CAMPS IN 1945, I WAS TAKEN BACK TO POWHATTAN MILL. WHEN I SEE THE KURDS AND THE BOSNIANS...THAT ROOM IS THERE!
IT'S LIKE ALL THE HORRIBLE ACTS THAT HUMANS ARE CAPABLE OF...SOMEHOW GAVE BIRTH TO SOME KIND OF...
THAT'S WHY I SAY... I'VE BEEN WAITING FOR YOU.
TH-THERE'S A BOX IN THAT TRUNK. GET IT FOR ME, WILL YOU, PLEASE?
THIS IS ALL THE EVIDENCE I'VE COLLECTED...OFFICIALLY AND UNOFFICIALLY.
UNOFFICIALLY?
I KNEW THE FIVE MURDERS IN '63 WERE BY THE SAME... PERSON... AS IN '33, BUT BY THEN THEY HAD ME ON A DESK PUSHING PAPERS AND WOULDN'T LET ME ANYWHERE NEAR THE CASE.
A PIECE OF THE REMOVED LIVER?
LEFT AT THE CRIME SCENE. BUT YOU KNOW, THAT'S NOT THE ONLY TROPHY HE TOOK WITH HIM.
FAMILY MEMBERS REPORTED SMALL PERSONAL EFFECTS MISSING IN EACH CASE ...A HAIRBRUSH IN THE WALTERS MURDER... A COFFEE MUG IN THE TAYLOR MURDER.
HAVE YOU EVER HEARD THE NAME EUGENE VICTOR TOOMS?

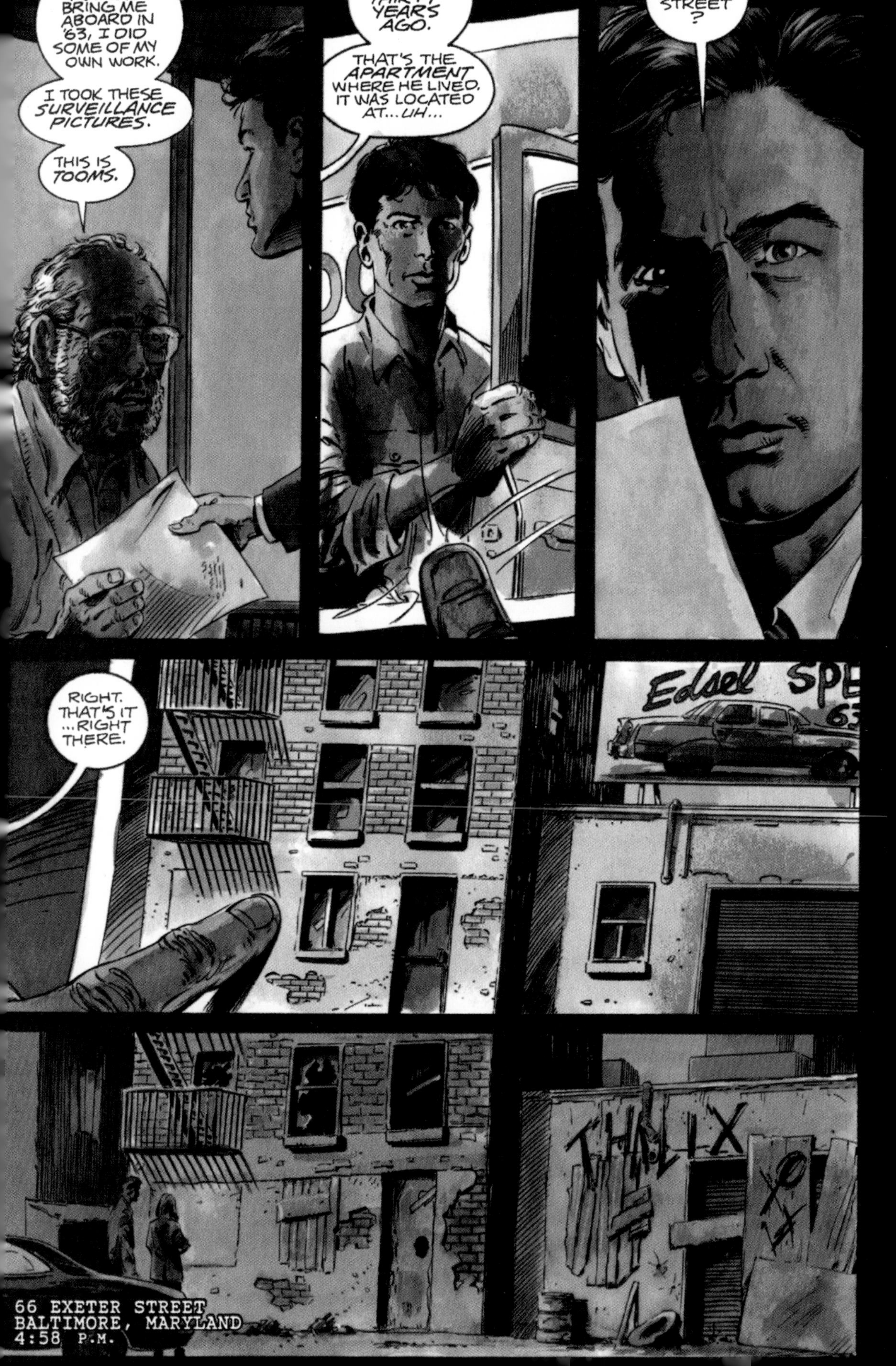
WHEN THEY WOULDN'T BRING ME ABOARD IN '63, I DID SOME OF MY OWN WORK.
I TOOK THESE SURVEILLANCE PICTURES.
THIS IS TOOMS.
'COURSE, THAT'S HIM THIRTY YEARS AGO.
THAT'S THE APARTMENT WHERE HE LIVED. IT WAS LOCATED AT... UH...
66 EXETER STREET?
RIGHT. THAT'S IT ...RIGHT THERE.
Edsel
66 EXETER STREET
BALTIMORE, MARYLAND
4:58 P.M.

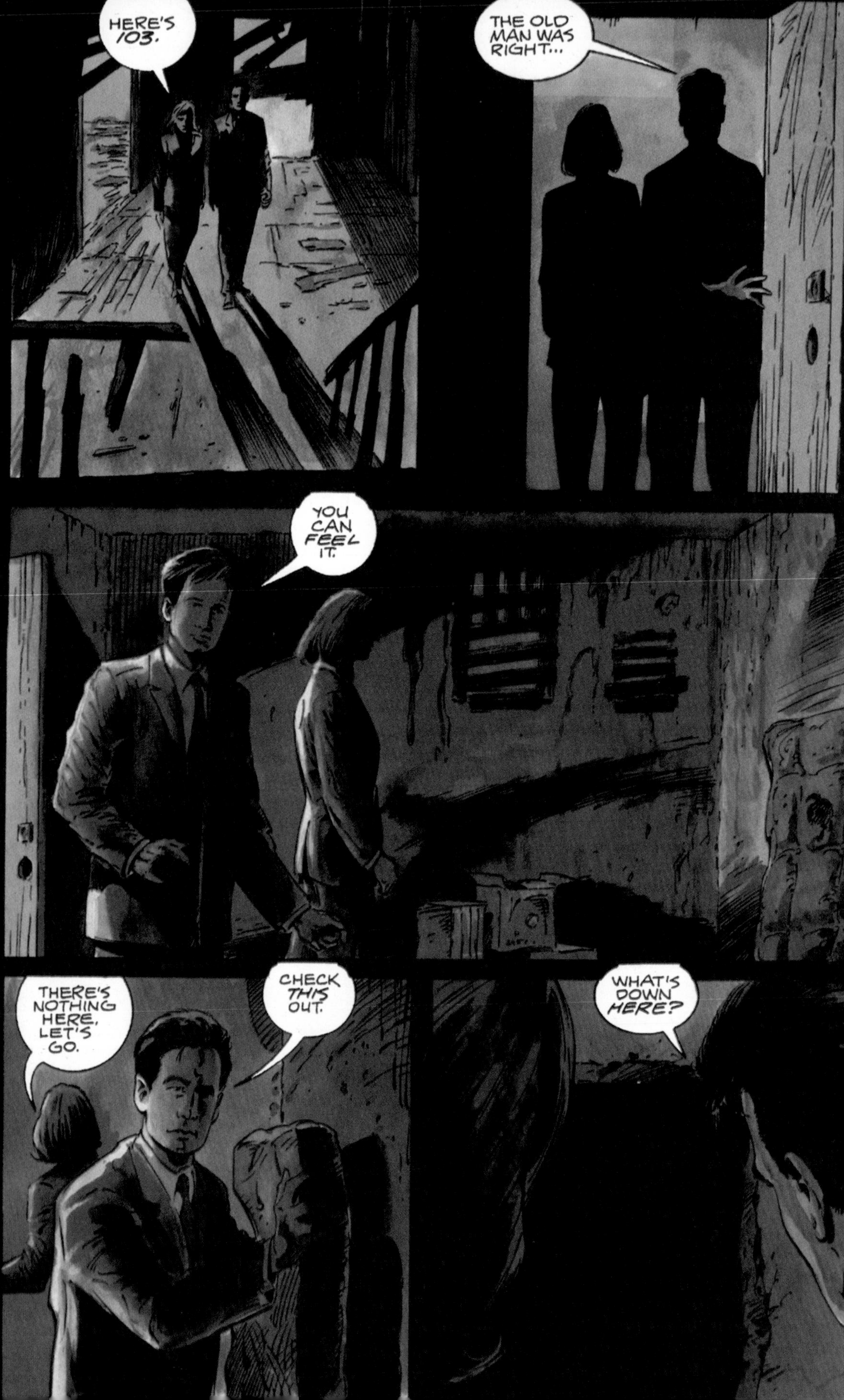
HERE'S 103.
THE OLD MAN WAS RIGHT...
YOU CAN FEEL IT.
THERE'S NOTHING HERE. LET'S GO.
CHECK THIS OUT.
WHAT'S DOWN HERE?

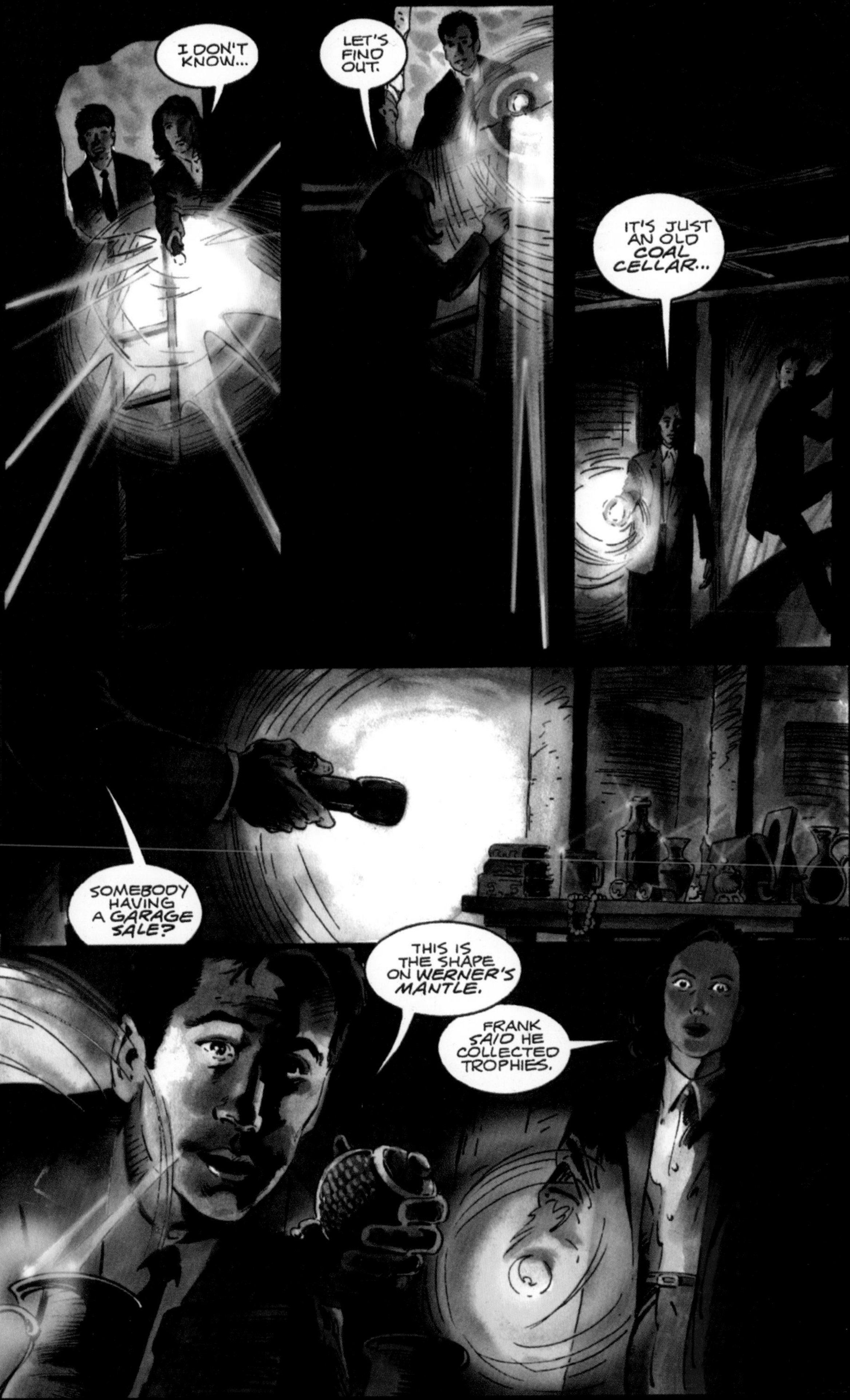
I DON'T KNOW...
LET'S FIND OUT.
IT'S JUST AN OLD COAL CELLAR...
SOMEBODY HAVING A GARAGE SALE?
THIS IS THE SHAPE ON WERNER'S MANTLE.
FRANK SAID HE COLLECTED TROPHIES.

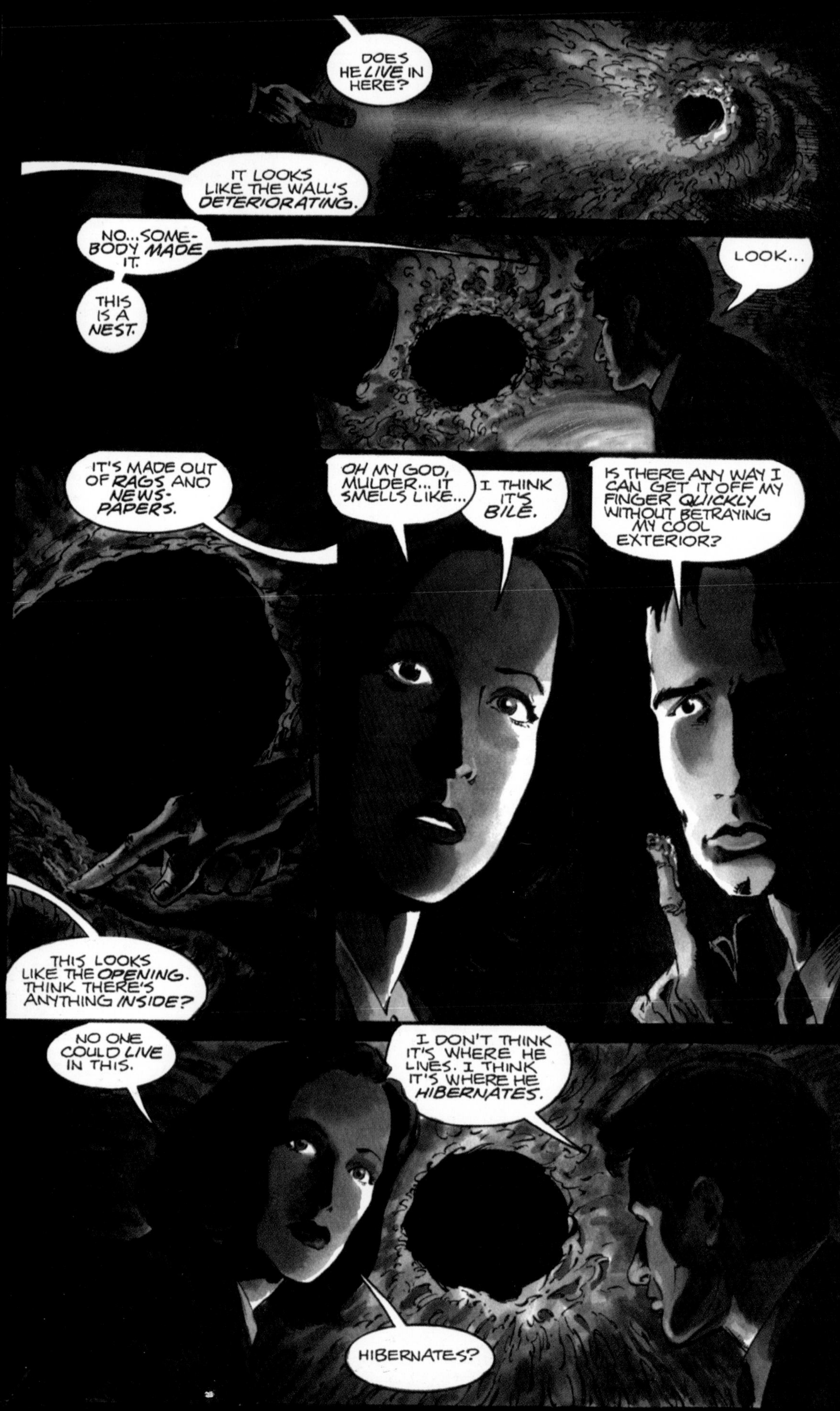
DOES HE LIVE IN HERE?
IT LOOKS LIKE THE WALL'S DETERIORATING.
NO... SOMEBODY MADE IT.
THIS IS A NEST.
LOOK...
IT'S MADE OUT OF RAGS AND NEWSPAPERS.
OH MY GOD, MULDER... IT SMELLS LIKE...
I THINK IT'S BILE.
IS THERE ANY WAY I CAN GET IT OFF MY FINGER QUICKLY WITHOUT BETRAYING MY COOL EXTERIOR?
THIS LOOKS LIKE THE OPENING. THINK THERE'S ANYTHING INSIDE?
NO ONE COULD LIVE IN THIS.
I DON'T THINK IT'S WHERE HE LIVES. I THINK IT'S WHERE HE HIBERNATES.
HIBERNATES?

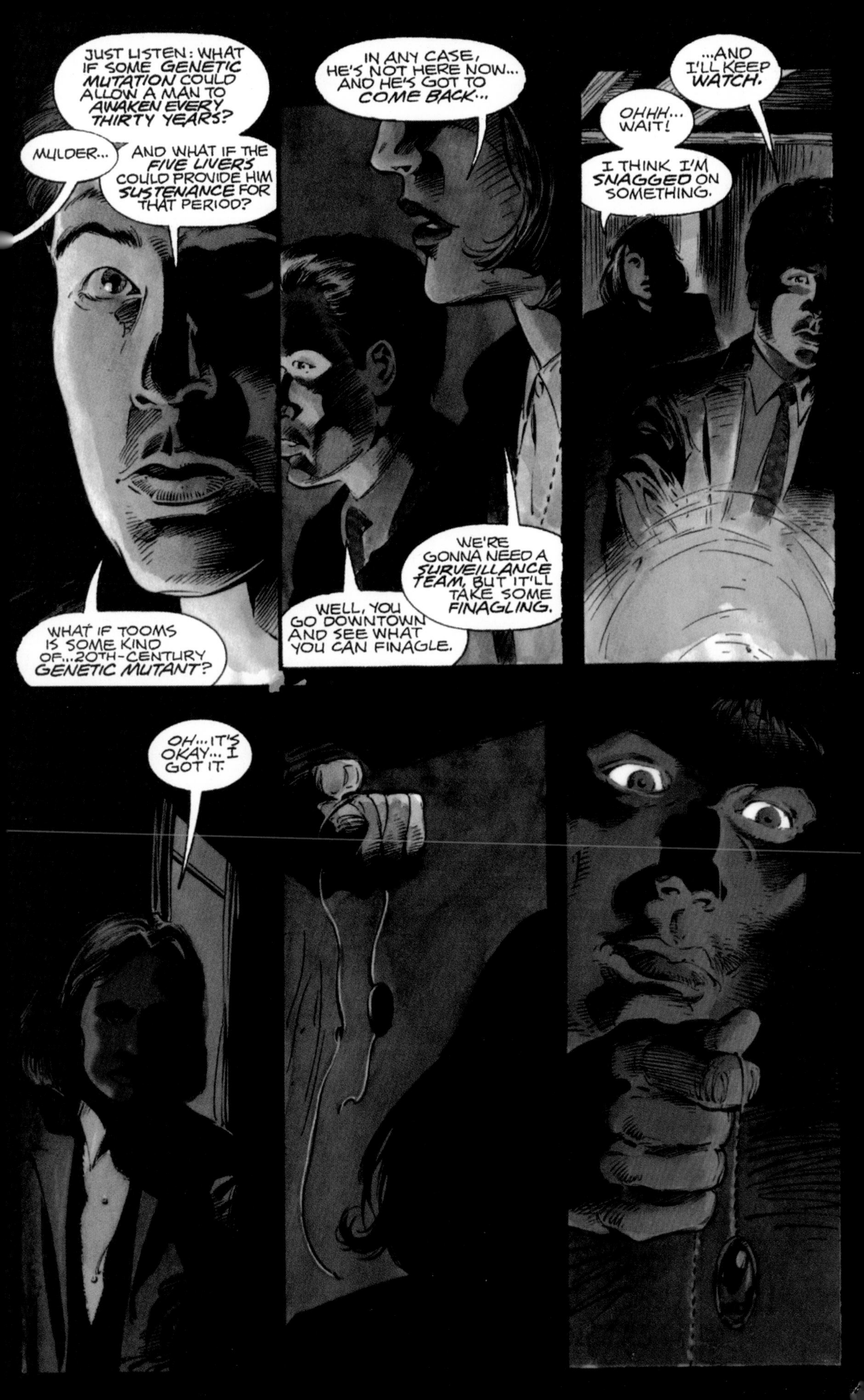
JUST LISTEN: WHAT IF SOME GENETIC MUTATION COULD ALLOW A MAN TO AWAKEN EVERY THIRTY YEARS?
MULDER...
AND WHAT IF THE FIVE LIVERS COULD PROVIDE HIM SUSTENANCE FOR THAT PERIOD?
WHAT IF TOOMS IS SOME KIND OF...20TH-CENTURY GENETIC MUTANT?
IN ANY CASE, HE'S NOT HERE NOW... AND HE'S GOT TO COME BACK...
WE'RE GONNA NEED A SURVEILLANCE TEAM, BUT IT'LL TAKE SOME FINAGLING.
WELL, YOU GO DOWNTOWN AND SEE WHAT YOU CAN FINAGLE.
...AND I'LL KEEP WATCH.
OHHH... WAIT!
I THINK I'M SNAGGED ON SOMETHING.
OH...IT'S OKAY... I GOT IT.

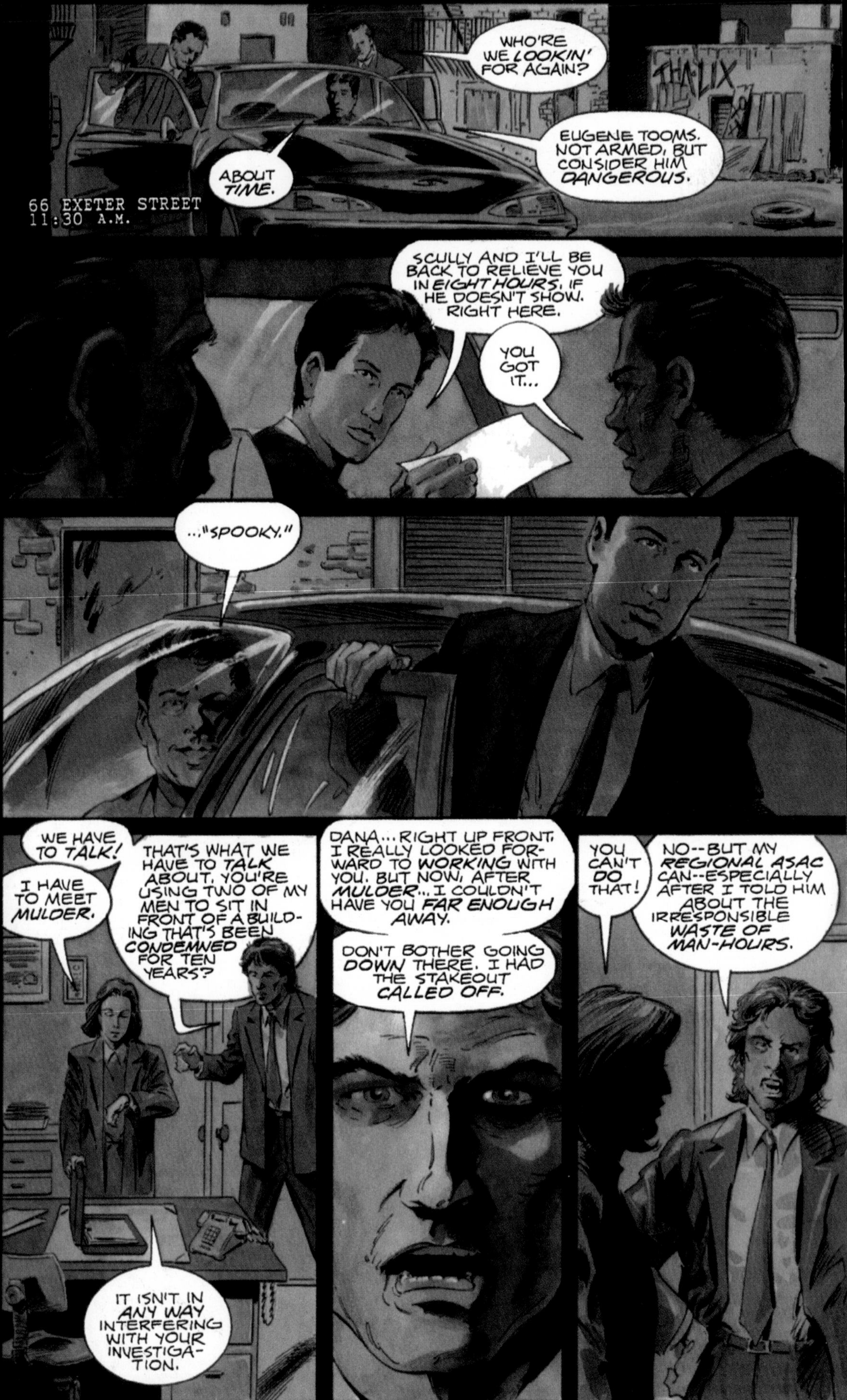
WHO'RE WE LOOKIN' FOR AGAIN?
EUGENE TOOMS. NOT ARMED, BUT CONSIDER HIM DANGEROUS.
ABOUT TIME.
66 EXETER STREET
11:30 A.M.
SCULLY AND I'LL BE BACK TO RELIEVE YOU IN EIGHT HOURS, IF HE DOESN'T SHOW. RIGHT HERE.
YOU GOT IT...
..."SPOOKY."
WE HAVE TO TALK!
I HAVE TO MEET MULDER.
THAT'S WHAT WE HAVE TO TALK ABOUT. YOU'RE USING TWO OF MY MEN TO SIT IN FRONT OF A BUILDING THAT'S BEEN CONDEMNED FOR TEN YEARS?
IT ISN'T IN ANY WAY INTERFERING WITH YOUR INVESTIGATION.
DANA... RIGHT UP FRONT, I REALLY LOOKED FORWARD TO WORKING WITH YOU. BUT NOW, AFTER MULDER... I COULDN'T HAVE YOU FAR ENOUGH AWAY.
DON'T BOTHER GOING DOWN THERE. I HAD THE STAKEOUT CALLED OFF.
YOU CAN'T DO THAT!
NO--BUT MY REGIONAL ASAC CAN--ESPECIALLY AFTER I TOLD HIM ABOUT THE IRRESPONSIBLE WASTE OF MAN-HOURS.

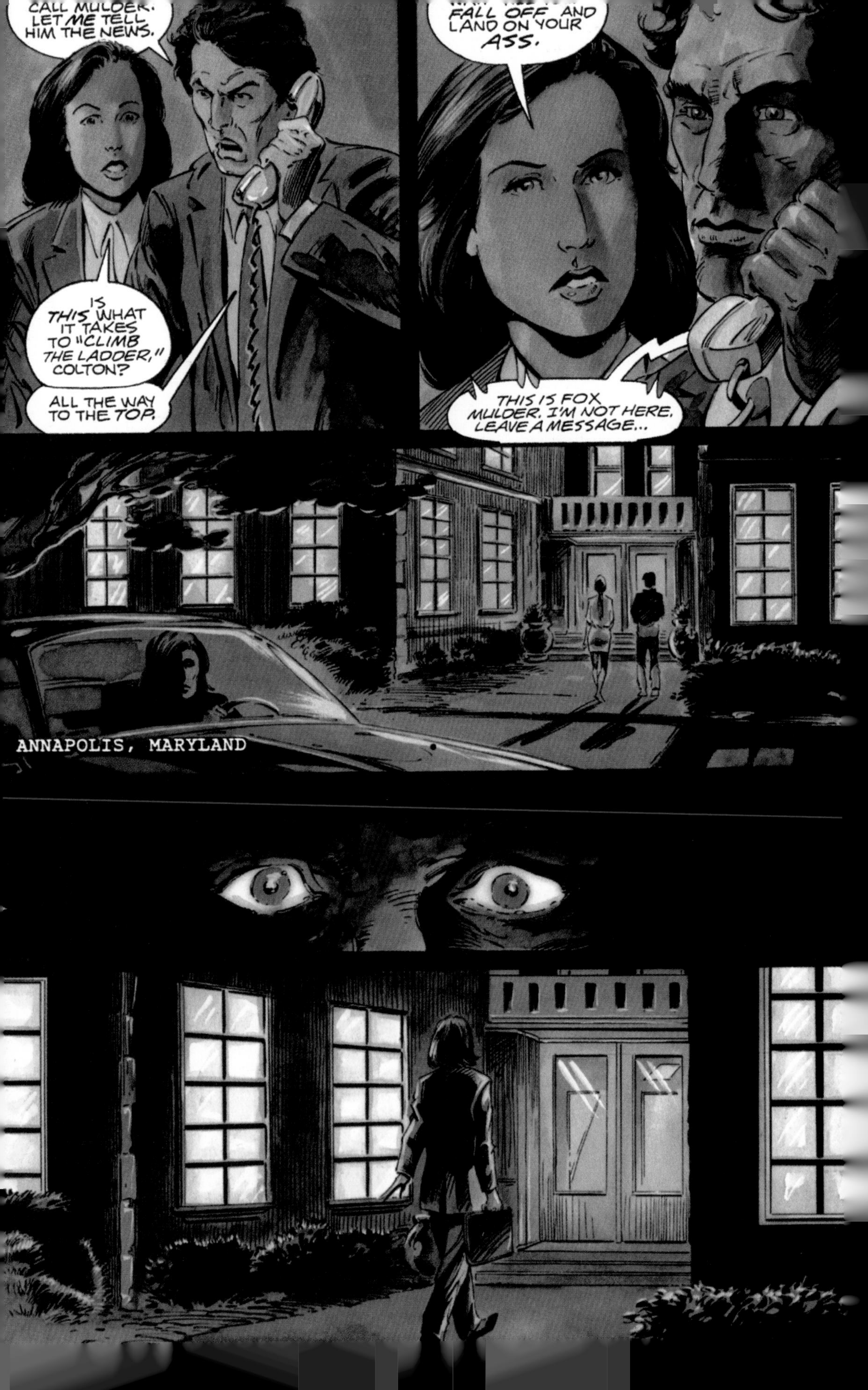
CALL MULDER. LET *ME* TELL HIM THE NEWS.
IS *THIS* WHAT IT TAKES TO "*CLIMB THE LADDER,*" COLTON?
ALL THE WAY TO THE *TOP.*
FALL OFF AND LAND ON YOUR *ASS.*
THIS IS FOX MULDER. I'M NOT HERE. LEAVE A MESSAGE...
ANNAPOLIS, MARYLAND

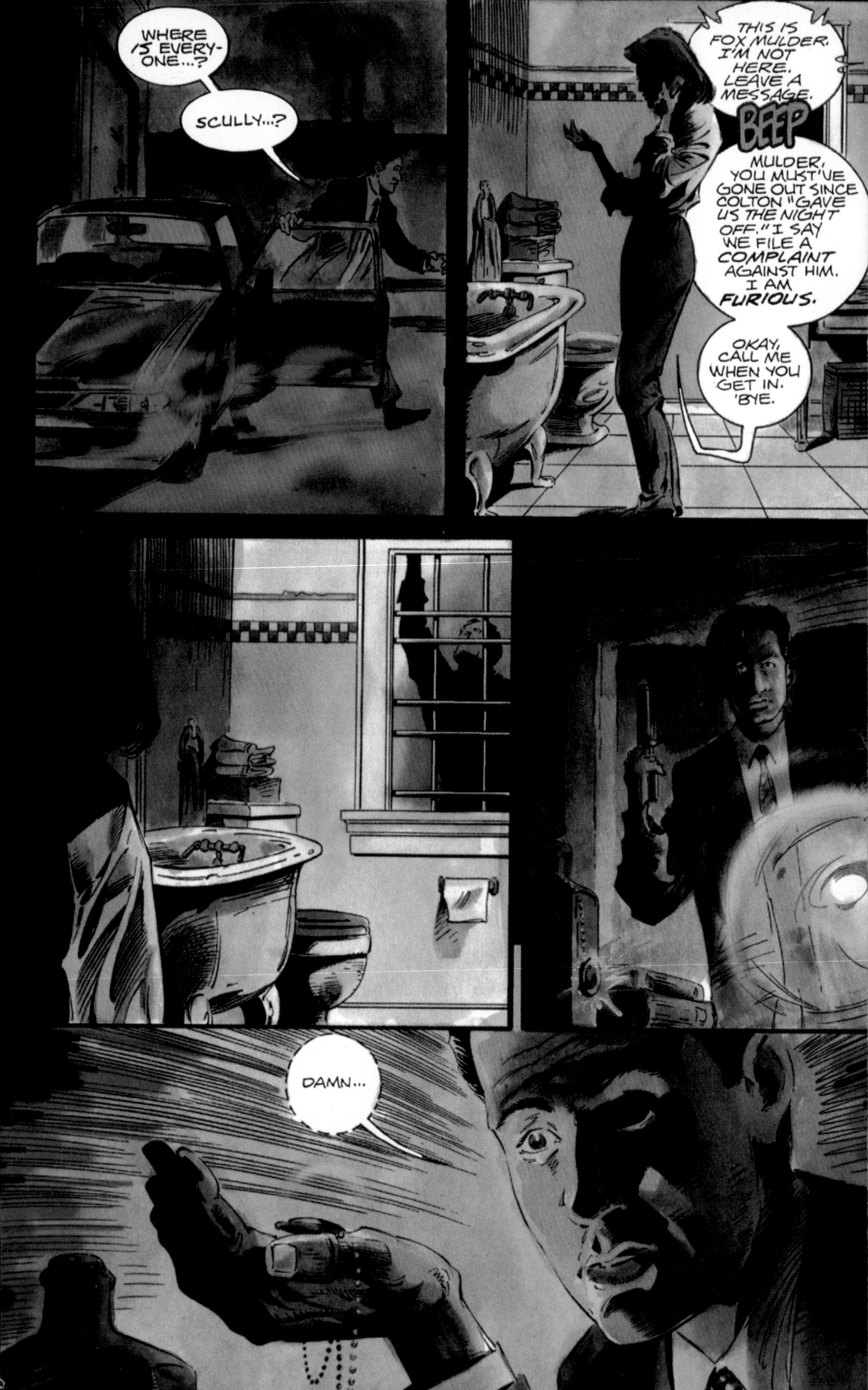
WHERE IS EVERY-ONE...?
SCULLY...?
THIS IS FOX MULDER. I'M NOT HERE. LEAVE A MESSAGE.
BEEP
MULDER, YOU MUST'VE GONE OUT SINCE COLTON "GAVE US THE NIGHT OFF." I SAY WE FILE A COMPLAINT AGAINST HIM. I AM FURIOUS.
OKAY, CALL ME WHEN YOU GET IN. 'BYE.
DAMN...

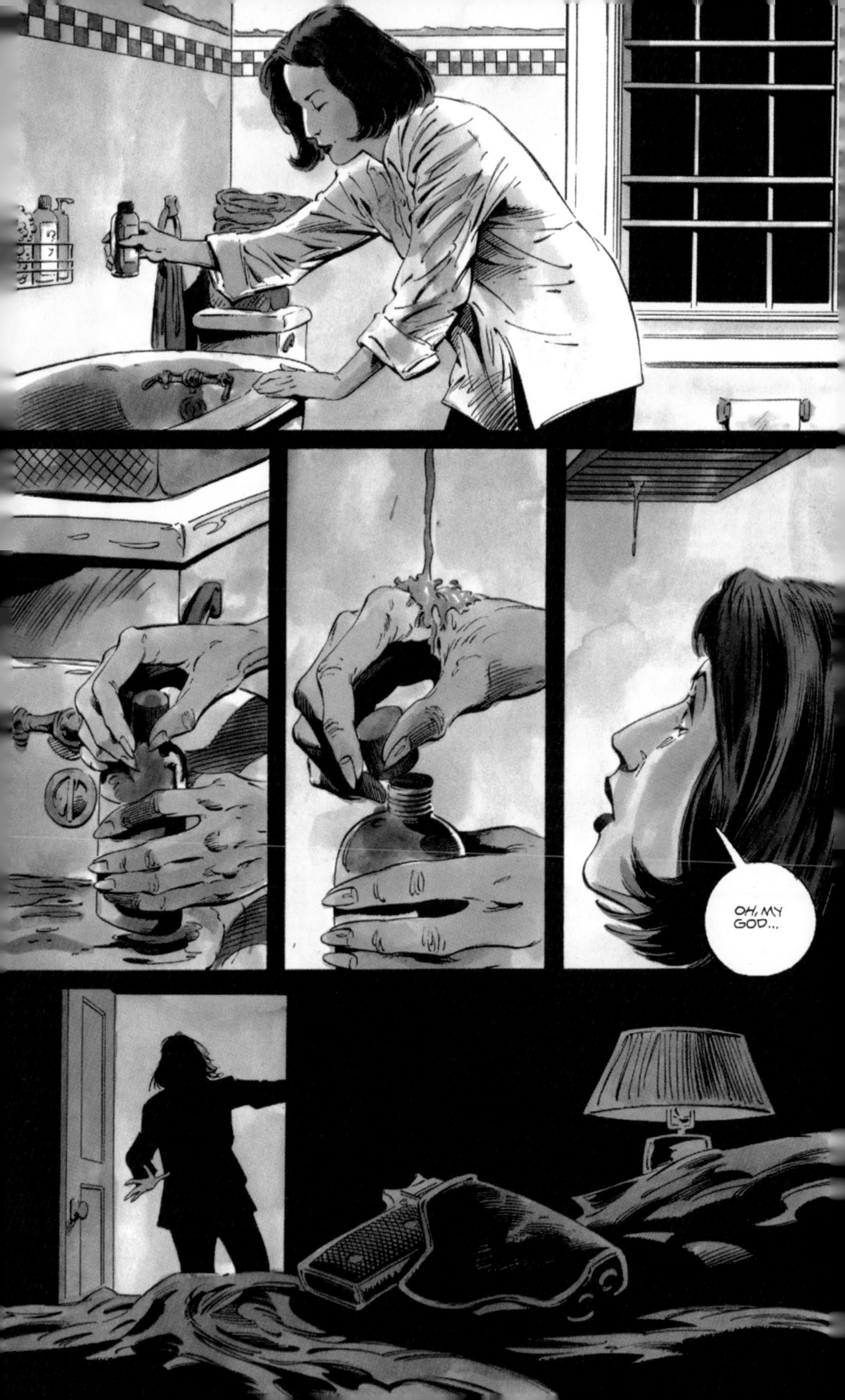
OH, MY GOD...

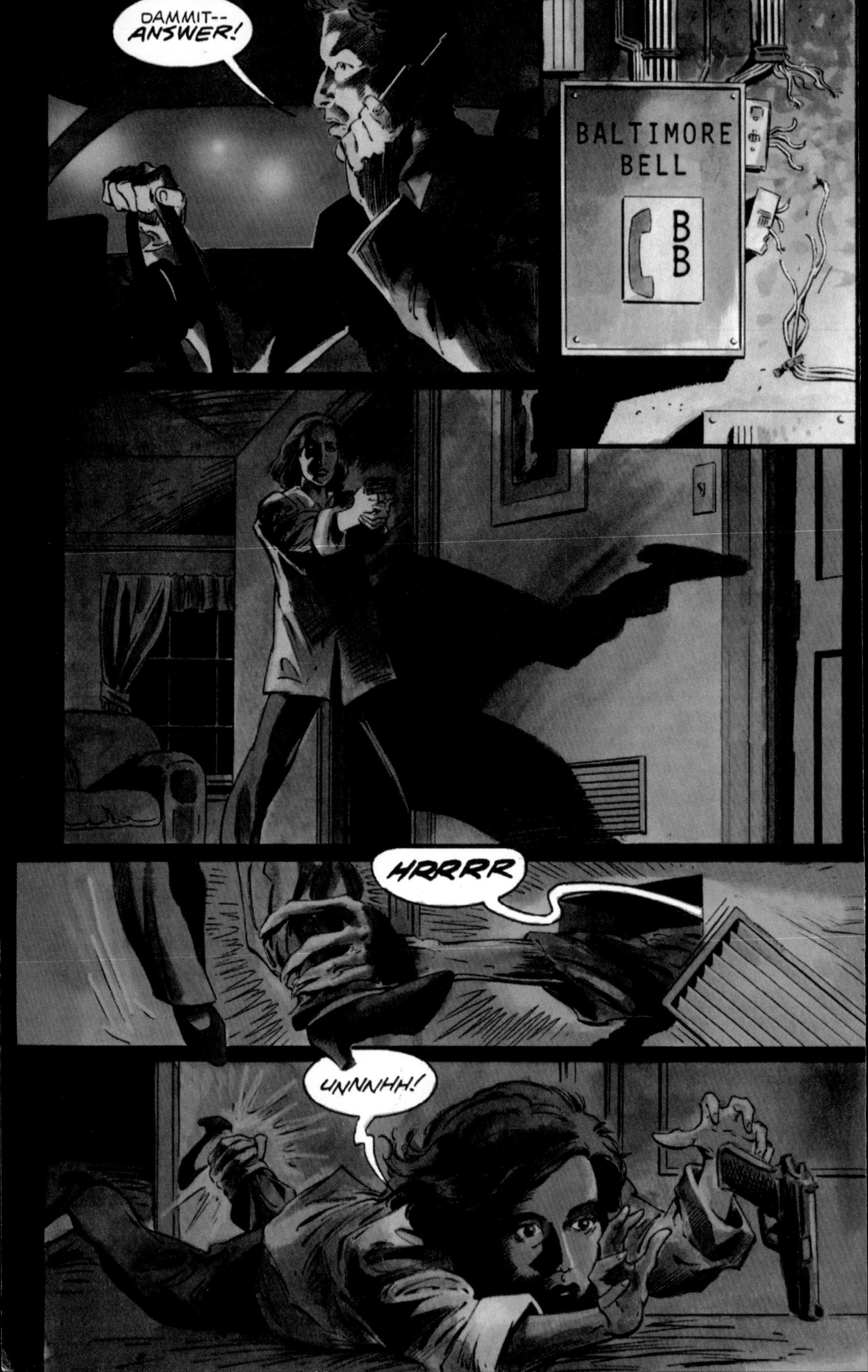
DAMMIT--
ANSWER!
BALTIMORE
BELL
BB
HRRRR
UNNNHH!

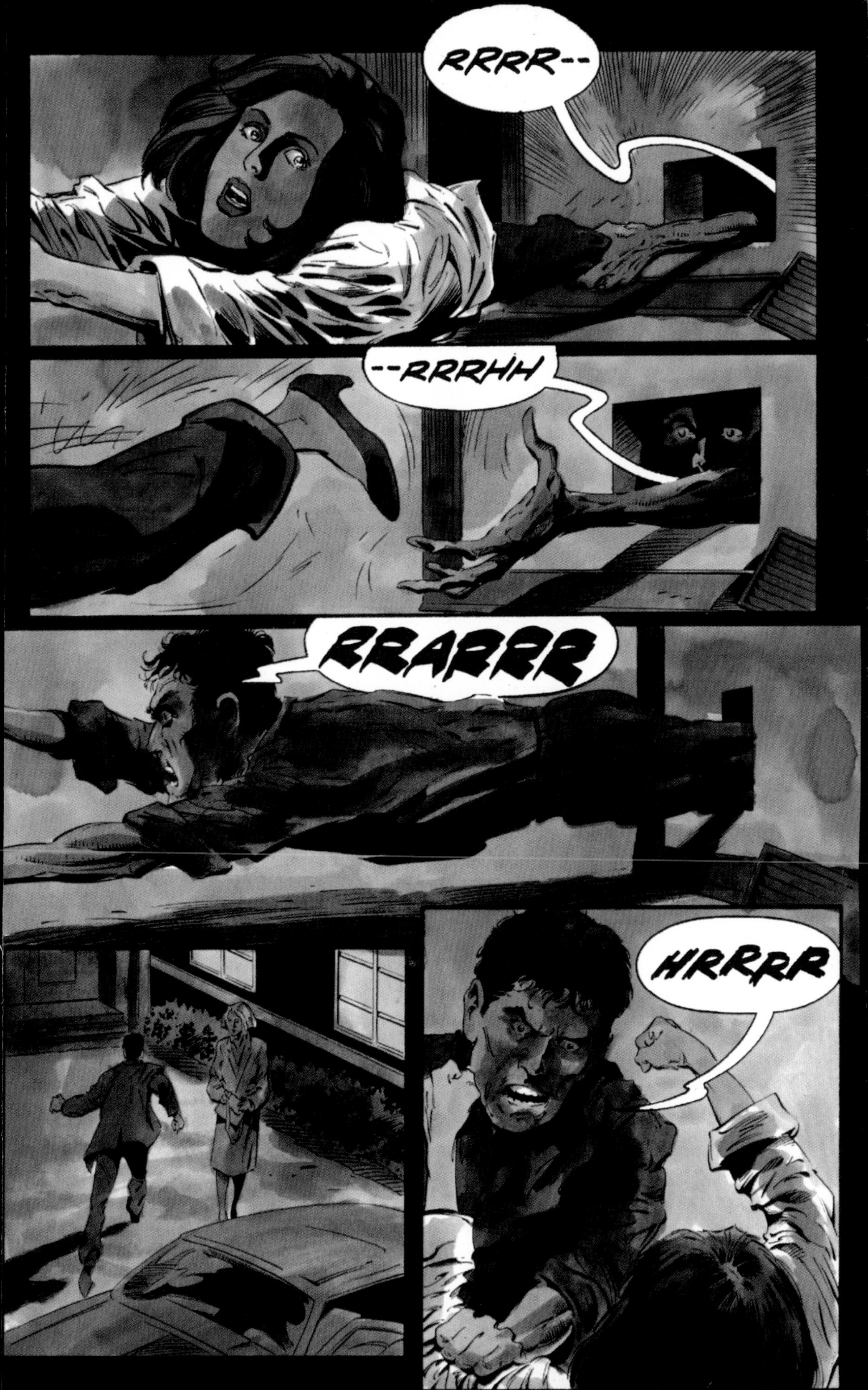
RRRR--
--RRRHH
RRARRR
HRRRR

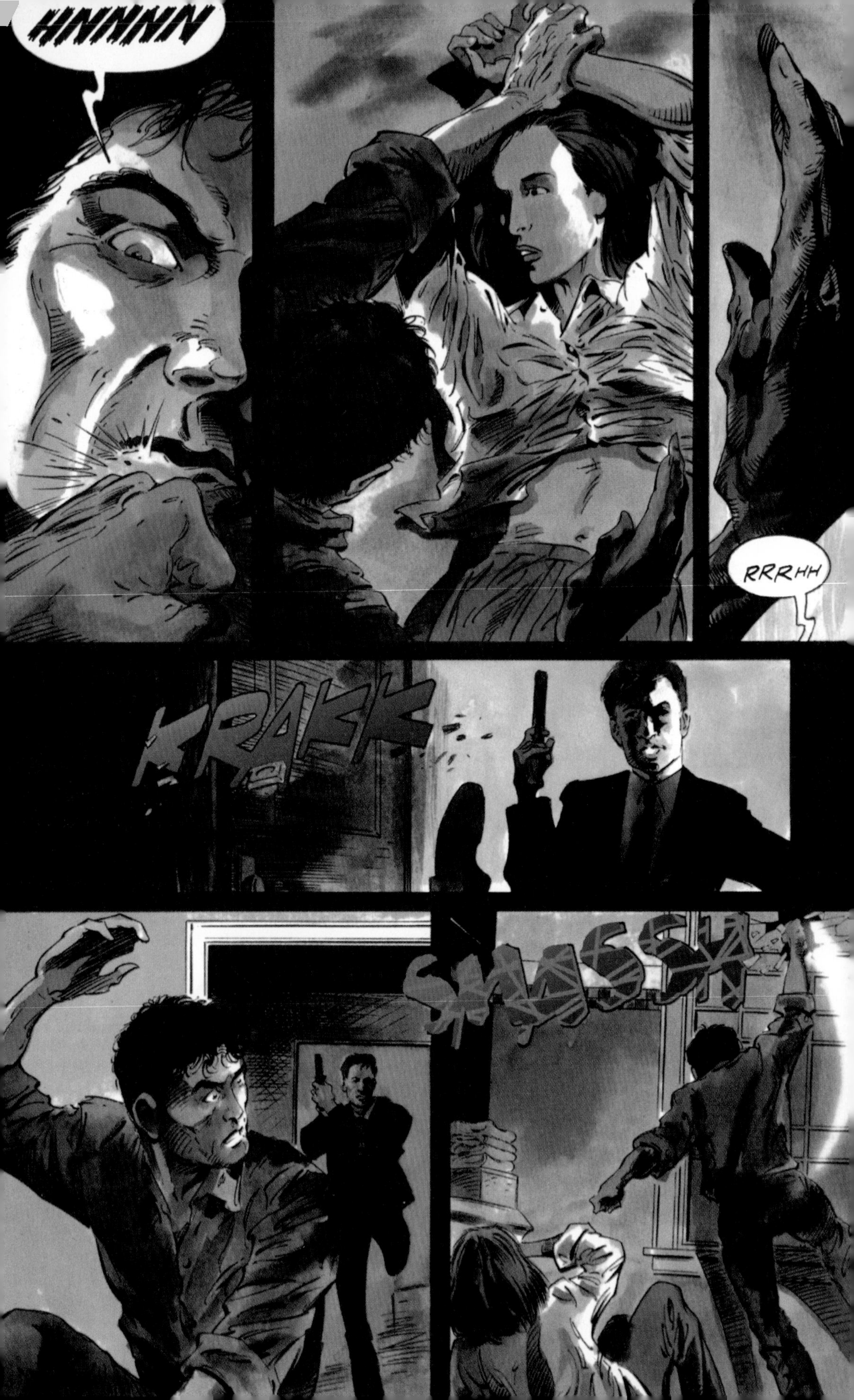
HNNNNN
RRRHH
KRAKK
SMASSH

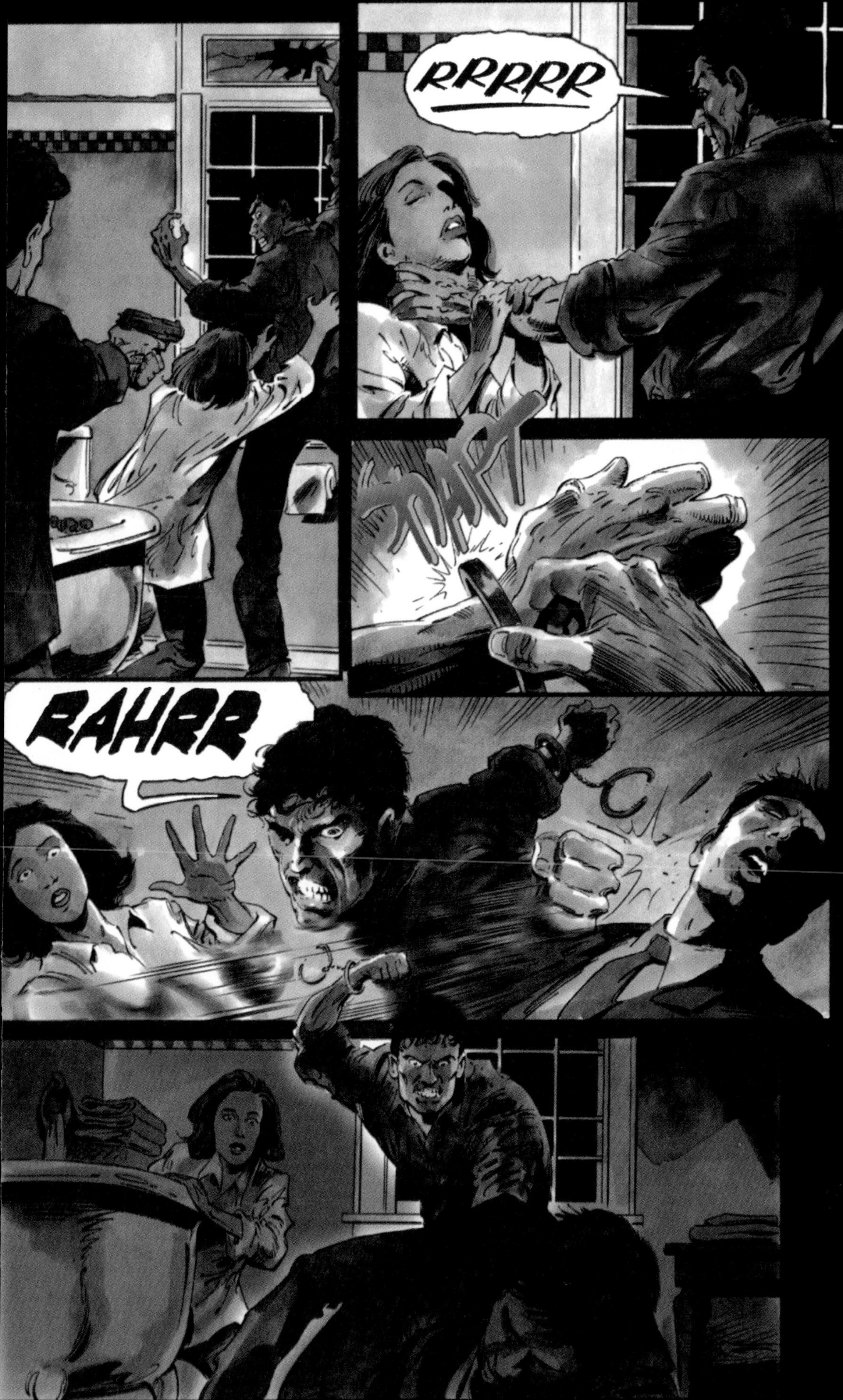
RRRRR
THAPT
RAHRR

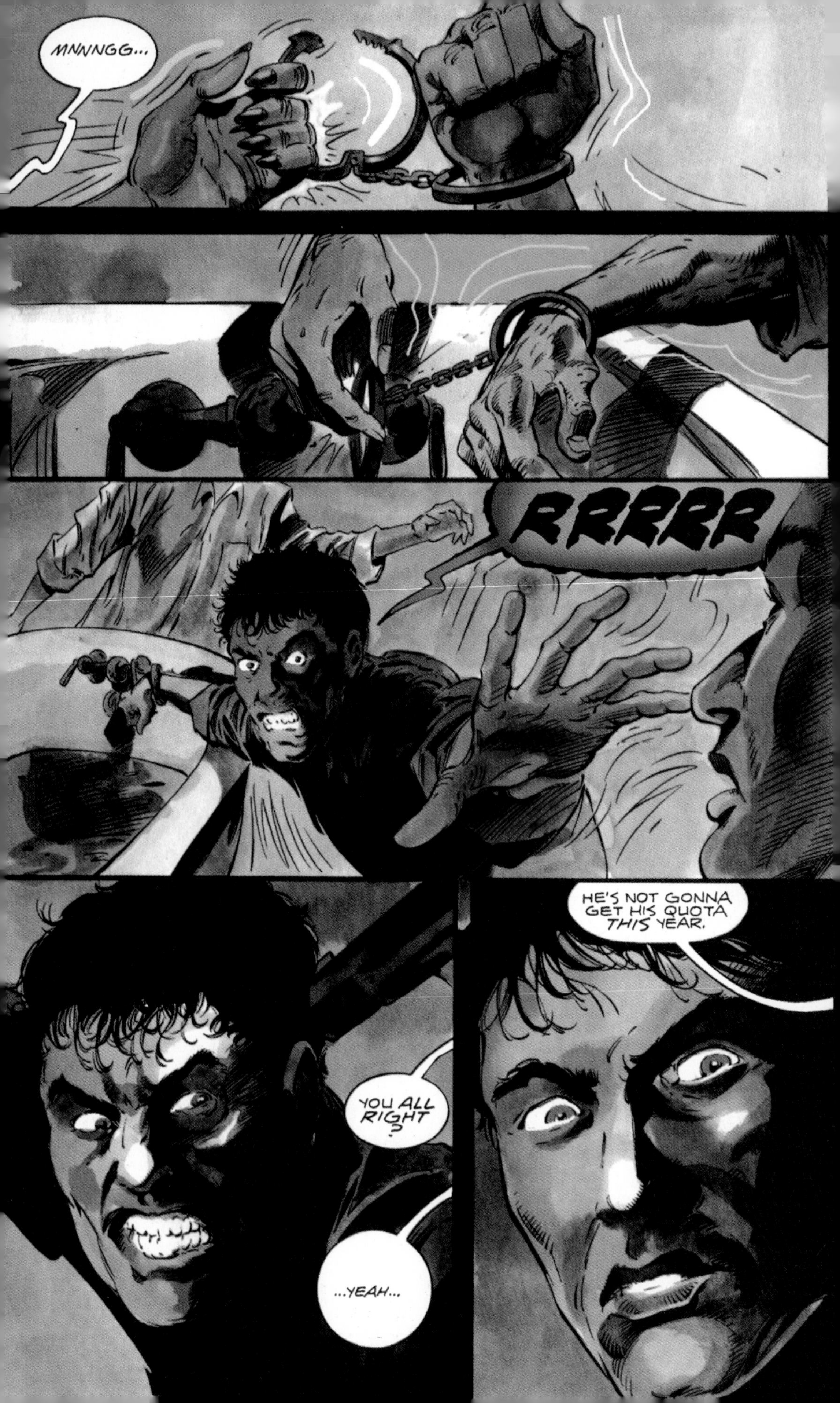
MNNNGG...
RRRRR
HE'S NOT GONNA GET HIS QUOTA THIS YEAR.
YOU ALL RIGHT?
...YEAH...

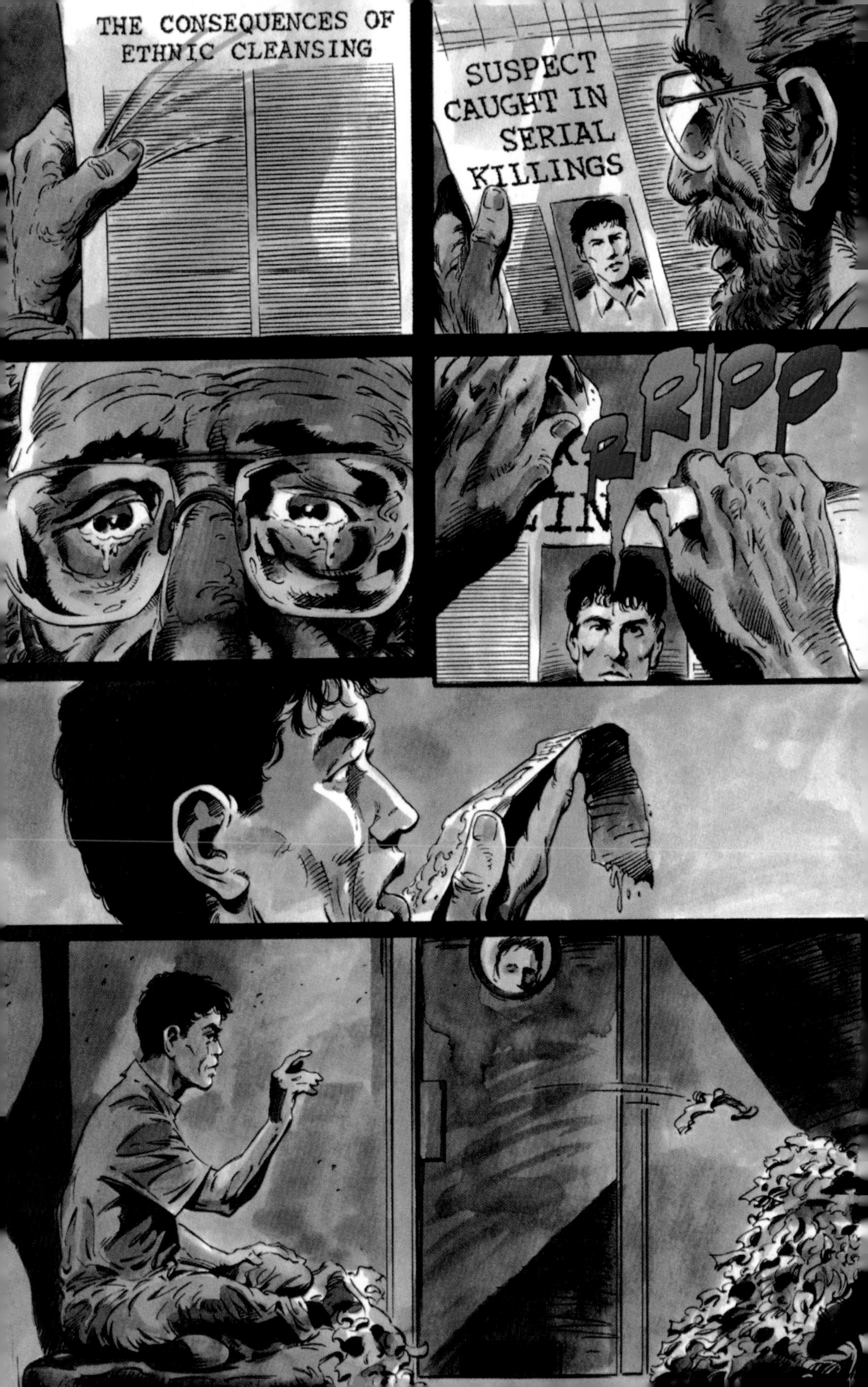
THE CONSEQUENCES OF ETHNIC CLEANSING
SUSPECT CAUGHT IN SERIAL KILLINGS
RRIPP

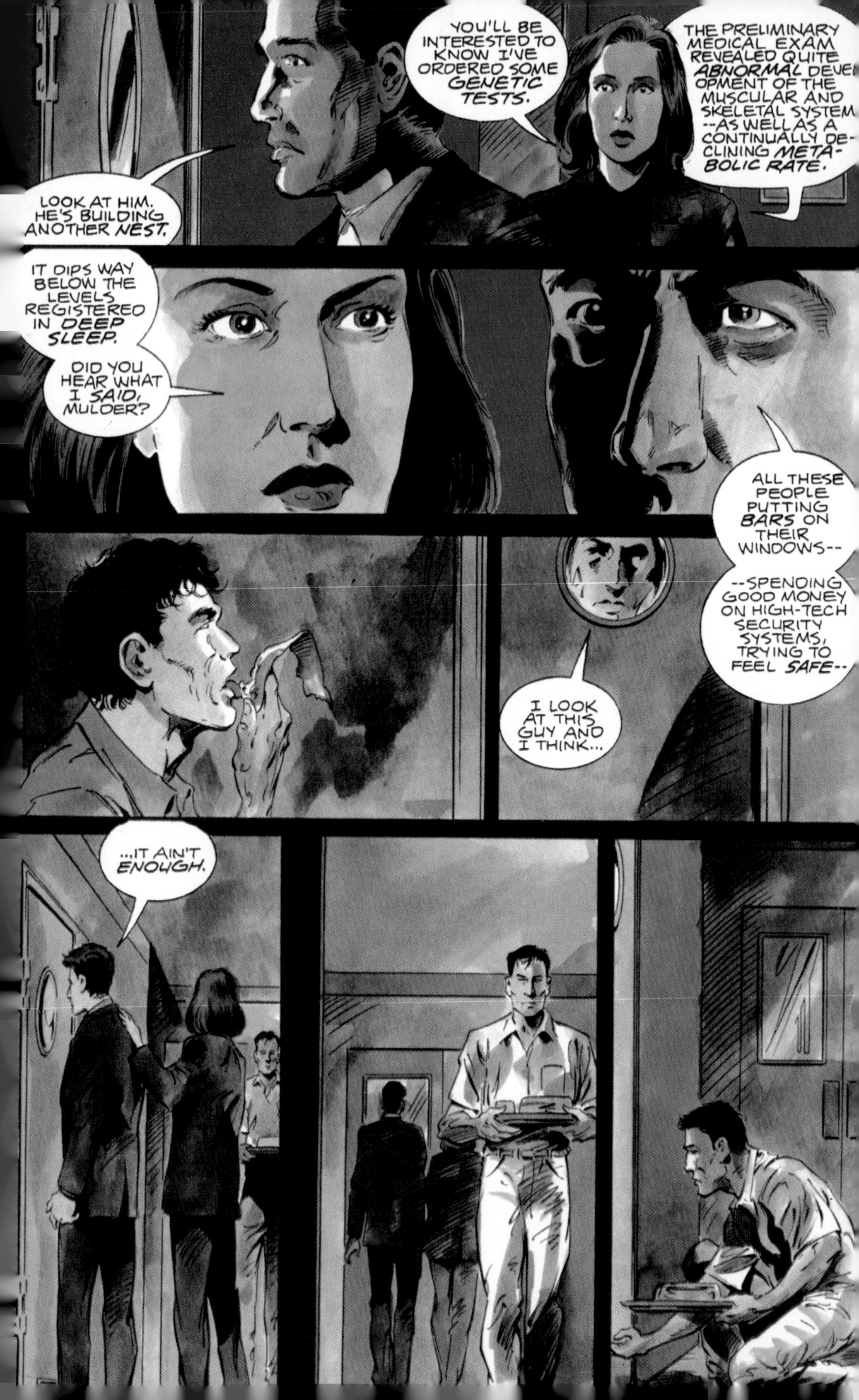
LOOK AT HIM. HE'S BUILDING ANOTHER NEST.
YOU'LL BE INTERESTED TO KNOW I'VE ORDERED SOME GENETIC TESTS.
THE PRELIMINARY MEDICAL EXAM REVEALED QUITE ABNORMAL DEVEL-OPMENT OF THE MUSCULAR AND SKELETAL SYSTEM --AS WELL AS A CONTINUALLY DE-CLINING METABOLIC RATE.
IT DIPS WAY BELOW THE LEVELS REGISTERED IN DEEP SLEEP.
DID YOU HEAR WHAT I SAID, MULDER?
ALL THESE PEOPLE PUTTING BARS ON THEIR WINDOWS--
--SPENDING GOOD MONEY ON HIGH-TECH SECURITY SYSTEMS, TRYING TO FEEL SAFE--
I LOOK AT THIS GUY AND I THINK...
...IT AIN'T ENOUGH.

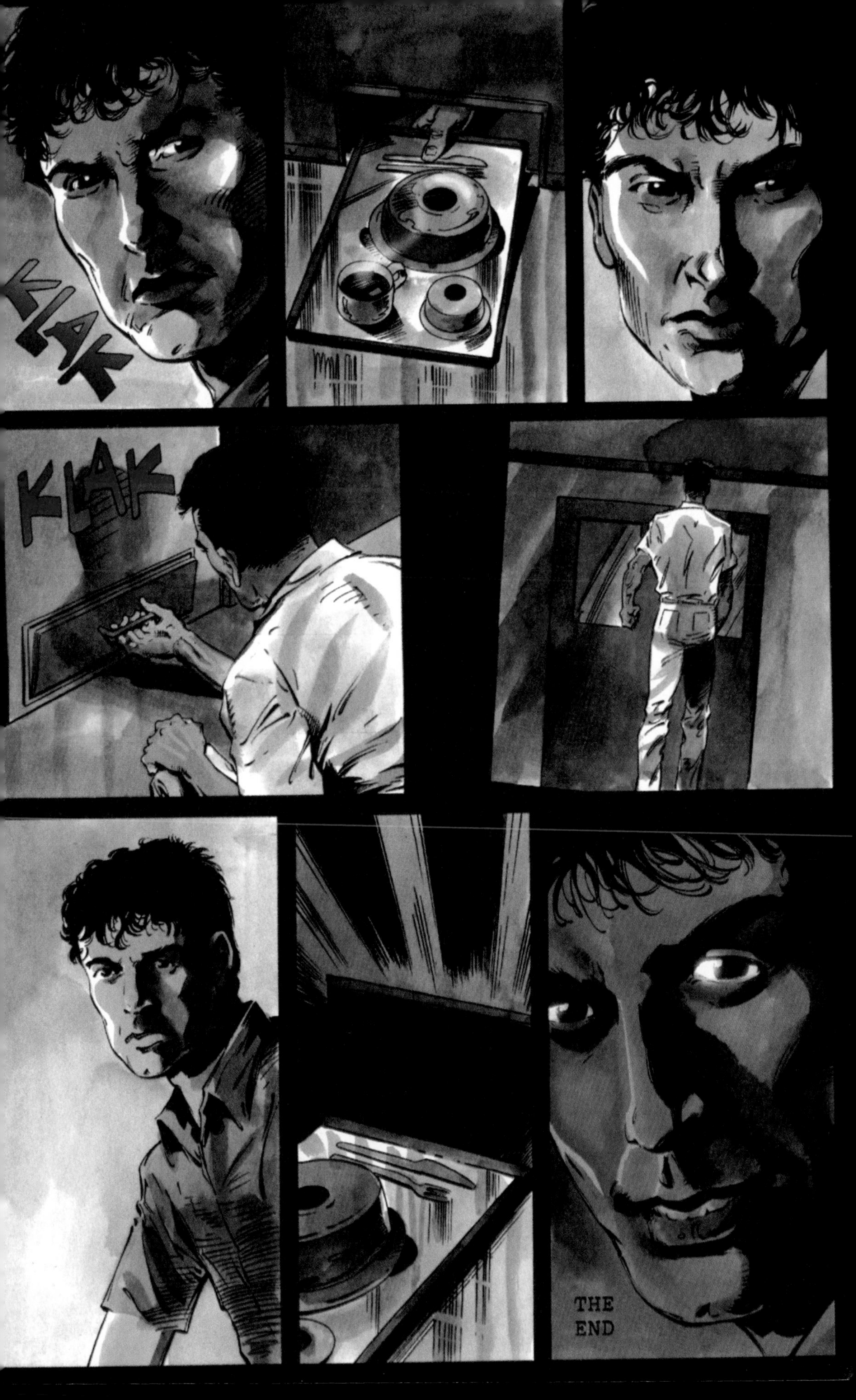
KLAK
KLAK
THE END

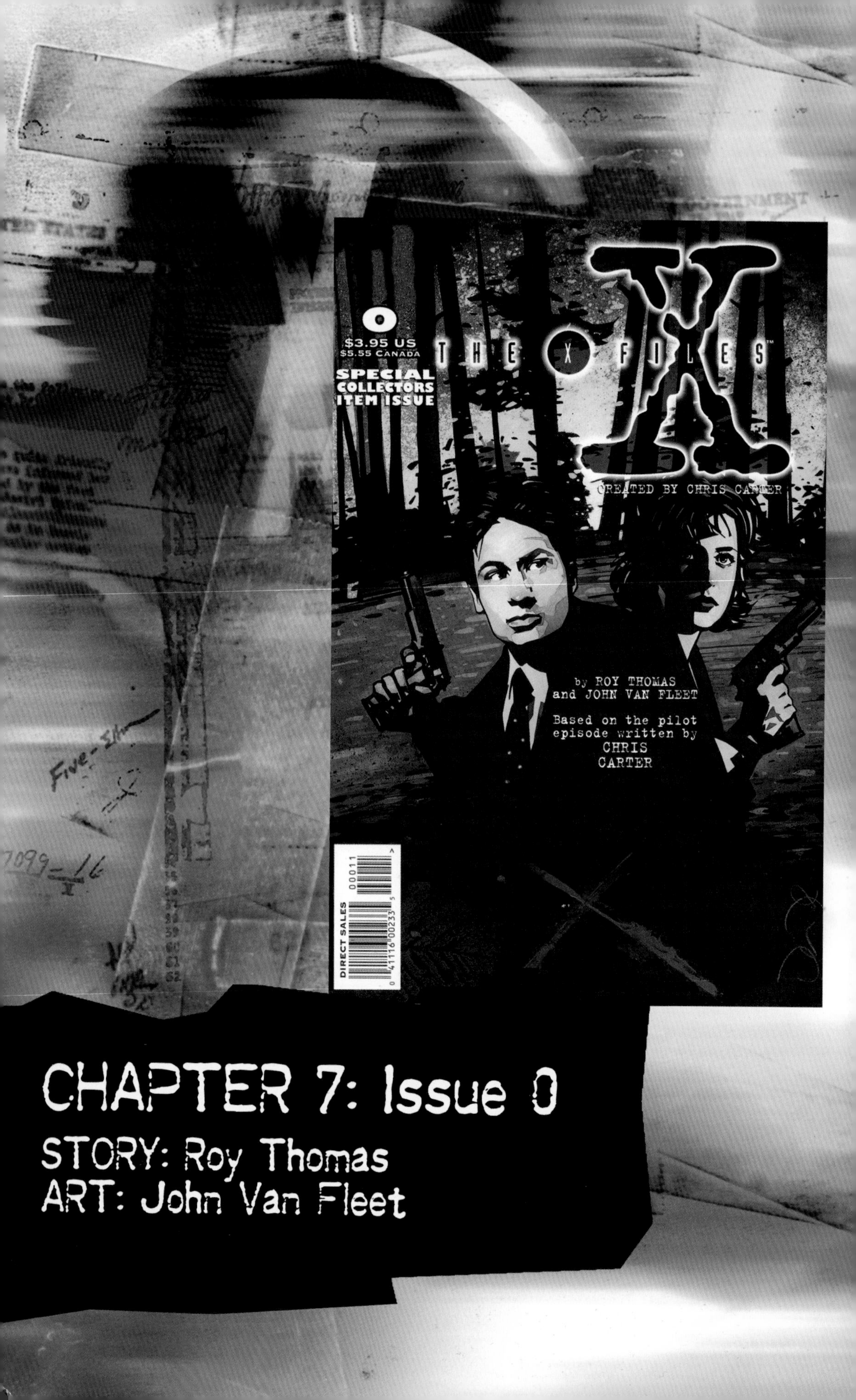
0
$3.95 US
$5.55 CANADA
SPECIAL COLLECTORS ITEM ISSUE
THE X FILES
CREATED BY CHRIS CARTER
by ROY THOMAS and JOHN VAN FLEET
Based on the pilot episode written by CHRIS CARTER
DIRECT SALES

CHAPTER 7: Issue 0

STORY: Roy Thomas
ART: John Van Fleet

THE FOLLOWING IS INSPIRED BY ACTUAL EYEWITNESS ACCOUNTS.

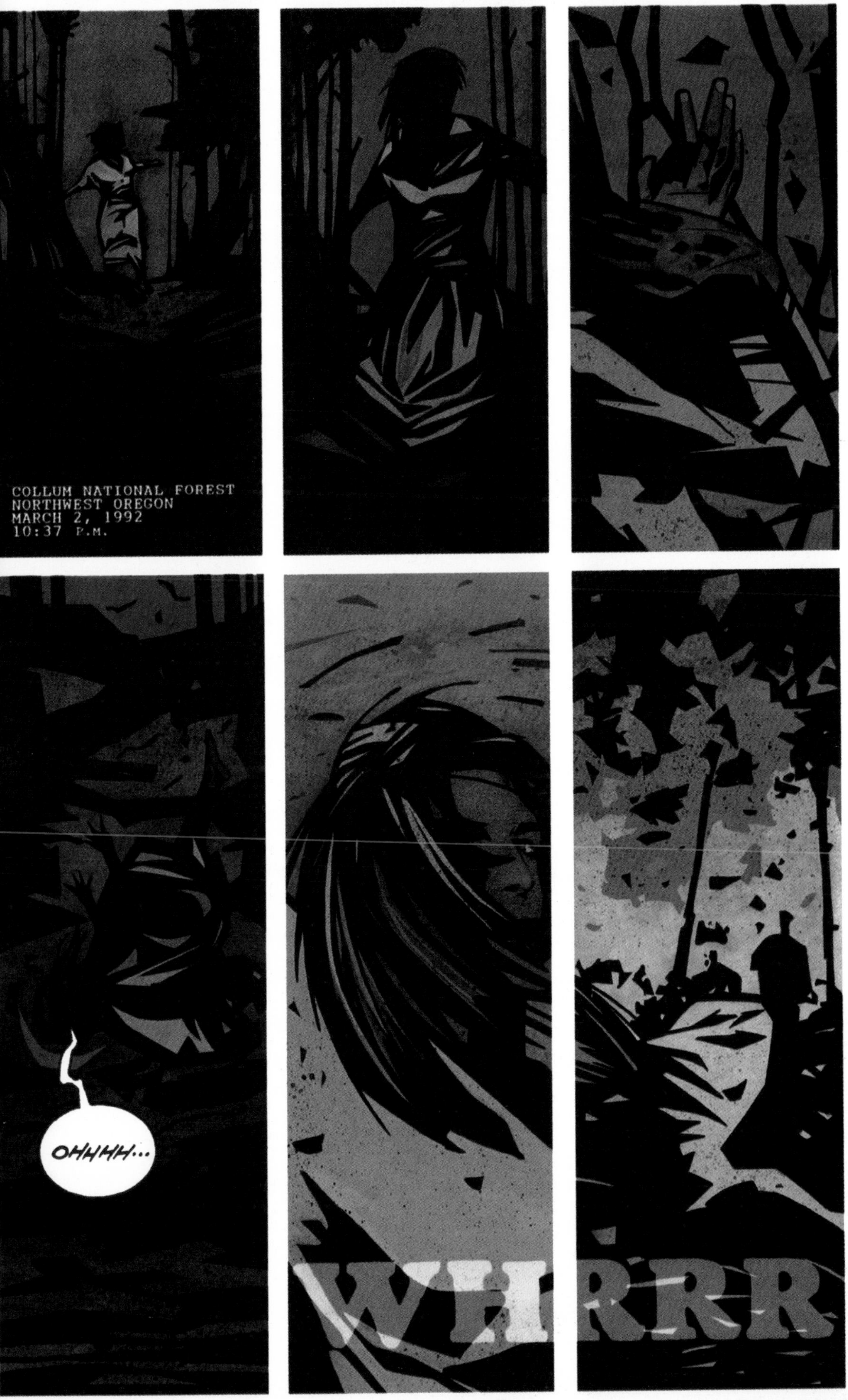
COLLUM NATIONAL FOREST
NORTHWEST OREGON
MARCH 2, 1992
10:37 P.M.
OHHHH...
WHRRR

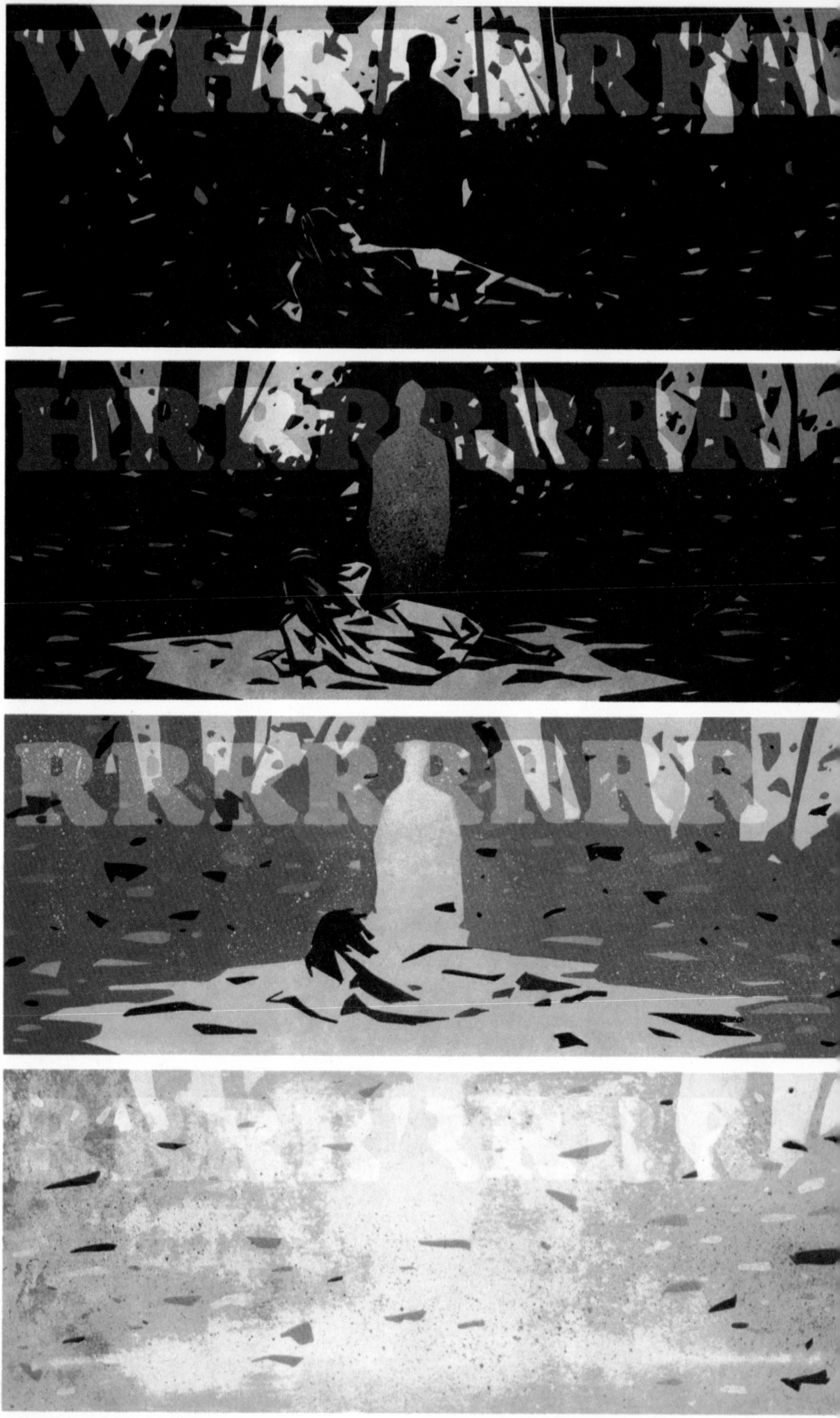
WHRRRRRR
HRRRRRRR
RRRRRRRR

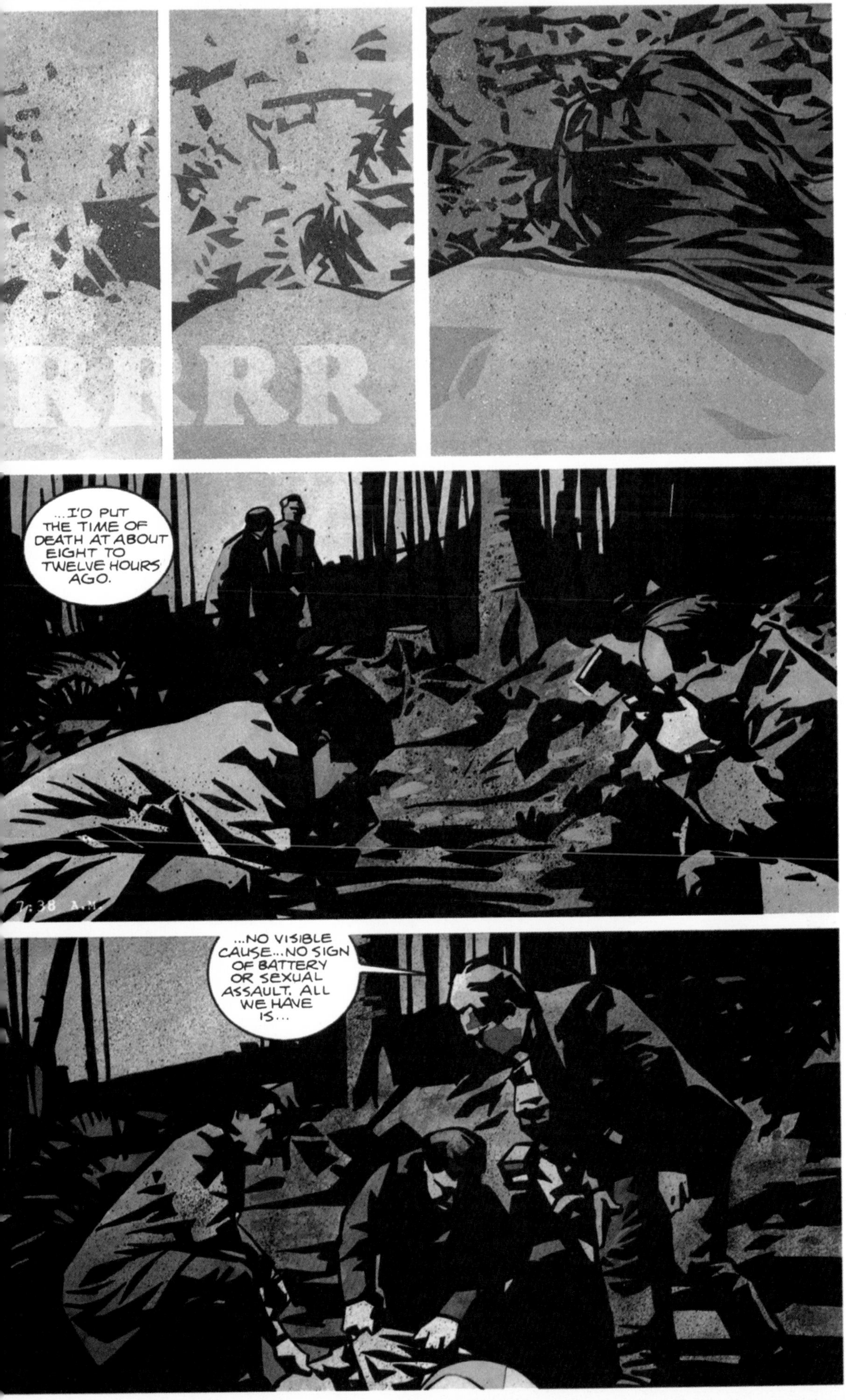
RRRRR
...I'D PUT THE TIME OF DEATH AT ABOUT EIGHT TO TWELVE HOURS AGO.
7:38 A.M.
...NO VISIBLE CAUSE...NO SIGN OF BATTERY OR SEXUAL ASSAULT. ALL WE HAVE IS...

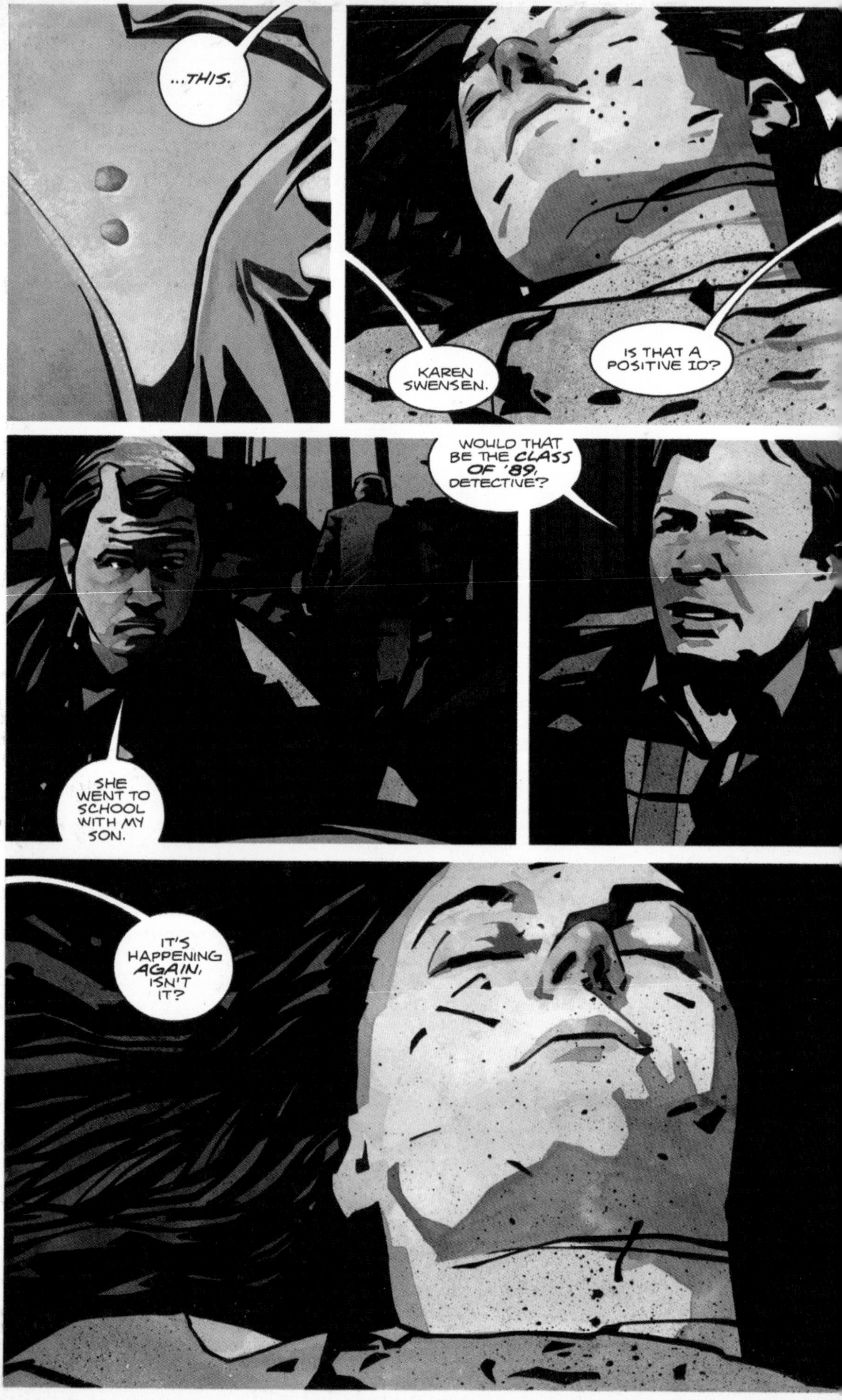
...THIS.
KAREN SWENSEN.
IS THAT A POSITIVE ID?
WOULD THAT BE THE CLASS OF '89, DETECTIVE?
SHE WENT TO SCHOOL WITH MY SON.
IT'S HAPPENING AGAIN, ISN'T IT?

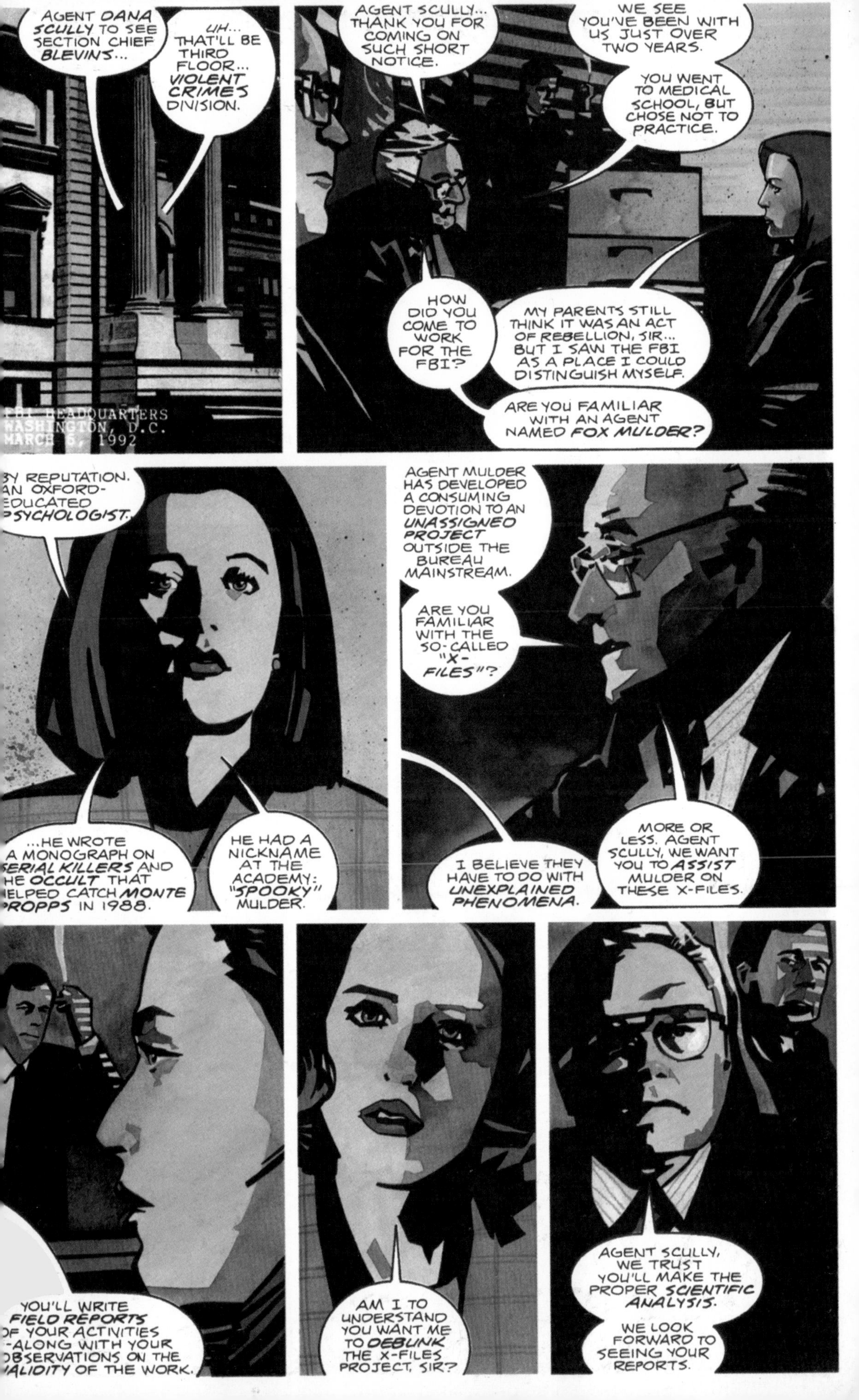
AGENT DANA SCULLY TO SEE SECTION CHIEF BLEVINS...
UH... THAT'LL BE THIRD FLOOR... VIOLENT CRIMES DIVISION.
FBI HEADQUARTERS
WASHINGTON, D.C.
MARCH 6, 1992
AGENT SCULLY... THANK YOU FOR COMING ON SUCH SHORT NOTICE.
WE SEE YOU'VE BEEN WITH US JUST OVER TWO YEARS.
YOU WENT TO MEDICAL SCHOOL, BUT CHOSE NOT TO PRACTICE.
HOW DID YOU COME TO WORK FOR THE FBI?
MY PARENTS STILL THINK IT WAS AN ACT OF REBELLION, SIR... BUT I SAW THE FBI AS A PLACE I COULD DISTINGUISH MYSELF.
ARE YOU FAMILIAR WITH AN AGENT NAMED FOX MULDER?
BY REPUTATION. AN OXFORD-EDUCATED PSYCHOLOGIST...
...HE WROTE A MONOGRAPH ON SERIAL KILLERS AND THE OCCULT THAT HELPED CATCH MONTE PROPPS IN 1988.
HE HAD A NICKNAME AT THE ACADEMY: "SPOOKY" MULDER.
AGENT MULDER HAS DEVELOPED A CONSUMING DEVOTION TO AN UNASSIGNED PROJECT OUTSIDE THE BUREAU MAINSTREAM.
ARE YOU FAMILIAR WITH THE SO-CALLED "X-FILES"?
I BELIEVE THEY HAVE TO DO WITH UNEXPLAINED PHENOMENA.
MORE OR LESS. AGENT SCULLY, WE WANT YOU TO ASSIST MULDER ON THESE X-FILES.
YOU'LL WRITE FIELD REPORTS OF YOUR ACTIVITIES --ALONG WITH YOUR OBSERVATIONS ON THE VALIDITY OF THE WORK.
AM I TO UNDERSTAND YOU WANT ME TO DEBUNK THE X-FILES PROJECT, SIR?
AGENT SCULLY, WE TRUST YOU'LL MAKE THE PROPER SCIENTIFIC ANALYSIS.
WE LOOK FORWARD TO SEEING YOUR REPORTS.

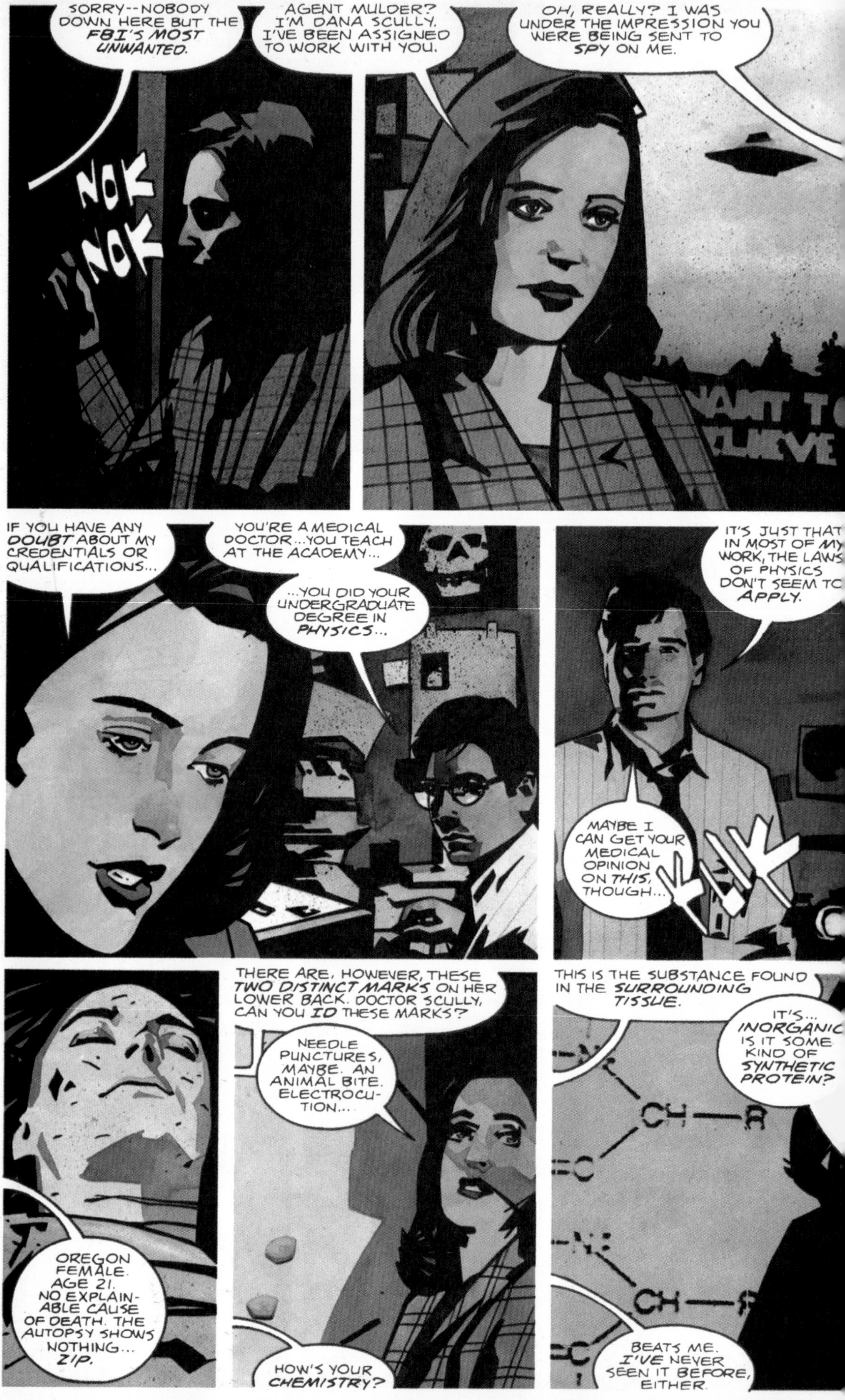
SORRY--NOBODY DOWN HERE BUT THE FBI'S MOST UNWANTED.
NOK NOK
AGENT MULDER? I'M DANA SCULLY. I'VE BEEN ASSIGNED TO WORK WITH YOU.
OH, REALLY? I WAS UNDER THE IMPRESSION YOU WERE BEING SENT TO SPY ON ME.
IF YOU HAVE ANY DOUBT ABOUT MY CREDENTIALS OR QUALIFICATIONS...
YOU'RE A MEDICAL DOCTOR... YOU TEACH AT THE ACADEMY...
...YOU DID YOUR UNDERGRADUATE DEGREE IN PHYSICS...
IT'S JUST THAT IN MOST OF MY WORK, THE LAWS OF PHYSICS DON'T SEEM TO APPLY.
MAYBE I CAN GET YOUR MEDICAL OPINION ON THIS, THOUGH...
OREGON FEMALE. AGE 21. NO EXPLAINABLE CAUSE OF DEATH. THE AUTOPSY SHOWS NOTHING... ZIP.
THERE ARE, HOWEVER, THESE TWO DISTINCT MARKS ON HER LOWER BACK. DOCTOR SCULLY, CAN YOU ID THESE MARKS?
NEEDLE PUNCTURES, MAYBE. AN ANIMAL BITE. ELECTROCUTION...
HOW'S YOUR CHEMISTRY?
THIS IS THE SUBSTANCE FOUND IN THE SURROUNDING TISSUE.
IT'S... INORGANIC. IS IT SOME KIND OF SYNTHETIC PROTEIN?
BEATS ME. I'VE NEVER SEEN IT BEFORE, EITHER.

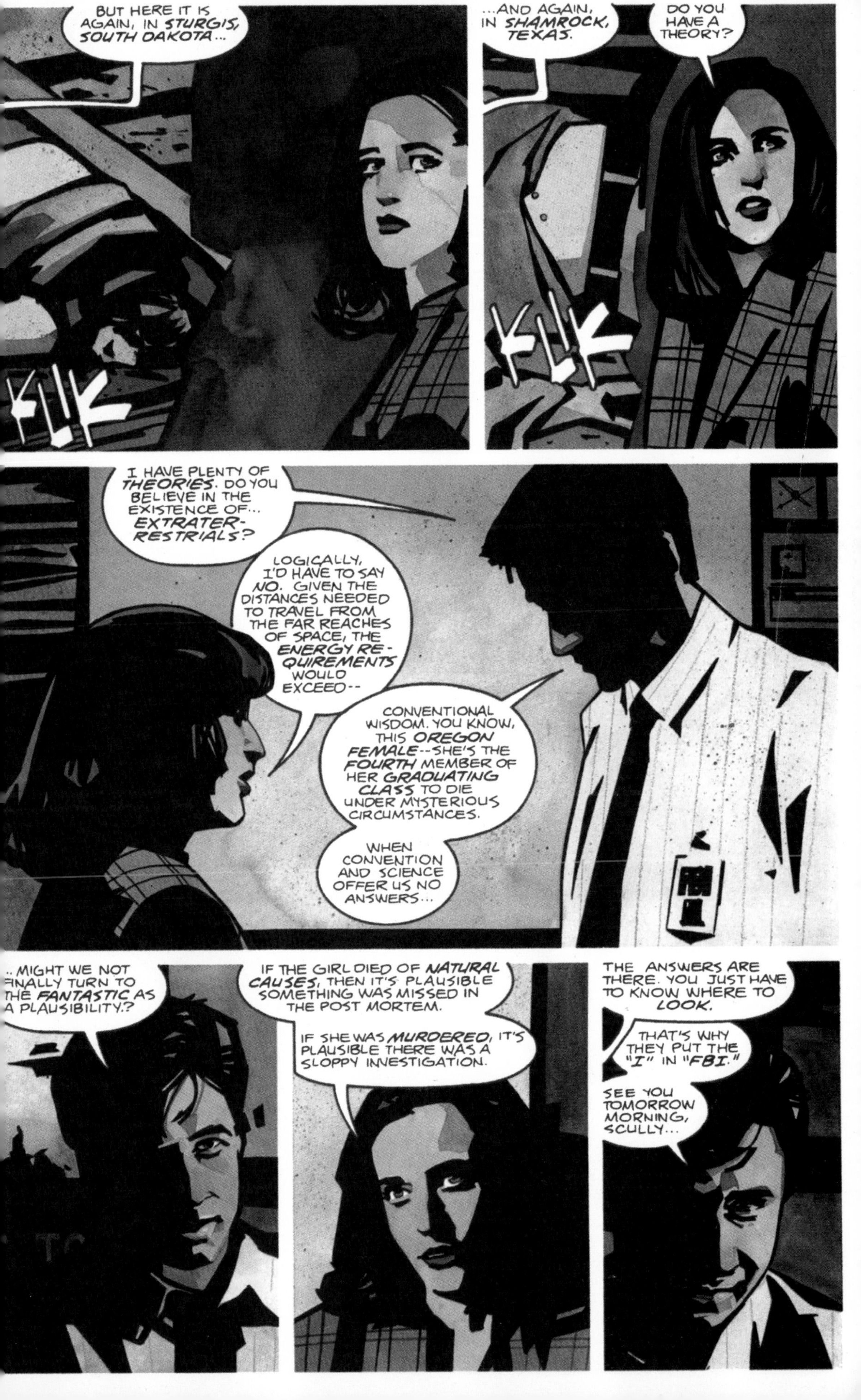
BUT HERE IT IS AGAIN, IN STURGIS, SOUTH DAKOTA...
KLIK
...AND AGAIN, IN SHAMROCK, TEXAS.
DO YOU HAVE A THEORY?
KLIK
I HAVE PLENTY OF THEORIES. DO YOU BELIEVE IN THE EXISTENCE OF... EXTRATER-RESTRIALS?
LOGICALLY, I'D HAVE TO SAY NO. GIVEN THE DISTANCES NEEDED TO TRAVEL FROM THE FAR REACHES OF SPACE, THE ENERGY RE-QUIREMENTS WOULD EXCEED--
CONVENTIONAL WISDOM. YOU KNOW, THIS OREGON FEMALE--SHE'S THE FOURTH MEMBER OF HER GRADUATING CLASS TO DIE UNDER MYSTERIOUS CIRCUMSTANCES.
WHEN CONVENTION AND SCIENCE OFFER US NO ANSWERS...
..MIGHT WE NOT FINALLY TURN TO THE FANTASTIC AS A PLAUSIBILITY.?
IF THE GIRL DIED OF NATURAL CAUSES, THEN IT'S PLAUSIBLE SOMETHING WAS MISSED IN THE POST MORTEM.
IF SHE WAS MURDERED, IT'S PLAUSIBLE THERE WAS A SLOPPY INVESTIGATION.
THE ANSWERS ARE THERE. YOU JUST HAVE TO KNOW WHERE TO LOOK.
THAT'S WHY THEY PUT THE "I" IN "FBI."
SEE YOU TOMORROW MORNING, SCULLY...

"WE LEAVE FOR THE VERY *PLAUSIBLE* STATE OF OREGON AT **8** A.M."

FORMER HONOR STUDENT'S BODY FOUND IN STATE PARK

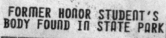

4TH TRAGIC FATALITY BEFALLS CLASS OF '89

I'D LIKE TO ASK ALL PASSENGERS TO FASTEN THEIR *SEAT BELTS*, AS WE'RE ABOUT TO BEGIN OUR DESCENT INTO--

EEEEE

WHAT THE HELL --?

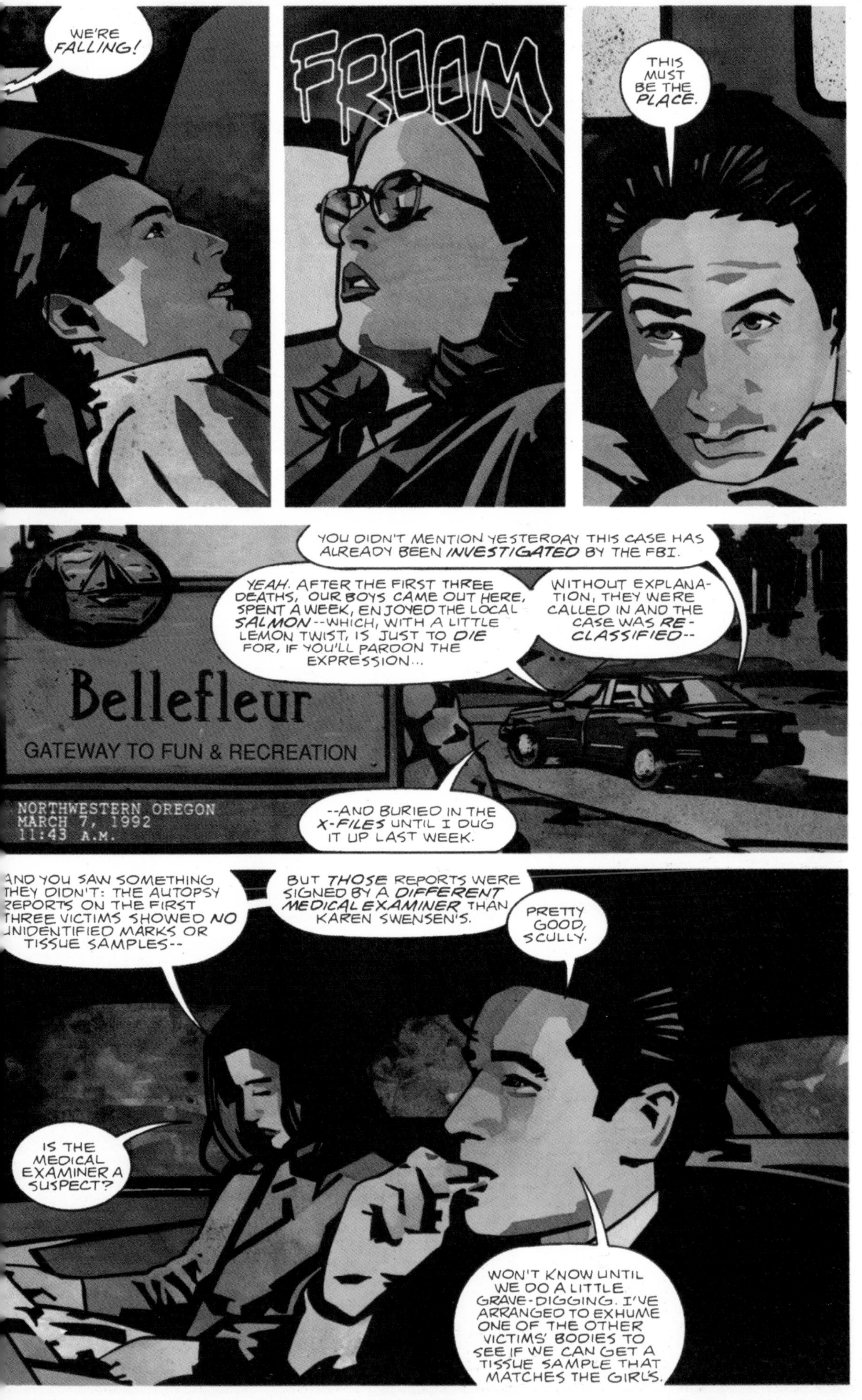
WE'RE FALLING!
FROOM
THIS MUST BE THE PLACE.
YOU DIDN'T MENTION YESTERDAY THIS CASE HAS ALREADY BEEN INVESTIGATED BY THE FBI.
YEAH. AFTER THE FIRST THREE DEATHS, OUR BOYS CAME OUT HERE, SPENT A WEEK, ENJOYED THE LOCAL SALMON--WHICH, WITH A LITTLE LEMON TWIST, IS JUST TO DIE FOR, IF YOU'LL PARDON THE EXPRESSION...
WITHOUT EXPLANATION, THEY WERE CALLED IN AND THE CASE WAS RE-CLASSIFIED--
Bellefleur
GATEWAY TO FUN & RECREATION
NORTHWESTERN OREGON
MARCH 7, 1992
11:43 A.M.
--AND BURIED IN THE X-FILES UNTIL I DUG IT UP LAST WEEK.
AND YOU SAW SOMETHING THEY DIDN'T: THE AUTOPSY REPORTS ON THE FIRST THREE VICTIMS SHOWED NO UNIDENTIFIED MARKS OR TISSUE SAMPLES--
BUT THOSE REPORTS WERE SIGNED BY A DIFFERENT MEDICAL EXAMINER THAN KAREN SWENSEN'S.
PRETTY GOOD, SCULLY.
IS THE MEDICAL EXAMINER A SUSPECT?
WON'T KNOW UNTIL WE DO A LITTLE GRAVE-DIGGING. I'VE ARRANGED TO EXHUME ONE OF THE OTHER VICTIMS' BODIES TO SEE IF WE CAN GET A TISSUE SAMPLE THAT MATCHES THE GIRL'S.

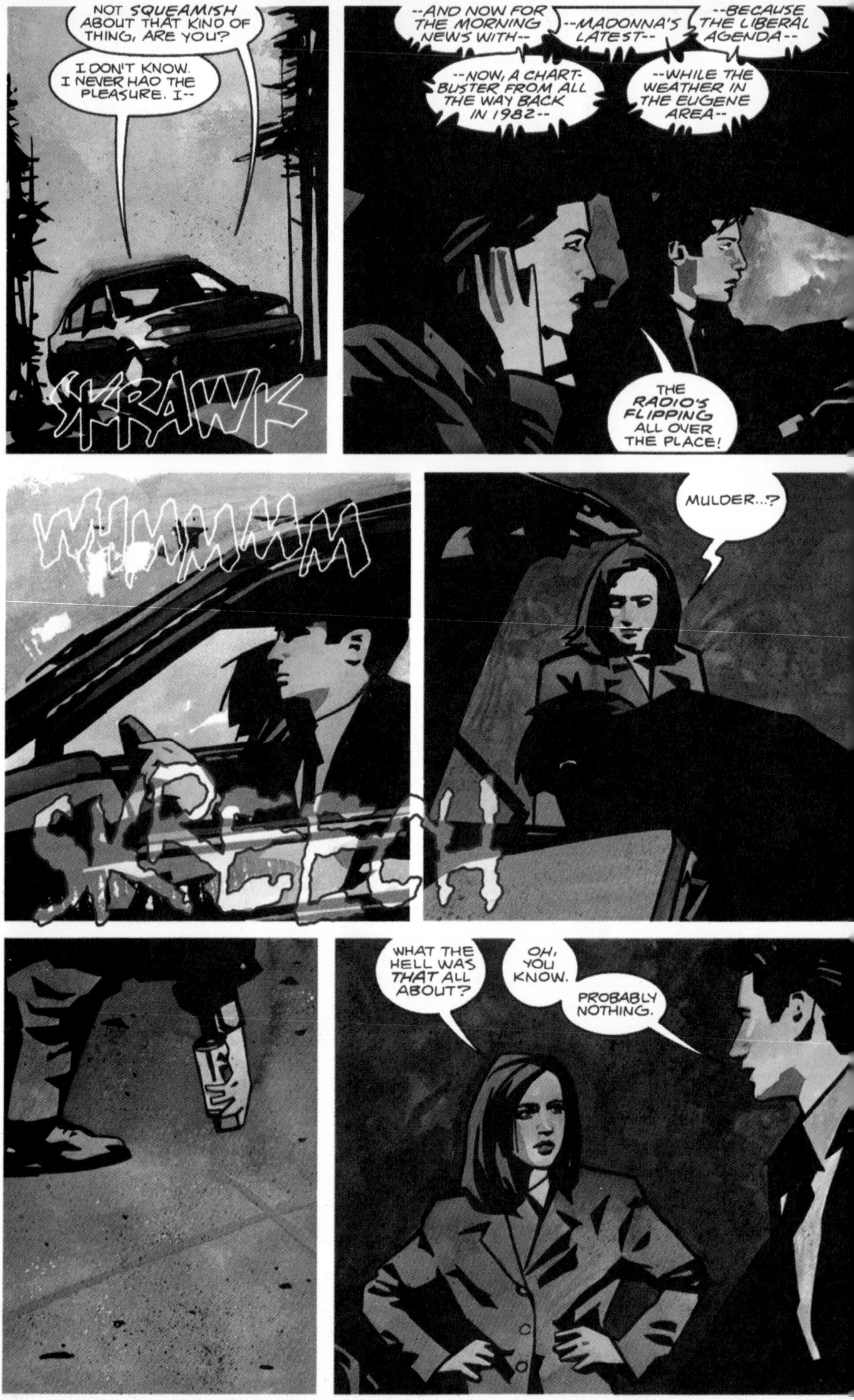
NOT SQUEAMISH ABOUT THAT KIND OF THING, ARE YOU?
I DON'T KNOW. I NEVER HAD THE PLEASURE. I--
SKRAWK
--AND NOW FOR THE MORNING NEWS WITH--
--MADONNA'S LATEST--
--BECAUSE THE LIBERAL AGENDA--
--NOW, A CHART-BUSTER FROM ALL THE WAY BACK IN 1982--
--WHILE THE WEATHER IN THE EUGENE AREA--
THE RADIO'S FLIPPING ALL OVER THE PLACE!
WHMMMM
SKREECH
MULDER...?
WHAT THE HELL WAS THAT ALL ABOUT?
OH, YOU KNOW.
PROBABLY NOTHING.

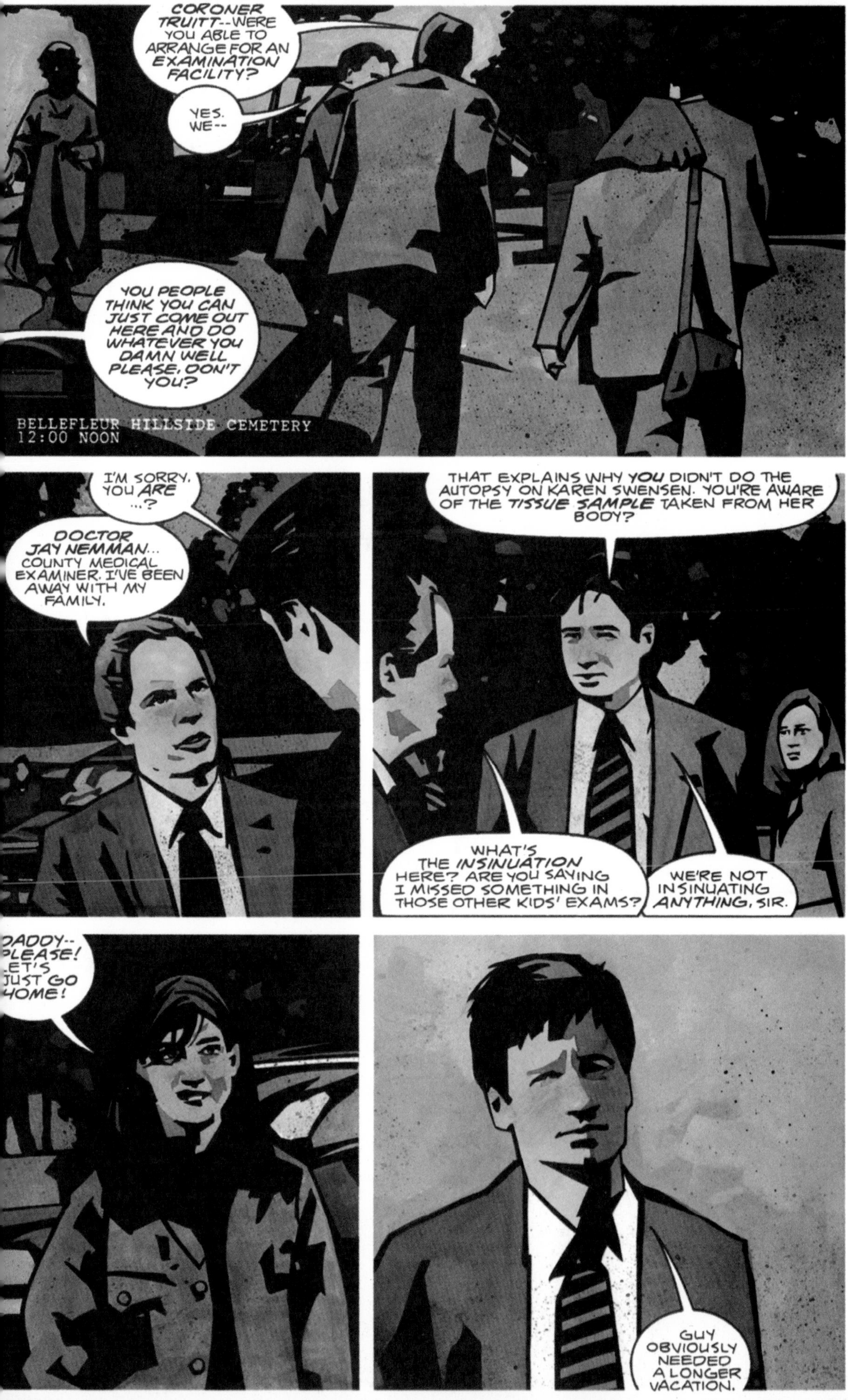
CORONER TRUITT--WERE YOU ABLE TO ARRANGE FOR AN EXAMINATION FACILITY?
YES. WE--
YOU PEOPLE THINK YOU CAN JUST COME OUT HERE AND DO WHATEVER YOU DAMN WELL PLEASE, DON'T YOU?
BELLEFLEUR HILLSIDE CEMETERY
12:00 NOON
I'M SORRY. YOU ARE ...?
DOCTOR JAY NEMMAN... COUNTY MEDICAL EXAMINER. I'VE BEEN AWAY WITH MY FAMILY.
THAT EXPLAINS WHY YOU DIDN'T DO THE AUTOPSY ON KAREN SWENSEN. YOU'RE AWARE OF THE TISSUE SAMPLE TAKEN FROM HER BODY?
WHAT'S THE INSINUATION HERE? ARE YOU SAYING I MISSED SOMETHING IN THOSE OTHER KIDS' EXAMS?
WE'RE NOT INSINUATING ANYTHING, SIR.
DADDY-- PLEASE! LET'S JUST GO HOME!
GUY OBVIOUSLY NEEDED A LONGER VACATION.

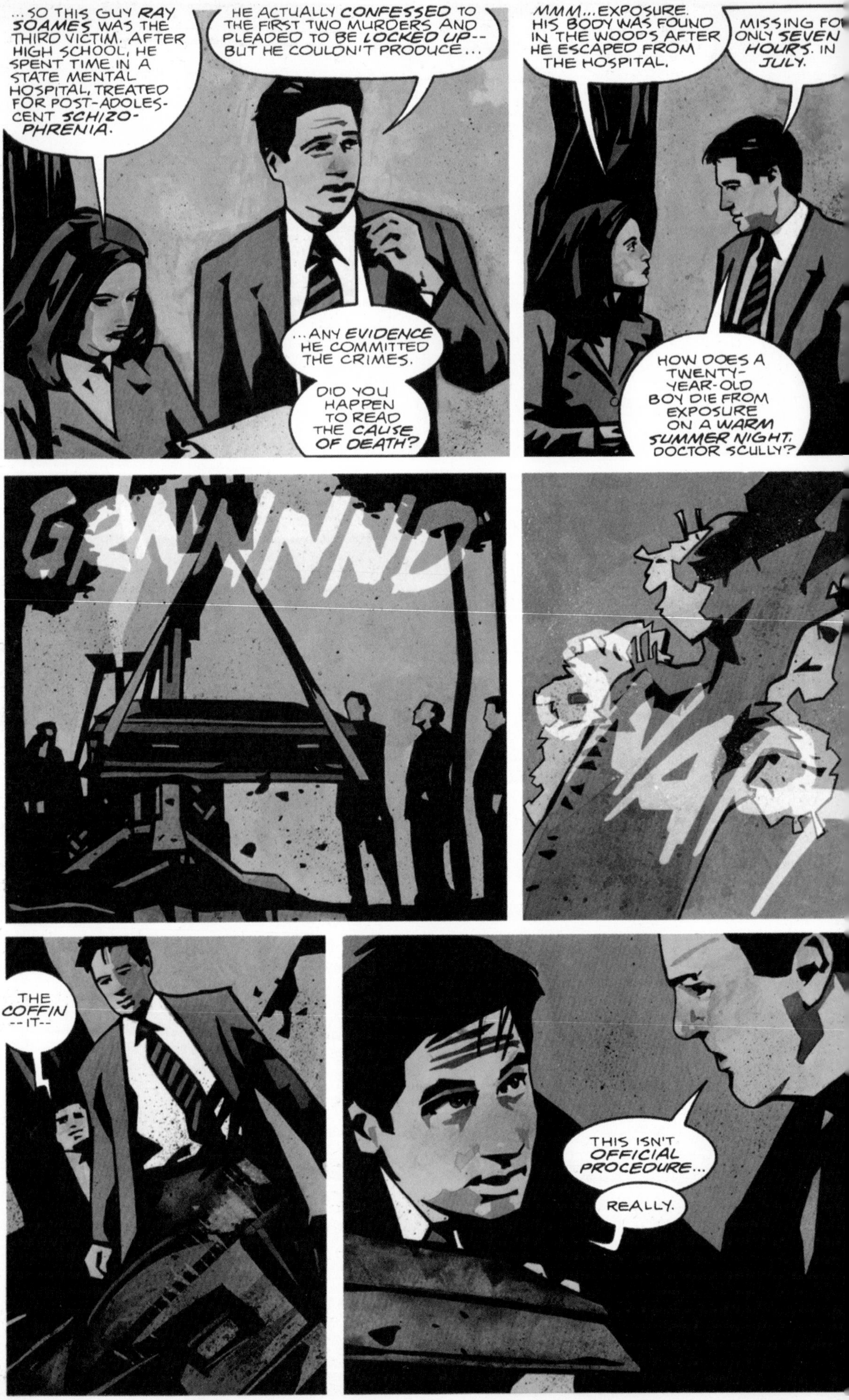
...SO THIS GUY RAY SOAMES WAS THE THIRD VICTIM. AFTER HIGH SCHOOL, HE SPENT TIME IN A STATE MENTAL HOSPITAL, TREATED FOR POST-ADOLESCENT SCHIZOPHRENIA.
HE ACTUALLY CONFESSED TO THE FIRST TWO MURDERS AND PLEADED TO BE LOCKED UP--BUT HE COULDN'T PRODUCE...
...ANY EVIDENCE HE COMMITTED THE CRIMES.
DID YOU HAPPEN TO READ THE CAUSE OF DEATH?
MMM... EXPOSURE. HIS BODY WAS FOUND IN THE WOODS AFTER HE ESCAPED FROM THE HOSPITAL.
MISSING FO ONLY SEVEN HOURS. IN JULY.
HOW DOES A TWENTY-YEAR-OLD BOY DIE FROM EXPOSURE ON A WARM SUMMER NIGHT, DOCTOR SCULLY?
GRNNNND
SNAP
THE COFFIN --IT--
THIS ISN'T OFFICIAL PROCEDURE...
REALLY.

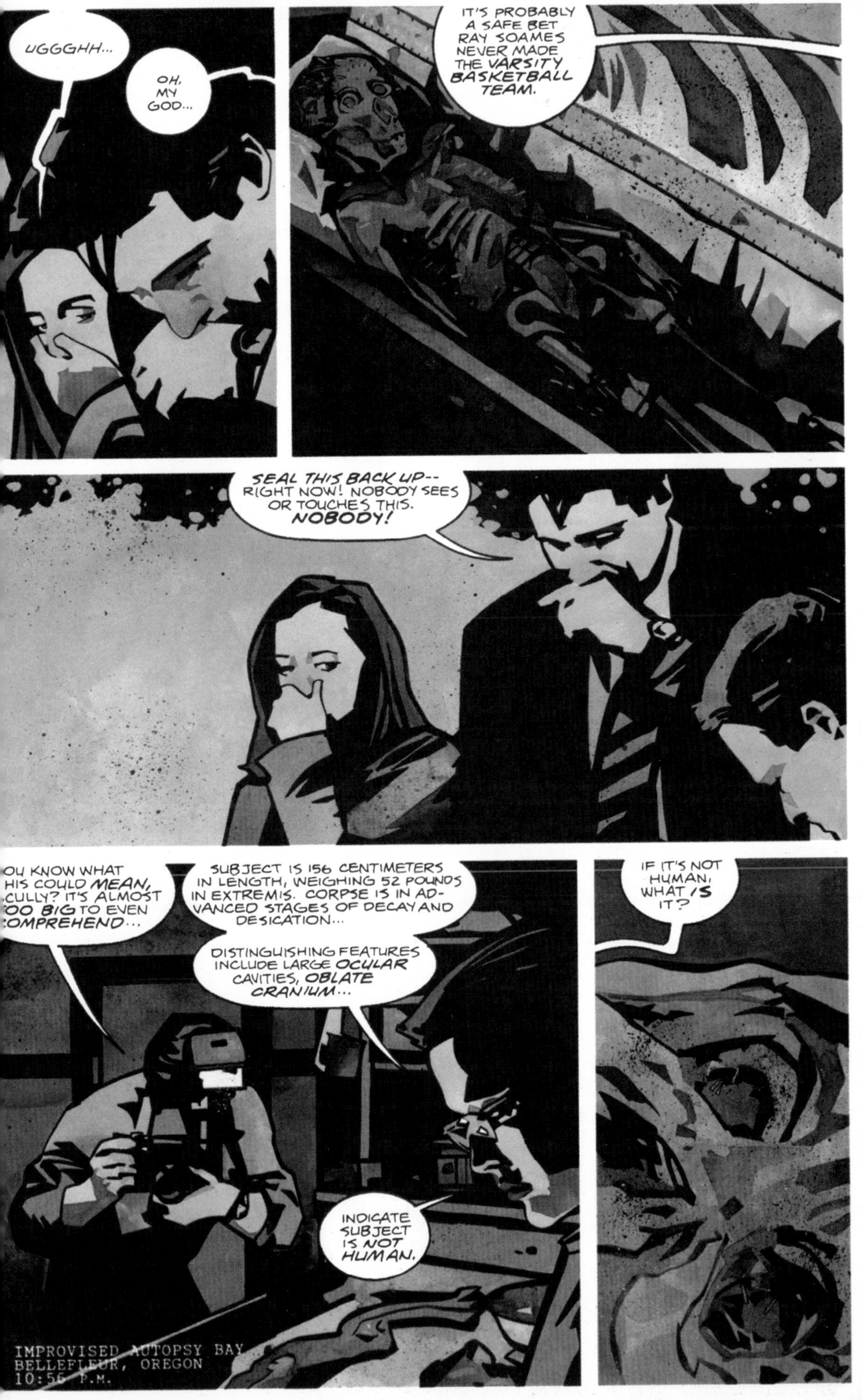
UGGGHH...
OH, MY GOD...
IT'S PROBABLY A SAFE BET RAY SOAMES NEVER MADE THE VARSITY BASKETBALL TEAM.
SEAL THIS BACK UP-- RIGHT NOW! NOBODY SEES OR TOUCHES THIS. NOBODY!
OU KNOW WHAT HIS COULD MEAN, CULLY? IT'S ALMOST OO BIG TO EVEN OMPREHEND...
SUBJECT IS 156 CENTIMETERS IN LENGTH, WEIGHING 52 POUNDS IN EXTREMIS. CORPSE IS IN ADVANCED STAGES OF DECAY AND DESICATION...
DISTINGUISHING FEATURES INCLUDE LARGE OCULAR CAVITIES, OBLATE CRANIUM...
INDICATE SUBJECT IS NOT HUMAN.
IMPROVISED AUTOPSY BAY
BELLEFLEUR, OREGON
10:56 P.M.
IF IT'S NOT HUMAN, WHAT IS IT?

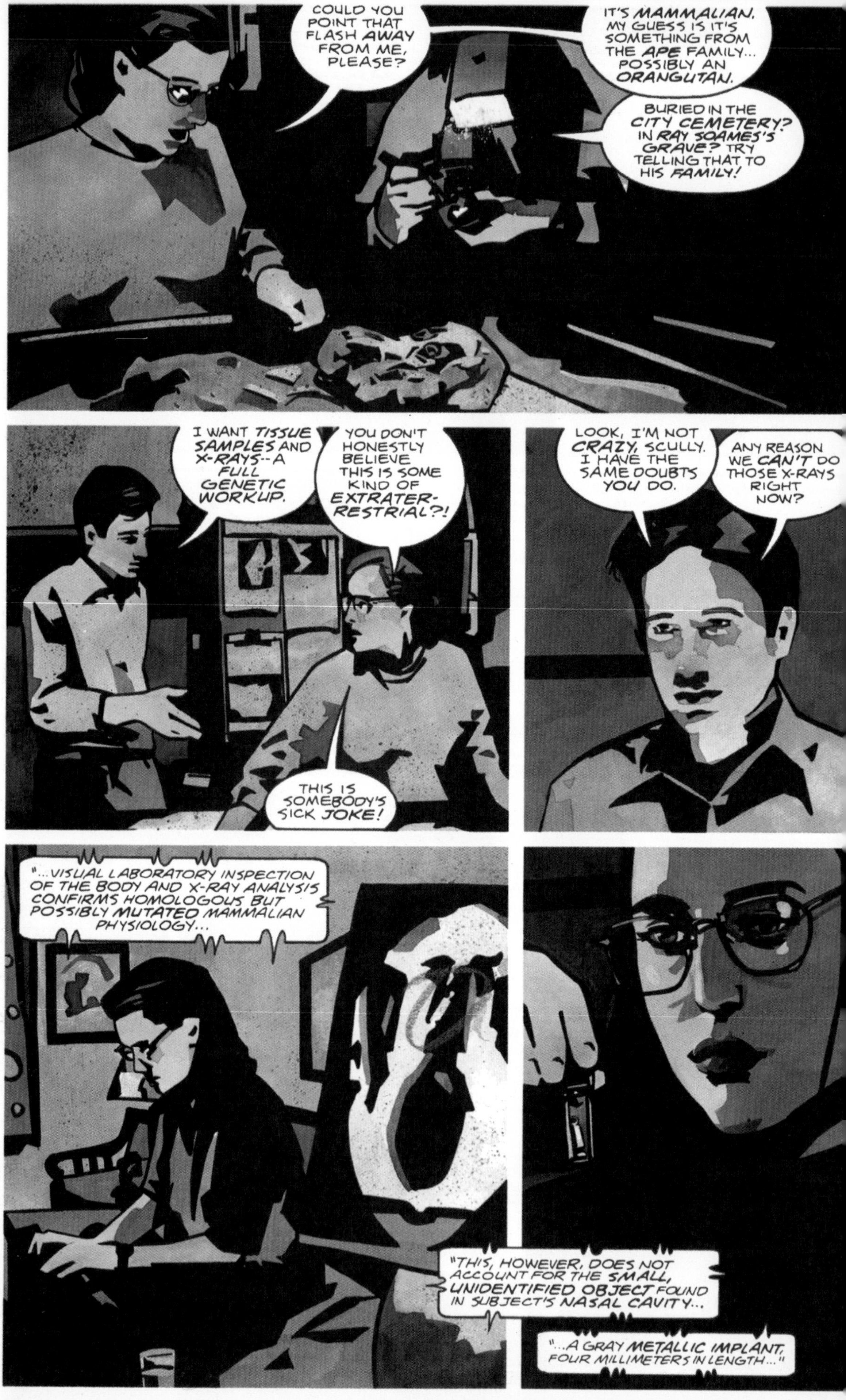

COULD YOU POINT THAT FLASH AWAY FROM ME, PLEASE?
IT'S MAMMALIAN. MY GUESS IS IT'S SOMETHING FROM THE APE FAMILY... POSSIBLY AN ORANGUTAN.
BURIED IN THE CITY CEMETERY? IN RAY SOAMES'S GRAVE? TRY TELLING THAT TO HIS FAMILY!
I WANT TISSUE SAMPLES AND X-RAYS--A FULL GENETIC WORKUP.
YOU DON'T HONESTLY BELIEVE THIS IS SOME KIND OF EXTRATER-RESTRIAL?!
THIS IS SOMEBODY'S SICK JOKE!
LOOK, I'M NOT CRAZY, SCULLY. I HAVE THE SAME DOUBTS YOU DO.
ANY REASON WE CAN'T DO THOSE X-RAYS RIGHT NOW?
"...VISUAL LABORATORY INSPECTION OF THE BODY AND X-RAY ANALYSIS CONFIRMS HOMOLOGOUS BUT POSSIBLY MUTATED MAMMALIAN PHYSIOLOGY...
"THIS, HOWEVER, DOES NOT ACCOUNT FOR THE SMALL, UNIDENTIFIED OBJECT FOUND IN SUBJECT'S NASAL CAVITY...
"...A GRAY METALLIC IMPLANT, FOUR MILLIMETERS IN LENGTH..."

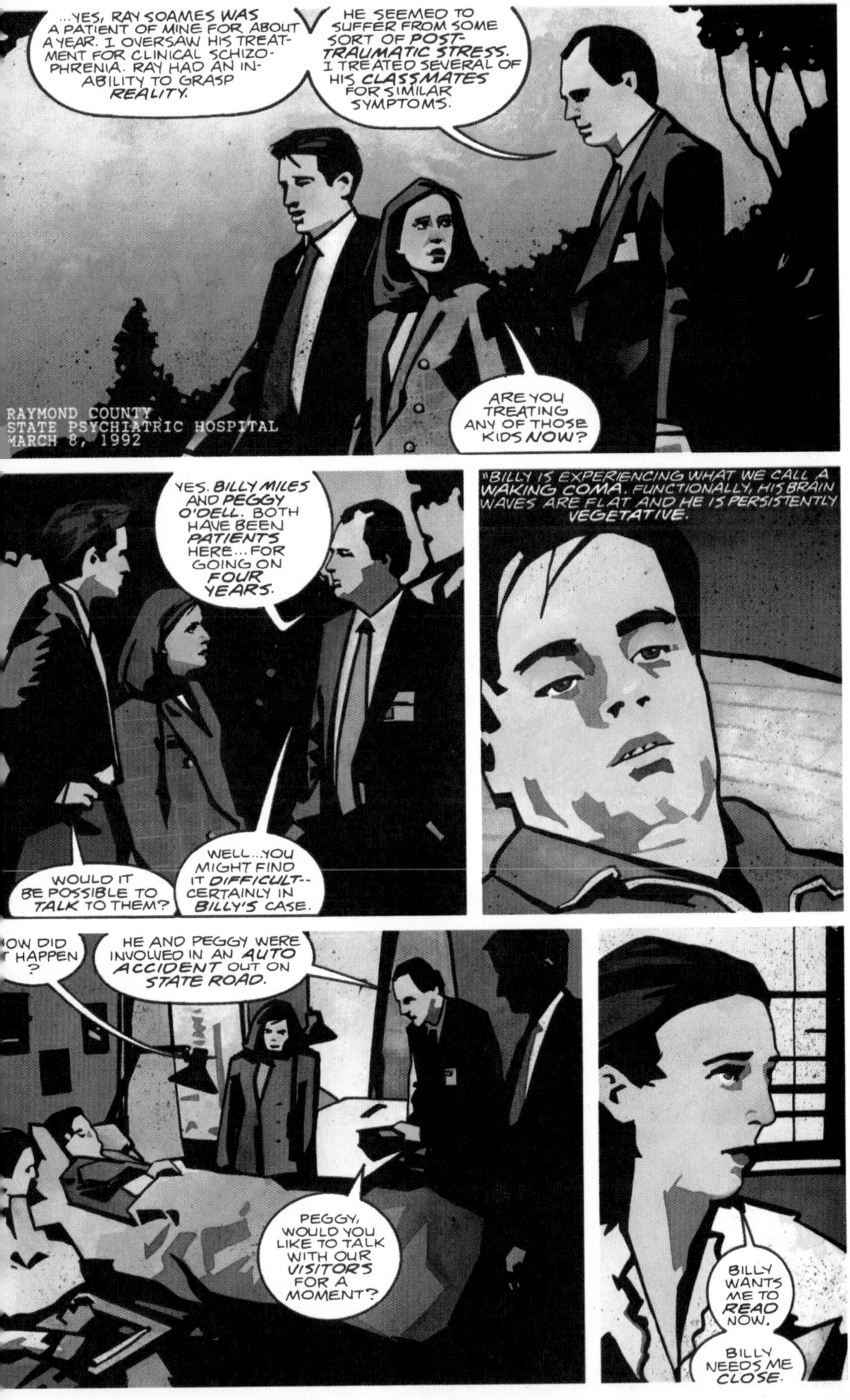
...YES, RAY SOAMES WAS A PATIENT OF MINE FOR ABOUT A YEAR. I OVERSAW HIS TREATMENT FOR CLINICAL SCHIZOPHRENIA. RAY HAD AN INABILITY TO GRASP REALITY.
HE SEEMED TO SUFFER FROM SOME SORT OF POST-TRAUMATIC STRESS. I TREATED SEVERAL OF HIS CLASSMATES FOR SIMILAR SYMPTOMS.
RAYMOND COUNTY
STATE PSYCHIATRIC HOSPITAL
MARCH 8, 1992
ARE YOU TREATING ANY OF THOSE KIDS NOW?
YES. BILLY MILES AND PEGGY O'DELL. BOTH HAVE BEEN PATIENTS HERE... FOR GOING ON FOUR YEARS.
WOULD IT BE POSSIBLE TO TALK TO THEM?
WELL... YOU MIGHT FIND IT DIFFICULT-- CERTAINLY IN BILLY'S CASE.
"BILLY IS EXPERIENCING WHAT WE CALL A WAKING COMA. FUNCTIONALLY, HIS BRAIN WAVES ARE FLAT AND HE IS PERSISTENTLY VEGETATIVE.
OW DID T HAPPEN?
HE AND PEGGY WERE INVOLVED IN AN AUTO ACCIDENT OUT ON STATE ROAD.
PEGGY, WOULD YOU LIKE TO TALK WITH OUR VISITORS FOR A MOMENT?
BILLY WANTS ME TO READ NOW.
BILLY NEEDS ME CLOSE.

DOCTOR, I'M WONDERING IF WE CAN DO A CURSORY MEDICAL EXAM ON PEGGY...

NO!

PEGGY, NO ONE'S GOING TO *HURT* YOU...

EEEE EAAA--

NOW, NOW, PEGGY... IT'S ALL RIGHT...

L-LET ME GO --!

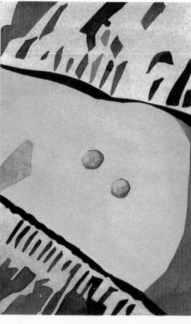

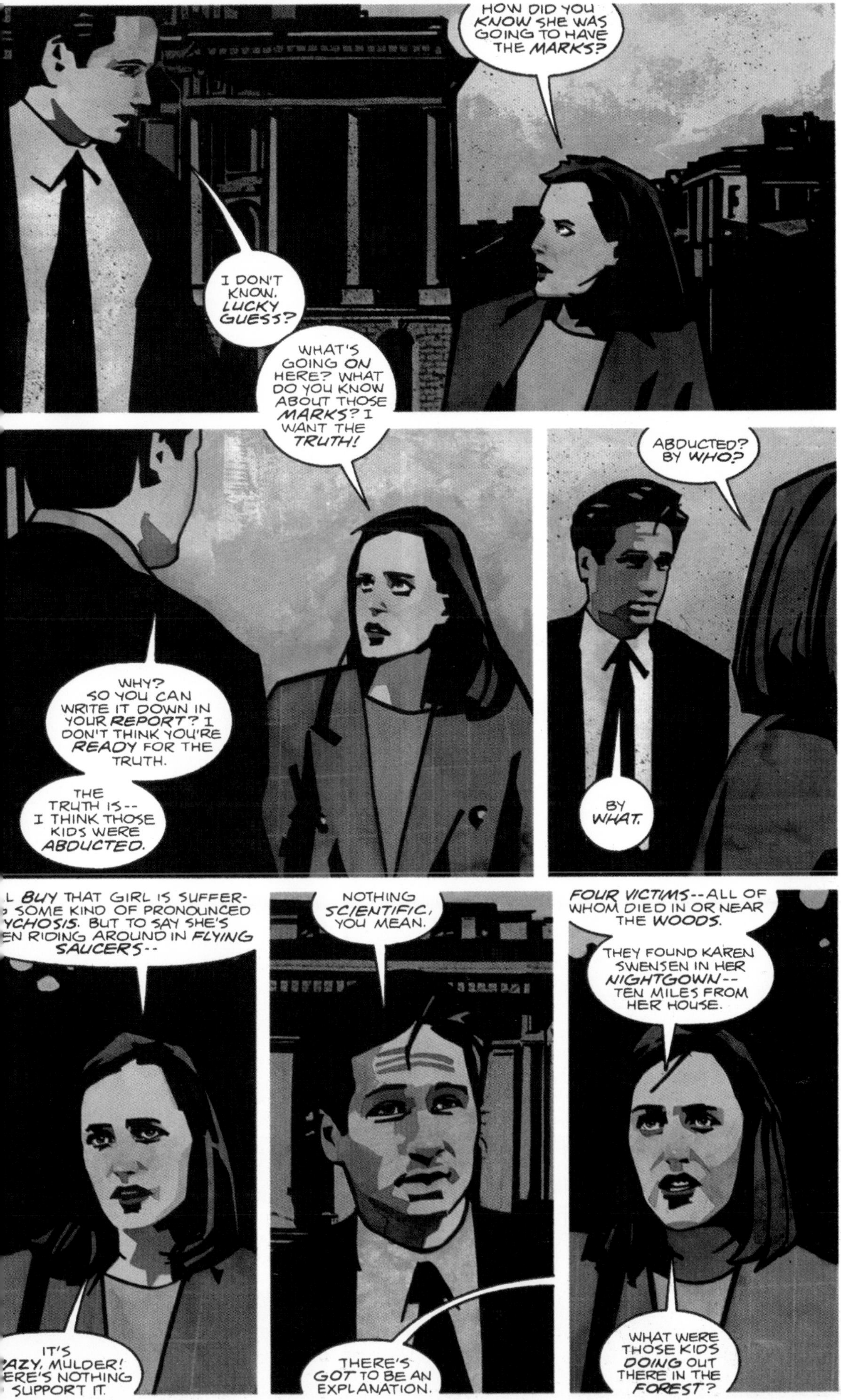
HOW DID YOU KNOW SHE WAS GOING TO HAVE THE MARKS?
I DON'T KNOW. LUCKY GUESS?
WHAT'S GOING ON HERE? WHAT DO YOU KNOW ABOUT THOSE MARKS? I WANT THE TRUTH!
WHY? SO YOU CAN WRITE IT DOWN IN YOUR REPORT? I DON'T THINK YOU'RE READY FOR THE TRUTH.
THE TRUTH IS-- I THINK THOSE KIDS WERE ABDUCTED.
ABDUCTED? BY WHO?
BY WHAT.
L BUY THAT GIRL IS SUFFER- SOME KIND OF PRONOUNCED YCHOSIS. BUT TO SAY SHE'S EN RIDING AROUND IN FLYING SAUCERS--
IT'S AZY, MULDER! ERE'S NOTHING SUPPORT IT.
NOTHING SCIENTIFIC, YOU MEAN.
THERE'S GOT TO BE AN EXPLANATION.
FOUR VICTIMS--ALL OF WHOM DIED IN OR NEAR THE WOODS.
THEY FOUND KAREN SWENSEN IN HER NIGHTGOWN-- TEN MILES FROM HER HOUSE.
WHAT WERE THOSE KIDS DOING OUT THERE IN THE FOREST?

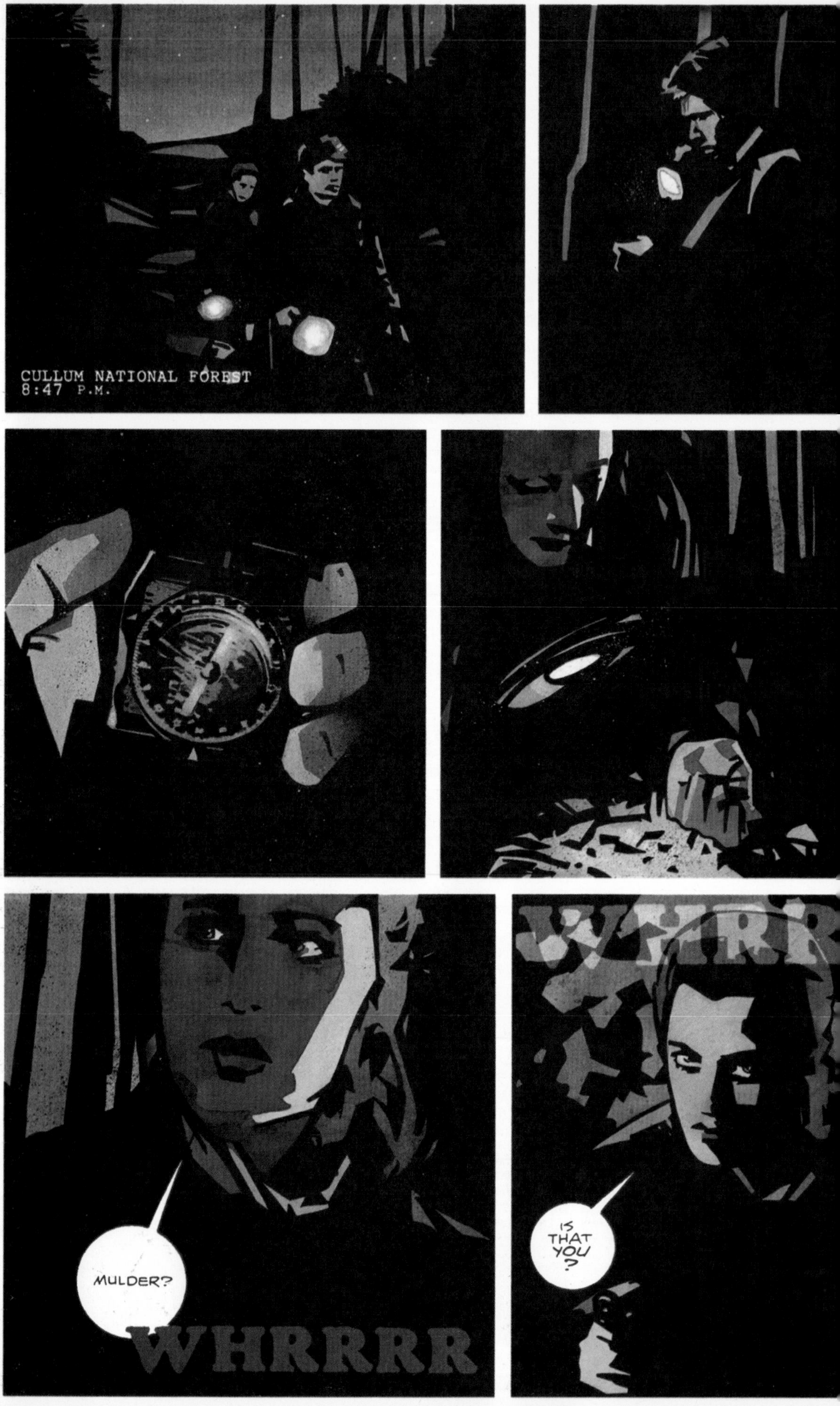
CULLUM NATIONAL FOREST
8:47 P.M.
MULDER?
WHRRRR
WHRR
IS THAT YOU?

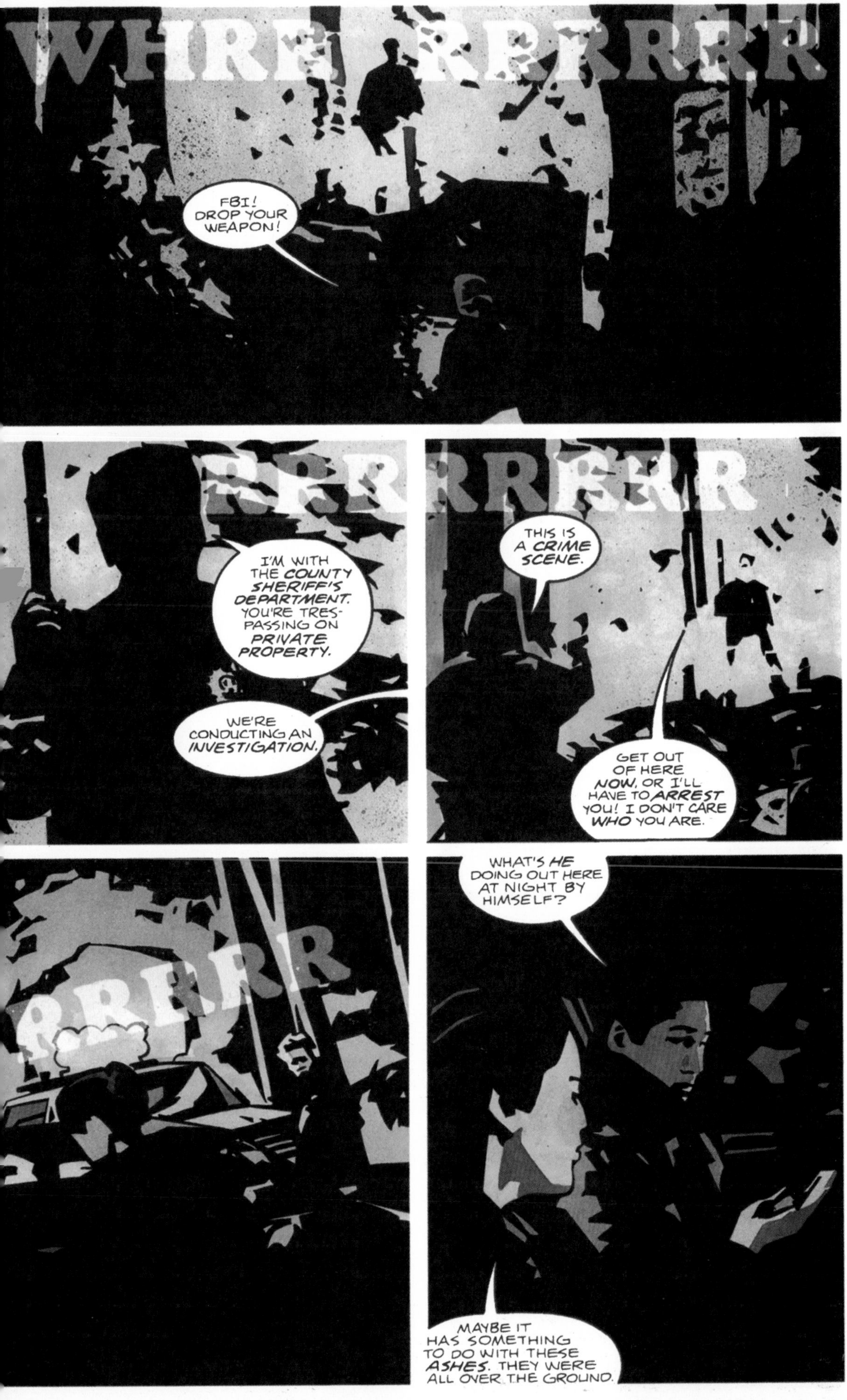
FBI! DROP YOUR WEAPON!
I'M WITH THE COUNTY SHERIFF'S DEPARTMENT. YOU'RE TRES-PASSING ON PRIVATE PROPERTY.
WE'RE CONDUCTING AN INVESTIGATION.
THIS IS A CRIME SCENE.
GET OUT OF HERE NOW, OR I'LL HAVE TO ARREST YOU! I DON'T CARE WHO YOU ARE.
WHAT'S HE DOING OUT HERE AT NIGHT BY HIMSELF?
MAYBE IT HAS SOMETHING TO DO WITH THESE ASHES. THEY WERE ALL OVER THE GROUND.

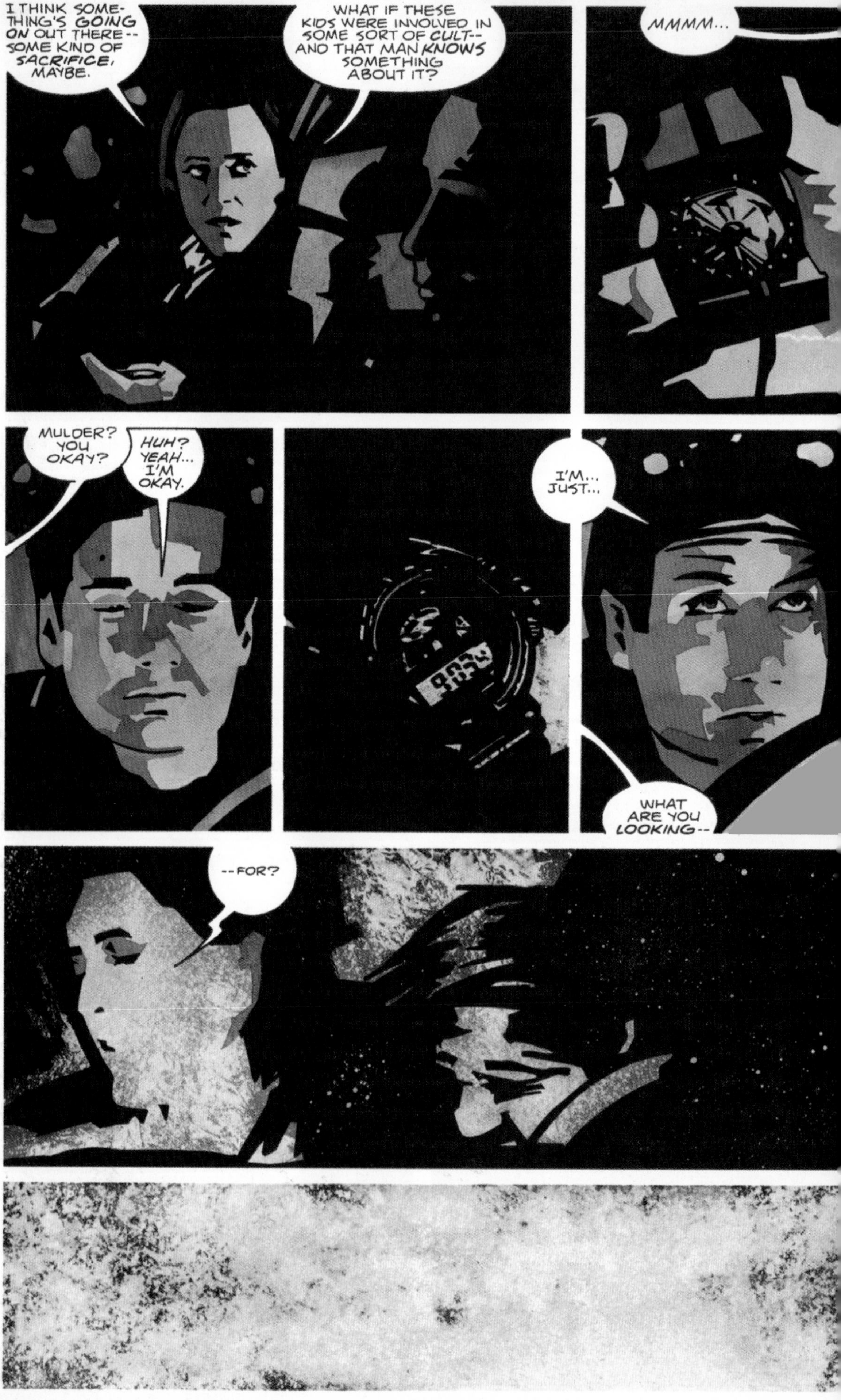
I THINK SOMETHING'S GOING ON OUT THERE-- SOME KIND OF SACRIFICE, MAYBE.
WHAT IF THESE KIDS WERE INVOLVED IN SOME SORT OF CULT-- AND THAT MAN KNOWS SOMETHING ABOUT IT?
MMMM...
MULDER? YOU OKAY?
HUH? YEAH... I'M OKAY.
I'M... JUST...
WHAT ARE YOU LOOKING--
--FOR?

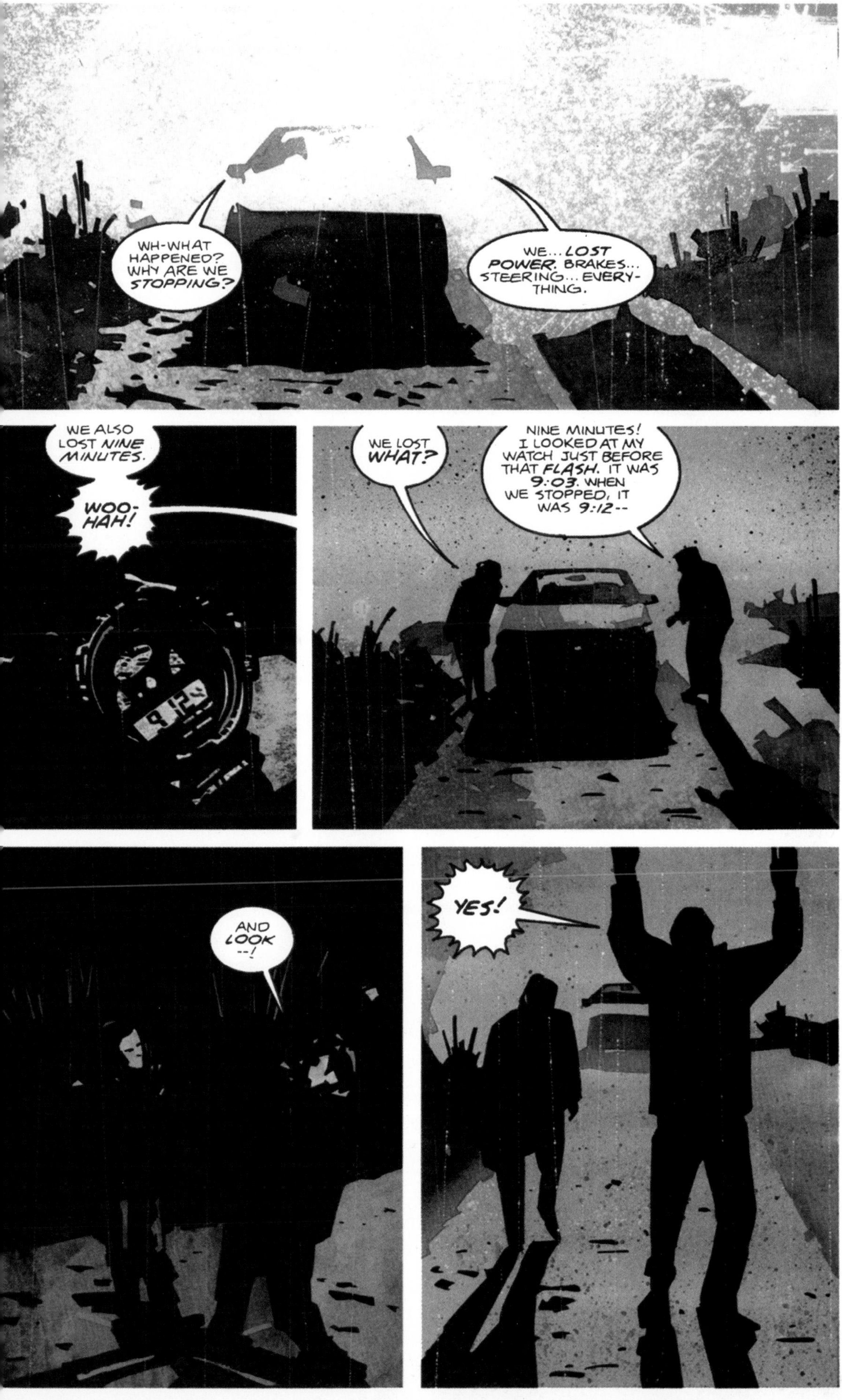

WH-WHAT HAPPENED? WHY ARE WE STOPPING?
WE... LOST POWER. BRAKES... STEERING... EVERY-THING.
WE ALSO LOST NINE MINUTES.
WOO-HAH!
WE LOST WHAT?
NINE MINUTES! I LOOKED AT MY WATCH JUST BEFORE THAT FLASH. IT WAS 9:03. WHEN WE STOPPED, IT WAS 9:12--
AND LOOK --!
YES!

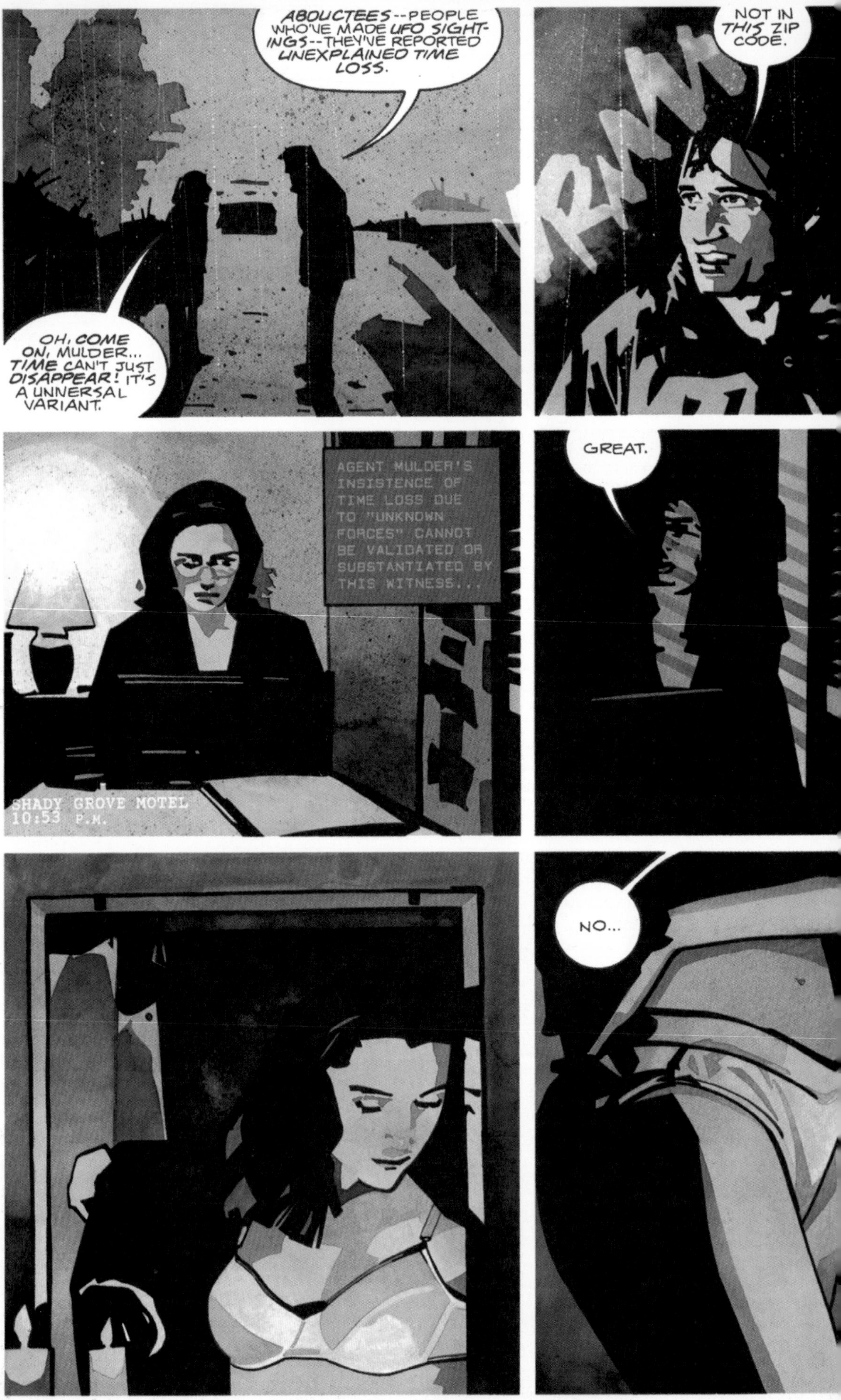
ABDUCTEES--PEOPLE WHO'VE MADE UFO SIGHTINGS--THEY'VE REPORTED UNEXPLAINED TIME LOSS.
OH, COME ON, MULDER... TIME CAN'T JUST DISAPPEAR! IT'S A UNIVERSAL VARIANT.
NOT IN THIS ZIP CODE.
AGENT MULDER'S INSISTENCE OF TIME LOSS DUE TO "UNKNOWN FORCES" CANNOT BE VALIDATED OR SUBSTANTIATED BY THIS WITNESS...
SHADY GROVE MOTEL
10:53 P.M.
GREAT.
NO...

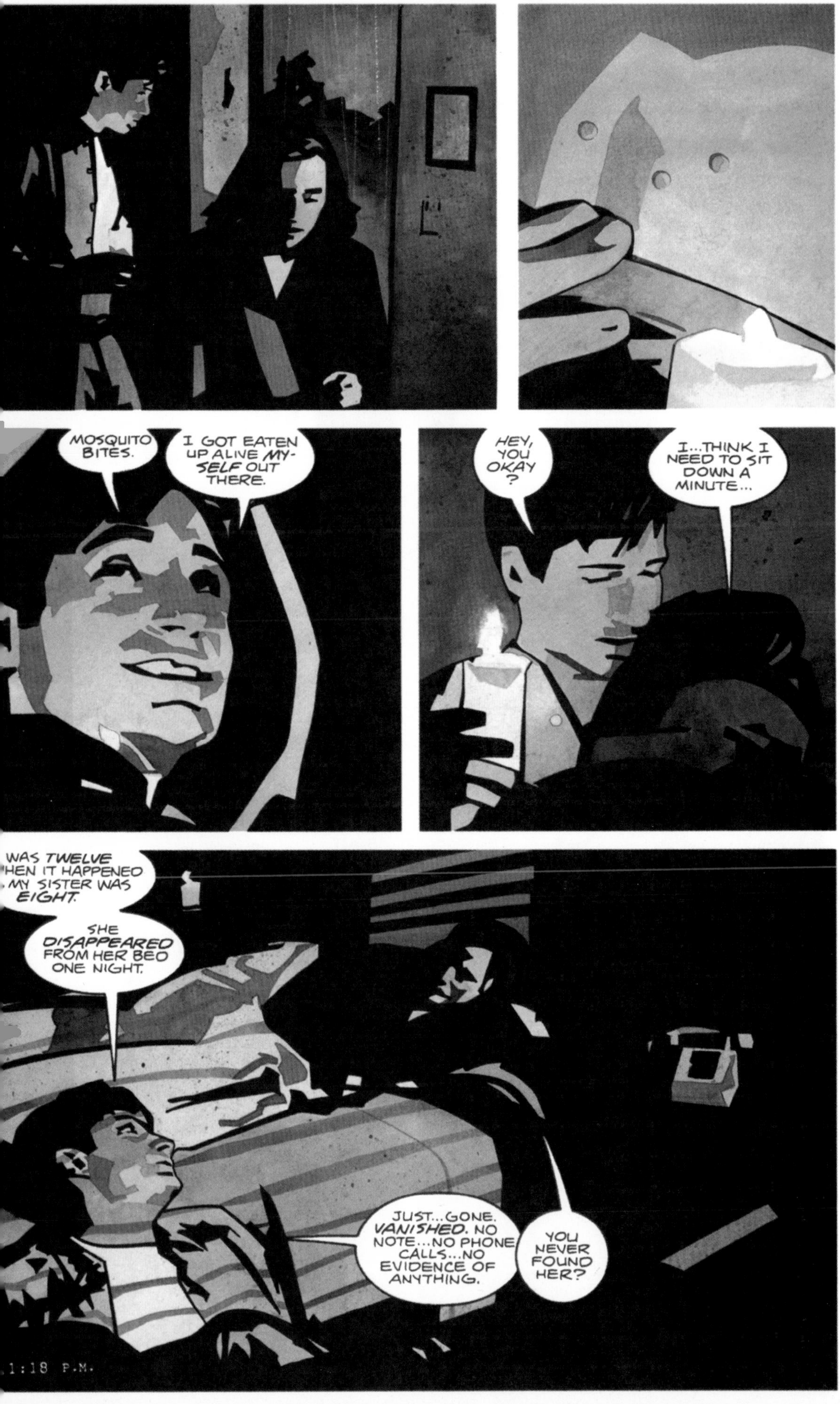
MOSQUITO BITES.
I GOT EATEN UP ALIVE MY-SELF OUT THERE.
HEY, YOU OKAY?
I...THINK I NEED TO SIT DOWN A MINUTE...
WAS TWELVE
HEN IT HAPPENED
MY SISTER WAS EIGHT.
SHE DISAPPEARED FROM HER BED ONE NIGHT.
JUST...GONE. VANISHED. NO NOTE...NO PHONE CALLS...NO EVIDENCE OF ANYTHING.
YOU NEVER FOUND HER?
1:18 P.M.

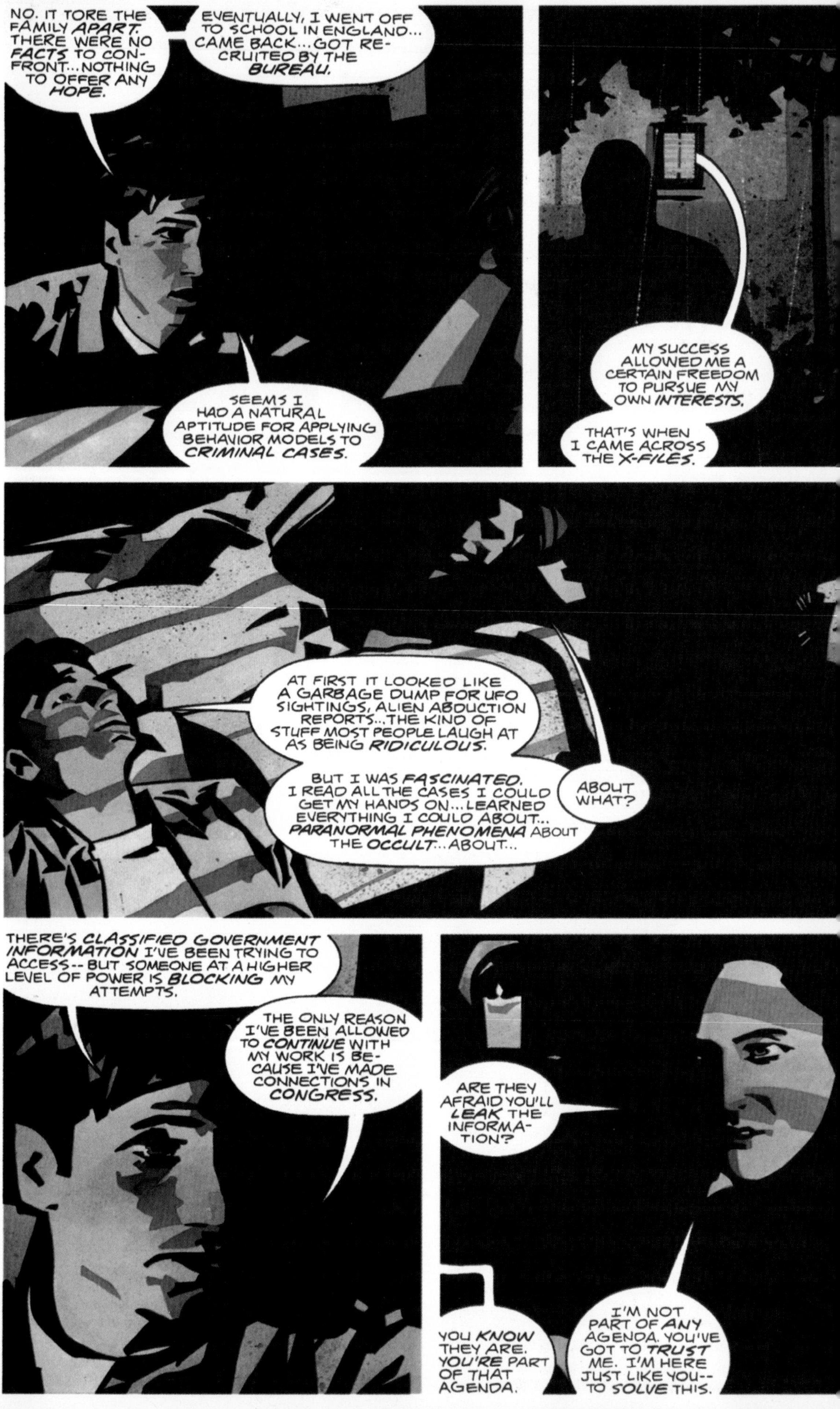
NO. IT TORE THE FAMILY APART. THERE WERE NO FACTS TO CONFRONT... NOTHING TO OFFER ANY HOPE.
EVENTUALLY, I WENT OFF TO SCHOOL IN ENGLAND... CAME BACK... GOT RECRUITED BY THE BUREAU.
SEEMS I HAD A NATURAL APTITUDE FOR APPLYING BEHAVIOR MODELS TO CRIMINAL CASES.
MY SUCCESS ALLOWED ME A CERTAIN FREEDOM TO PURSUE MY OWN INTERESTS.
THAT'S WHEN I CAME ACROSS THE X-FILES.
AT FIRST IT LOOKED LIKE A GARBAGE DUMP FOR UFO SIGHTINGS, ALIEN ABDUCTION REPORTS... THE KIND OF STUFF MOST PEOPLE LAUGH AT AS BEING RIDICULOUS.
BUT I WAS FASCINATED. I READ ALL THE CASES I COULD GET MY HANDS ON... LEARNED EVERYTHING I COULD ABOUT... PARANORMAL PHENOMENA ABOUT THE OCCULT... ABOUT...
ABOUT WHAT?
THERE'S CLASSIFIED GOVERNMENT INFORMATION I'VE BEEN TRYING TO ACCESS -- BUT SOMEONE AT A HIGHER LEVEL OF POWER IS BLOCKING MY ATTEMPTS.
THE ONLY REASON I'VE BEEN ALLOWED TO CONTINUE WITH MY WORK IS BECAUSE I'VE MADE CONNECTIONS IN CONGRESS.
ARE THEY AFRAID YOU'LL LEAK THE INFORMATION?
YOU KNOW THEY ARE. YOU'RE PART OF THAT AGENDA.
I'M NOT PART OF ANY AGENDA. YOU'VE GOT TO TRUST ME. I'M HERE JUST LIKE YOU-- TO SOLVE THIS.

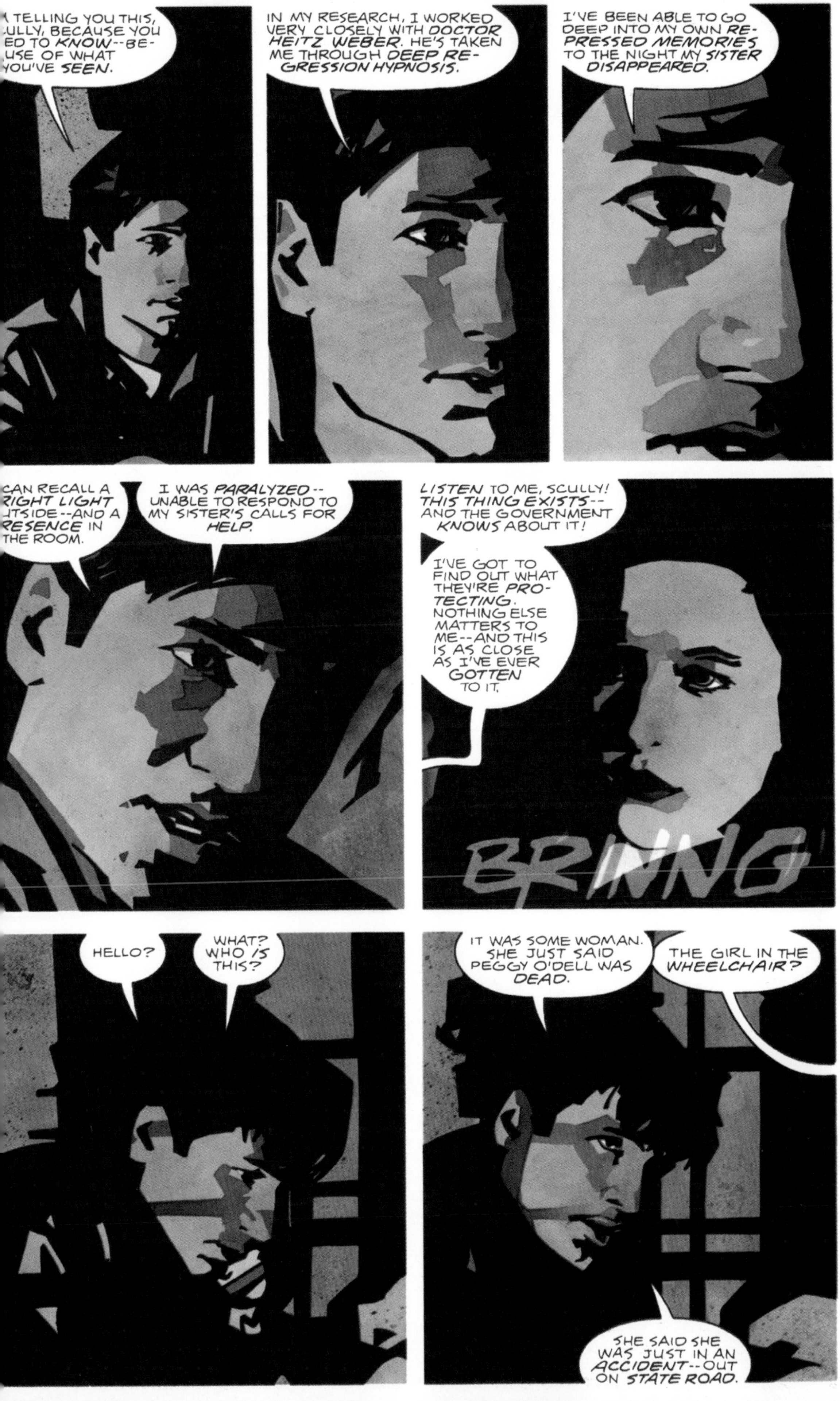

TELLING YOU THIS, ULLY, BECAUSE YOU ED TO KNOW--BE- USE OF WHAT YOU'VE SEEN.
IN MY RESEARCH, I WORKED VERY CLOSELY WITH DOCTOR HEITZ WEBER. HE'S TAKEN ME THROUGH DEEP RE- GRESSION HYPNOSIS.
I'VE BEEN ABLE TO GO DEEP INTO MY OWN RE- PRESSED MEMORIES TO THE NIGHT MY SISTER DISAPPEARED.
CAN RECALL A RIGHT LIGHT UTSIDE--AND A RESENCE IN THE ROOM.
I WAS PARALYZED-- UNABLE TO RESPOND TO MY SISTER'S CALLS FOR HELP.
LISTEN TO ME, SCULLY! THIS THING EXISTS-- AND THE GOVERNMENT KNOWS ABOUT IT!
I'VE GOT TO FIND OUT WHAT THEY'RE PRO- TECTING. NOTHING ELSE MATTERS TO ME--AND THIS IS AS CLOSE AS I'VE EVER GOTTEN TO IT.
BRINNG
HELLO?
WHAT? WHO IS THIS?
IT WAS SOME WOMAN. SHE JUST SAID PEGGY O'DELL WAS DEAD.
THE GIRL IN THE WHEELCHAIR?
SHE SAID SHE WAS JUST IN AN ACCIDENT--OUT ON STATE ROAD.

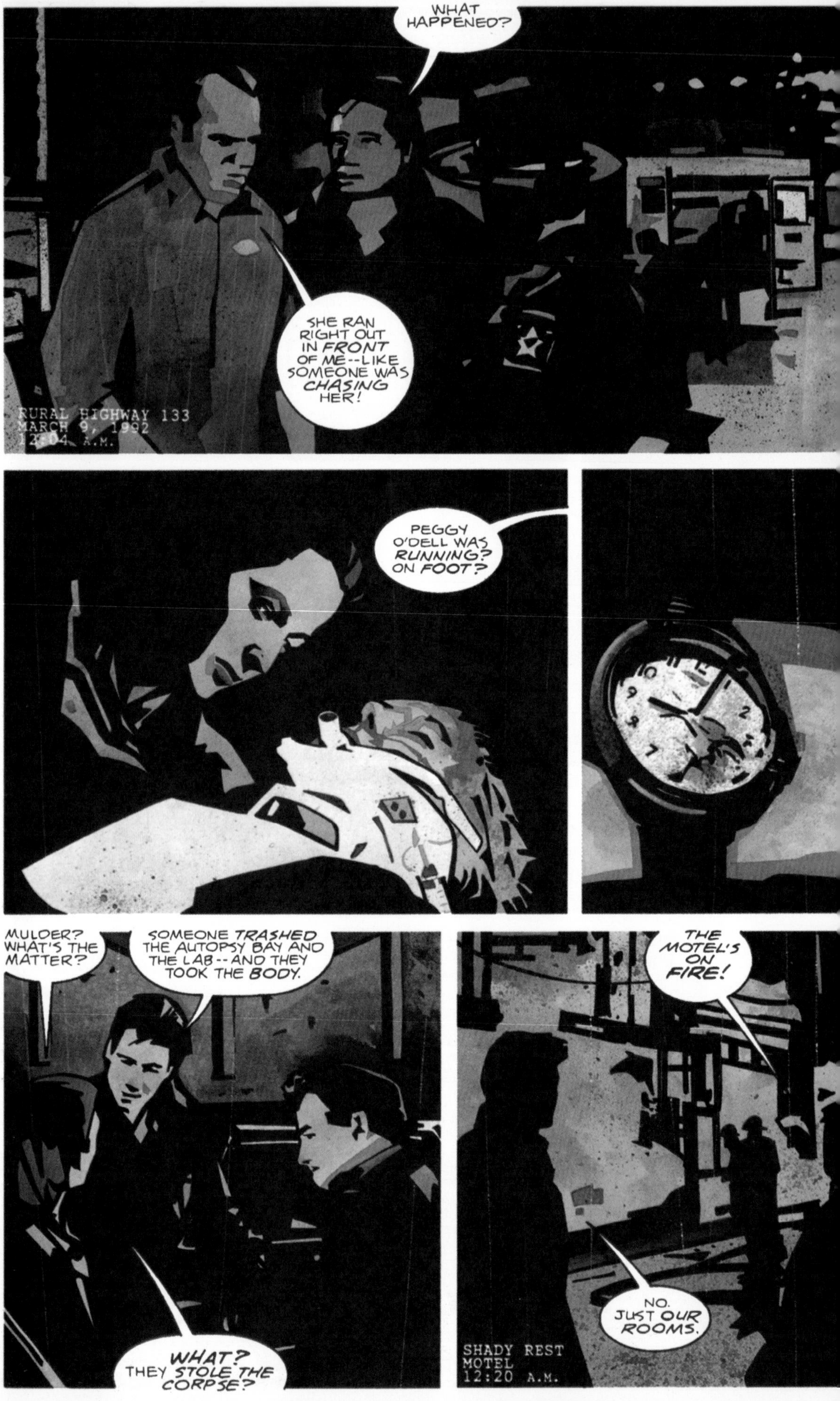
WHAT HAPPENED?
SHE RAN RIGHT OUT IN FRONT OF ME--LIKE SOMEONE WAS CHASING HER!
RURAL HIGHWAY 133
MARCH 9, 1992
12:04 A.M.
PEGGY O'DELL WAS RUNNING? ON FOOT?
MULDER? WHAT'S THE MATTER?
SOMEONE TRASHED THE AUTOPSY BAY AND THE LAB--AND THEY TOOK THE BODY.
WHAT? THEY STOLE THE CORPSE?
SHADY REST
MOTEL
12:20 A.M.
THE MOTEL'S ON FIRE!
NO. JUST OUR ROOMS.

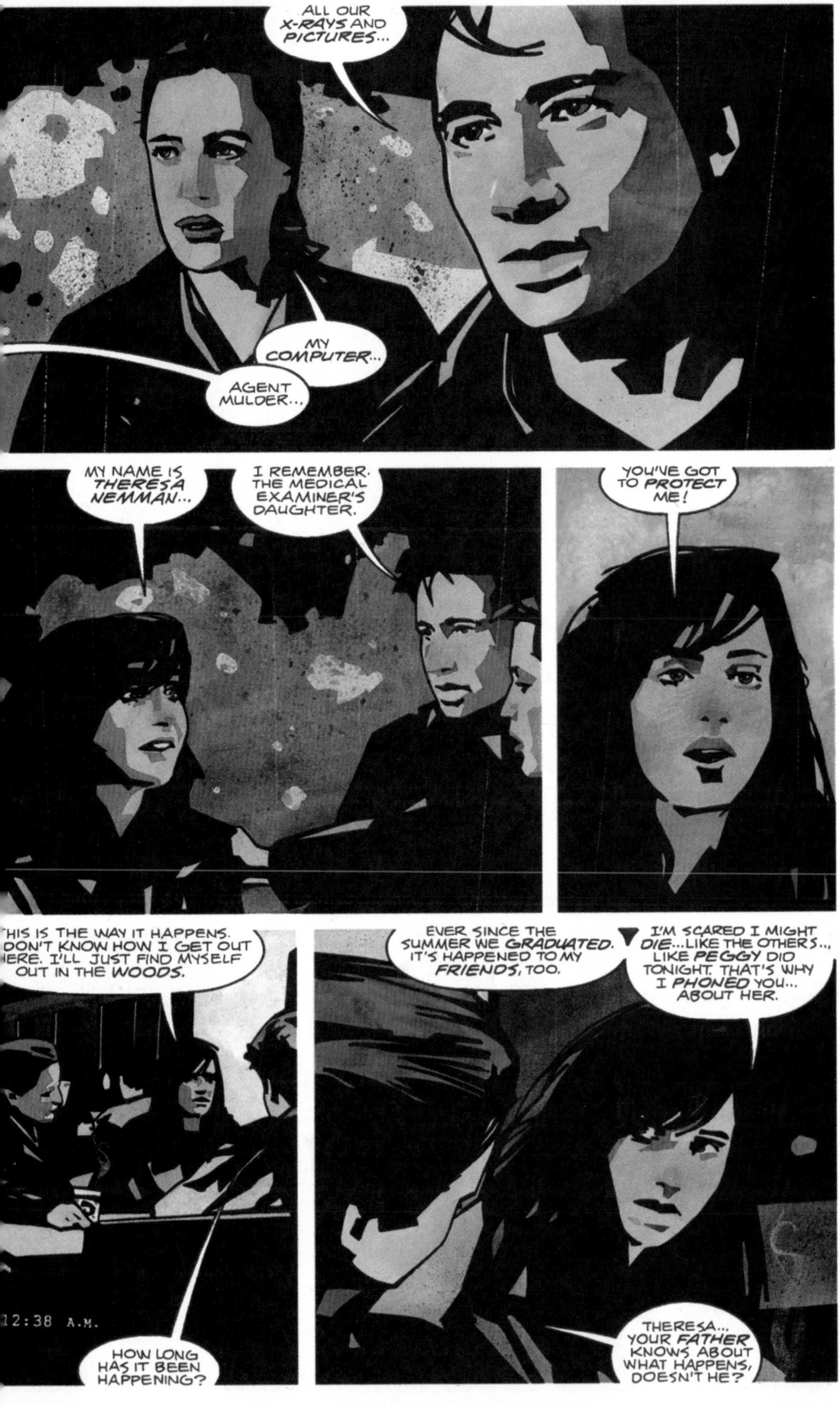
ALL OUR X-RAYS AND PICTURES...
MY COMPUTER...
AGENT MULDER...
MY NAME IS THERESA NEMMAN...
I REMEMBER. THE MEDICAL EXAMINER'S DAUGHTER.
YOU'VE GOT TO PROTECT ME!
THIS IS THE WAY IT HAPPENS. DON'T KNOW HOW I GET OUT HERE. I'LL JUST FIND MYSELF OUT IN THE WOODS.
12:38 A.M.
HOW LONG HAS IT BEEN HAPPENING?
EVER SINCE THE SUMMER WE GRADUATED. IT'S HAPPENED TO MY FRIENDS, TOO.
I'M SCARED I MIGHT DIE...LIKE THE OTHERS... LIKE PEGGY DID TONIGHT. THAT'S WHY I PHONED YOU... ABOUT HER.
THERESA... YOUR FATHER KNOWS ABOUT WHAT HAPPENS, DOESN'T HE?

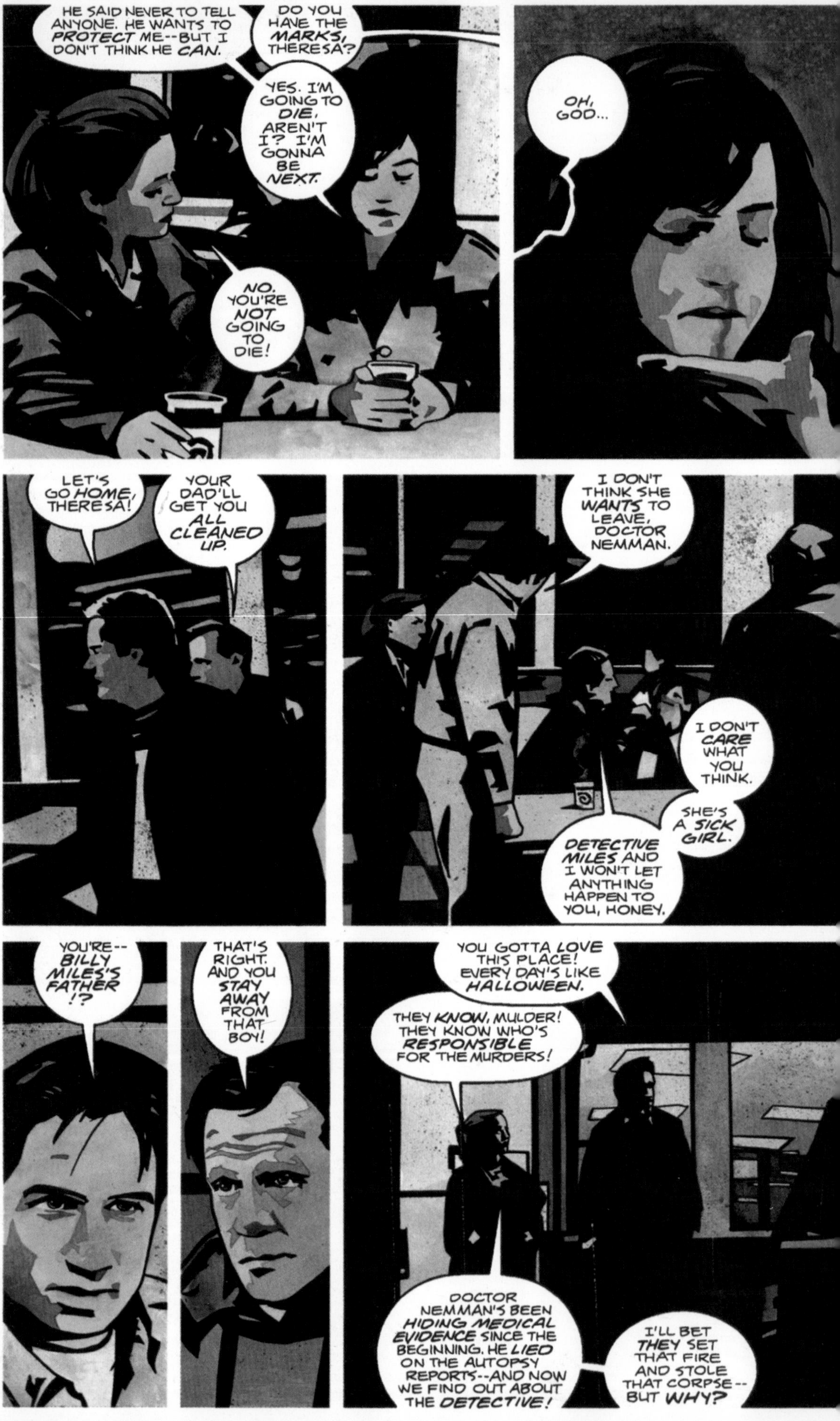
HE SAID NEVER TO TELL ANYONE. HE WANTS TO PROTECT ME--BUT I DON'T THINK HE CAN.
DO YOU HAVE THE MARKS, THERESA?
YES. I'M GOING TO DIE, AREN'T I? I'M GONNA BE NEXT.
NO. YOU'RE NOT GOING TO DIE!
OH, GOD...
LET'S GO HOME, THERESA!
YOUR DAD'LL GET YOU ALL CLEANED UP.
I DON'T THINK SHE WANTS TO LEAVE, DOCTOR NEMMAN.
I DON'T CARE WHAT YOU THINK.
SHE'S A SICK GIRL.
DETECTIVE MILES AND I WON'T LET ANYTHING HAPPEN TO YOU, HONEY.
YOU'RE-- BILLY MILES'S FATHER !?
THAT'S RIGHT. AND YOU STAY AWAY FROM THAT BOY!
YOU GOTTA LOVE THIS PLACE! EVERY DAY'S LIKE HALLOWEEN.
THEY KNOW, MULDER! THEY KNOW WHO'S RESPONSIBLE FOR THE MURDERS!
DOCTOR NEMMAN'S BEEN HIDING MEDICAL EVIDENCE SINCE THE BEGINNING. HE LIED ON THE AUTOPSY REPORTS--AND NOW WE FIND OUT ABOUT THE DETECTIVE!
I'LL BET THEY SET THAT FIRE AND STOLE THAT CORPSE-- BUT WHY?

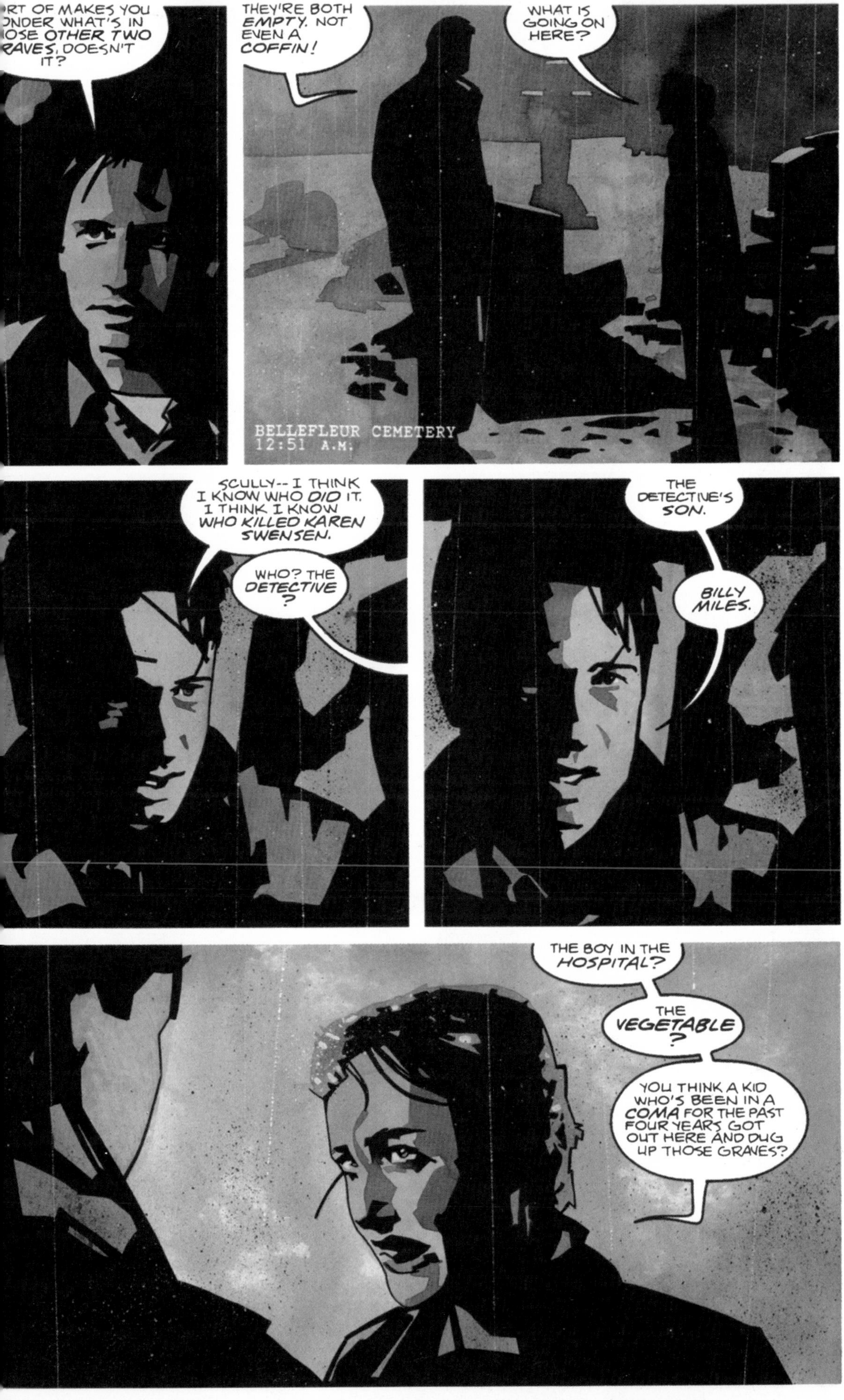
RT OF MAKES YOU
ONDER WHAT'S IN
OSE OTHER TWO
RAVES, DOESN'T
IT?
THEY'RE BOTH EMPTY. NOT EVEN A COFFIN!
WHAT IS GOING ON HERE?
BELLEFLEUR CEMETERY
12:51 A.M.
SCULLY-- I THINK I KNOW WHO DID IT. I THINK I KNOW WHO KILLED KAREN SWENSEN.
WHO? THE DETECTIVE?
THE DETECTIVE'S SON.
BILLY MILES.
THE BOY IN THE HOSPITAL?
THE VEGETABLE?
YOU THINK A KID WHO'S BEEN IN A COMA FOR THE PAST FOUR YEARS GOT OUT HERE AND DUG UP THOSE GRAVES?

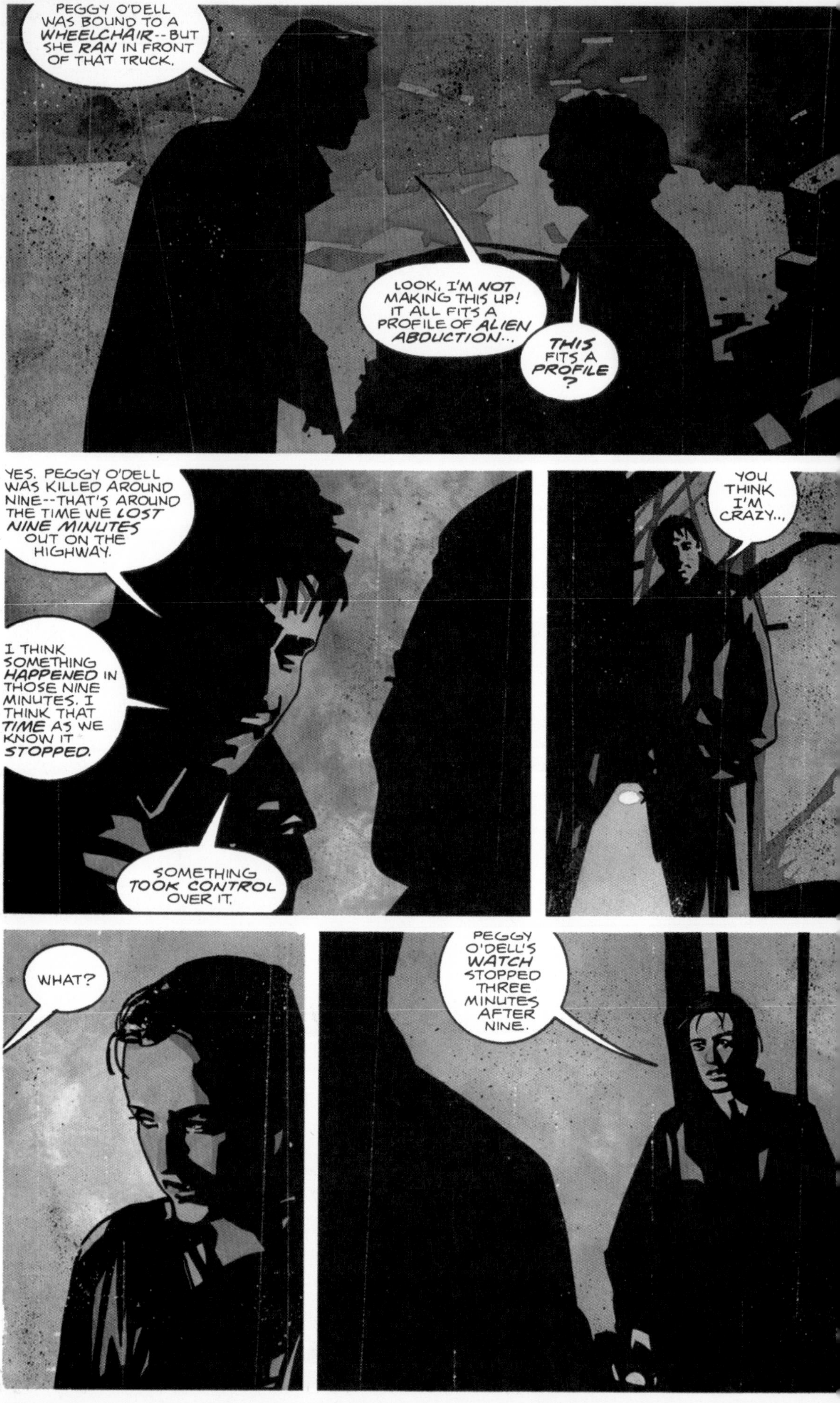
PEGGY O'DELL WAS BOUND TO A WHEELCHAIR-- BUT SHE RAN IN FRONT OF THAT TRUCK.
LOOK, I'M NOT MAKING THIS UP! IT ALL FITS A PROFILE OF ALIEN ABDUCTION...
THIS FITS A PROFILE?
YES. PEGGY O'DELL WAS KILLED AROUND NINE--THAT'S AROUND THE TIME WE LOST NINE MINUTES OUT ON THE HIGHWAY.
I THINK SOMETHING HAPPENED IN THOSE NINE MINUTES. I THINK THAT TIME AS WE KNOW IT STOPPED.
SOMETHING TOOK CONTROL OVER IT.
YOU THINK I'M CRAZY...
WHAT?
PEGGY O'DELL'S WATCH STOPPED THREE MINUTES AFTER NINE.

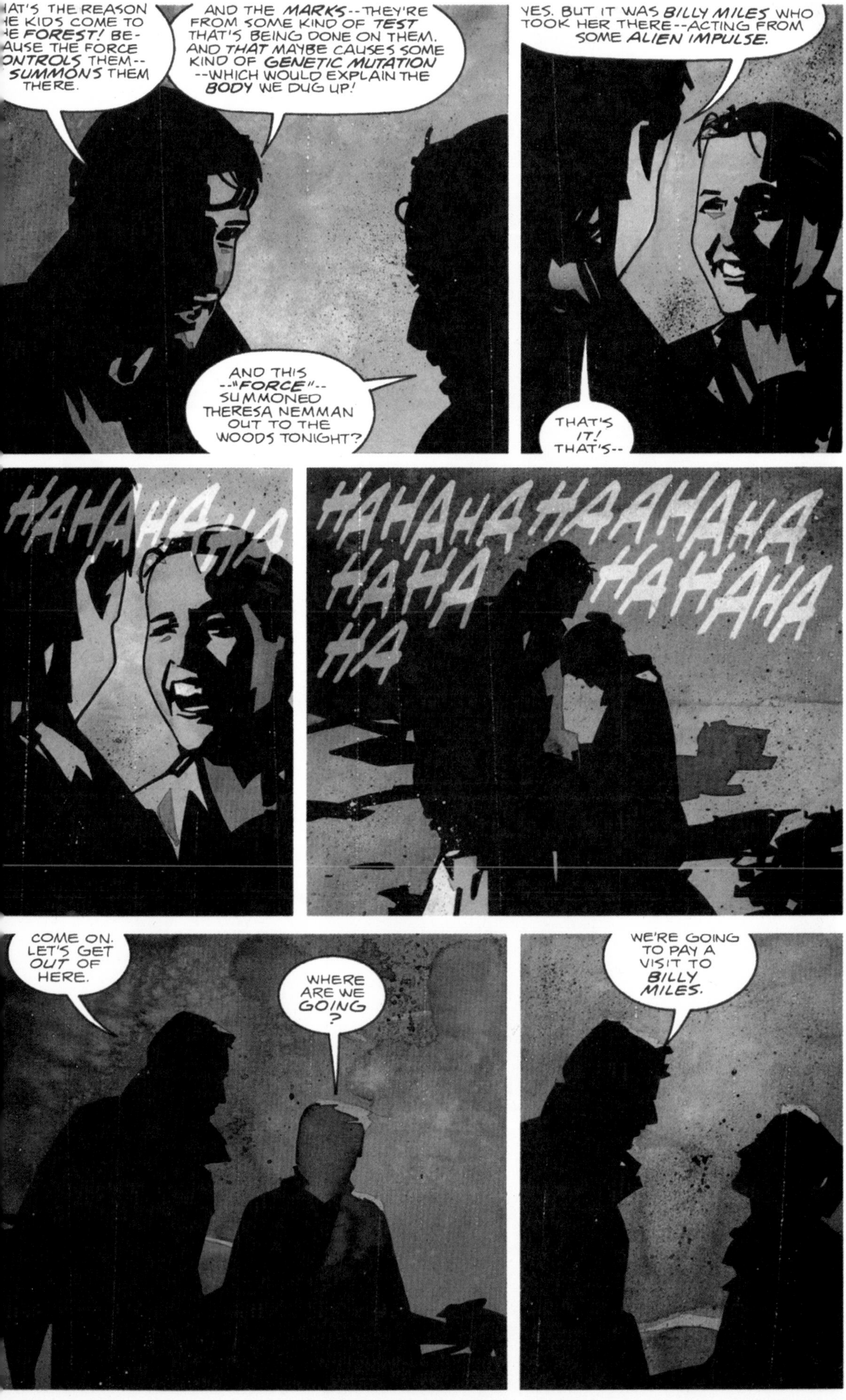
HAT'S THE REASON HE KIDS COME TO HE FOREST! BE-AUSE THE FORCE ONTROLS THEM-- SUMMONS THEM THERE.
AND THE MARKS--THEY'RE FROM SOME KIND OF TEST THAT'S BEING DONE ON THEM. AND THAT MAYBE CAUSES SOME KIND OF GENETIC MUTATION --WHICH WOULD EXPLAIN THE BODY WE DUG UP!
AND THIS --"FORCE"-- SUMMONED THERESA NEMMAN OUT TO THE WOODS TONIGHT?
YES. BUT IT WAS BILLY MILES WHO TOOK HER THERE--ACTING FROM SOME ALIEN IMPULSE.
THAT'S IT! THAT'S--
HAHAHAHA
HAHAHAHAHAAHAHAHA HAHA HA HAHAHA
COME ON. LET'S GET OUT OF HERE.
WHERE ARE WE GOING?
WE'RE GOING TO PAY A VISIT TO BILLY MILES.

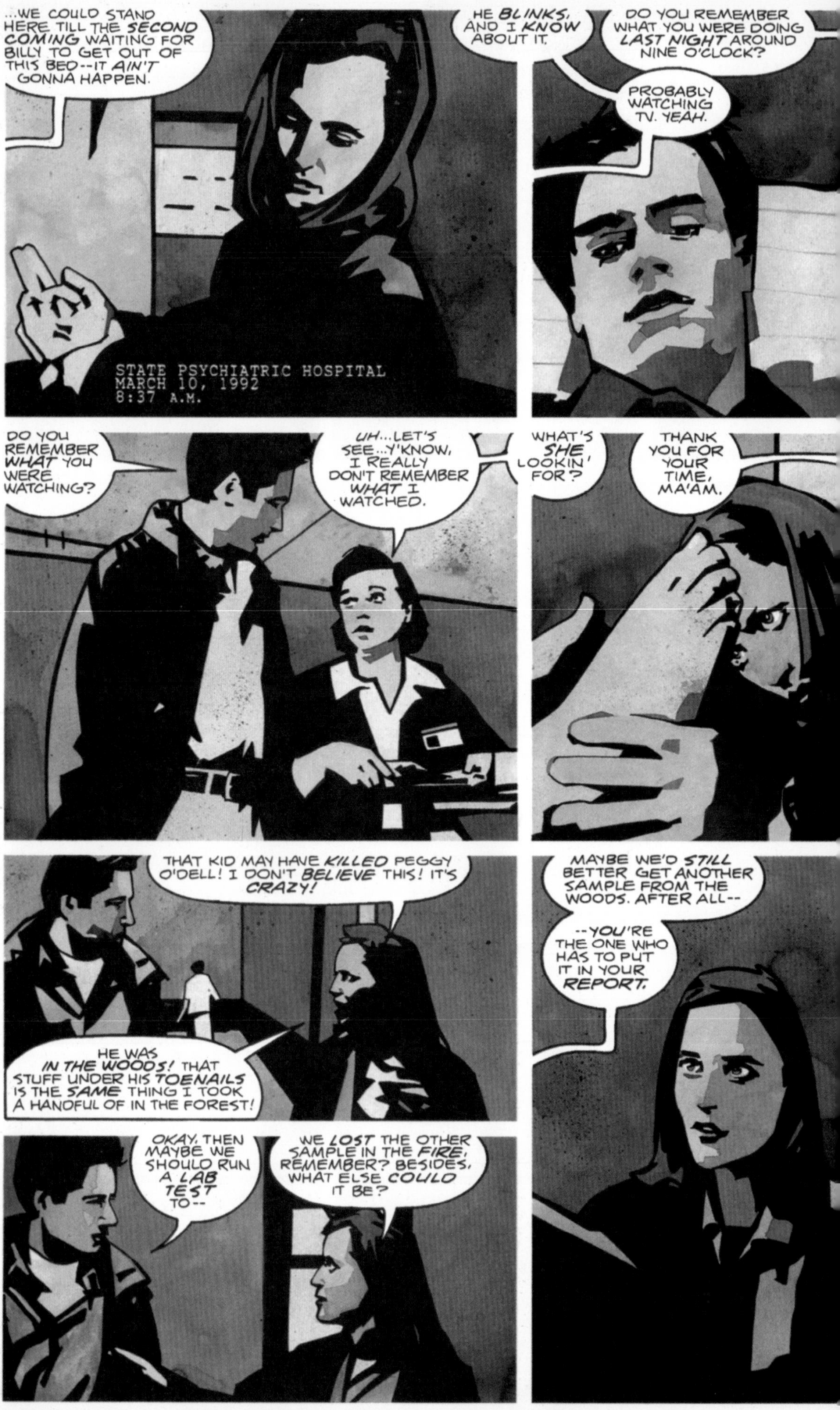
...WE COULD STAND HERE TILL THE SECOND COMING WAITING FOR BILLY TO GET OUT OF THIS BED--IT AIN'T GONNA HAPPEN.
STATE PSYCHIATRIC HOSPITAL
MARCH 10, 1992
8:37 A.M.
HE BLINKS, AND I KNOW ABOUT IT.
DO YOU REMEMBER WHAT YOU WERE DOING LAST NIGHT AROUND NINE O'CLOCK?
PROBABLY WATCHING TV. YEAH.
DO YOU REMEMBER WHAT YOU WERE WATCHING?
UH...LET'S SEE...Y'KNOW, I REALLY DON'T REMEMBER WHAT I WATCHED.
WHAT'S SHE LOOKIN' FOR?
THANK YOU FOR YOUR TIME, MA'AM.
THAT KID MAY HAVE KILLED PEGGY O'DELL! I DON'T BELIEVE THIS! IT'S CRAZY!
HE WAS IN THE WOODS! THAT STUFF UNDER HIS TOENAILS IS THE SAME THING I TOOK A HANDFUL OF IN THE FOREST!
OKAY. THEN MAYBE WE SHOULD RUN A LAB TEST TO--
WE LOST THE OTHER SAMPLE IN THE FIRE, REMEMBER? BESIDES, WHAT ELSE COULD IT BE?
MAYBE WE'D STILL BETTER GET ANOTHER SAMPLE FROM THE WOODS. AFTER ALL--
--YOU'RE THE ONE WHO HAS TO PUT IT IN YOUR REPORT.

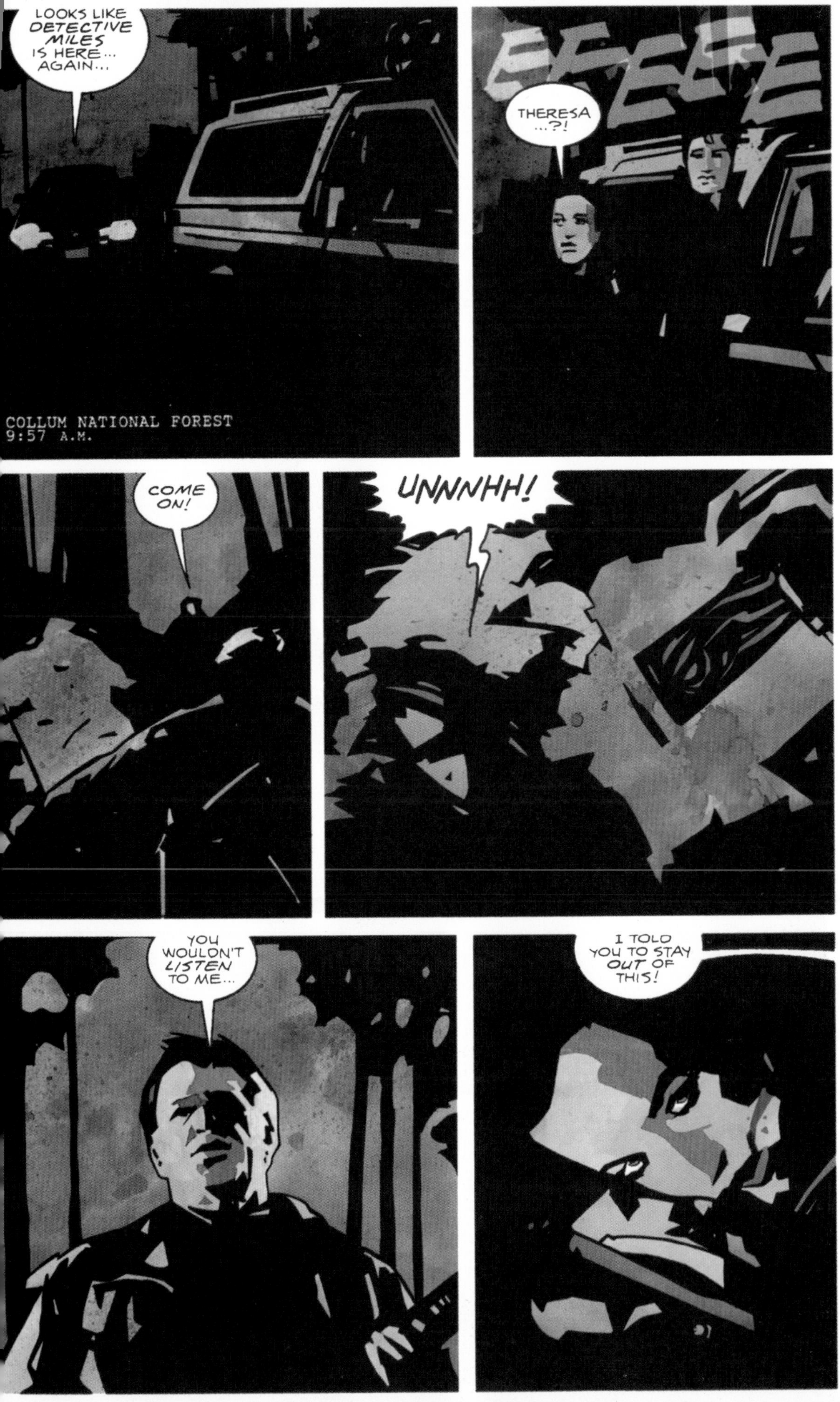
LOOKS LIKE DETECTIVE MILES IS HERE... AGAIN...
COLLUM NATIONAL FOREST
9:57 A.M.
THERESA ...?!
COME ON!
UNNNHH!
YOU WOULDN'T LISTEN TO ME...
I TOLD YOU TO STAY OUT OF THIS!

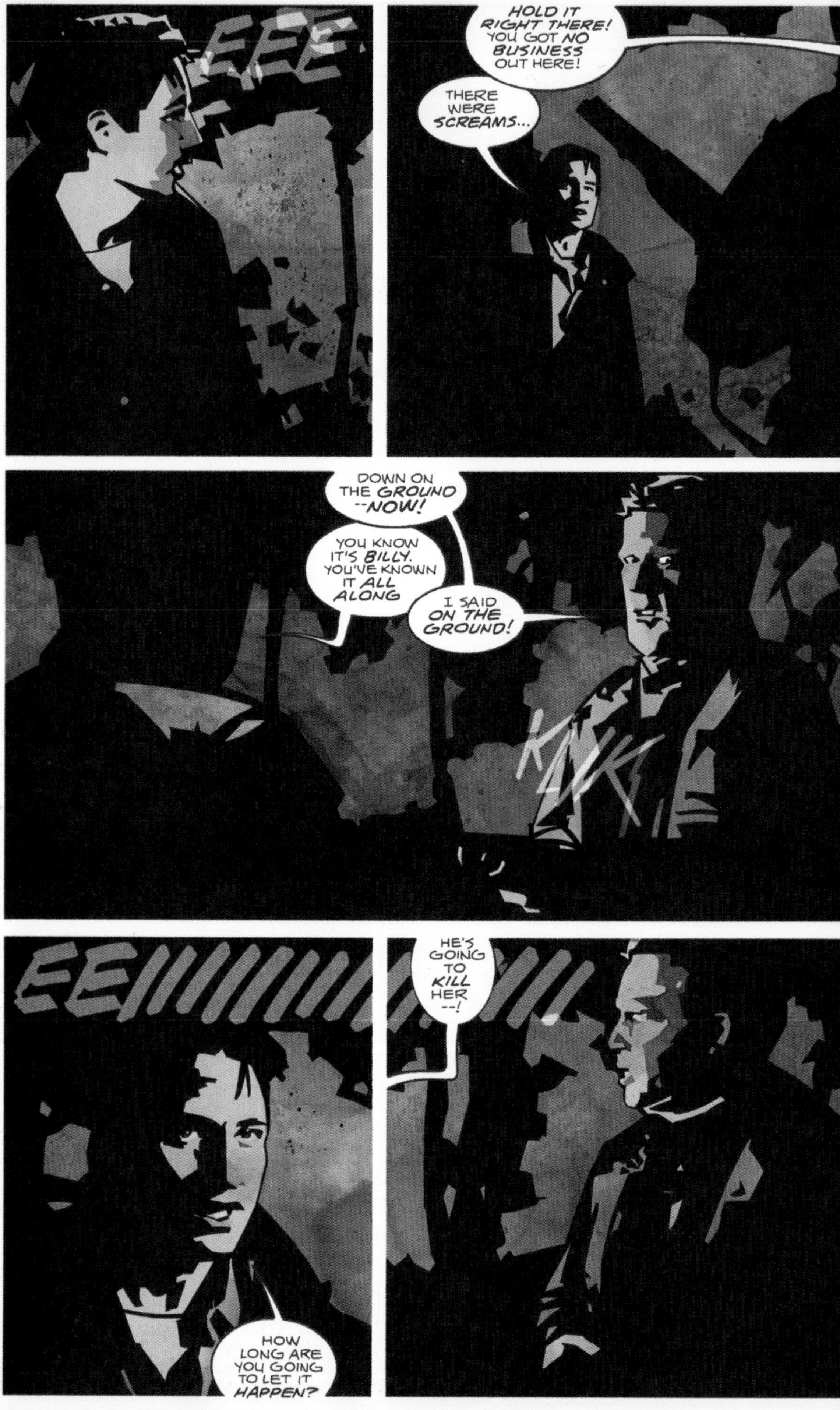
HOLD IT RIGHT THERE! YOU GOT NO BUSINESS OUT HERE!
THERE WERE SCREAMS...
DOWN ON THE GROUND --NOW!
YOU KNOW IT'S BILLY. YOU'VE KNOWN IT ALL ALONG
I SAID ON THE GROUND!
HOW LONG ARE YOU GOING TO LET IT HAPPEN?
HE'S GOING TO KILL HER --!

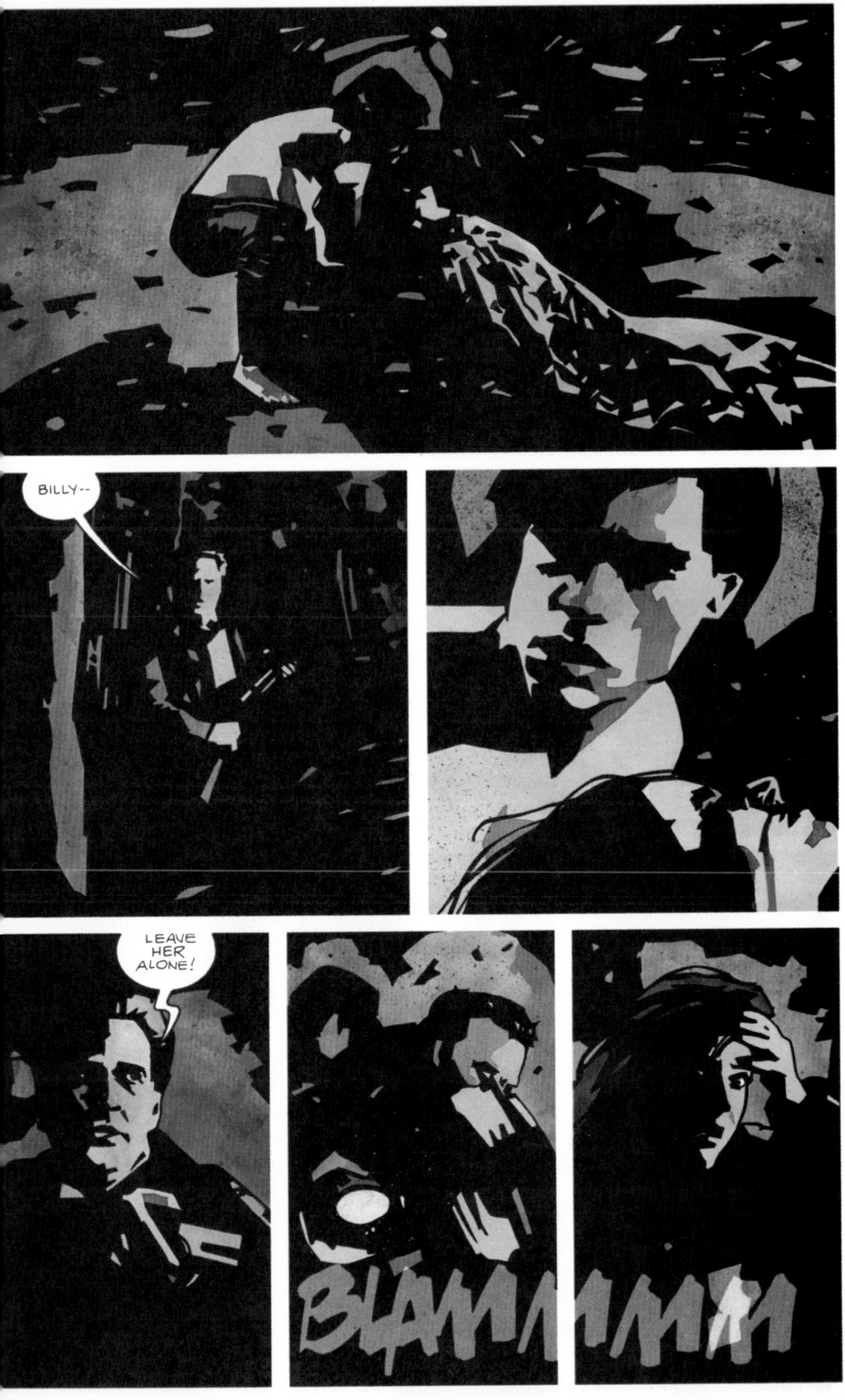
BILLY--
LEAVE HER ALONE!
BLAMMMMM

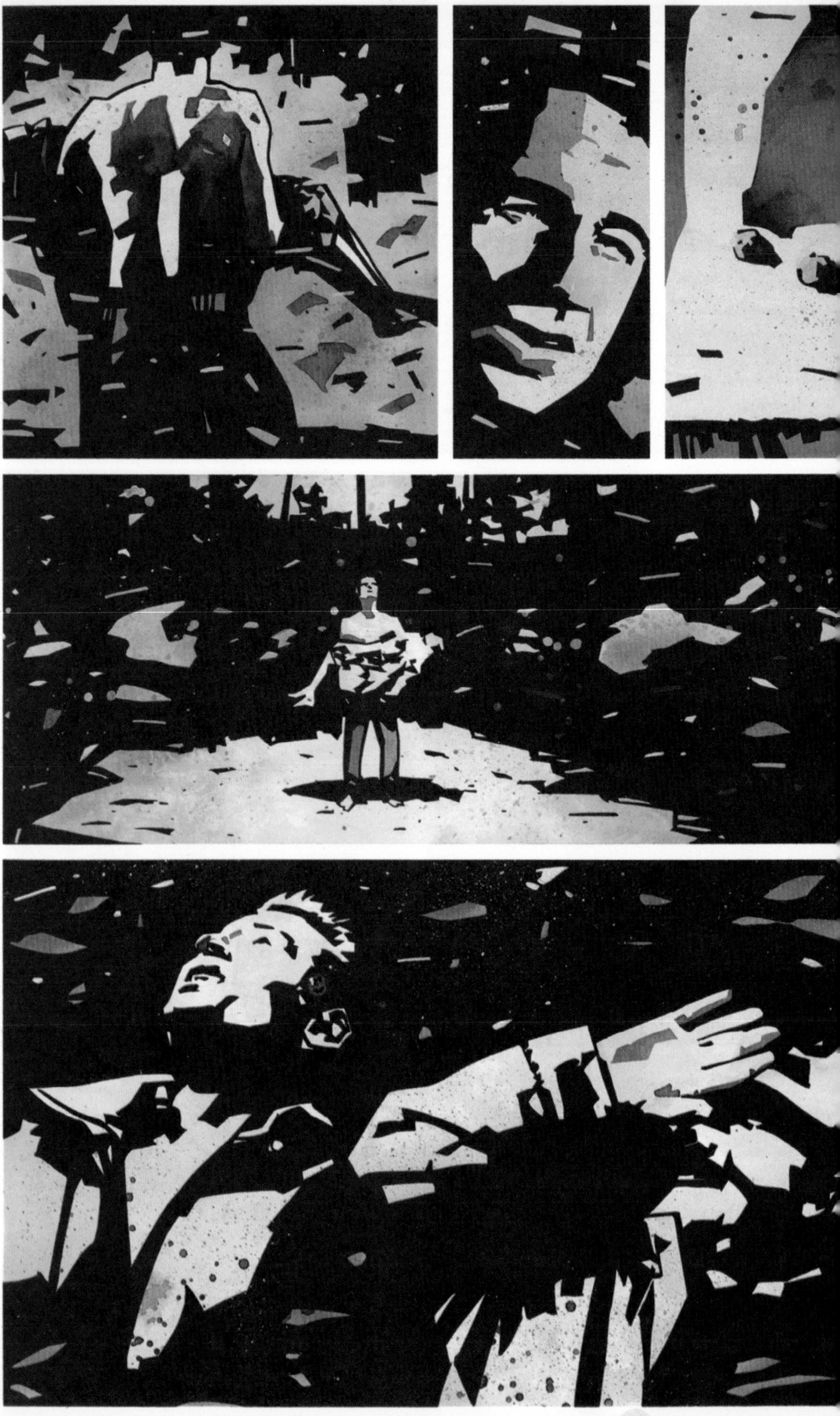

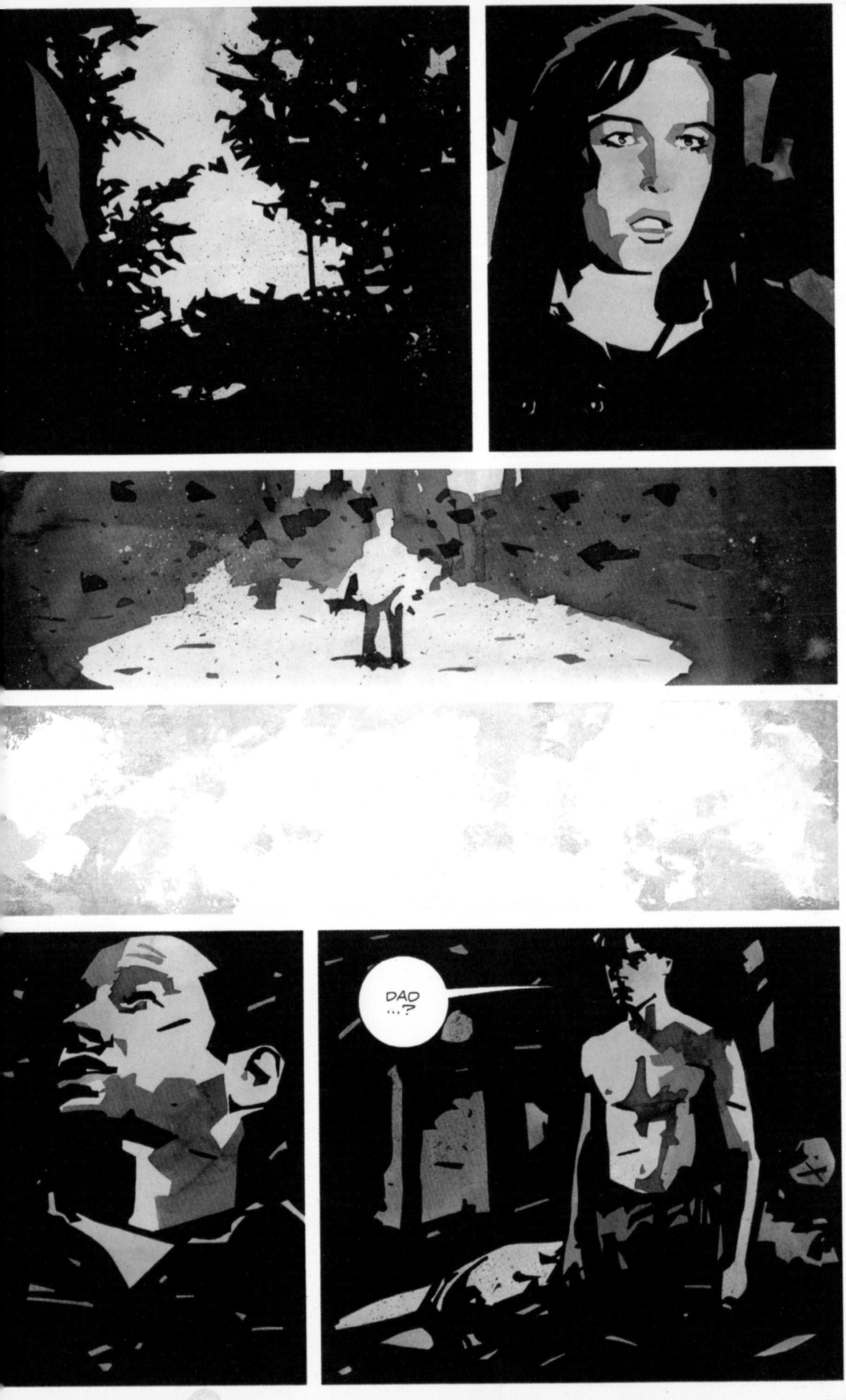
DAD ...?

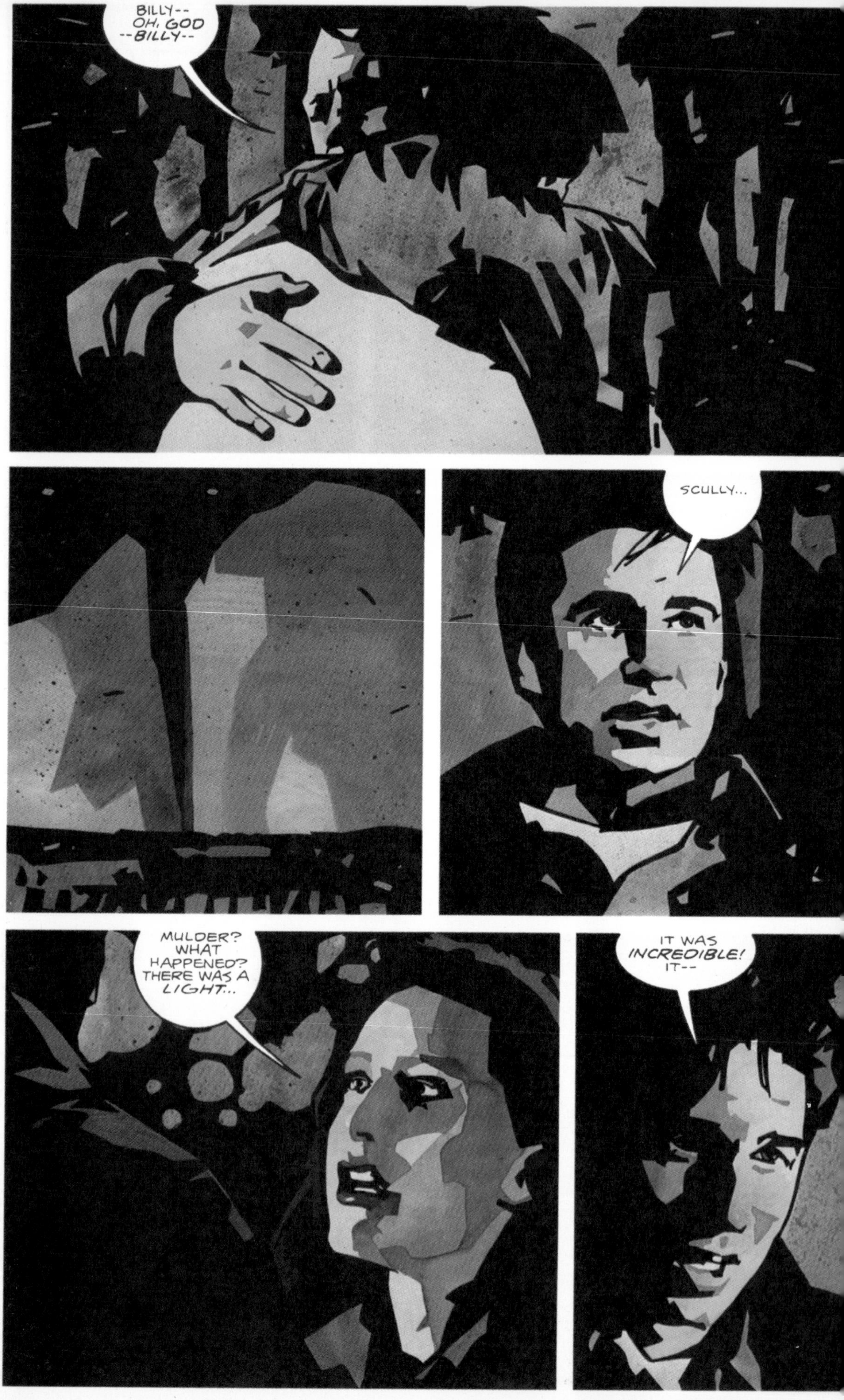
BILLY-- OH, GOD --BILLY--
SCULLY...
MULDER? WHAT HAPPENED? THERE WAS A LIGHT...
IT WAS INCREDIBLE! IT--

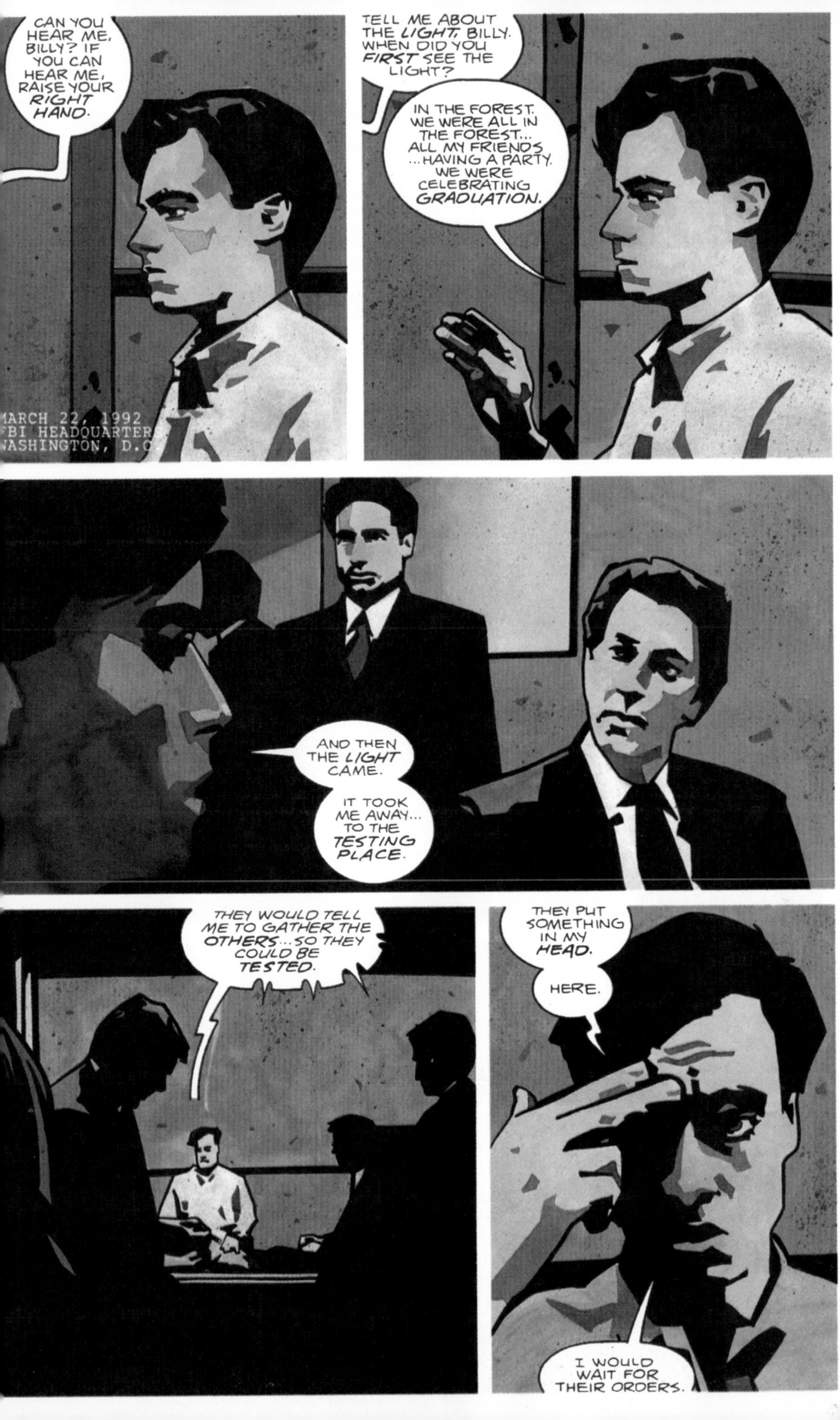
CAN YOU HEAR ME, BILLY? IF YOU CAN HEAR ME, RAISE YOUR RIGHT HAND.
MARCH 22, 1992
FBI HEADQUARTERS
WASHINGTON, D.C.
TELL ME ABOUT THE LIGHT, BILLY. WHEN DID YOU FIRST SEE THE LIGHT?
IN THE FOREST. WE WERE ALL IN THE FOREST... ALL MY FRIENDS ...HAVING A PARTY. WE WERE CELEBRATING GRADUATION.
AND THEN THE LIGHT CAME.
IT TOOK ME AWAY... TO THE TESTING PLACE.
THEY WOULD TELL ME TO GATHER THE OTHERS...SO THEY COULD BE TESTED.
THEY PUT SOMETHING IN MY HEAD.
HERE.
I WOULD WAIT FOR THEIR ORDERS.

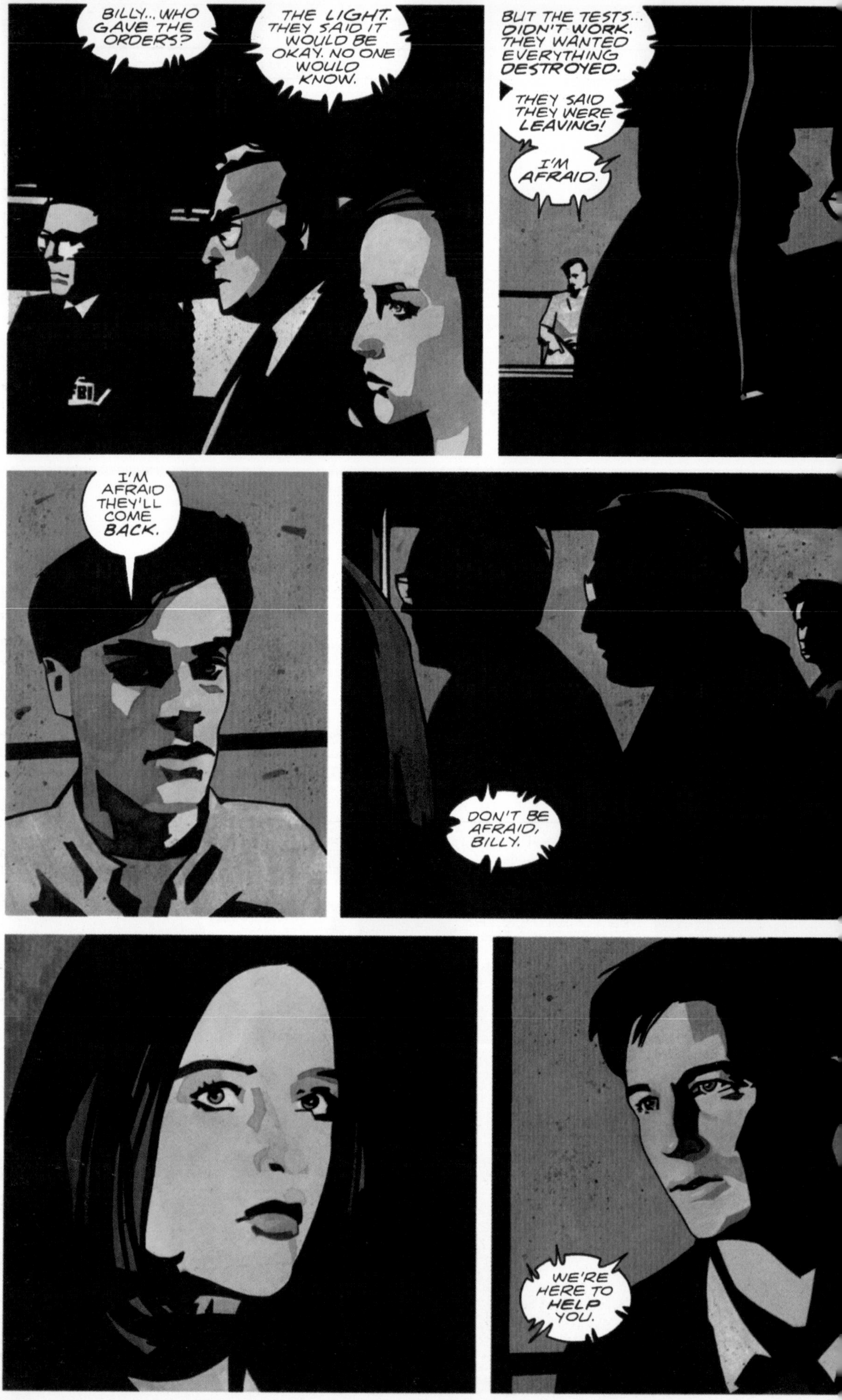
BILLY... WHO GAVE THE ORDERS?
THE LIGHT. THEY SAID IT WOULD BE OKAY. NO ONE WOULD KNOW.
FBI
BUT THE TESTS... DIDN'T WORK. THEY WANTED EVERYTHING DESTROYED.
THEY SAID THEY WERE LEAVING!
I'M AFRAID.
I'M AFRAID THEY'LL COME BACK.
DON'T BE AFRAID, BILLY.
WE'RE HERE TO HELP YOU.

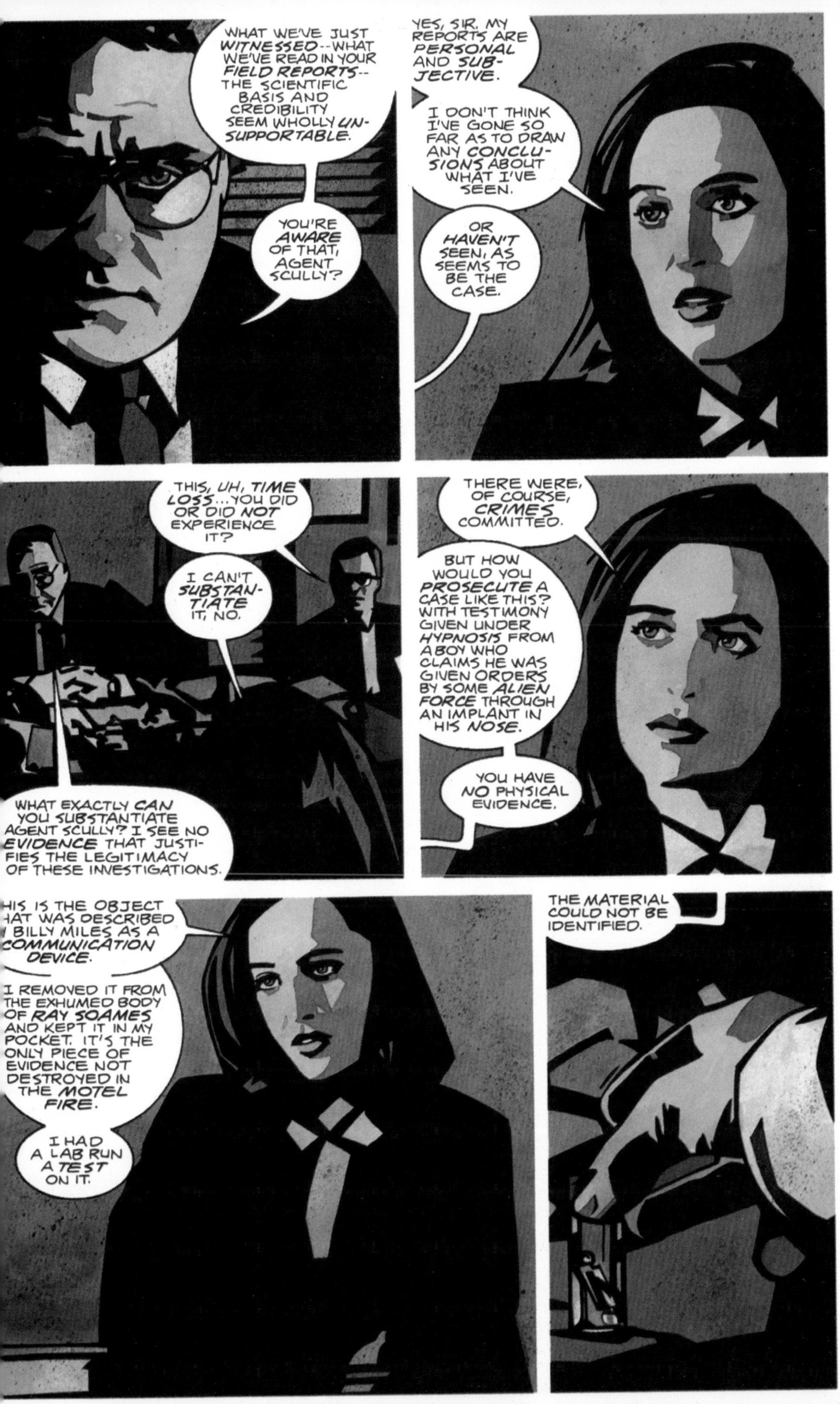
WHAT WE'VE JUST WITNESSED--WHAT WE'VE READ IN YOUR FIELD REPORTS--THE SCIENTIFIC BASIS AND CREDIBILITY SEEM WHOLLY UN-SUPPORTABLE.
YOU'RE AWARE OF THAT, AGENT SCULLY?
YES, SIR, MY REPORTS ARE PERSONAL AND SUB-JECTIVE.
I DON'T THINK I'VE GONE SO FAR AS TO DRAW ANY CONCLU-SIONS ABOUT WHAT I'VE SEEN.
OR HAVEN'T SEEN, AS SEEMS TO BE THE CASE.
THIS, UH, TIME LOSS...YOU DID OR DID NOT EXPERIENCE IT?
I CAN'T SUBSTAN-TIATE IT, NO.
WHAT EXACTLY CAN YOU SUBSTANTIATE AGENT SCULLY? I SEE NO EVIDENCE THAT JUSTI-FIES THE LEGITIMACY OF THESE INVESTIGATIONS.
THERE WERE, OF COURSE, CRIMES COMMITTED.
BUT HOW WOULD YOU PROSECUTE A CASE LIKE THIS? WITH TESTIMONY GIVEN UNDER HYPNOSIS FROM A BOY WHO CLAIMS HE WAS GIVEN ORDERS BY SOME ALIEN FORCE THROUGH AN IMPLANT IN HIS NOSE.
YOU HAVE NO PHYSICAL EVIDENCE.
HIS IS THE OBJECT HAT WAS DESCRIBED BILLY MILES AS A COMMUNICATION DEVICE.
I REMOVED IT FROM THE EXHUMED BODY OF RAY SOAMES AND KEPT IT IN MY POCKET. IT'S THE ONLY PIECE OF EVIDENCE NOT DESTROYED IN THE MOTEL FIRE.
I HAD A LAB RUN A TEST ON IT.
THE MATERIAL COULD NOT BE IDENTIFIED.

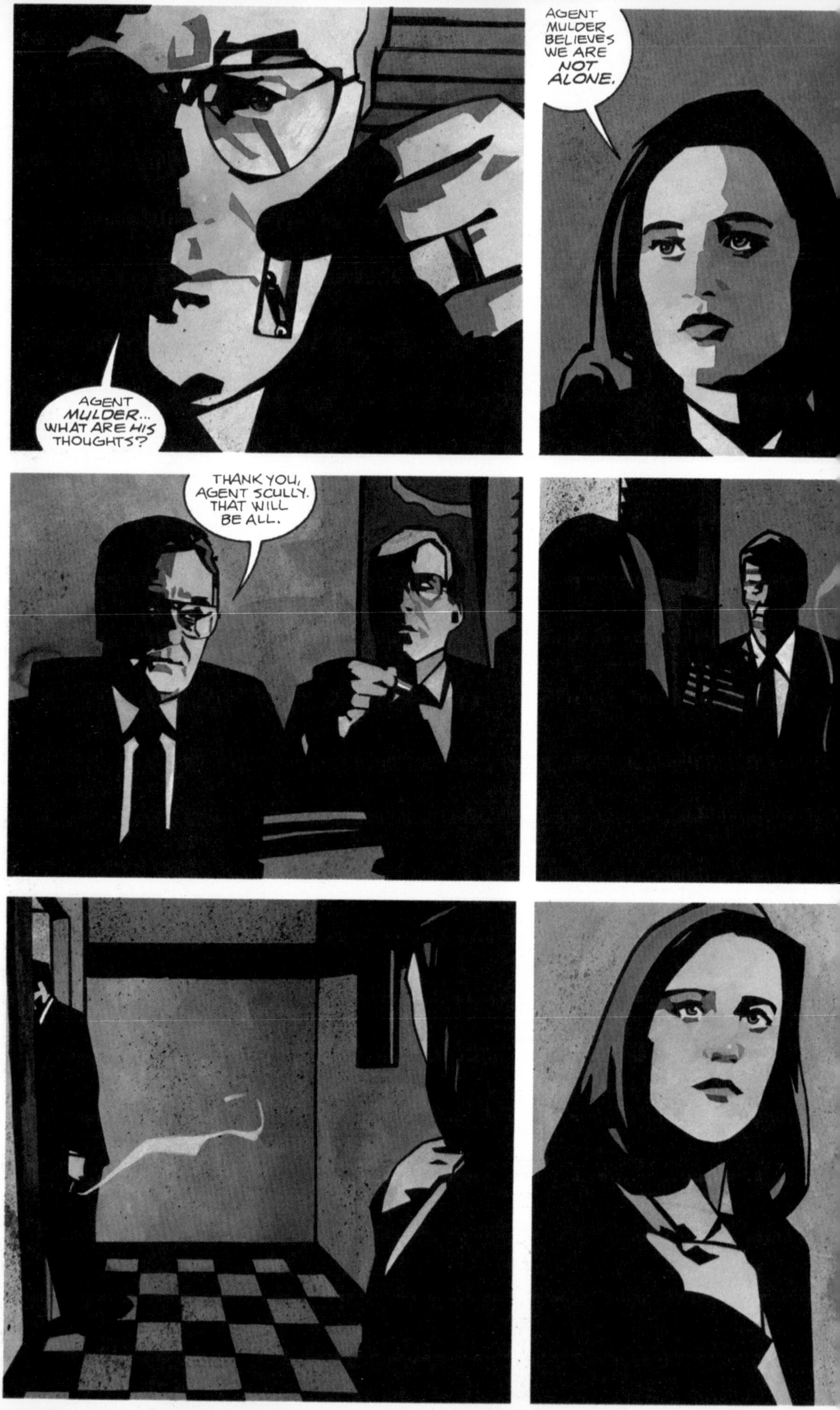
AGENT MULDER... WHAT ARE HIS THOUGHTS?
AGENT MULDER BELIEVES WE ARE NOT ALONE.
THANK YOU, AGENT SCULLY. THAT WILL BE ALL.

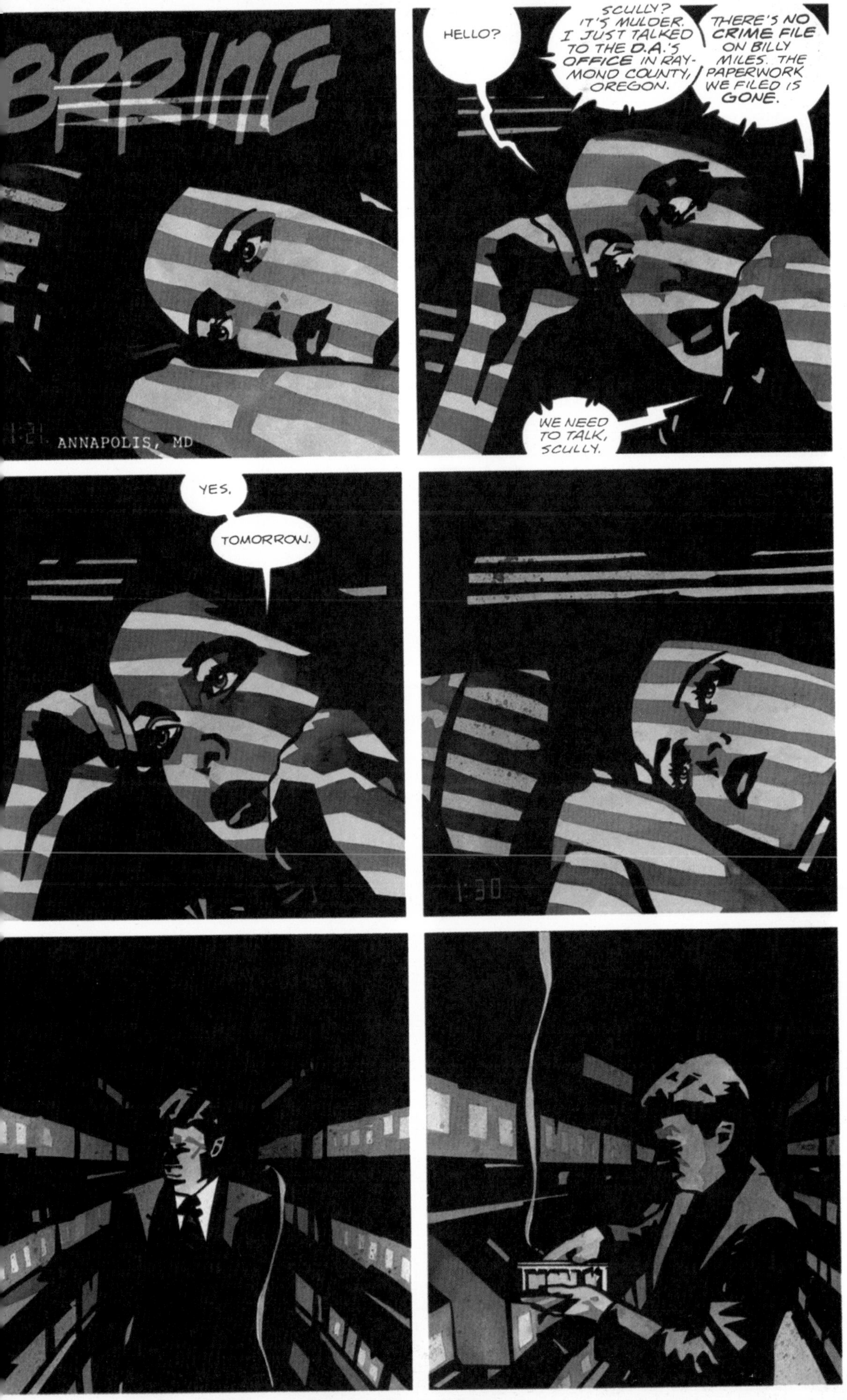
BRRING
1:21 ANNAPOLIS, MD
HELLO?
SCULLY? IT'S MULDER. I JUST TALKED TO THE D.A.'S OFFICE IN RAYMOND COUNTY, OREGON.
THERE'S NO CRIME FILE ON BILLY MILES. THE PAPERWORK WE FILED IS GONE.
WE NEED TO TALK, SCULLY.
YES.
TOMORROW.
1:30

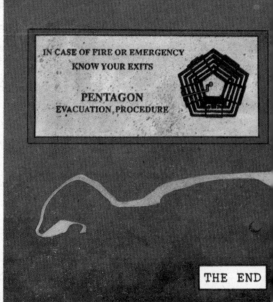

IN CASE OF FIRE OR EMERGENCY
KNOW YOUR EXITS

PENTAGON
EVACUATION PROCEDURE

THE END